Challenge or Surrender?

Juan de la Cuesta Hispanic Monographs

FOUNDING EDITOR
Tom Lathrop†
University of Delaware

PUBLISHER
Michael P. Bolan
University of Delaware

EDITOR
Michael J. McGrath
Georgia Southern University

EDITORIAL BOARD
Vincent Barletta
Stanford University

Annette Grant Cash
Georgia State University

David Castillo
State University of New York - Buffalo

Gwen Kirkpatrick
Georgetown University

Mark P. Del Mastro
College of Charleston

Juan F. Egea
University of Wisconsin - Madison

Sara L. Lehman
Fordham University

Mariselle Meléndez
University of Illinois at Urbana - Champaign

Eyda Merediz
University of Maryland

Dayle Seidenspinner-Núñez
University of Notre Dame

Elzbieta Sklodowska
Washington University in St. Louis

Noël Valis
Yale University

Challenge or Surrender?
Female Responses to Spain's
Gendered Power Imbalance in
Emilia Pardo Bazán's Feminist Short Stories

by

PATRICIA RAMSAY

Juan de la Cuesta
Newark, Delaware

No portion of this book may be reproduced in any form without permission from the publisher.
For permission contact: libros@juandelacuesta.com.

Copyright © 2025 by Linguatext, LLC. All rights reserved.

Juan de la Cuesta Hispanic Monographs
An imprint of Linguatext, LLC.
103 Walker Way
Newark, Delaware 19711 USA
(302) 453-8695

www.JuandelaCuesta.com

MANUFACTURED IN THE UNITED STATES OF AMERICA

ISBN: 978-1-58871-411-4

Table of Contents

Acknowledgments 7
Introduction 9

1 Emilia Pardo Bazán: *Feminista y cuentista* 27

2 The Pitfalls of Love and Devotion 65
   "El árbol rosa", "Comedia" 67
   "El zapato", "La redada", "El encaje roto" 78
   "Los pendientes", "Posesión" 90

3 Ruled by Head or Heart? 103
   "Apólogo", "La dama joven" 105
   "Las cutres", "Coleccionista" 120
   "Saletita", "El mascarón" 131

4 Don Juan's Downfall 144
   "Cenizas", "Remordimiento" 151
   "El aviso", "El cinco de copas" 161
   "Dalinda", "El pajarraco" 170

5 Galician Tales 184
   "El molino", "El aire cativo", "La santa de Karnar" 189
   "La capitana", "La hoz", "Un destripador de antaño" 206

Conclusion 227
Works Cited 235
Appendix: Publication Details 251
Index 253

Acknowledgments

A BOOK SUCH AS this takes time to complete, and I am indebted to my family and to the many friends and colleagues who have been with me and supported and contributed to this project over the years, whether directly or indirectly. However, I would like to thank Nicola Gilmour and Claudia Bernardi in particular, for their expertise, advice, and criticism as they encouraged and helped me through the initial drafting and proofreading stages.

This has been an amazing journey of discovery, of seeking feminist-slanted subtexts in Emilia Pardo Bazán's imaginatively crafted texts and relating them to both her Spanish *fin de siècle* world and, more than a century later, our own. Some of Pardo Bazán's concerns have been addressed but many, sadly, are still ongoing today. It is my hope that this volume will give readers a glimpse of Pardo Bazán's extraordinary abilities and that it will also encourage others to read and discuss her short story narratives. With "more than six hundred" stories to choose from, the door is still wide open!

Any translations in this text not otherwise acknowledged are my own.

Introduction

She was not a lighthouse, but a mirror.

- Ronald Hilton
The Centenary of Emilia Pardo Bazán

During her lifetime the Spanish writer Emilia Pardo Bazán (1851–1921) penned "cientos y cientos de cuentos [que] constituyen un caso excepcional sin precedentes, que asombra y hace impensable el hecho de que una sola persona haya podido escribir tal cantidad de relatos tan diferentes y variados" [hundreds and hundreds of short stories, the sheer number of them is unprecedented; it is almost unthinkable that a single person could have created such a diversified collection] (Paredes Núñez "Estudio" 1: 5).[1] This publication analyses twenty-five of these short stories that have been selected for the portrayals of their respective female protagonists. In each story there is at least one woman who, in some way either challenges, or is overcome by one of the gendered inequalities that were historically embedded into *fin de siècle* Spanish society. Four of these gendered inequities in particular, and the protagonist's responses to them will be focused on. The first is the Spanish code of honor, where men are active, valiant and indomitable and women passive and virginal; the second is the *ángel del hogar* construct, in which the woman was expected to be a paragon of altruism and abnegation and defined only as a wife or a mother (Jagoe 25); the third, the broad societal acceptance of the sexual double standard and lastly, the way in which *el qué dirán*, the anonymous neighborhood gossip, monitored women's behavior. Pardo Bazán, as a feminist and intellectual,

---

1   Two recent compilations of Pardo Bazán's short stories now represent the definitive collections, *Cuentos completos* (1990) and *Obras completas* (2004). Excerpts from the original texts are quoted from the former, unless otherwise noted. All references to these two collections follow the format: volume: page, and the contractions *CC* and *OC* may be used.

publicly railed against all of these, and I will argue that her short stories were among her most effective channels of dissemination for her often unpopular feminist ideas.

Cristina Fernández Cubas aptly comments on Pardo Bazán's stories: "Lo que no puede decir en cartas o artículos—y hay pocas cosas que no se atreva a decir en cartas y artículos—lo expone en forma de cuento" [What she cannot say in letters or articles—and there are few topics that she does not dare to expound on in her letters or articles—she incorporates into a short story] (51). I maintain that it was Pardo Bazán's exceptional literary abilities that enabled her to use these narratives to incorporate and promulgate her feminist beliefs, including difficult and even distasteful topics, without offending the sensibilities of her readers. Despite the widespread social acceptance of the aforementioned gendered inequities, Pardo Bazán was able to critique them in much of her short fiction and thereby promote her views to hundreds of thousands of readers. Furthermore, Pardo Bazán's questioning of the gendered injustices detailed in the following chapters would have been considered unacceptable in the Spanish society of the time for dissemination through other means.

As we will see, Pardo Bazán does not shrink from using her stories to emphasize the social and physical harm to multitudes of Spanish women resulting from the sexual double standard. This widely accepted gendered inequity features in almost half of the narratives examined in this publication, although only six of the stories were selected with this topic specifically in mind. Its presence in multiple other stories gives an indication of her concern at the insidious behavior of predatory men in *fin de siècle* Spanish society.

The popular press offered Pardo Bazán a platform for over 400 of her short stories, which were read, or perused, even if in passing, by many thousands of mainly middle-class households.[2] Through many of these stories Pardo Bazán communicated her feminist viewpoint, even if often couched in the ambiguity of a sub-text, which the reader constructs for themselves, imagining or interpreting "what is *not* said or *not* done (and *how* it is not

---

2   An example is *El Imparcial*, a Madrid daily newspaper which in the early twentieth century had a circulation of 130,000 copies that were distributed not only throughout Spain but also in major European and South American cities. 149 of Pardo Bazán's short stories—about a quarter of her entire output—were printed in this one newspaper (Carlos Blanco 120), while a further 143 were printed in *Blanco y Negro* which, in 1896, had a circulation of 45,000 (Charnon-Deutsch *Pose* 103, Paredes Núñez 4: 456-59).

said or done), what may be implied, suggested or hinted, what is ambiguous, marginal, ambivalent, evasive, emphasised or not emphasised" (Cuddon 877). Pardo Bazán addressed gendered inequalities in her society, together with the often-deleterious effects that these inequalities caused in a Spanish woman's life, and through this literary platform, she was able to directly address the men who had the power to change their society if they so wished.

Approaches to Pardo Bazán's œuvre

Numerous biographers and literary critics have attested to the quality of Pardo Bazán's literary work. Her œuvre is immense: twenty novels, twenty novellas, poetry, hundreds of literary, social and scientific essays, and more than six hundred short stories of which, as Ronald Hilton observed, a rapid review "would be scarcely more than a catalogue" ("Concept" 329). It was two early novels, *Los pazos de Ulloa* (1886) and *Madre naturaleza* (1887) using a masculine narrative voice, that established Pardo Bazán as a serious novelist and attracted considerable critical attention. Indeed, in the 1990s Janet Pérez commented that these two works had attracted almost 80% of the critical scrutiny dedicated to Pardo Bazán's work ("Winners" 347), and it was largely on the reputation of these works that she became the only female writer of her generation to be accepted as part of the Spanish literary canon. It can also be added that it was the reputation that Pardo Bazán had built up as a novelist that later ensured the ready reception of her stories in the popular press. A few decades on, much of Pardo Bazán's literary output, including many of her other novels, novellas and short stories, remains largely untapped. Pardo Bazán's acclaim as a novelist notwithstanding, it is her short stories that concern us here. The exact number of these is unknown; the imprecise "more than six hundred" is a widely quoted phrase. Today, more than a century after her death, new stories (and essays) are still being rediscovered as newspapers and magazines from Spain and the wider Spanish-speaking world continue to be digitized and their contents made widely available.[3]

Although Pardo Bazán's short stories may have become increasingly accessible, meaningful analyses of these works were late in appearing as this immense trove of short fiction was almost ignored until about the 1980s. Since then, scholars have published a steady stream of books and articles commenting on and analyzing her narratives. Even so, as I selected stories for this project, I came to two realizations. The first was that very few of the six hundred plus texts had drawn serious critical analysis. The number has grown

---

3   The Galician literary journal *La Tribuna*, which focusses on Pardo Bazán's life and writings, regularly publishes these recently digitized narratives.

during the last few decades, but I estimate that it would still be in double, not triple figures. The second realization was how different the approaches taken by various critics were. Paredes Núñez considers that the sheer number of stories precludes any meaningful study of them as a collection ("Estudio" 1: 7), and it seems clear that aspiring critics of Pardo Bazán's work must create both their own selection of stories and a rationale for their study.

I have identified two broad analytical approaches to Pardo Bazán's stories. The first is a thematic survey of the entire opus, which comments, necessarily briefly, on several hundred works. Despite Paredes Núñez's pessimistic assessment, Ángeles Quesada Novás (2005) and Ruth Noya Taboada (2016) have both successfully taken this approach, compiling stories on love and violence respectively, and providing a useful overview of those themes in Pardo Bazán's work, although there is necessarily little substantive analysis of the hundreds of individual texts that are mentioned by name.[4] Quesada Novás, in particular, provides valuable surveys of themes such as anger or jealousy that are relevant to the present study. The second approach undertakes analysis of narratological aspects in selected narratives: Susan M. McKenna (story endings), Joyce Tolliver (discourse analysis) and Susan Walter (narrative framing) have all published excellent studies in this line. The methodologies that these three scholars have employed have proved inspirational for my own analyses.

However, I have chosen a third path for my study, one that combines both of the above approaches, analyzing 25 stories in both thematic and narratological detail, a small number when considered against Pardo Bazán's total output but, I believe, a significant number when considered against the existing corpus of analyses of her stories to date.[5] As a reaction to this relatively limited range of Pardo Bazán stories covered by scholars, I believe that it is important to include texts that have received little critical attention. To that end, I would consider only about four or five of the 25 stories included

---

4   Quesada Novás includes 180 texts in her indexes, and the individual texts mentioned in Noya Taboada's work number in the hundreds.

5   The 25 narratives were chosen after reading about 300 stories and selecting those in which female protagonists made significant decisions. The Don Juan selection offered a different slant, and there were sufficient stories incorporating specifically Galician matters to form a separate chapter. Some Pardo Bazán collections were read in their entirety; other reading was guided by indexes such as that in Efraín E. Garza's *Las manifestaciones del amor en cuentos de Pardo Bazán*, which lists 60 titles (7-9), and various articles, including Janet Pérez's "Winners, Losers and Casualties in Pardo Bazán's Battle of the Sexes" which mentions no fewer than 72 female-focussed narratives.

here as well-known.⁶ My in-depth analysis of the other 20 constitutes an important addition to Pardo Bazán scholarship and forms a significant plank of my methodological framework, which is based on close reading, defined by J. A. Cuddon as "[d]etailed, balanced and rigorous critical examination of a text to discover its meanings and to assess its effects" (142).⁷ I concur with Annette Federico's observation that a good literary critic "has to take his personal experience of life and his limited knowledge of the world into a formal and self-contained space created in another person's mind". She asserts that we must read the text in a way that "extends our appreciation of the aesthetic features of a work, shows us something of what it may mean, and opens it up for critical debate." This, in her view, sums up "a good close reading" (2, 6) and this is what I aspire to in the chapters that follow.

There is no set way in which to do this, although this fact has not deterred numerous eminent writers and critics from offering suggestions. Virginia Woolf (1882–1941) acknowledges the unique insights that any one critic possesses and instructs potential readers and critics to follow their own instincts, to use their own reason and come to their own conclusions ("Read" 64). Another prominent literary figure, W. H. Auden (1907–73), offers guidelines by way of a rhetorical question: "What is the function of a critic?" Three of the answers he does provide include: to give a "reading" of a work that increases the reader's understanding of it; to throw light upon the process of artistic "Making"; and to illustrate the relation of art to life, to science, to economics, ethics, religion, and so on (8-9).

My own analytical methods embrace Woolf's sentiments and embody Auden's observations. Pardo Bazán's individual short fictional works can be read and considered in their entirety by the reader. Furthermore, because I believe that in a short story every word deserves attention, I begin with an intensive examination of the text.⁸ When this is done, the story itself is taking shape, a process poetically described by Woolf as floating "to the top of the mind as a whole" ("Read" 75), and I, as the critic, am able to express my understanding of the narrative and its intricacies. My argument is that Pardo Bazán crafted each of these selected stories with two objectives in mind: the

---

6   These are "La dama joven" (1885), "Un destripador de antaño" (1890), "El encaje roto" (1897) and "Remordimiento" (1892).

7   Close reading was first discussed in the work of I. A. Richards (1893–1979) and is expounded in his book *Principles of Literary Criticism*.

8   Edgar Allan Poe (1809–49), writing about short stories, observed that "[i]n the whole composition there should be no word written, of which the tendency, direct or indirect, is not to the one pre-established design" (127).

first, to create a widely acceptable, publishable narrative and the second, to mirror in these narratives the challenges faced by Spanish women as they responded to various gendered inequities of their society. Identifying the manner in which Pardo Bazán was able to undermine seemingly acceptable narratives to convey subversive messages to her contemporary readers is a major part of each analysis. My aim is to elucidate the connection between her "art" as a storyteller (à la Auden's third point) to aspects of her society. This book contributes significantly to the existing literature on Pardo Bazán's œuvre, both by bringing to light some lesser-known works and by providing a critical interpretation of them based on these methods and principles.

Pardo Bazán's stories cannot be easily classified. Even the titles of her own collections provide ironic or sardonic twists on the theme itself. "Apólogo", for example included by the author in *Cuentos de amor*, does mention marriage, but it is certainly not a love story, and in *Cuentos trágicos*, the "tragedy" suffered by "El pajarraco", a serial womanizer, appears to be that he eventually gets married. The thematic scope of Pardo Bazán's short stories is broad, including historical incidents and persons, re-worked mythologies, politically themed narratives, fantastic and imaginative tales and the "everyday", where the focus is on one small object or incident. Most take place in Spain, but some are set in far-flung lands. Many evince what Joyce Tolliver describes as "a certain unsettling quality" and few are comfortable stories with happy endings (*Cigar* 12).

A significant number of Pardo Bazán's stories promulgate her feminist beliefs, focusing, in one way or another, on female protagonists who inevitably encounter, for better or worse, the historical gendered conventions of Spanish society alluded to earlier. It is this group of women-centered stories that interested me when I was selecting stories for this work. Additionally, in the 25 narratives I have chosen, almost every female protagonist exerts her agency, thereby making an independent decision about the direction of her life; some decisions have positive outcomes, while others are disastrous.

Pardo Bazán's feminist short fiction emphasizes both the limited options for women who are unhappy with their situation and the marginalization that unmarried women may experience if they are forced into the world to fend for themselves. This statement also connotes the magnitude of Pardo Bazán's self-imposed task of informing and educating the Spanish reading public about the gendered injustices in contemporary society and thereby encouraging radical social change. We will also see the lack of autonomy in nineteenth-century Spanish women's lives, that Pardo Bazán formally addressed in her 1889 essay "The Women of Spain", communicated in the individual stories as they are analyzed.[9]

A number of the stories in this collection portray women who improve their lives by exercising their own agency and challenging or rebelling against the patriarchal norms that constrain them, thereby disregarding any societal expectations of female submission to male authority. For other females portrayed, including those who submit to selfish male demands, there are less fortunate outcomes. In one way or another, almost all these fictional women can be considered non-traditional, in terms of the prevailing, gendered middle-class *ángel del hogar* model and the expected observance of the historical Spanish code of honor (to be discussed in Chapter 1) forced on women by Spanish society of the time. Many of the narratives also incorporate one or more sub-texts that invite the readers to consider feminist and social issues in a less direct manner. There were, in fact, several ways that the narratives could have been grouped into chapters and, despite my confidence in the final decisions, some individual stories could have fitted into more than one chapter due to the significant commonalities they all share.

Sources

Connecting the stories in this collection to the historical and social context of their settings and the time of their production is an important part of the analyses. Pardo Bazán's own life has been thoroughly documented, with three recent biographies by Pilar Faus (2003), Eva Acosta (2007) and Isabel Burdiel (2019) being particularly informative. Carmen Bravo-Villasante's 1962 book was the first of the modern biographies of Pardo Bazán to appear, followed by Walter T. Pattison's in 1971, and I have also made use of these works. Nelly Clémessy (1981) has concentrated on Pardo Bazán's novels, while Cristina Fernández Cubas (2001) and Inés Alberdi (2013) have written shorter accounts of the writer's life for a wider audience. Nevertheless, it is noticeable (and for me, puzzling) that, apart from a few pages in total in each of two early works, Bravo-Villasante and Pattison, there is scarcely a mention of Pardo Bazán's career as a short story writer, even in the substantial biographies of Acosta, Burdiel and Faus.

---

9   The "Women of Spain" was commissioned by and published in the respected London literary magazine *Fortnightly Review* in 1889. The following year, it was translated into Spanish, retitled as "La mujer española", and reprinted in *La España Moderna*. The text was slightly modified for its local readership and also included a preface detailing the circumstances of the original essay's publication.

In my discussion I have drawn upon many publications, including Maurice Hemingway and Pattison, among others, who have produced succinct and scholarly analyses of Pardo Bazán's novels, the two published collections of her most important feminist essays, edited and introduced by Leda Schiavo (1976) and Guadalupe Gómez-Ferrer (2018) respectively, while Maryellen Bieder's "Women, Literature, and Society: The Essays of Emilia Pardo Bazán" (Glenn and Mazquiarán de Rodríguez 25-54) has provided a comprehensive overview of these writings. Martha Zarate's *Emilia Pardo Bazán's Articles in La Nación, El Imparcial and La Epoca: A Bibliographic Guide* (2002) offers a useful précis of more than four hundred essays and Julia Biggane's *In a Liminal Space: The Novellas of Emilia Pardo Bazán* (2000) comprises a literary analysis of Pardo Bazán's twenty novellas. Studies by Walter, McKenna, Quesada Novás and Tolliver have already been mentioned and Margot Versteeg and Susan Walter have edited a volume entitled *Approaches to Teaching the Writings of Emilia Pardo Bazán* which provides imaginative articles whose aim is to educate and inform future generations of Pardo Bazán scholars while providing valuable critical insights. Tolliver (*Torn Lace and Other Stories* [1996]) and Linda Willem (*Náufragas y otros cuentos* [2010]) have also published annotated selections of Pardo Bazán's feminist short stories.

Connections with "The Women of Spain"

In the fictional narratives that I have selected, many of the female protagonists, with the exposure of their imperfections and failure to measure up to the traditional angelic womanly behavior expected by Spanish society, reflect in various ways the imperfect lives of the "real-life" women described by Pardo Bazán in her essay "The Women of Spain". In her essay, Pardo Bazán notes the strengths and weaknesses of various classes of Spanish women throughout the country, often highlighting the problems that society has created for these women. Pardo Bazán was very much aware that in *fin de siècle* Spain this nebulous concept of "perfection" in a woman had developed over many centuries, as I will trace in Chapter 1, and it existed primarily in the eye of a theoretical male beholder. By the mid-nineteenth century, this woman had evolved to become the submissive and compliant *ángel del hogar*, of whom examples in the real world (as "The Women of Spain" amply demonstrates) were few and far between.

The essay itself was inspired by the writer's observations of women (and their menfolk) in the society around her. In it Pardo Bazán notes that "in Spain to put in writing matters which are admitted by everybody in conversation often amounts to an act of courage" and that, when writing for non-

Spanish readers in particular, "the obligation of speaking the truth becomes even stronger" (779). Addressing Spain's past, she observes that in the eighteenth century the women of the country were pious, deferential and naïve, living in "absolute submission to paternal and conjugal authority, religious practices and complete self-effacement" (880). A century on, she asserts, no matter how liberal and advanced a Spanish man's ideas may be in general, his thoughts as to the ideal woman are less so. She is not to be found in the future, but in the past: "The model wife is still the same as she was a hundred years ago ... a combination of the qualities of the stoic and the angel ... within a crystal barrier which should separate her from the world through the help of ignorance" (882-83).

There is a crucial feminist statement in "The Women of Spain" that is pertinent to understanding the situation of many of the female protagonists in the narratives discussed here. Pardo Bazán avers that since "the faults of the Spanish woman must, to a great degree, be imputed to the man ... it would be neither just nor reasonable to hold her entirely responsible" (779). The truth of this sentiment will become evident as the different stories are analyzed in the chapters that follow. In all but a few of these tales, the degree of control and compliance that men demanded from women is well demonstrated, as are the lack of female agency and the submissiveness of many of these women.

"The Women of Spain" also alludes to a number of social and political factors that are outside the scope of this work, such as education and suffrage but, more importantly for my purposes, it does include and emphasize Pardo Bazán's personal disdain for the "double moral standard that prevails for the two sexes" (883, 887). Atavism, discussed in some detail in Chapter 1, is also alluded to in the essay as Pardo Bazán, almost casually, mentions "the despotic and jealous temper natural to the African races" (884). This is a controversial topic, foregrounded in "Apólogo" in Chapter 3 in relation to the treatment of women and also implied in three further stories.

On reading Pardo Bazán's discussion of the different "women of Spain", her views on social class become obvious, displaying "finely delineated distinctions of social strata" (Bieder "Family" 32). Pardo Bazán's "women of Spain" are all categorized (a nineteenth-century obsession), from the Queen down to the lowliest agricultural worker. Working-class women do not escape Pardo Bazán's observant eye; they are the "common people", encapsulating the "national character" of the country. Furthermore, they can be divided into "at least ten or twelve different popular female types" (899). These regional "types" are enumerated, as townswomen or countrywomen, and by region and province. For example, Pardo Bazán describes the *chulas* of Madrid as having "hasty and reckless tempers and all the fervor of unbridled passions" (900), while Andalusians, in her opinion, are "more timid and religious" (901). She ends by speaking of her own province, Galicia, where women are often seen carrying out intensive farm-work liberated from the home, not due to a desire for a freer way of life, but rather as a matter of survival.

As the different stories are analyzed, we will observe that many of the matters of class and regional differences raised in "The Women of Spain" can be found in Pardo Bazán's fictional narratives. By echoing this reality in her stories, her reading public is presented with fictional representations of "real-life" women, whom they would recognize, but few of whom would even come close to the ideal of the *ángel del hogar*. In the real world, in Pardo Bazán's view, this figure existed only in patriarchal fantasies. Bieder observes that, in the majority of Pardo Bazán's novels, female characters tend to reinforce and affirm existing patriarchal social values ("Authority" 473), but my examination of the women in Pardo Bazán's short stories will show that, while this may be true in respect to her longer fiction, an analysis of these shorter narratives will reveal multiple examples of challenges, even rebellion, against Spain's male-dominated status quo. In the stories discussed here very few of the protagonists conform to traditional social mores; in fact, many of the women characters actively and, sometimes dramatically, confront and resist them. In stories such as these, Pardo Bazán conveys a novel, subversive feminist viewpoint to her readers, presenting a different take on reality.

Challenge or Surrender? Two Different Responses

The protagonists who resist societal expectations are strong, independent women, who exert their own agency and, by doing so, challenge the norms of their society—*mujeres fuertes*, [independent women] to use Ann K. Hills's nomenclature (172). This phrase has positive overtones. However, along with the "good women", among Pardo Bazán's characters there are also examples of *mujeres fuertes* capable of criminal behavior. An obvious contrast to the *mujer fuerte* is the *mujer débil* [fragile, easily broken], a woman who succumbs and submits to prevailing patriarchal pressures. Women who align with this description are also represented here: some lose their honor, while others lose their lives or are maimed. Another point is notable: when the 25 stories are viewed as a whole, the majority of the female characters' actions appear to be in response to those of the men they are confronted with at the time. It is here that the truth of Pardo Bazán's statement concerning the degree to which a woman's behavior is in response to the man with whom she has associated with becomes clear, as compliance with male wishes often results, or threatens to result, in an outcome that is contrary to the woman's best interests.

Literary Style and Other Narrative Elements

Pardo Bazán's short stories, the majority of which were written in the last three decades of her life, reveal the full range of her ability to deploy different literary styles, an ability that was criticized and ridiculed by some of her contemporary male critics who accused her of being merely a "follower of fashion" (Gilmour 148). The coeval literary convention was that Spanish women writers were expected to promote the patriarchal *ángel del hogar* stereotype in their work. However, Pardo Bazán composed many of her short story narratives with discernible feminist sub-texts, and the interplay of these sub-texts with the dominant narratives subverts and challenges societal norms (Tolliver *Cigar* 13). This strategy is evident in many of the stories discussed here, with established literary styles and genres manipulated to create both a dominant surface reading that can be seen in some way to conform to the patriarchal mores of her society, and a less obvious sub-text that conveys a feminist message.

As this selection of stories was made on a thematic basis, factors such as style (as well as length and publication date) necessarily fall randomly within the chapters. On examination, the selection revealed examples of almost every recognized literary style of the nineteenth century. However, it is Realism, a style that that Pardo Bazán fully embraced in the late nineteenth century, which dominates, with almost twenty of the stories being either wholly or partially Realistic narratives. While this is discussed in greater detail in Chapter 1, it is worth quoting Pardo Bazán here as she states her particular view of Realism's words and wish lists. She extolled the style: "[O]ur national realism ... that is indirect and unconscious ... legitimate and profoundly human, so that like man himself [it] contains spirit and matter, heaven and earth" ("Spanish Realism" 264). A more prosaic definition of Realism is provided by Sister Mary Francis Slattery, who states that the style is an "illusion of exact correspondence with reality" portraying the "fragmented, flawed world of quotidian experience" (55). The breadth of daily human experience that is portrayed in the following stories will be shown to attest to the truth of both definitions, and I will explore this further in Chapter 1. Pardo Bazán also employs many other literary styles, but their usage, as will be demonstrated, will largely be to achieve a particular purpose in a narrative or to deliver a message that would appear to be too blunt to be expressed in a realist text.

Naturalism, found sparingly in the stories in this collection, is a term first used in its literary sense by Émile Zola (1840–1902) and is based on an atheistic philosophy "which sought the ultimate principle, if at all, in nature" (Brown 1). As discussed at length in the following chapter, this was a stance that Pardo Bazán, an avowed Catholic, modified in her own literature, with Lou Charnon Deutsch observing that Pardo Bazán characters always retained their free will (*Strategies* 85). Literary Romanticism is another important style in nineteenth-century Spanish literature, but in these particular stories it is largely confined to the treatment of the Don Juan figure, where Pardo Bazán's representations depict him in Romantic terms as "a Promethean rebel, fired by never-satisfied desire ... the polar opposite of the selfless, compliant, passionless feminine ideal" (Kirkpatrick *Románticas* 23). There are some Gothic tropes—mist and fog, ancient graveyards and abbeys, and mysterious, shadowy monks—which can be combined with Romanticism, in order to create certain impressions, and examples of this writing can be seen in a few of these narratives. However, the final story, featuring a *destripadora* and the desecration of a corpse is presented as a full-blown Gothic narrative, where the tropes serve to disguise unpopular and unsavory truths.

Pardo Bazán has also used other minor styles and genres. One story takes the form of a Fantastic narrative, set in its own alien world in which the reader must enter and accept as reality, and here, as with the Gothic style, unwelcome truths are presented to the reader. She also employed *Costumbrismo* from time to time. The name refers to a style of early nineteenth-century prose that concentrates on regional *costumbres*—customs and habits. Although often sentimental, the narratives are set in the real world, with subjects viewed through the eyes of an idealistic third-person narrator. Again, there is only one story entirely in this style, and *costumbrista* passages are discernible in other narratives. Sentimentalism and idealism also typify the *folletín*, a serialized romantic novella of which there is a single example. Pardo Bazán's understanding of each of these styles and her literary strategies will be the subject of extensive discussion shortly. As mentioned above, more than one narrative style can be observed in some texts and, more importantly, Pardo Bazán often manipulates and adapts styles, and their established tropes, and deploys them for her own purposes. One example is her treatment of the *folletín* where the trope of the traditional "happy ending" is subverted by replacing it with an ambiguous conclusion.

Pardo Bazán also uses allusions and intertexts in many of these narratives. Allusions are direct or indirect references within the text, regardless of the literary style, that bring another train of thought to the reader's mind relating to people, places, literary or cultural subjects etc., while an intertext is an entirely different narrative introduced as part of the plot itself; a striking example is observed in "La dama joven" in Chapter 3.

Another key element of the discussion will be the role of the narrative voice in the stories. Pardo Bazán is well known for her third-person narration, a style that her readers were comfortable with and accepted, but a surprising number of the selected texts feature first-person narration, in both masculine and feminine voices. The settings of the narratives also vary widely with urban locations predominating in the first chapters. Other tales are set in smaller towns: one encounter takes place in a prison cell, and the Galician stories discussed in Chapter 5 are largely rural. Overall, the narratives range across Spain's social classes, from representations of wealthy upper middle-class women to one of a woman who appears to be a pauper. This is, in some ways, an eclectic mix of stories, but the four thematic chapters and the secondary threads that link pairs or trios of stories together within the chapters provide an original analysis of largely unknown Pardo Bazán stories. It will be demonstrated that each of these narratives, either overtly or subversively, reflects some of the difficulties faced by women that Pardo Bazán observed in her own society and, in fictionalizing both these difficulties and her protagonists' responses to them, she has offered her readers an opportunity to connect the tale to their own world.

Roadmap to the Chapters

This work is structured with the present Introduction providing a broad overview of the entire work followed by five numbered chapters, The first, Chapter 1, "Emilia Pardo Bazán: *Feminista y cuentista*", provides the methodological framework for the four later analytical chapters. In this first chapter I outline relevant aspects of Pardo Bazán's life and literary achievements and situate her work within nineteenth-century Spanish society and its literary milieu. Included in this chapter is a detailed analysis of Spanish literary movements and Pardo Bazán's interpretations and handling of these different styles in order to achieve her objective for a particular narrative. The chapter focusses largely on the last thirty years or so of Pardo Bazán's life and on the feminist beliefs that began to dominate much of her literary output from the early 1890s onwards. In addition, I discuss two relatively short-lived, but significant, publishing enterprises at the beginning of this decade, Pardo Bazán's literary magazine *Nuevo Teatro Crítico* (1891–93) and the *Biblioteca de la Mujer* (1892–93, 1913). The fates of these two ventures are discussed in some detail, and I will demonstrate that their failures led to Pardo Bazán's increased focus on her short story production from this time onwards.

As already alluded to at the start of this introduction I also discuss four important societal conventions and practices that recur in these narratives. The first is the Spanish code of honor, with its fifteenth-century origins still impacting nineteenth-century Spanish society. This is followed by a discussion of the restrictive *ángel del hogar* paradigm, based on sixteenth-century Catholic teachings that, together with aspects of the honor code, evolved into the expected behavior pattern for *fin de siècle* middle-class Spanish women. As a corollary to the behavior patterns required by these two models, a third societal factor, the sexual double standard, became an accepted reality for many Spaniards. About half of the stories analyzed in this work address this problem, either overtly or in a more indirect way. *El qué dirán*, the community voice of judgment that frequently underpins the stories, is a fourth important societal influence, being a traditional feature of every Spanish community. Chapter 1 highlights its power in Spanish society, particularly in relation to women, before moving on to the stories themselves in subsequent chapters.

The four analytical chapters are themed according to the different situations represented in the women's lives, with further linkings between pairs or trios of stories within each analytical chapter. Chapter 2, "The Pitfalls of Love and Devotion" brings together and analyzes stories depicting women in a relationship with a man whom, in the end, they do not marry. Almost all the male protagonists in this chapter have a crippling character defect, and their actions place each of the female protagonists in a situation where they must determine their own future. Several of the narratives can be read against the grain to reveal a feminist perspective on the situations depicted. Social issues, such as the rights of single women and their legal position in society are raised, together with the ideal of the "angel in the house" model that underpins the societal expectations of the various, mainly middle-class, protagonists. In the opening pair of narratives, "El árbol rosa" (1921) and "Comedia" (1904), the female protagonists each meet a man who has noticed her in a public place and is intent on seduction, while the women view the men as a potential *novio* [fiancé/partner]. "El árbol rosa" portrays a strong female character who holds to her wish to protect her reputation by meeting in the public eye in the Parque de Buen Retiro. "Comedia" offers a contrast with the female protagonist being a naïve and easily deceived young woman, whose story ends tragically.

In the same chapter a trio of stories, "El zapato" (1911), "La redada" (1900) and "El encaje roto" (1897), form the second grouping. They all have strong female protagonists who break their engagements by challenging their respective fiancés directly and publicly. The stories in the final pair of this second chapter, "Los pendientes" (1909) and "Posesión" (1895), are unusual tales. "Los pendientes" is a fantasy narrative that can be read as an extreme parody of the *ángel del hogar* figure, while "Posesión", based loosely on a historical document, is set during the early years of the Inquisition, and consists largely of a power struggle between a woman accused of heresy and her inquisitor.

The stories in this chapter foreground social class, a woman's education (or, more accurately, the lack of it), and expectations of submission and gendered behavior. "Comedia" illustrates the consequences of poverty and ignorance for young women, while the trio of rebellious fiancées illustrate the reality that wealth may offer a woman some freedom. Breaking from the Realist style that dominates these short stories, Pardo Bazán employs fantasy, which at times borders on horror in the final two stories to critique patriarchally imposed behavior patterns.

Three pairs of stories are analyzed in Chapter 3, "Ruled by Head or Heart?" "Apólogo" (1898) and "La dama joven" (1855) form the first pair, "Las cutres" (1910) and "Coleccionista" (1910) the second, and the third pair consists of "Saletita" (1898) and "El mascarón" (1915). All of the female protagonists discussed in this chapter are alone in the world, having to make important decisions about their immediate and long-term futures. In the first story of each pair, the protagonists make rational and logical decisions, while the protagonists in the second narrative of each pair act according to their emotions. In addition, in each of these narratives there is at least one significant sub-text that invites the reader to consider a secondary societal or literary matter in the light of the main narrative.

In "Apólogo" the protagonist is an accomplished and successful operetta singer considering an offer of marriage from an intensely jealous man who forbids her to work after marriage. Resisting his demands, she takes dramatic action to protect herself and her career. In "La dama joven", a nineteenth-century romantic *folletín* in which the traditional happy ending is questioned, the protagonist decides between marriage and a stage career. Two dissimilar stories, "Coleccionista" (1912) and "Las cutres" (1910), form the second pair and are united by the perceived eccentricities of the female protagonists, as observed by the respective character observer-narrators. These stories also share "defiant endings" which supply insights that "disrupt the content" (McKenna 99) and both illustrate the immense pressure that *el qué dirán* placed on women. In the last two stories presented in this chapter, the single female protagonists are seeking security in their lives. "Saletita", the first tale, centers on a wealthy older *indiano* who arrives on the doorstep of his former girlfriend, now a middle-aged, widowed shopkeeper, living with her teenaged daughter.[10] In "El mascarón", the female protagonist, also a widowed shopkeeper in her forties longing for male company, is murdered during Carnival. The portrayal of the female protagonists discussed in Chapter 3 reflects a concern on Pardo Bazán's part for women on the fringes of society who lack male support through no apparent fault of their own. The female characters illustrate that women can, and do, act in their own interests. However, I will show that if their actions are driven by their emotions rather than reason, the outcome may be less than satisfactory.

In Chapter 4, "Don Juan's Downfall", Pardo Bazán uses different writing styles and literary techniques to foreground the plight of the women targeted by Don Juans, with a Romantic aesthetic and Romantic attitudes underpinning several of the narratives. I will analyze those aspects of Romanticism that Pardo Bazán used to undermine the figure of the traditional Don Juan. Each of the three pairs of narratives analyzed here exposes different aspects of the amorality of these men. Spanish society's almost universal acceptance of a male-biased sexual double standard aids and abets these would-be Don Juans in their endeavors. The six stories underscore Pardo Bazán's critical views of deceitful seducers such as these, and the subsequent dishonor and humiliation that the actions of predatory males inflicted upon thousands of Spanish women. The first pair, "Cenizas" (1902) and "Remordimiento" (1892), both portray Don Juan as an old man. In these stories the Don Juan's attentions prove fatal to the intended victims. In the second pair, "El aviso" (1897) and "El cinco de copas" (1893), Pardo Bazán uses the literary device of *deus ex machina* where apparently supernatural events save Don Juan's intended victims. "El aviso" is notable for the introductory narrator's overt denunciation of philandering men, voicing truths that, as the quotation from Fernández Cubas earlier in this chapter reminds us, would be difficult for Pardo Bazán to express openly. In "El cinco de copas" the reader must decide if the narration is the delusion of a sleepless and tormented man or a divine miracle. The two young female protagonists ultimately avoid, perhaps by chance, humiliation at the hands of their would-be seducers.

In the final two stories discussed in Chapter 4, "Dalinda" (1906) and "El pajarraco" (1912), the intended victims retaliate against the Don Juans, and in a reversal of tradition, it is the Don Juan figure who is left publicly humiliated. Dalinda, the protagonist of the eponymous story, defends her

---

10   An *indiano*, in the context of Pardo Bazán's stories, is a Spanish returnee from Latin America. Pardo Bazán's representations of this figure, as discussed in Chapter 3, portray older, wealthy men.

right to protect herself, while the intended victim of "El pajarraco" patiently organizes the indignity that ends the Don Juan's ignominious career. All six of the Don Juans in these stories are ultimately unsuccessful in their seduction attempts. Throughout her literary career Pardo Bazán repeatedly condemned donjuanesque behavior. The narratives in this chapter confirm that, despite the almost universal acceptance of predatory male behavior in her society, with presumably at least some of her male readership being among these predators, Pardo Bazán was prepared to confront these men directly with her message. In these stories she deliberately diminishes the traditional Romantic heroism of the figure, and, in addition, provides a degree of awareness and agency to several of her female characters.

The six stories of Chapter 5, "Galician Tales", are grouped in threes rather than pairs and were selected from the hundred plus Pardo Bazán stories set in the province of Galicia. The first three depict honest, hardworking, and well-meaning women of the province, followed by a darker, more violent trio of women in the second. The storylines are particularly concerned with the peculiar cultural and social factors faced by all Galicians in the late nineteenth century, which largely determined the fates of many of the province's inhabitants. There is a focus on the Galician customs, legends, and legendary female figures of the province, with snippets of the Galician language—*galego*—included in some.

The first three stories, "El molino" (1900), "La santa de Karnar" (1891) and "El aire cativo" (1919), illustrate the actions of honorable, law-abiding women whose decisions better their own lives and often the lives of those around them. The first, an example of Pardo Bazán's use of *costumbrismo* incorporates the legend of *La Santa Compaña*. The protagonist is a decisive female miller, feminine yet simultaneously exhibiting the "unwomanly" characteristics of bravery, fearlessness and physical strength. "El aire cativo" features a confident and rational young woman who supports herself by making deliveries. In this story's unexpected ending Pardo Bazán underscores the hold that the provincial legends have on even apparently strong and rational Galician women. "La santa de Karnar", which presents several interesting female protagonists, is centered on a nineteenth-century recluse, locally regarded as a miracle-working saint, although her character is not the focus of the tale. Two of the female characters, a mother and an older, blind woman are portrayed as single-minded and decisive. Furthermore, a subtext appears late in the narrative that focuses on the problematic dichotomy between faith and reason. Few of these women, despite their "unfeminine" mindset, are able to dismiss local folklore entirely.

The protagonists of the final three stories discussed in this chapter commit acts of violence, and the narratives exhibit a marked naturalistic tendency in the brutal and realistic depiction of that violence, according to Lou Charnon-Deutsch, who names each story but offers no further discussion of them ("Naturalism" 73). The first, "La capitana" (1902), is modelled on a real-life historical figure, a female bandit leader, whose men prey on small rural traders. The presumably murderous actions of the female laborer who is the protagonist of "La hoz" (1922), the second story discussed in this section, are driven by jealousy. In the final story, "Un destripador de antaño" (1890), Pardo Bazán re-works a Galician legend, narrating it as a Gothic horror tale centering on the brutal killing of an orphaned girl by her aunt. By deploying the Gothic style, Pardo Bazán articulates an unpalatable vision of the violence and brutality engendered by the Galician class system that would not be acceptable to her readers if it were presented in a realist manner.

The stories in this chapter all portray strong, self-assured, female protagonists, qualities that challenge the norms imposed on the urban middle-class women who would be reading them. These Galician women, who represent a cross section of the province's society, could be as violent as the men, a fact that Pardo Bazán also portrayed in other similar stories, and she is prepared to hold these violent women to account for their actions. All but two of the stories analyzed in depth in Chapters 2-5 feature women protagonists who, in some way challenge, defy or surrender to the conventions of their respective classes and societies—women who are largely the antitheses of *ángeles del hogar*. Additionally, these fictional protagonists depict the characteristics and imperfections that Pardo Bazán observed in her society, real women whose actions had been influenced or provoked in some way by the men in their society. The analysis will demonstrate that each of Pardo Bazán's defiant women protagonists exercises her own agency and makes her own decisions that affect her future. For some of the women, the decisions they make will better their lives; for others, their choices will have a less fortunate outcome.

I contend that Pardo Bazán, as a feminist and writer of fiction, made her greatest impact on Spanish literature and on her society through her production of widely read, accessible, and relatable stories such as these. They are all narratives that portray in detail the harsh realities of Spanish life, including the historical, gendered injustices that continued to dominate nineteenth-century Spanish society hampering women's freedoms. These are narratives that, in fact, portray a panoply of "fictional 'Women of Spain'" that matches those of the author's real-life observations of her countrywomen.

1
Emilia Pardo Bazán: *Feminista y cuentista*

> En la reivindicación de los derechos de la mujer [son] [p]az, calma, razón, paciencia, constancia, las únicas armas para conseguir el fin. Lento el progreso, lentísimo; ... Como los viajeros alpinistas, que necesitan abrir en la roca el hueco para colocar el pie, pero acaban por llegar a la cumbre y plantar en ella su bandera los defensores del derecho de la mujer avanzan solitarios, jamás cansados, aprovechando las mismas asperezas para ganar terreno y culminar su obra verdaderamente redentora.
>
> [The only weapons that will bring about the indication of women's rights are peace, calm, reason, patience and perseverance. Progress is slow, extremely slow. ... Just as mountaineers open a new foothold in a rock in order to take the next step towards the summit and on reaching it plant their flag there, defenders of women's rights advance on their own solitary path, never tiring, overcoming the challenges to gain ground and complete their truly redemptive work.]
>
> - EMILIA PARDO BAZÁN
> *Sobre los derechos de la mujer*

IN 1914, TOWARDS THE end of her life, Pardo Bazán was interviewed for the prestigious Madrid magazine *La Esfera* by El Caballero Audaz, the pseudonym of the journalist José Mariá Carretero Novillo (1887-1951). During the interview Pardo Bazán was asked "¿Qué opina usted sobre el femenismo?" [What are your views on feminism?] and her reply was, arguably, one of her clearest and most overt statements on this topic:

> Yo soy una radical feminista. Creo que todos los derechos que tiene el hombre debe tenerlos la mujer ... En los países menos adelantos es donde se considera a la mujer bestia de apetitos y carga. Los hombres en España alardean de aparecer siempre preocupados por el amor de las mujeres, y no puede haber mayor obstáculo que éste para el avance de la mujer [I am a radical feminist. I believe that all the rights that men have should

also be held by women ... In lesser developed countries, women are considered objects of lust and domestic servants. Spanish men boast of their preoccupation with their sexual conquests, and there can be no greater obstacle than this to the advancement of women]. (*La Esfera*, no. 7, pp. 6-8)

Some twenty years previously, in 1893, in a eulogy for the renowned Spanish feminist Concepción Arenal, Pardo Bazán publicly expressed her negative views of the *ángel del hogar* model, and all that it represented. For both Arenal and Pardo Bazán the construct of the *ángel* was the "verdadero obstáculo para que la mujer se transforme y se complete; [un] obstáculo serio y terrible" [the true stumbling block for a woman who wished to change and fulfil herself; it was a far-reaching and formidable obstacle] ("Arenal" 210). It is precisely these views that Pardo Bazán voiced so publicly that underpin, in one way or another, the short stories analyzed in this book, stories that foreground women who either challenge their society's gendered "ideals" of the *ángel del hogar* or are consumed by them.

As an avowed feminist Pardo Bazán had set herself apart from the mainstream of her society, never having accepted for herself the conventions that governed women's behavior, particularly that of middle-class women. Throughout her adult life, now well-documented by her biographers, Pardo Bazán exercised her agency, making and acting on her own decisions while railing against two deeply entrenched and intertwined gendered social mores—the Spanish code of honor (which in practice, encompassed the sexual double standard) and *el ángel del hogar*—that affected the day-to-day behavior of a high proportion of Spanish women. As every story discussed here makes some reference to either or both of these they will be examined in some detail in the pages that follow, as will *el qué dirán*, the "community watchdog" which, in reality, served to enforce social standards, particularly in smaller neighborhoods where it had a power that the subject of the gossip was largely unable to combat; its impact appeared to be particularly severe on women who challenged patriarchal expectations.

This chapter will also cover Pardo Bazán's post-1890 feminist-inspired publishing career, with a brief discussion of her literary magazine *Nuevo Teatro Crítico* (1891–93) and her *Biblioteca de la mujer* (1892–93, 1913). Both were successful, to a greater or lesser degree, but had limited impact, although the former did reinforce Pardo Bazán's name and literary credentials. Her subsequent focus on short story production and her success in disseminating these stories will also be discussed. An appreciation of the manner in which

Pardo Bazán manipulated her writing to create narratives with feminist subtexts is key to understanding the tales analyzed in these pages. One approach used in this way was Pardo Bazán's use of framed stories, where a second story is embedded in the opening story.

Other means involved her subversion of established narrative and generic styles, an overt presentation of the figure of the *mujer fuerte*, and an emphasis on the lamentable fates of deceived women protagonists. Pardo Bazán's skillful use of a variety of literary techniques, including tropes, allusions and intertexts which subvert the text in an entirely different manner, is also part of the discussion that follows, with an emphasis on how these strategies helped to introduce subversive feminist messages to her stories. Realism, the dominant literary novelistic style of the period, is examined in some detail, together with a discussion concerning Pardo Bazán's male-voiced Realist writing, with its potential for subversion. This is followed with an examination of other literary styles found in these stories. Finally, as so many of the stories chosen here are set in Galicia, we will consider Pardo Bazán's Galician stories, her ambivalent status as a Galician writer, and the polemics surrounding this status in the province itself.

The Development of the *Ángel del Hogar* in Spain

The stories at the center of this study are set between the early years of the nineteenth century and the first two decades of the twentieth, with one exception, "Posesión", a historical tale. All, either directly or obliquely, refer to the two traditional pillars of Spanish society at that time, the Spanish honor code and the *ángel del hogar*. The first is an integral part of the social fabric, part and parcel of patriarchy, not exclusive to Spain, however, the Hispanic concern is often much more apparent than that of other cultural traditions ("Honor" 273). The Spanish honor code of the nineteenth century had its origins in the Counter-Reformation, a European-wide period of Catholic revival that, it was hoped, would challenge the protestant Reformation. It began in 1545 with the Council of Trent and ended in 1781 (Bungener xxiv-xxxvii). Since 1492, Spain had identified closely with Catholicism and during the counter-reformation period of "revival", which Gwendolyn Barnes-Karol calls a "culture of control", the clergy were focused on imbuing Spanish men with ideological views that emphasized control of their daughters and wives in order to protect them from worldly temptations (51). Sermons stressed this matter to the contemporary population but, in retrospect, published clerical opinions were the most influential factor in restricting women's position in Spanish society for the greater part of the next four centuries. Shubert and Álvarez Junco state that it was only in the 1970s that the Spanish state asserted its independence from the Catholic Church (288-89).

Three well-known clerical publications have survived. The first text is Juan de Espinosa's *Diálogo en laude de las mujeres* (1580) which, as Anne J. Cruz notes, credits women with natural virtue (195). The second is *La perfecta casada* (1583) by Fray Luis de León (1527–91), which was inspired by Proverbs 31 in the Bible, a passage that lists the attributes of a virtuous wife, an ideal (but ultimately imaginary) woman that the biblical writer longed for. Originally penned as a private essay, *La perfecta casada* was later published in book form; it was well received and remained popular in Spain for several hundred years. It emphasizes wifely silence, honesty, absolute fidelity, piety, thrift, lack of vanity and motherly care of the children. In addition, the woman's central place in the home but not beyond it is stressed, despite the physical and monetary freedom that the biblical wife appears to have had as she "considers a field and buys it [and] out of her earnings she plants a vineyard" (Prov. 31. 16 *New International Version*). The place of the husband in relation to the wife is also firmly stated: a wife is a gift from God to the husband. It is her duty to do her husband's bidding, and the concluding paragraph assures the reader that a woman who follows the book's teachings will obtain her heavenly reward (León 119, 152). The reader is left with the overwhelming impression that Fray Luis considered women to be morally, physically and intellectually inferior to men, but also potentially powerful in their negative impact, capable of corrupting a man by their mere physical presence in the public sphere (León 10-11).

The third text is that of Juan de la Cerda, a Franciscan friar, who taught at length on the upbringing of daughters. In his 1599 treatise *Vida política de todos los estados de mugeres*, de la Cerda urges parents to be like dragons in guarding their daughters and states that young girls who are hidden and enclosed keep their honor unblemished, but in venturing outside they often become sullied, earning themselves a bad name. He adds that young women should avoid being seen by men, who, for their part, are apt to become involved in activities which cause young women serious harm if they also participate in them (f. 424 r).

Mary Elizabeth Perry explains that the treatment of women in this age was defined by two of Juan de la Cerda's recommendations: the literal enclosure of women in their houses or convents and the metaphorical enclosure of their lives in terms of passivity and obedience to men. If a woman deviated from social norms, she brought shame, not just to herself, but to her family. While the degree of enclosure for women relaxed somewhat over the centuries, the principle remained firmly embedded in the Spanish social psyche. In other words, the "gendered honor" that arose from these teachings was a burdensome social code that victimized women, with their honor based solely on the apparent absence of disgraceful behavior, particularly illicit sexual activity (Perry 124-25).

From these readings, it is seen that in early modern Europe honor for women was a preeminently sexual matter, while for men honor was judged by positive actions, with reputations being built on asserting oneself and controlling women. Perhaps the most succinctly expressed definition of this dichotomy is provided by Mandrell when he says that honor is "that which accrues to men but inheres in the comportment of women" ("Honor" 44). He refers to the idea of man as "one whose manliness stems from *making* and *doing*, as opposed to woman for whom it is a question of *being* and *existing*" (279-80). Thus, first and foremost, the Spanish notion of female honor stressed abstinence from sexual activity. With the loss of her virginity, a girl or woman diminished or extinguished her prospects of marriage and her hopes of a respectable and honorable womanhood. Paradoxically, the ultimate assessment of a woman's worth depended to a great degree on the integrity of the men with whom she associated, both by choice and by chance.

Anne Cruz observes that "these prescriptive and proscriptive codes were also written by men with their own interests in mind" (206). She further notes that, because "conclusions as to the historical status and welfare of women [are] all gleaned from male-centered texts", it is hard to discern what a woman's status and welfare might or might not really have been (206). Cruz continues: "In writing about women, men wrote about (male) desires: the demarcation of feminine absence in the text, then, ultimately ensures male presence" (206). This remained a complaint from progressive women for centuries, as Simone de Beauvoir (1908–1986) observed: "Representation of the world, like the world itself, is the work of men; they describe it from their own point of view, which they confuse with absolute truth" (133). Teachings set out by fifteenth- and sixteenth-century churchmen, who demanded sexual purity for women, were repeated and emphasized during the next two centuries by their clerical successors, setting an almost unattainable standard for a Spanish woman, who had no option but to comply.

Spanish women's lives became even more restricted in the nineteenth century when a further male-authored work, "The Angel in the House" (1854–62), an epic poem by the Englishman Coventry Patmore (1823–1896), was taken to heart by Western European men. The poem extols a form of "subjection, masked by the ideology of female domesticity" (Kirkpatrick

"Tradition" 353), and set out his middle-class Victorian expectations of women: docile, devoted and domesticized wives and mothers, paragons of virtue. Nina Auerbach considers that "three cherished Victorian institutions" were responsible for this British "angel" model: "the family, the patriarchal state, and God the Father" (1).

However, Spain's second pillar of *fin de siècle* Spanish society, *el ángel del hogar*, was not merely a response to a popular, somewhat sentimental nineteenth-century English poem. Although Spain may have used that label, the ideology behind it, as we have seen, had largely been adopted into Spanish society some time before. Intertwined with the code of honor, the nineteenth-century *ángel del hogar* was the culmination of more than four centuries of Spain's own historical development, with Auerbach's third institution "God the Father"—in the case of Spain, the Catholic church—from the sixteenth century onwards being largely responsible for its existence. Fray Luis de León's *La perfecta casada*, discussed above, remained popular and, in addition, María del Pilar Sinués de Marco, a notable Spanish writer, expressed these same sentiments in *El ángel del hogar* (1859).[1] Sinués's book was regarded as the "standard", detailing acceptable behavior for an ideal Spanish middle-class woman: a perfect wife and mother. This woman was submissive, a pious Catholic, obedient to her husband and forgiving of any of his infidelities. Many facets of this ideal of true femininity were, in fact, well established in Spain before 1850 (Kirkpatrick "Tradition" 344), but the popularity of Sinués's publication, reprinted regularly until 1881, ensured the widespread dissemination of this "angel" construct.

Sinués, and other women writers of the period, also presented the woman's role as that of a spiritual leader within the home. This diffuse and impossible ideal is described by A. Pirala in the women's magazine *La Moda Elegante Ilustrada*: a woman is "el vínculo de los más nobles afectos, la reguladora del orden y de la economía, el iris de paz, la inspiradora del contento y bien estar de todos" [the one who affectionately binds her family together, who keeps her household and its finances operating smoothly, one who radiates peace and ensures the contentment and well-being of all] (Jagoe 58). Joan M. Hoffman argues that this superhuman ideal created the social and literary model of a delicate, compliant, chaste, reticent and selfless being, but also one who was at the same time weak and repressed, needing protection,

---

1   There is no obvious evidence that Pardo Bazán was influenced in any way by Patmore's poem, but Burdiel notes that Sinués appropriated the title for her own book, which appeared soon after the first section of the poem had been published (412).

which all too easily became control. The nineteenth-century woman may have been an angel, she states, but she was an "angel without wings" ("Ángel" 28).

In comparing the sixteenth- and nineteenth-century writings on "ideal women" by "self-proclaimed authorities", Bridget A. Aldaraca has identified a shift in the reasoning behind the male rationale for women's behavior from the sixteenth-century work of Fray Luis to the nineteenth century. In every era, the woman is instructed to be modest, industrious, thrifty and (later) *ilustrada* [learned], but the true difference is marked by the idea that middle-class nineteenth-century woman's existence "begins and ends at her doorstep". In 1790, Doña Josefa Amar y Borbón published a paper which seems to suggest the existence of a greater freedom for women a century earlier. Amar y Borbón states that the "physical space of the house is no longer primarily a strongbox for the husband's possessions; it has been given a social content, and the social life in which the woman participates is no longer the harem-like exclusion of Fray Luis' enclosure" (qtd. in Aldaraca *Hogar* 31). This report indicates that eighteenth-century Spanish society was more relaxed about the physical situation of a woman than it had been previously. However, by the nineteenth century, Aldaraca notes that the woman was again defined "territorially, by the space which she occupies" (*Hogar* 27).

The *ángel del hogar* figure is often generalized as a middle-class woman who is married, a mother, housebound and supported by her husband, but Roberta Johnson, citing Alejandro San Martín, a nineteenth-century Spanish politician, is arguably closer to reality, stating that "there is no middle-class where women are concerned, only two widely divergent social classes: the rich woman and the poor woman, just as in feudal times. The painful difference is that the girl born and educated in the middle-class is poorer and more helpless than the country girl" ("*Concepts*" 92). Johnson adds that a century or so later Ubaldo Martínez Veiga reiterates this sentiment, but he also comments that working-class women who are left on their own can look for work, giving them an advantage over middle-class women in the same situation (73). Multiple Pardo Bazán short stories illustrate this: for example, the female protagonists in "Comedia", "Dalinda" and "La dama joven", which will be discussed in later chapters, are on their own in the world and find employment as a nursemaid, a waitress and a seamstress, respectively.

During the late nineteenth century, another, more modern figure, the hysteric, developed and became conflated with the *ángel del hogar* ideology. During the late 1870s, pseudo-scientific studies by the French psychoanalytic clinician Jean-Marie Charcot (1825–93) pronounced that women were susceptible to hysteria, a definable medical condition, which further reinforced the male rationale for the submission of Spanish middle-class women. Spanish proponents of the *ángel del hogar* model used a diagnosis of hysteria to confirm their beliefs in the hypersensitivity of the female nervous system and, therefore, a woman's unsuitability for any activity in the public realm. The female tendency towards hysteria, the bursting out of sublimated and repressed sexual energy, supposedly accounted for a woman's need to be both protected by a man and prevented from accessing education and the professions (Aldaraca "Medical" 401-405). Aldaraca concludes that socially constructed categories, such as hysteria, operate "in the realm of ideology to exercise control over the categorized group by those who define the category" (410-11). This was certainly true in Spain where this model was directed largely towards middle-class women and girls. Its effect was deployed as a further rationalization of their existing exclusion from the public sphere, their rudimentary education, and their exclusion from the professions ("Medical" 410-11).

Jennifer Smith furthers this discussion as she explains a perceived connection between a woman's religious experience leading to signs of hysteria, and she notes Pardo Bazán's addition to the debate and her disapproval thereof:

> [El hombre liberal] le prohíbe [a la mujer] ser librepensadora, mas no le consiente arrobos y extremos místicos. Detrás de la devota exaltada ve el padre, hermano, o marido alzarse la negra sombra del director espiritual un rival en autoridad. ... Así es que de todas las prácticas religiosas de la mujer, la que el hombre mira con más recelo es la confesión frecuente [A liberal man forbids his wife to be a free thinker, and also frowns upon religious or mystical extremes. Behind an ecstatic mystic the father, brother, or husband sees the black shadow of her spiritual director, a rival in authority. ... So, of all the religious practices of the woman, the one that the man regards with the most jealousy is frequent confession]. ("La mujer española" 91)

Smith continues, recounting findings of nineteenth-century medical professionals who correlate both spiritual love and unrequited love in a woman with outbreaks of hysteria. However, following through the examples that Smith discusses, one thread appears constant; the mystical experiences all follow an orthodox Catholic theology, centering on the figure of Jesus. As we shall see in "Posesión", the final story of Chapter 2, Pardo Bazán both used and subverted this theory by setting the tale in a previous era, one when Inquisitors solicited confessions from female heretic mystics who were asked to confess that their spiritual unions were sexual transgressions (66-70).

Pardo Bazán was one of several nineteenth-century Spanish women who actively promoted feminist ideas which, at their heart, encouraged women to claim the right to be responsible for their own decisions and act accordingly, thus challenging these established masculine views of domesticity and male control. The foregrounding of women's agency in the stories in this work highlights one aspect of Pardo Bazán's efforts to "normalize" a woman's independent decision-making.[2] As far as women's rights were concerned, *fin de siècle* Spain lagged behind the rest of Europe, the United States and even New Zealand. As stated above, the Spanish female behavioral legacy was one of submission to males in authority. The concepts of the male public and female private spheres and the cult of domesticity were regarded as moral prescriptions which women were supposed to respect. A Spanish woman's role was to get married and be a good wife and a good mother: "Her realm was the home: beyond was the realm of men" (Shubert *Social* 33). The feminist philosopher Diana T. Myers views this submissive upbringing as inimical to a girl's interests, explaining that cultural norms are established long before young girls are able to assess the desirability of choice as a life-shaping influence and, as a result, many young women will be predisposed to accept a subordinate social position.

EL QUÉ DIRÁN AND THE SOCIAL CONTROL OF WOMEN

With this restrictive, chaste behavioral pattern for women embedded in society, *el qué dirán*, the power of public opinion, expressed as community gossip, acts as an enforcer of these values. *El qué dirán* is a familiar theme in Pardo Bazán's short stories and it is discussed in connection with many texts in this work. Critical neighborhood gossip is certainly not confined to Spain. However, in Pardo Bazán's time Spain was largely rural, with a multitude of small, scattered towns in which it was hard to be anonymous. Women were often targeted for criticism, but men sometimes attracted negative public attention too, particularly persistent Don Juans and males perceived to be "unmanly". *El qué dirán* is a control mechanism that can be socially useful, particularly in smaller communities, contributing to social stability and cultural continuity and discouraging deviance (Gilmore *Aggression* xi). However, in Pardo

---

2   Christine Arkinstall's *Spanish Female Writers and the Freethinking Press* (1879–1926) provides a detailed account of these Spanish feminist activists.

Bazán's feminist stories, it is usually portrayed as a negative and destructive force that often leaves women victimized.

David D. Gilmore has written on this topic, drawing from his experiences in Andalusia, but I believe that the core of his argument can be applied to all Spanish communities and indeed beyond, to wider Western Europe and the Americas. He describes *el qué dirán*, "what they will say", as "covert aggression", verbal and indirect. It takes the form of whispers and innuendos; a rolling, snowballing wave of slander designed to damage an individual (*Aggression* 12, 55). During his studies Gilmore encountered eleven different Spanish words or phrases related to the practice of *el qué dirán;* this surprisingly large number gives the reader some indication of the complexity of the topic.[3]

Spanish men gossip among themselves when they gather in bars, taverns, and barbershops while the women in smaller communities tend to be housebound. Nevertheless, despite this restriction, women find reasons to gather and talk among themselves in the street or at the local markets.[4] People fear this talk, even as they participate in it, as it always corresponds to the worst paranoid fantasy of persecution—what the "worst" of the *malas lenguas* [scandalmongers] will say. Facts may be good, but hearsay is better "since it can be embroidered" (*Aggression* 34, 66). Gilmore depicts this community gossip as "a kind of ever-present Greek chorus ... full of arrogant justice ... but without a drop of mercy. ... It is the arbiter of social life and death, a threatening and therefore sinister thing [appearing] everywhere and nowhere, all men and women helpless before it, with no appeal" (34). Pardo Bazán often uses this anonymous Greek chorus in her short fiction as a literary technique to highlight the actions of women protagonists who have not conformed to the societal mores expected of them.

---

3   Criticar, rajar, darle la lengua, chismorear, paliquear, corte el traje, charlar, hablar oculto, contar, cuchichear, murmurar (*Aggression* 69-74).

4   One of Pardo Bazán 's stories not included here, "El indulto" (1883), narrates a rumor that illustrates this point: "Pero ¿de veras murió?"/-preguntaban las madrugadoras a las recién llegadas./-Si, mujer.../-Yo lo oí en el mercado.../-Yo, en la tienda...,/-¿A ti quién te lo dijo?/-A mí, mi marido./-¿Y a tu marido?/-El asistente del capitán./-¿Y al asistente?/-Su amo.../ Aquí ya la autoridad pareció suficente y nadie quiso averiguar más, sino dar por firme y valedera la noticia" [But, did he really die? the early risers asked those who had just arrived./ Yes. I heard it at the market./ Me? I heard it at the shop./ Who told you?/ My husband told me./ And who told your husband?/ The captain's orderly./ And who told the orderly?/ His boss./ At this point the source appeared sufficiently authoritative; no one attempted to learn more and everyone just accepted the news as reliable and valid] (1: 125).

Pardo Bazán's Public Persona

In her essays, short stories and public speaking, Pardo Bazán railed against the constraints that Spanish women experienced in their society, a society "based on the belief that the male is the superior sex and many of the social institutions and much social practice ... organized to reflect this ... so that the belief in male supremacy 'comes true'" (Spender 3). Pardo Bazán viewed language and writing "not as contested territory, but as her birthright, independent of her gender" (Bieder "Literary" 23). With her fiction employing male-voiced narrative and the feminist-leaning content of her short stories, essays and interviews, Pardo Bazán distanced herself from the norms and rhetoric of self-effacement that most other women writers had adopted. On the one hand, she was a living fulfilment of her arguments for equality with men; on the other, she was seen to be breaching the firmly established boundaries of gender activity, thus provoking a polemical response to her work (Bieder "En-gendering" 475). Considering this, it was hardly surprising that sharp criticism and controversy after controversy, now documented by her biographers, followed Pardo Bazán for the remainder of her life.

One of the first (of many) misogynous criticisms of Pardo Bazán's work appeared in 1879 when her first novel, *Pascual López: Autobiografía de un estudiante de medicina*, was published. The reviewer, Manuel de la Revilla y Moreno (1846–1881), a prominent literary critic, commented that Pardo Bazán, like an undesirable freak of nature possessed "el cerebro de un hombre en un cráneo femenino" [the brains of a man in the head of a woman]. Nevertheless, he grudgingly concluded his review with: "Siga por ese camino la señora Pardo Bazán y ocupará lugar distinguido entre nuestros novelistas" [if Pardo Bazán continues on this path she will occupy a distinguished place among our novelists] (*El Globo* 1,532, p. 1). Leopoldo Alas (Clarín) (1852–1901), Pereda, and Emilio Bobadilla (Fray Candil) (1862–1921) were three of those heavily involved in later personal attacks on Pardo Bazán's person and her works, couching their arguments in such a way that it was often impossible for Pardo Bazán to rebut them. One example is Alas's remark about *Los pazos de Ulloa* (1886): that no woman could produce a good Naturalist narrative, his implication being that either the novel was substandard, or that Pardo Bazán was not a proper woman—or perhaps both (Tolliver *Cigar* 23). Pereda compared the "immoral" protagonist of *Insolación* (1889) to Pardo Bazán herself, and Bobadilla referred to Pardo Bazán derisively as "mucho hombre" [quite a man] (*Cigar* 21). Occasionally she did respond directly to the criticisms; at other times she put it to the criticizing men that, as a woman, she was unable to respond (Tolliver "Distinguished" 221). Tolliver comments that this disparagement is "the price that she paid for using the 'distancing' form of address rather than the 'engaging narrations' of the sentimental novelists" (*Cigar* 34).

Nicola M. Gilmour addresses this dilemma of public perception that feminist *fin de siècle* writers faced. Pardo Bazán, characterized as "masculine" by critics because of her writing style, appeared to brush aside these inevitable personal insults and to remain impervious, "como estatua de mármol" [like a marble statue], to the mudslinging and criticism levelled at her by "los malos y los necios" [the stupid and the nasty] (Pardo Bazán "Educación" 174). However, in her private life she demonstrated a more conventional femininity, with her steadfast Catholicism and nationalist leanings, her fashionable dress and her culinary and household skills, all the while continuing to pen the greater part of her fiction in a male-voiced narrative, and under her own name, rather than a male pseudonym (Gilmour 149-53, 155).

Pardo Bazán's Feminist Publishing Ventures

Since childhood, Pardo Bazán had personally ignored the patriarchally-approved legacy of submission ("Apuntes" 25) and, towards the end of the nineteenth century, as her own feminist views developed, she appeared eager to disseminate them, either overtly, through her public speaking and in her essays, or more subtly in many of her short stories. The 1890s were a turning point for Pardo Bazán and this dissemination of her feminist ideals. In 1890 her father died and, inheriting his papal title, she became a countess, moved her family from Galicia to Madrid—a vibrant, literary-minded city at that time—and embarked on a prolific career in publishing. Between 1891 and 1912, Pardo Bazán collected and published eleven volumes of her short stories; from 1891 until 1893 she single-handedly wrote and produced a monthly literary magazine *Nuevo Teatro Crítico*; and the following year she launched a book series, *Biblioteca de la mujer*. During that same decade Pardo Bazán continued to write, adding to her already published twenty or so books another forty fiction and non-fiction volumes. At the same time hundreds of her articles and essays were also disseminated in various newspapers and literary magazines (Bravo-Villasante 309-26). Pardo Bazán's own *Nuevo Teatro Crítico*, and *Biblioteca de la mujer*, alongside two prominent literary magazines, *La España Moderna* (founded by Pardo Bazán's acquaintance José Lazaro Galdiano) and *La Ilustración Artística*, provided public platforms for the widespread circulation of many of her feminist essays, in which she plainly advocated for gendered equality in Spanish society.

Arguably, one of her greatest achievements was her single-handed authorship and production of *Nuevo Teatro Crítico*. There were thirty issues in all, each of about a hundred pages, which Pardo Bazán self-published between January 1891 and December 1893, using them to discuss subjects that she considered to have been neglected or glossed over in the press. Her aim was to educate a Spanish public that she viewed as "joven e inculto" [immature and uninformed] (Varela Jácome 159). The title, *Nuevo Teatro Crítico*, was a personal tribute to the Benedictine monk Benito Jerónimo Feijóo y Montenegro (1676–1764), of whom Pardo Bazán had been a long-time admirer.[5] Each issue featured at least one short story or serialized novella, a critical literary review of a recent book or play, a biography or obituary of a noted author, travel commentaries, historical essays, religious commentaries, fine art reproductions, an essay on a contemporary social or political theme and Pardo Bazán's own contributions to the polemics of the day, such as the literary feud between the two noted Spanish writers Juan Valera y Alcalá (1824–1905) and Ramón Campoamor (1817–1901). It was a publication which offered readers "las más diversas materias y asuntos" [distinctly diverse topics and issues] (Cornide Ferrant 329). Pardo Bazán's feminist essays in this magazine are singled out by Tolliver, who describes them as "uncompromising attacks on the gender mores of her time" (*Cigar* 64),[6] and Geraldine Scanlon describes this set of essays as being Pardo Bazán's "most obvious contribution to the feminist debate of the time" ("Gender" 230). In addition, Scanlon provides an extensive analysis of much of Pardo Bazán's "fresh and vigorous" literary criticism in *Nuevo Teatro Crítico* (234-243).

Most importantly, in Benito Varela Jácome's opinion, *Nuevo Teatro Crítico* provided Pardo Bazán with a platform to defend her own work, which she did zealously (160-61). In addition, she now had the opportunity to publish, without editorial censure, material which transgressed the moral boundaries of the time. Short stories, such as "No lo invento" (1891), which deals frankly with necrophilia, a topic that is still taboo more than a century later, and "Cuento primitivo" (1893), in which Pardo Bazán subverts the biblical story

---

5   Feijóo's own magazine, published between 1726 and 1740, was titled *Teatro crítico universal o discursos varios en todo género de materias para desengaño de errores comunes*.

6   Rocio Charques Gámez's *Los artículos feministas en el Nuevo Teatro Crítico de Emilia Pardo Bazán*, offers an analysis of eight feminist essays that appear in *Nuevo Teatro Crítico*: *La Biblioteca de la mujer*, "Concepción Arenal", "La cuestión académica", "El destino de la mujer", "La educación del hombre y la de la mujer", "La educación femenina", "Mujer y trabajo" and "*Tristana*".

of Adam and Eve by presenting it from a feminist perspective, are two examples of such provocative narratives. Three stories examined here, "La santa de Karnar", "El cinco de copas" and "Remordimiento", appear in volumes 4, 26 and 27 respectively. While the premise of the first and third of these tales is completely different, both feature a female protagonist who openly confronts and questions a man of some standing, on his own ground. Both protagonists acquit themselves well, thus challenging the accepted feminine behavioral mores of the day. "El cinco de copas" is a damning indictment of donjuanesque behavior, as it details the impunity of a would-be seducer targeting the naïve fifteen-year-old daughter of his friend.

Nuevo Teatro Crítico did make a considerable impact on the cultural life of the day, and it also consolidated Pardo Bazán's reputation as a serious literary critic and a member of the literary élite (Scanlon "Gender" 245). The success of this enterprise, while it lasted, gave Pardo Bazán great satisfaction. She artfully noted in the "Crónica Literaria" section of the March 1892 issue that she had recently noted a strange entry in the press headed "Gran fracaso", [Great Failure] detailing the closure of another literary magazine, *La revista*, "[p]or dificultades editoriales que no se han podido vencer, ha fracasado últimamente un gran proyecto literario ... una Revista crítica, redactada exclusivamente por Valera y Menéndez y Pelayo" [because of insurmountable editorial difficulties, a great literary project has recently failed ... the literary magazine edited by Valera and Menéndez y Pelayo] (85). Pardo Bazán laments its closure "más que nadie" [more than anything] before making it quite clear to her readers, that *her* successful magazine "no ha sido descabellada" [has not suffered the same preposterous fate] (86).

Pardo Bazán was keenly aware of the dearth of readily available feminist literature in the Spanish language and, in order to remedy this by informing and educating her compatriots she created a library of feminist literature, the *Biblioteca de la mujer*. She spent years planning for its publication, and her hopes for the success of this undertaking were immense. Six titles were published during the first year, 1892, and a further three were added in 1893, two of which were reprints of Pardo Bazán's own work.[7] Pardo Bazán advertised

---

7   The *Biblioteca de la mujer* comprised: *Vida de la Virgen María* María de Jesús de Ágreda (1892), *La esclavitud femenina* John Stuart Mill (1892), *Novelas* María de Zayas y Sotomayer (1892), *Reinar en secreto (La Maintenón)* Padre Mercier (SJ) (1892), *Historia de Isabel la Católica* Gonzalve de Nervo (1892), *Instrucción de la mujer cristiana* Juan Luis Vives (1892), *La revolución y la novela en Rusia* Emilia Pardo Bazán (1893 [1887]), *Mi romería* Emilia Pardo Bazán (1893 [1888]), *La mujer ante el socialismo* August Bebel (1893), *La cocina española antigua* Emilia Pardo Bazán

a further ten volumes, but they never appeared, and the *Biblioteca de la mujer* seemed to have folded.[8]

Twenty years later she concluded the series with two self-authored cookbooks, with a "rueful admission of failure appended to the first" (Wood 608). She expressed her frustration at the apparent lack of interest in her crusade in a much-quoted letter to the Director of *La Voz de Galicia* saying that when she founded the Women's Library, her objective was to disseminate reputable foreign feminist writings throughout Spain. In the end, she concluded that Spanish women appeared not to care about such matters. If, occasionally, a Spanish woman did mix in politics, she would ask for several quite different things, but none that directly interested or affected her as a woman. She adds "he resuelto prestar amplitud a la Sección de Economía Doméstica de dicha Biblioteca, y ya que no es útil hablar de derechos y adelantos femeninos, tratar gratamente de cómo se prepara escabeche de perdices y la bizcochada de almendra" [I have resolved to create a Home Economics Section of the above Library and, since it is useless to talk about women's rights and feminist advances, I am providing instructions for preparing marinated partridges and almond sponge cake] (Bravo-Villasante 280-81).

Pardo Bazán appeared to have been influenced by the English philosopher John Stuart Mill's 1869 essay "The Subjection of Women" which she included in her *Biblioteca de la mujer* in Spanish translation, and she reinforced his feminist message in her own essay "Del amor y la Amistad" published in *Nuevo Teatro Crítico*. In particular she responded to Mills's views on the inferior status of women and his musings on their capabilities of what they would be capable of if, like men, they were allowed to choose their own path and develop physically, morally and intellectually with total spontaneity. His conclusion was that the observable differences between the character and aptitudes of women and those of men, may very well be the product of circumstances, rather than a difference in natural intelligence (188).

Despite Pardo Bazán's best efforts with her magazine, it was the question of financial practicalities that brought it to a close: "*El Nuevo Teatro Crítico* fue un fracaso económico. La tirada de mil ejemplares era demasiado ambiciosa" [*Nuevo Teatro Crítico* was an economic failure. Printing a thousand copies was far too ambitious] (Buriel 455). A similar problem befell the *Biblioteca de la Mujer*. Three thousand copies of each volume were printed

---

(1913) and *La cocina española moderna* Emilia Pardo Bazán (1913). There was a full twenty years between the first nine volumes and the two Pardo Bazán cookbooks that completed the project.

8 Gareth Wood lists these proposed books (617).

but only the first book, which was relatively conservative in tone, sold well. Later volumes proved less popular and were even given away to subscribers of *Nuevo Teatro Crítico* (Wood 618). Nevertheless, "la coruñesa no entrega todos sus afanes a la causa feminista" [the lady from La Coruña was not channeling all her efforts into to this feminist cause] (Acosta 365) and, by 1894, she had largely turned her attention away from these enterprises. They had allowed her to disseminate explicitly feminist material, but she had come to realize that their impact was limited. Yet, fifteen years later she was still encouraging her readers to purchase copies and a 1908 advertisement in *Retratos y apuntes literarios* indicated that her *biblioteca* would still serve "para completar el conocimiento científico, histórico y filosófico de la mujer en todas las épocas y en todas las literaturas" [to complete a woman's scientific, historical and philosophical knowledge from every era and every style of literature] (Acosta 496-97).

Pardo Bazán had entered the Spanish literary scene a decade before with the publication of *La cuestión palpitante* (1883) and her responses to the ensuing and often acrimonious polemic demonstrated her willingness and ability to engage on an equal footing with some of her fiercest critics. However, the *Biblioteca de la mujer* and *Nuevo Teatro Crítico*, particularly the latter, cemented Pardo Bazán's place in this arena and showcased her as a versatile and successful writer, placing her at the forefront of both the Spanish public and literary worlds.

Pardo Bazán was by no means the only Spanish feminist publisher of her time. Arkinstall reports that "some twenty serious periodicals edited by and for women" were published during the last third of the nineteenth century (13). Many were traditional, focusing on feminine sacrifice, abnegation, modesty and virtue. However, the Barcelona-based, *La Ilustración de la Mujer* (1883–87), signaled a change of focus, being founded by Josefa Pujol de Collado and Dolores Monsedá de Maciá on "the defense of and struggle for women's rights" (13). The nineteenth-century feminist concerns of Pardo Bazán and the other women who have been mentioned were influenced by eighteenth-century enlightenment ideas about women, of men such as Feijóo, Charles Fourier (1772–1837), Immanuel Kant (1724–1804) and the aforementioned nineteenth-century John Stuart Mill (1806–1873). Following from this, Spanish feminist theory was uniquely tinged with social class consciousness when compared to feminist thought in other European countries and in the United States. This was especially true in the late nineteenth century and into the twentieth century, when Spain was finally beginning to catch up economically and socially with the European industrializing nations.

In Pardo Bazán's writings that do not overly emphasize social class overtly, her observations usually address the default middle-class (Johnson *Concepts* 92). This was not unusual and a Spanish women's press with a working-class orientation did not emerge until the twentieth century (Arkinstall 13).

Pardo Bazán as *cuentista*

From 1890 onwards and overlapping somewhat with her feminist publishing projects, Pardo Bazán embarked on her career as a *cuentista*.[9] Her narratives "[e]ntrelazan múltiples discursos sociales, económicos, matrimoniales, religiosos y psicológicos en torno a la construcción de la mujer española" [interweaved multiple social, economic, matrimonial, religious and psychological discourses concerning the make-up of the Spanish woman] (Bieder "Discurso" 96). I concur with the suggestion put forward by Porfirio Sánchez about Pardo Bazán's foray into the short story at this later stage of her career. He points out that the innate brevity and ephemeral nature of a story published in a newspaper or magazine, where over 400 of Pardo Bazán's stories originally appeared, allowed her a freedom to experiment with both literary styles and controversial topics that fell outside traditional novelistic conventions (314).

During the next three decades, until her death in 1921, Pardo Bazán's short stories would reach many thousands of readers, both in Spain and the wider Spanish-speaking world, a stark contrast to the limited circulation of her early feminist essays. Yet, towards the end of her life Pardo Bazán remained dismayed by the lamentable response of women when their menfolk made fun of feminist ideas: "¡[L]as mujeres! se crispaban, se escandalizaban, se deshacían en protestas de sumisíon a la autoridad viril. ... Eran las peores enemigas de las que pensábamos revindicarnos de derechos" [Women! They became agitated, scandalized, and dissolved into protests of submission to masculine authority. ... They were the worst enemies from whom we thought

---

9 During the previous decade Pardo Bazán had only published about a dozen stories, with approximately half of them incorporating a feminist slant that was at odds with the prevailing patriarchal mores. "La Borgoñona" (1883) relates a young girl's religious calling—as a friar, "El indulto" (1883) is a veiled critique of the gendered Spanish justice system, "La mayorazga de Bouzas" (1886) recounts a tomboyish mayorazga's cruel revenge on her husband's lover, "Morrión y Boina" (1889) tells of a man who claims that his wife's poetry is his own and "Primer amor" (1883) hints at sexual desire in an elderly spinster. Stories such as these, interspersed among more conservative tales, offered a more subtle and oblique feminist perspective than her essays and *Biblioteca* volumes.

we would claim our rights] (*La Nación de Buenos Aires* 1322). In her oratory and in her essays, she had campaigned persistently to change the attitudes which prevented women from stepping outside their traditional boundaries—in her view, a woman's opportunity for an education that was equal to that of a male, and the acceptance of their presence outside the domestic sphere should be uncontested rights.

Pardo Bazán certainly achieved at least one of her campaign aims for herself. Of the more than six hundred stories that she wrote during her lifetime a number offered an oblique feminist slant. They addressed her concerns about the gender-biased society of her time from a different, more accessible angle and were well represented among the more than four hundred that were published in Spain's most prominent newspapers and literary journals. Pardo Bazán employed a range of literary techniques to incorporate feminist sub-texts into texts whose content, on the surface, appeared to be patriarchally acceptable. Her male readers may not have welcomed the unapologetic feminism of Pardo Bazán's own journal and the *Biblioteca*, but the popularity of her stories, evident by the sheer number accepted for publication, did place her various disguised feminist messages in front of them. Among her readers were the men who had the power, if they wished to use it, to change aspects of Spain's patriarchal system to one that was more gender equitable.

Narrative Techniques in Pardo Bazán's Short Fiction

Although the majority of Pardo Bazán's stories were written in a Realist style (discussed later in this chapter), often drawn from her own observations or from *sucedidos,* incidents that she had either read or heard about, she exhibited a mastery of every literary style.[10] As I will show in the coming chapters Pardo Bazán was able to subtly manipulate style conventions to achieve a particular effect in a narrative in order to reach a defined section of her readership . Bieder describes this technique thus: "[Pardo Bazán] is set apart from her contemporary female writers by her ability to manipulate the conventions of generic traditions to produce different and at times competing effects in the reader. Her manipulation of the accepted conventions deflects recognized narrative strategies enabling them to fulfil unexpected functions ("En-gendering" 474). An earlier American poet, Emily Dickinson (1830–

---

10   In the Preface to her collection *Cuentos de amor,* Pardo Bazán defends her use of *sucedidos,* arguing that she has arranged the stories *her* way, sometimes "por gusto y capricho" [to my liking] but at other times when recent events are involved, "por respetos á la vida privada ajena" [out of respect for people's privacy] (351).

1886), of whom Pardo Bazán may or may not have been aware, had also articulated this practice: "Tell all the truth but tell it slant. ... The Truth must dazzle gradually" (563), an "instruction" ably carried out by Pardo Bazán as she shaped and slanted the familiar Spanish literary conventions in order to achieve her feminist-inspired literary objectives.

Framed narratives with their "stories within stories" structure, are one vehicle that Pardo Bazán uses to introduce subversive ideas. Nine of such framed stories are discussed: "El aviso", "Cenizas", "El cinco de copas", "Coleccionista", "Las cutres", "Un destripador de antaño", "El encaje roto", "Remordimiento" and "La santa de Karnar". A short explanation of this literary technique will clarify the terminology of the construct and provide an understanding of the differing roles of the narrators. In a framed story, a narrator introduces the first tale. while a second tale is often, (but not always) related by a second narrator. In the narratives in this selection, the second story is the main story and is not subordinate to the first, other than syntactically (Moger 315). Currently, there are at least three different approaches to naming the two narrators, who each adopt a different level of discursive authority. The first is Angela S. Moger's nomenclature of "narrator persona" and "internal narrator" (315). The second, which Susan Walter explains in detail, uses the terms "public narrator" and "private narrator" (*Frames* 34-38). The third, which Walter herself uses (following Mieke Bal) employs "embedding narrator" and "embedded narrator". I prefer to use this third approach using "embedding" and "embedded" narrators, as they refer directly to the respective narrator's entry levels in a particular narrative (*Frames* 36-38).

In a framed story, the embedding narrator creates their own voice; their role is to address the reader and, in so doing, bring the fictional world into existence, thus performing a public act. In four of the stories this narrator becomes the narratee, acting as an internal audience for the central story that unfolds in the embedded narrative. The second, embedded narrator is normally a character in the text, bound to the fictional world and dependent upon it to speak. When this narrator speaks, it can only be to others inside the fictional context. Each narrator brings their own ideology to bear, and it is these narratorial interactions themselves that contribute to the reader's interpretation of the tale (Lanser *Act* 138). Two mutually exclusive points of view are thus able to be presented in the story, propelling the reader into acting as mediator. These literary conversations, often including widely divergent opinions, draw the reader in and force them to determine meaning as they attempt to make sense of the seemingly arbitrary juxtaposition of frame and framed (Moger 321, 324). Walter further comments that a frame adds "something more" to a narrative, and one of these added elements may be a voice of social judgment (*Frames* 53).

Pardo Bazán often uses this literary device of embedded narratives to introduce a veiled critique of socially imposed gender inequities (Walter *Frames* 22, 39), and this critique, or sub-text, may contain an entirely different message and be read in an entirely different way from the surface text (Lanser "Feminist" 348-49). Pardo Bazán was only too aware that Spain's *fin de siècle* worldview was predominantly patriarchal, and her readers expected an authoritarian male voice in their literature. This expected male voice in the majority of Pardo Bazán's stories provided a point of identification with, or a point of entry to, the stories for male readers who may have been unable or unwilling to process the undertones and subtleties of female-voiced framed sub-texts directly (Thomas 83). There are very few female voices in Pardo Bazán's framed stories, with "El encaje roto" being the only known story to employ female narrators at both levels of narration. "Cenizas" uses a gender-neutral embedding narrator, as does "La santa de Karnar" (although the embedded narrator is a woman), while the embedding narrator of "Remordimiento" is female-voiced (but there is an interesting corollary to that statement, which I will explain in Chapter 4).

Sandra M. Gilbert and Susan Gubar assert that as nineteenth-century European feminist writing was emerging, the female writer's focus was changing. They eschewed the path of women who wrote for a readership of "'mere' women, like themselves", and also that of those who mimic men by disguising their identity. Their seminal 1979 work, *The Madwoman in the Attic: the Woman Writer and the Nineteenth-Century Literary Imagination* (1979), focusses on nineteenth-century women authors who circumvent these strategies, noting that they all "dealt with central female experiences from a specifically female perspective" and that they create submerged meanings, "hidden within or behind the more accessible 'public' content of their works" (72). In effect, they revised male genres, "using them to record their own dreams and their own stories in disguise." As the orthodox plot recedes, "another plot, hitherto submerged in the anonymity of the background, stands out in bold relief" (73, 75). A perusal of Pardo Bazán's feminist works makes it apparent that these findings of Gilbert and Gubar are particularly noticeable in many of her short stories as she worked within the system with the aims of informing and educating her readership with such "disguised" narratives. For McKenna, Pardo Bazán, employing strategies such as those outlined above, "repeatedly stretched and tested the limits of traditional social and literary boundaries while simultaneously maintaining a semblance of coexistence with the dominant ideology" (100).

Pardo Bazán's Female Characters

Although Pardo Bazán's novelistic protagonists largely conform to patriarchal values, María Elena Ojea Fernández argues that the female protagonists of Pardo Bazán's short stories often defy patriarchal expectations, either overtly or covertly. She adds that the Pardo Bazán female protagonist who challenges her traditional role is portrayed as "la mujer fuerte", who can be contrasted with Pardo Bazán's submissive protagonists "que le sirve para criticar la injustica del sistema patriarchal" [whose function is to censure the injustice of patriarchal ideology] (172). Ojea Fernández asserts that the female protagonists in Pardo Bazán's short stories are "mucho más comprometidos y progresistas—en relación al tema femenino—que sus novelas largas" [far more committed and progressive—in relation to feminist matters—than in her full-length novels] (173). Examples of both "strong" female protagonists who reject the restrictions of their society and "submissive" protagonists who remain trapped helplessly within them, can be identified in the narratives discussed in the following chapters.

Pardo Bazán's treatment of the strong protagonists illustrated her progressive feminist stance and set her writing apart from contemporary mainstream nineteenth-century Spanish women writers who, with a few exceptions, modelled their protagonists on "ideal women" who, by definition, deferred to their menfolk. Ojea Fernández's concept of the *mujeres fuertes* should be distinguished from the widely accepted model of the *Nueva Mujer Moderna*, or New Woman. *Mujeres fuertes* exist across all social classes. Their actions vary from the seemingly insignificant, altering only the moment, to those that change the course of their lives. Sometimes the women's decisions are positive; at other times they can have tragic results. However, each decision, good or bad, is made deliberately, without recourse to male advice. This differs from the New Woman, a cultural representation arising in the early 1900s that gradually became incorporated into societal values and the collective imaginary surrounding gender norms as women adapted to new social, political, economic and demographic contexts. Above all, it was a middle-class concept where women had greater access to areas of public activity, such as education, culture and new sectors of the labor market, thus enhancing their personal and professional options (Nash 31-32).

Allusions and Intertexts

In addition to her subversion of literary genres, framing techniques and use of familiar female societal models, Pardo Bazán utilizes her learning to reinforce her feminist viewpoint. The depth of her literary and artistic knowledge cannot be underestimated: "[F]ew contemporary Spanish men, let alone women, were able to match the breadth of Pardo Bazán s interests, her reading or her experience" (Bieder "Literature" 29). It is from this well of knowledge that Pardo Bazán draws, enriching her texts with constant references to history, world-wide literatures and literary tropes, hagiography, art and music. Allusions and intertextual references abound in her short stories. Ritva Leppihalme defines an allusion as a "[t]acit reference to another literary work, to another art, to history, to contemporary figures, or the like" (6). Allusions employ pre-formed linguistic material in either its original or a modified form, or proper names in order to convey an often-implicit meaning (3). An allusion may be only a single word in a sentence, such as "Cerezal" in "El zapato" (3: 424), but, to a reader familiar with a particular reference, an unspoken scenario or implication is brought to mind.

Four stories presented in this work have allusions to fairytales. Three, "El zapato", "La dama joven" and "Un destripador de antaño" allude to "Cenicienta" [Cinderella], while "El aire cativo" brings to mind "El principe rana" [The Frog Prince]. Only in "La dama joven" is the fairytale referenced directly; in the others a marriage prospect together with a ballroom and a shoe, a forlorn, overworked young orphan, or a kiss are sufficient for the reader to recall these well-known tales. Pardo Bazán's use of fairytales to effect subversions in her short stories follows an historical precedent. Melissa Ashley explains that the original fairytales were feminist critiques of patriarchal society created by seventeenth-century French female writers, such as Baroness Marie Catherine d'Aulnoy. Their central theme was subversive—the critique of arranged marriage with the heroines becoming agents of their own destinies. The customs and conventions that constrained women's freedom and agency were unsettled by exaggeration, parody, reversed gender roles (which in these texts are difficult to miss), references to classical myths and fables and medieval chivalry codes. Ashley adds that the patriarchy was critiqued with the male figures—kings and fathers—being represented as passive, ineffective and unreasonable. In a fairytale the female reader is invited to imagine the greatest freedom in her life, the freedom to choose whom to love, which is one of the main points that Pardo Bazán is making in "El zapato" and "La dama joven" in particular.

"La dama joven" also incorporates an intertextual reference to Adelardo López de Ayala's 1878 play *Consuelo*, while intertexts with Tirso de Molina and Zorrilla's theatrical versions of *Don Juan* are either directly referenced or alluded to throughout the six stories examined in Chapter 5. Pardo Bazán recalls E. T. A. Hoffmann's short story "Der Sandmann" in the introduction to "Un destripador de antaño", immediately setting the darker tone that the narrative will deliver. Another three stories, "Comedia", "Posesión" and "El aviso", allude to Francisco José de Goya's artwork. Pardo Bazán was passionate about art, and was particularly knowledgeable about Goya, presenting a lecture on his work to the Academia de Bellas Artes in 1901. "Comedia" references a swarm of bats, which recalls Goya's *Capricho 43*, an aquatint etching, "El sueño de la razón produce monstruos" [The Dream of Reason Creates Monsters]. The disheveled state of the condemned female protagonist in "Posesión" alludes to another from the same series, *Capricho 24*, "No hubo remedio" [There Was No Remedy], which portrays a disheveled woman astride a donkey traveling to her death at the stake. In "El aviso", the purple, leaden sky is described as resembling that depicted in the "célebre boceto de Goya" [Goya's famous etching] (1: 402), surely referring to the dome fresco of the Real Ermita de San Antonio de la Florida, a neoclassical chapel in central Madrid, (and since 1919, Goya's final burial place). In brief, her multiple cultural references extend across a variety of literary genres and artistic formats.

From a different perspective, many of Pardo Bazán's stories were published in magazines, such as *Blanco y Negro* and *La Ilustración Artística*, that employed artists to illustrate their texts. In most instances the artwork was decorative rather than informative, simply illustrating a scene from the tale, but there are two stories in this selection where the illustration reinforces a particular message from the story. "El molino" tells of a capable, hardworking miller, able to match the men around her both emotionally and physically, and thus demonstrating male attributes. However, the illustration alongside the text depicts a blonde, shapely and attractive young woman, albeit with bare feet. This reinforces Pardo Bazán's sub-text, of a feminine *mujer fuerte*, who is in control of her life. The other illustration is of an Andalusian man in "El mascarón", dressed in a Carnival outfit, and presented as a Berber of ill-repute, foreshadowing an atavistic sub-text to the narrative before the reader has even begun the story. It is unknown if these image selections were authorial or editorial, but either way, in both tales the picture influences the story. Pardo Bazán's use of this multiplicity of literary and artistic devices throughout these 25 stories not only enriched her texts, but it also offered her a subtle way of transmitting a secondary message that served as a reminder to her readers of the many gendered inequalities in Spanish society.

Considering the breadth of scholarship that Pardo Bazán incorporated into her short fiction her ideal reader appears to be an educated male, as familiar with Spanish literary styles and genres as she was, and the literary tropes incorporated in the texts would resonate immediately with this demographic. The aforestated mental "shorthand" enables complex scenarios from the original literary works to be expressed in few words and to be understood immediately by this ideal reader. "Comedia", with its introduction of Golden Age Drama tropes, enables a Realist narrative to be understood on an entirely different level, while the introductory tropes in "La dama joven" establish it as a *folletín*, a style that would appeal particularly to female readers. Centuries of *refundiciones* [re-workings] of the original Don Juan tale have provided Spanish literature with multiple tropes and stock characters—such as the friends of the protagonist in "Dalinda" for example, who the reader knows will do all in their power to help Don Juan seduce his victim. Gothic tropes have their place in these stories too, hinted at in "Cenizas" and patent in "Un destripador de antaño". A knowledge of the origins of Pardo Bazán's numerous tropes can take a reader's understanding of a story to a different level.

Many of Pardo Bazán's short story titles, contain or suggest allusions to a related, but unvoiced topic. For Pardo Bazán, a title was not only "un simple elemento identificativo y 'convencional' sino que destaca como acto perlocutivo con una triple función: persuasiva, provocadora y publicitaria" [a simple identifying and 'conventional' element but able to stand out as a perlocutionary act with a triple function: to persuade, to be provocative and to promote] (Martínez Arnaldos 453). In numerous narratives, Pardo Bazán's titling suggests connections and strategies for literary analysis and, for the reader, alternative interpretations of the text. Manuel Martínez Arnaldos cites Roland Barthes on the importance of titles: "El título ... es una cuestión a resolver que implica un código hermenéuetico" [The title ... is a matter of creating an unspoken exegesis {for the reader}] (453). The titles of some of the stories discussed in this study are straightforward, such as "El zapato", which names an object that forms a focus of the tale. Others, such as "El pajarraco", have a second meaning that becomes apparent as the story progresses, while still others, such as "Comedia", suggest a particular approach for analysis.

Atavism

Atavism is another lens that Pardo Bazán uses to communicate indirectly with her readers as characters whose origins or racial disparity caused them to be regarded as "outsiders" are introduced into her writings. It is, according to Elizabeth J. Ordóñez, "a discourse that essentializes non-European peoples as racially inferior", a view that seamlessly blends into nineteenth-century Spanish liberal thinking (23). In the late nineteenth century, both scientific writings and the popular press expounded views on atavism, heredity and organic memory, so it can be seen that, by adopting this attitude to non-European peoples, Pardo Bazán was a woman of her times. Brian J. Dendle states that Pardo Bazán "accepts almost without question the unverifiable speculations which contemporary biologists and ethnologists passed off as scientific laws" (30).[11] In similar vein, Charnon-Deutsch, while acknowledging that a few of Pardo Bazán's works are undeniably racist, asserts that she does remain within the mainstream of the thinking of her contemporaries who were all grappling with these ideas as they challenged the traditional Catholic doctrines of free will and monogenesis ("Theory" 147).

The intricate issue of racial disparity had been on Pardo Bazán's mind for a decade before her short stories that included this matter were published. In "Women of Spain" (1889) she distinguishes between *madrileñas* and *andaluzas*, [women from Madrid and Andalucia] with the latter exhibiting a "preponderance of the Semitic or African descent" ("Women" 904). Pardo Bazán continues: the Castilians are mixed Iberian-Celtic; the Basques are separate again, and the "purely Celtic division" are from Asturias and Galicia. She praises the personal characteristics of this latter group such as tender-heartedness and fidelity to their husbands (904), here suggesting that ethnic origin and temperament are linked.

Lou Charnon-Deutsch describes Pardo Bazán's instances of atavism as "haphazard", and suggests that it was perhaps appealing, particularly in her short stories, for the more prosaic reason that it functioned as a shortcut for defining a person's worth, personality traits or physical attributes ("Atavism" 145).[12] Atavism is foregrounded in "Apólogo", where it becomes an integral

---

11   Dendle defines atavism as "the reproduction of the moral or physical qualities of ancestors, however remote" (18) and Charnon-Deutsch, expressing the same ideas, states that the theory of organic memory is that memory and heredity are indivisible; we "remember" our ancestors in our bodies and may ... inherit their ... emotional proclivities ("Theory" 143).

12   In addition to the works with atavistic content discussed here, other examples of Pardo Bazán's introduction of the theme include: "Atavismos" (1912), the play *El becerro de metal* (1906, staged 1922), "Benito de Palermo" (1899), "El buen judío" (1910), "Corpus" (1899), *Una cristiana-La prueba* (1890), *Un drama* (1895), "Entre razas" (1898), *Finafrol* (1909), "La novela de Raimundo" (1898), "Maldición gitana" (1897), "El malvís" (1915), *El niño de Guzmán* (1899), "Los padres del santo" (1898),

part of the story and arises either openly or in a more veiled manner in "El árbol rosa", "Los pendientes" and "El mascarón". Bieder addresses this topic, offering a caution to the modern reader who may be offended by Pardo Bazán's atavistic writing. She states that the cultural assumptions and reading strategies that readers bring to a text do change over time. Much of what offended *fin de siècle* readers is now commonplace in contemporary Western society, and vice versa ("Insolación" 899).

Pardo Bazán, Literary Style and Genre

This section outlines the salient points of the chief literary styles as employed and interpreted by Pardo Bazán in her nineteenth- and early twentieth-century Spanish prose writing. Although Pardo Bazán is best known as one of Spain's leading nineteenth-century Realist fiction writers, she demonstrated a mastery of many literary styles and one of my arguments is that that it is in Pardo Bazán's short stories that the full range of her ability to manipulate established literary styles is demonstrated. In 1883, at the beginning of her literary career, Pardo Bazán herself had stated in *La cuestión palpitante* that "los períodos literarios nacen unos de otros, se suceden con orden ... no basta el capricho de un escritor, ni de muchos, para innovar formas artísticas; han de venir preparadas, han de deducirse de las anteriores" [literary periods are born one from the other, following in order ... the whim of one writer, or even many, is not sufficient to innovate fresh artistic forms; they have to be "primed", they must be developed from what has gone before] (8), and over her lifetime she demonstrated that with her deep understanding of Spain's literary history she could use and, if she wished, subvert any of the accepted styles for her own purposes.

Realism

The majority of the narratives discussed in this work are written in a Realist style and today Pardo Bazán is best known as one of Spain's leading nineteenth-century writers of Realist fiction. In fact, she is widely regarded as the only noteworthy female Realist.[13] Mandrell asserts that, historically, the effect of Spanish *costumbrismo*, which was popular well into the nineteenth

---

"La ventana cerrada" (1901) and "Vidrio de colores" (1998). This is by no means an exhaustive list.

13 Both Mandrell ("Realism" 3) and Torrecilla (98) name Leopoldo Alas (Clarín), Benito Pérez Galdós and Pardo Bazán as the leading Spanish Realist writers of the nineteenth century. Stephen Miller also includes Pardo Bazán in his listing of ten notable Realist writers of this period (410), while Zamostny lists her among

century, was to delay the move in Spain towards a Realist program of representation ("Realism" 94 n. 11). He further observes that in Spain, the earlier Romantic style was never fully repudiated as it was in other countries, but rather it was drawn into the Realist novel. The result of this "absorption" of Romanticism was that, within the Spanish canon, Romantic features, such as nostalgia and respect for tradition, became inextricably imbricated in nineteenth-century Spanish Realist fiction (99). There were also other factors, both literary and non-literary that affected Spain's late adoption of Realism. The first is the delayed rise of the middle-class, Realism's principal subject matter, during the period of Spain's slow and belated industrialization (Rutherford 271–74). The second is that canonical Spanish writers such as José María de Pereda (1833–1906) and Valera y Alcalá resisted the influence of French Realism. Jesús Torrecilla describes these early Spanish Realists reformulating some of the fundamental principles of the French movement, not from an individual but from a collective "Spanish" point of view, with the goal of appropriating the movement and shaping it to conform to Spanish literary taste (103).

It was Benito Pérez Galdós, Pardo Bazán's close friend, in his 1870 essay "Observaciones sobre la novela contemporánea en España" ["Observations Regarding the Contemporary Spanish Novel"] who provided the outlines for Spanish realism. He proposed using the style to create a genuinely Spanish modern literature rooted in authentic national tradition, free from foreign, particularly French, influences (Torrecilla 100). Realism grew in popularity in Spain, with the 1880s being the most intensive decade of long and short Realist narrative (Miller 417). It was adopted and developed by women writers and women readers in Spain from its beginnings and, as a genre, it reached out to a much wider social range, in terms both of readership and of characters represented, than earlier more élite forms of literature, such as poetry and drama (Morris 3-4).

Miller describes Realism as a style that created socio-mimetic fictions centered on the typical or representative people, manners, conflicts and particular times, places and settings of regional and national life (410), while Erich Auerbach considers that the central achievement of realist writing is the "serious treatment of everyday reality [and] the rise of lower-class protagonists as subject matter" (cited in Morris 48). Although literary realism imitates life, it is not a slice of life but a "representational form" and, as such, can never be identical with that which it represents (Morris 4). It records

---

the "firmly canonical": Pérez Galdós, Pardo Bazán, Pio Baroja, Ramón del Valle Inclán, Miguel de Unamuno and Ramón Gómez de la Serna (5).

experience, activities and emotions objectively, and without obvious authorial comment or condemnation, including activities and emotions regarded as sinful. In conservative Catholic Spain this was seen by some as apparently shamelessly promoting immorality and condoning evil—a stance that raised problems for Realist novelists, including Pereda and Valera, who held traditional Catholic moral values—and was particularly problematic for women writers such as Pardo Bazán (Rutherford 271-74).

The complex handling of time as historical process in narrative is another facet of Realist writing which is of particular importance in both the writing and analysis of short stories. Some stories, as Norman Friedman notes, are short because the material is of small compass, while others are of broader scope and may be abbreviated in order to maximize the artistic effect ("Short" 102).[14] Analepses, or flashbacks, and prolepses, or anticipatory sequences are the literary techniques that achieve anachrony, and Realism may also use external analepses and prolepses beyond the temporal span of the main narrative. This ordering of time allows the writer to meet a reader's expectations of the orderly sequence required for intelligibility (Morris 106). The third-person narration of Realist texts is able to convey the multiple, often contradictory levels of sensory, emotional and rational awareness that mingle to constitute subjective reality. Realism enables a many-layered complexity of perspective, voice, temporality and particularity to be achieved in a prose narrative (Morris 118).

Spanish Realism was a male-dominated domain, even if written by women. Narrators were predominantly third-person or male-voiced, and Pardo Bazán tended to follow this pattern. Early in her career she documented her views on Realist writing:

> Si es real cuanto tiene existencia y verdadera y efectiva, el realismo en el arte nos ofrece una teoría más ancha, completa y perfecta que el naturalismo. Comprende y abarca lo natural y lo espiritual, el cuerpo y el alma, y concilía y reduce á unidad la oposición del naturalismo y del idealismo racional. En el realismo cabe todo, menos las exageraciones y desvaríos de dos escuelas extremas, y por precisa consecuencia, exclusivistas [If everything that exists that is true and effective is real, realism in art offers us a broader, more complete and perfect theory than naturalism

---

14   For example, of the Pardo Bazán stories that I discuss, I consider "La redada" and "Apólogo" to be two representative examples of stories of "small compass", and "Remordimiento" and "El cinco de copas", where the storyline ranges over several years, to be representative of N. Friedman's second category.

does. It grasps and encompasses the natural and the spiritual, the body and the soul, and reconciles and creates a unity from the opposition of naturalism and rational idealism. Everything fits in realism—except the exaggerations and delusions of two extreme schools—that is to say, the exclusivists]. (*Cuestión* 151)

Pardo Bazán's belief that in the literary domain there is no distinction between men and women set her apart from the majority of her female contemporaries, women writers, the *literatas*, whose output was aimed at a female readership and reinforced the patriarchal *ángel del hogar* construct (*Cuestión* 366). Bieder explains Pardo Bazán's approach: "By adopting male-voicing, [she] creates no disruption for her readers on the surface ... she writes within and for a patriarchal society" and adds that this practice allows Pardo Bazán to address the same broad readership as her male contemporaries ("En-gendering" 475). Miller addresses, in some detail, the advantages of Pardo Bazán's position as the only major female Realist. One is that her male-voiced narratives prevented her work being pigeonholed in book series and periodicals reserved for women writers and audiences. Another is that writing within and for a patriarchal society gained her access to the same publishing venues as the male Realist writers. Additionally, Pardo Bazán's deliberate use of male narrators and perspectives enabled her to recreate the "touchstone" reality of Spanish society, which she could undermine by means of a subtle twist of viewpoint at the end that suddenly placed the narrated action in a woman-sensitive light (420).

Indeed, in some of Pardo Bazán's stories the male-voiced narrative itself is subversive, delivering unpopular statements. There are two examples of this in the following chapters: in "El aviso" the priest delivers a diatribe against the activities of philandering men, who, among other things, spread venereal disease, information which is both an uncomfortable truth for many of her male readers, and a difficult subject for a woman to opine on openly. The second example is in "Un destripador de antaño" as a Galician cathedral canon disparages his working-class parishioners, a harsh sentiment, which, as I will show in Chapter 5, Pardo Bazán appears to have deliberately included here in order to critique Galician authorities. By having male characters of some status deliver those statements Pardo Bazán provides them with a gravitas that, for her readership, would otherwise be missing.

Naturalism

Pardo Bazán's early novels were chiefly in a Naturalist style, and they established her reputation in Spain as a serious writer. However, she had particular views about Naturalism which, in some respects differed significantly from those of the French writer Émile Zola (1840–1902), and in 1884 she penned *La cuestión palpitante* as a response to the French Naturalist writers and their works.[15] Zola himself, as he was interviewed about Pardo Bazán's *La cuestión palpitante,* observed that he was unable to hide his surprise at the fact that Pardo Bazán, a married woman, was both a fervent and militant Catholic, and at the same time also a naturalist. His only explanation of the hearsay surrounding Pardo Bazán was that her naturalism could only have been purely formal, artistic, and literary (Mandrell "Realism" 98). French Naturalist novelists viewed the world as an impartial scientist would, with empirical observation being preferred to imagination. Both supernatural explanations of the physical world and absolute standards of free will and morality were rejected while nature and human experience were treated as deterministic and mechanical processes (Lehan 529). I concur with James Mandrell's explanation of Pardo Bazán's position that her staunch Catholicism and her doctrinaire faith in the possibility of individual will account for her inability to accept the deterministic slant of Zola's theories. Mandrell considers that Pardo Bazán's Naturalism, as was probably the case of all Naturalistic tendencies in Spain, was more stylistic or technical—perhaps modal is a better word than generic ("Realism" 97-98). While there are no stories in this work that could be described as wholly naturalistic, Charnon-Deutsch mentions Naturalism in relation to "La dama joven" and I will also show that specific episodes in each of the final trio of stories can be described as naturalistic in their brutality.

Romanticism

Romanticism arrived in Spain in the early nineteenth century, later than most other Western European countries, but due to Spain's political and social climate, was not fully taken up until the 1830s or 40s (Kirkpatrick

---

15 Pardo Bazán's early novels, *Un viaje de novios* (1881), *La Tribuna* (1883), *El cisne de Vilamorta* (1885), *Los pazos de Ulloa* (1886) and *La madre naturaleza* (1887) follow the Naturalist style. *La cuestión palpitante*, in addition to stating Pardo Bazán's Naturalist views, also showcased the breadth and depth of her historical and stylistic European literary knowledge, ranging, for example, from the work of the fourteenth century Geoffrey Chaucer (1340s–1400) to her coeval English, French and Spanish writers.

Románticas 1-2). In some of her short stories Pardo Bazán used this style for specific effects; here we find it chiefly in Chapter 4 where the male protagonists model their behavior on the Romantic figure of Don Juan, famously characterized in Tirso de Molino's (1579–1648) seventeenth-century drama *El burlador de Sevilla y convidado de piedra*. The term "romantic writing" was first used in the Middle Ages where it denoted a popular story, suggestive of the old romances, written in the vernacular (indeed, Lilian Furst notes that modern French still retains *roman*, a novel) (*Romanticism* 12). Legions of critics have attempted to "define" Romanticism—from the "sentimental melancholy" and "vague aspiration" of William Lyon Phelps (1865–1943) to George Sand's (1804–1876) "emotion rather than reason; the heart opposed to the head" (Furst 3-4).

Romanticism, according to Marlon B. Ross, is not simply a collection of works published between two arbitrary dates. Rather, it is a masculine phenomenon, seen as "a complex of values and beliefs, a set of structural, thematic and generic tendencies, an approach to the world with its own assumptions and aims, an ideology, however contentious and diverse its proponents". He adds that these men were writing in order "to reconfirm their capacity to influence the world in ways socially-historically determined as masculine" (29). Susan Kirkpatrick explains that "[t]he Romantic's commitment to making the individual subject the standpoint from which the world was viewed gave the movement a deeply introspective character" (*Románticas* 10). Ross echoes this point of view, stating that Romantic poets were on a quest "for self-creation, self-comprehension, for self-positioning that is unprecedented in literature" (26). The Don Juan figure of the Romantic era, with links to both Prometheus and to Lucifer, in common with other male romantic heroes, demands liberty and power without moral restraints (Kirkpatrick *Románticas* 10, 14). Pardo Bazán expounds her own views of the Romantic movement in the fourth chapter of *La cuestión palpitante* where she praises the Romantic "revolution", naming practically every European proponent of the style as she does so. She offers singular praise to the Spaniards Campoamor and Bécquer, two later romantics, before, somewhat ambivalently, roundly condemning romantics as "díscolos y sediciosos hasta lo sumo" [utterly wayward and seditious] and ridiculing the clothes and the lives of deceased romantic writers in a very personal way (35). I will show in my analyses of the stories in Chapter 4 that this ambivalence towards Romanticism will be used to undermine the romantic subject of Don Juan himself.

Gothic

Gothic writing, in Abigail Lee Six's opinion, is difficult to "categorize" and can be variously described as a text with Gothic elements or conventions, a mode, or a text that employs specific literary techniques. Gothic stories can blur boundaries as they appropriate features of other genres, resulting in Gothic being a mode with notoriously "fuzzy" edges (148). Maggie Kilgour observes that the main concern of the Gothic is not to "depict character but to create a feeling or effect in its readers by placing them in a state of thrilling suspense and uncertainty" (6).

Spanish readers considered the Gothic novel of the early 1800s to have been "popular" rather than serious fiction, however this opinion altered in the 1830s, when Spanish translations of E.T.A. Hoffmann's (1786–1882) works appeared.[16] They influenced a group of literary writers, notably Pedro de Madrazo (1816–1898) and Gertrudis Gómez de Avellaneda (1814–1873). Gothic tropes are a literary strategy that enables a writer to deliver uncomfortable information to a reader and still "keep responsibility for the content at a safe distance from his own standing" (Six 66) and, as these tropes became more recognized in Spanish fiction, Gothic narratives became a tool for later writers, including Pardo Bazán, to articulate or criticize ideas whose representation would not be acceptable in the prevailing realist mode (Aldana Reyes 113, 118). I argue that this point is essential to understanding Pardo Bazán's use of the style in "Un destripador de antaño" in particular, and several tropes that are incorporated into to this tale will be examined as the narrative analysis develops. Isolated Gothic tropes can also be observed in "Los pendientes", "Cenizas", "El cinco de copas" and "La santa de Karnar", and they will be commented on as they occur.

Costumbrismo

As with the Gothic style, there is only one tale presented here, "El molino", which Pardo Bazán herself categorized as being in the *costumbrista* style, but *costumbrista*-style writing is noted in "Coleccionista", "La santa de Karnar", "La capitana" and "Un destripador de antaño" where I will show that Pardo

---

16   "Der Sandmann" (1816), arguably, Hoffmann's most noted story, is a Gothic tale that was also used to instil terror into children and several of its tropes can be identified in Pardo Bazán's text. Hoffmann was among the first writers to use the short story to present "pleasurable horrific and startling effects" (Aldana Reyes 113). Pardo Bazán was well acquainted with the works of Hoffmann. Chapter 4 of Romero López's book details both Hoffmann's works in Pardo Bazán's personal library and her use of these works in her fiction (41-47).

Bazán uses it to create a specific effect in the reader's mind. Javier Jiménez traces the development of *costumbrismo* from its early eighteenth-century British and French roots: "It is a style that takes different elements from everyday life to construct an amalgam that becomes the typical, or even the national, whether a character or a place. ... [T]here is an interpretation or view of society transmitted through the image portrayed ... positively representing local character and tradition, identifying the local community's shared values" (57-58).

Costumbrismo as a corollary of Romanticism was fully established as a distinctive literary genre in Spain in the 1830s (Iarocci 387). The *cuadro de costumbres* (a brief sketch of social manners), with a "distinctive mimetic register of *costumbrismo*" (Iarocci 381), was a literary genre concerned with the depiction of an inherently Spanish way of life in a manner tolerable to a society and culture suspicious of anything that failed to uphold a perspective on public and personal morality that was incompatible with that advocated for and espoused by Catholic doctrine (Mandrell "Realism" 94).

Costumbrista stories later evolved to the form of a brief newspaper article aimed at a middle-class reading public. The object of representation, initially focused on abstract universal human nature, turned towards human subjects enmeshed in a specific time and place (Iarocci 387). A literate narrator becomes the measure of the reality as he attempts to document "slices of life" for his readers. The stories tend to reflect a fundamentally bourgeois view of an external world that was unfamiliar to the predominantly middle-class perspective of the readers.

Taking Fernán Caballero's novel *La gaviota* as a typical *costumbrista* text, Mandrell states that the protagonists are types, composites of various individuals: "todas las personas que componen la sociedad, prestan al pinto de costumbres cada cual su rasgo, que unidos todos como un mosáico, forman los tipos que presenta al público" [Various individuals unite, as the tiles in a mosaic do, to form the literary character that the writer presents to the public] ("Realism" 95). He continues: "The idealizing tendencies that are found in the writings of the *costumbristas* ... meant that reality as such was not portrayed, that the transcription of present-day reality was a glossing over of the real world of the middle and lower classes as a means of approaching some type of abstract social ideal" ("Realism" 95).

Paredes Núñez classifies Pardo Bazán's *costumbrismo* narratives as "cuentos directos", where the narrator not only configures the structure of the tale but is also its essence. He describes it as a narrative with a storyline that passes through "the subjective sieve" of the narrator's intentions, resulting in the transmission of the narrator's perspective to the reader. However, he appears to disparage the style somewhat when he refers to these narratives as "meros cuadros costumbristas" [simplistic *costumbrista* tales] (1: 48).

Pardo Bazán's *costumbrista* narratives in this publication, in my opinion, model the style of Ramón de Mesonero Romanos (1803–1882), one of *costumbrismo*'s most esteemed Spanish exponents whose "irony is light and … is rarely mean spirited. His tone is commonsensical, his outlook is practical … his even-tempered judgments model the satisfied comfort of the class he represents" (Iarocci 388). Additionally, as we will see in the relevant stories Pardo Bazán makes her own use of the style.

Lo Fantástico

"Los pendientes", one of thirteen of Pardo Bazán's narratives classified by Paredes Núñez as *Cuentos de fantasía*, is the only story included here that truly represents this style, although elements of Fantasy are also present in "Posesión". As with the Gothic style, Fantasy has a genre-specific didactic potential, which makes it possible to question the status quo more profoundly and indirectly than in Realist literature. Christopher Owen and Amy Crawford argue that this is because the non-realistic elements permit these works to criticize otherwise untouchable social and institutional systems of power. Equally importantly, they also allow topics to be discussed that would normally be unacceptable in a Realist work (16). Farah Mendlesohn describes such stories as "immersive fantasies", set in their own worlds that function on all levels as complete worlds, impervious to external influences, with an omniscient narrator making straightforward observations that express interest in rather than amazement at the fantastic elements of the story (59-60).

Folletín

The *folletín*, or *novela por entregas*, of which there is again only one example—"La dama joven"—refers to the market-induced fragmentation of a novel, published in a specific section of a newspaper; a practice that was well-established in Spain during the 1840s (Martí-López 71).[17] The literary *folletín* is characterized structurally by a simple vocabulary and syntax, with short, fragmented paragraphs, the latter due, in part, to the fact that writers were paid by the line. Action and dialog predominate over description and narration, and stock characters, including virtuous priests, predominate over psy-

---

17   The rise in popularity of the *folletín* in Spain paralleled the rise of the popular press and is explained in detail in Botrel's "La novela por entregas: unidad de creación y de consumo" (111-155).

chologically differentiated ones. Thematically, good and evil are demarcated, honorable certainties are emphasized and, at the conclusion, the female protagonist, usually a virtuous orphan, will be happily married (Martí-López 71-72). Michael Nimetz summarizes this typical ending rather more bluntly: "[T]he tribulations of pulp heroines disappear in the last instalment with a wave of a magic wand" (69). Pardo Bazán puts this sentiment to particular use in "La dama joven".

Pardo Bazán, a Galician Writer?

In this final section I wish to examine Pardo Bazán's relationship with her native province, focusing particularly on its unique cultural and literary histories. She had spent the first fifteen years of her life in Galicia, and she lived both there and in Madrid after her marriage, drawing on her origins for much of her novelistic work. The Galician people, their lifestyles, beliefs, and customs permeate fourteen of her twenty novels and over a hundred of her six hundred or so short stories (with almost half of the narratives examined in this work being set in Galicia). Nevertheless, in Galicia itself Pardo Bazán was shunned by the writing fraternity because she wrote solely in Spanish, rather than the Galician language, *galego*.[18] In addition, they asserted that she transgressed the conservative feminine code of Galician literature, which epitomized, in Manuel de Murgía's words, the characteristics of "dulzura, vaguedad y melancolía" [benevolence, incertitude and melancholia] (qtd. in Gonzáles Arias 107). Even today. an anti-Pardo Bazán sentiment is still evident among some of the province's writers—António Medeiros comments that in the early 2000s a nationalist-left Galician asserted to him that Pardo Bazán was a "bourgeois and *españolista* writer who didn't have anything to do with Galicia" (109).

Paredes Núñez suggests that Pardo Bazán's reasons for using Spanish were not political, ideological or artistic, but rather pragmatic, in order to achieve a wider dissemination of her work (Realidad 12-13). Pattison also holds this view: "If she did not withdraw into the narrow field of literature in the Galician language, it was in order to meet the challenge head-on, to reach a wide audience and to prove her competence to all Spain" (21). Similarly, Ordóñez has suggested that Pardo Bazán may have compromised cer-

---

18   There is a consensus that for the three main Spanish regional literatures, Basque, Catalan and Galician, the literary tradition and history of each area is constituted by the use of its regional language, thus excluding works in Spanish from the Galician canon. Conversely, works in the Spanish canon must be written in Spanish (Castilian) (Gabilondo 250-51).

tain aspects of her identity, in this case her affinity for Galicia, to negotiate acceptance by male writers (Gabilondo 257-58). But perhaps the most straightforward explanation of Pardo Bazán's use of Spanish is her own, that her knowledge of Galician was insufficient. She states bluntly: "[T]ropiezo con la dificultad del diálogo" [I run into difficulties with dialogs] ("Apuntes" 81). The result was that Pardo Bazán was excluded from her own province's official literature. Ironically Murgía, the father of the *Rexurdimento,* never wrote in Galician himself, although some of his works were subsequently translated into that language (Pereira Muro 76).[19]

As Pardo Bazán was establishing her position as one of the foremost writers in Spain, she was at the same time, with her numerous Galician novels and stories, contributing to the construction of the Galician-Spanish literary tradition as we know it today (Rodríguez Gonzáles). Her decision to write in Spanish and work with conventional Spanish publishers ensured that the readership of her Galician-based texts reached far beyond the minority of Spaniards who were fluent in *galego* (Sotelo Vázquez 310). However, as a Galician author, Pardo Bazán's problems were greater than matters of language or themes. As was to happen many times in her life, differences became personal, often resulting from her own deliberate statements and attitudes, which created an on-going, difficult, often contentious relationship with the Galician literary world. In her tribute to Rosalía de Castro (1885), for example, Pardo Bazán articulated her "nationalist, centralist Spanish ideology" by arguing that "hoy castellano [es] nuestro verdadero idioma" [nowadays Spanish is Spain's appropriate language] (Gabilondo 256). She added that Galician poets, in effect, compose in Galician "lo que pensaron en distincta lengua" [words that had come to mind in another language] and condemned Galician as a subaltern dialect of the illiterate, not a language of culture (*Tierra* 11, 8). With Pardo Bazán's arguably condescending views towards the Galician language and Galician writers, the torrid critical response she received is hardly surprising.

Conclusion

As I have argued above, Pardo Bazán's late nineteenth-century feminist views were strongly held, and she developed many strategies to disseminate them. Initially she achieved this through her two publishing endeavors. The first

---

19   The *Rexurdimento* was a movement led by Manuel de Murgía, beginning in 1863, that revived nationalist Galician identity, language, literature and culture. It was inspired by the publication of *Cantares gallegos* by Murgía's wife, Rosalía de Castro (1837–1885), a Galician post-Romantic writer and poet (Tenriero Prego 106).

was a literary magazine *Nuevo Teatro Crítico*, which also offered her an uncensored platform for her writing and further enabled her to participate in the literary polemics of her day, and the second was her production of ten re-printed feminist books in her *Biblioteca de la mujer*. *Nuevo Teatro Crítico* did establish Pardo Bazán as a serious writer and literary critic, but both enterprises were short lived. It is no coincidence that it was at this point that she markedly increased her short story output. H. G. Wells (1866–1946) is reputed to have stated that the 1880s and 1890s was the period where "short stories broke out everywhere" (Hanson *Short* 34). Indeed, this was the exact moment when Pardo Bazán began to pen short stories in earnest, and the Spanish popular press, essential for the circulation of these works, was well established. The short story form was considered a particularly appropriate vehicle for the expression of "the ex-centric, alienated vision of women", as they expressed their "difference of view" (Hanson "Re-reading" 3). Clare Hanson explains that these female short story writers see things differently from men and express what would otherwise remain hidden. They feel a sense of alienation from their dominant patriarchal cultures and, by using this story form, they can express such alienation more effectively than they could in novelistic prose ("Re-reading" 3). I have outlined the most important literary techniques that Pardo Bazán employed to embed her "alienated vision" in her short stories and thus indirectly challenge the gender-based inequalities of her society, and I will discuss these techniques in greater detail in the textual analyses that follow.

In the following chapters I will show that from the 1880s onward Pardo Bazán addressed the lack of an overt response to her feminist crusade for emancipation with this more subversive strategy—embedding her message in fictional narratives that would be read by thousands. By using this approach, she would not only entertain her readers but also educate and make them aware of the deleterious effects of the gendered injustices in her society. *Mujeres fuertes*, strong female protagonists who exercise their agency, feature in many of these stories. In other stories different situations are depicted where women suffer as a result of their inability to resist the wishes or selfish demands of their male companions, or as a response to verbal pressure from their communities. Women's decisions (like those of males) can be good or bad and, as many of these tales fictionalize the world Pardo Bazán observed around her, both outcomes are reflected in the often-subversive tales that will be discussed in the next four chapters. However, there is one common factor among these women: be they *mujeres fuertes* or *mujeres débiles*, there are very few indeed who even come close to the ubiquitous *ángel del hogar* model, who existed only in the Spanish patriarchal imagination.

2
The Pitfalls of Love and Devotion

> Many things happen (according to the proverbe)
> betweene the Cup and the Lippe.
>
> - WILLIAM LAMBARDE
> *A Perambulation of Kent* (1576)

AS WE HAVE SEEN, in *fin de siècle* Spain the ideal bourgeois woman was married and raising a family of devout Catholic children, and girls were brought up to believe that they were destined to follow this model. Many middle-class marriages were arranged by the families of the prospective bride and groom, and these arrangements were presented as a fait accompli to the couple. Pardo Bazán's own marriage to José Quiroga Pérez de Deza was such a one,[1] and there are plentiful examples of such situations in her short stories.[2] Other women found their own partners, while a minority did not wish to marry: some never received marriage proposals and other young women entered convents. Early marriage was common— the age of consent during the *fin de siècle* was thirteen—and a significant number of women who married older men were widowed at a young age. If these women did not remarry, they could well spend the balance of their lives facing the same problems as their unmarried sisters.

---

1   Burdiel details the backgrounds and assets of the Pardo Bazán and Quiroga Pérez de Deza families and comments "[f]ue un matrimonio benedecio por las familias de ambos, o al menos así lo aparece. ... De los sentimientos de los novios no conocemos nada" [it was a union looked upon agreeably by both families, or at least it appeared that way. ... We know nothing about the sentiments of the young couple themselves] (69).

2   Examples include "El árbol rosa", "La aventura" (1899), "La boda" (1909), "Champaña" (1898), "La dama joven", "Feminista" (1909) and "Remordimiento".

The seven stories discussed in this chapter feature unmarried women protagonists who have chosen a particular romantic relationship. In this chapter, as indeed in all the subsequent chapters, I have selected each of these narratives on the basis of the female protagonist's actions and her reasoning, (or lack of it), for her decisions. This has resulted in an eclectic juxtaposition of literary styles; if a particular style warrants further analysis it will be discussed as appropriate.

The female protagonist's individual situations in this first chapter represent a variety of the unforeseen problems and pitfalls that arise in real-life romances and engagements; here none result in marriage. These narratives starkly highlight two of the options available to Spanish women in the *fin de siècle*: to accept their traditional role as a wife or to challenge the expected female norms and perhaps attain a degree of independence, usually at a price. In every story, there is at least one female protagonist who deliberately exercises her agency and makes a particular life-changing decision. Some decisions have positive outcomes while others have dire consequences.

In the first pair of stories, "El árbol rosa" and "Comedia", each female protagonist responds differently to a man she encounters in a public place. Pursued by these men, the young women fall in love with them, and after a relatively short time, their thoughts turn towards a lasting commitment. The men, on the other hand, have different objectives—seduction, followed by abandonment. Milagros, the protagonist of "El árbol rosa", refuses to be seduced by her acquaintance, while in "Comedia" Lorenza is deceived by Mariner, succumbs to his wishes, and subsequently kills herself. The second section of this chapter focusses on three short stories: "El zapato" "La redada", and "El encaje roto". In each of these tales the female protagonist comes to a sudden realization that life with the man she is about to marry would be intolerable. Their fiancés are driven by jealousy or anger, and the destructiveness of these emotions in relationships is highlighted. These women all take charge of their situations, ending their engagements publicly and dramatically. The final pair of stories analyzed in this chapter are "Los pendientes", a Fantasy tale, and "Posesión", whose imagined ending verges on a horror scene. In both narratives Pardo Bazán takes the depictions of the protagonists to the point of disbelief. Claraluz, the protagonist in "Los pendientes", is a devoted, obedient and angelic *novia* who mutilates herself to please the man she loves. By contrast, the antagonist, Mara, is an exotic and seductive public dancer who pays a high price for her infidelity. Dorotea, the condemned female protagonist of "Posesión", is an aspiring nun who, instead of becoming a "bride of Christ", imagines herself becoming the "bride of Satan" and she will burn at the stake because of that.

"El árbol rosa" and "Comedia": Undying Love or Seduction?

"El árbol rosa" and "Comedia" foreground two naïve, motherless young women who are the objects of attention from men who have seen them in a public space and then approached them. However, the two women's actions both during the ensuing courtships and later, after realizing that they have been both deceived and abandoned, demonstrate two very different outcomes that reflect their upbringings and the strength of their characters. Milagros, the protagonist of "El árbol rosa", questions her suitor's insistence on privacy for their meetings and, indeed, by the end of the story, questions his very identity. When the young man disappears without warning from her life, she has the inner strength to put the romantic interlude into perspective and move on with her life. Lorenza, the protagonist of "Comedia" is entranced and then deceived by the man who has sought her out. He is a traveling actor who does manage to seduce her. She is stunned when he tells her that not only is he moving on, but also that he is married. Unlike Milagros, Lorenza does not have the inner strength to deal with these facts and she commits suicide.

A male's deception of a single woman by wooing and then abandoning her is a frequent theme in many of Pardo Bazán's stories. Some men, like the protagonists of these two stories are not depicted in the text as serial seducers but rather as sexual opportunists, and they can be read as exposing the sexual double standard of middle-class Spain.[3] It has been established earlier that a young Spanish woman's honor lies in her virginity, while, in Pardo Bazán's own words, a man "considers himself a superior being, authorized to throw off every yoke and question all authority and to arrange his life on an elastic moral system of his own making" ("Women" 884). Some men are married and simply seeking a temporary distraction, like Mariner in "Comedia", and mystery surrounds others, like Raimundo Corts in "El árbol rosa", who appears and then disappears without revealing his true identity. Nevertheless, the liaison is long enough for Milagros Alcocer to fall hopelessly in love with him.

"El árbol rosa" is perhaps best known for the fact that it is Pardo Bazán's last published story. It appeared in the feminist-oriented *Raza Española* in

---

3   Other men, often modelling themselves on literary Don Juans, pride themselves on the number of their sexual conquests; their stories, and the downfalls of the men in these tales, will be discussed in Chapter 4.

June 1921, a month after Pardo Bazán's death, in an edition dedicated to her memory that contained a selection of her writings, interspersed with eulogies from prominent Spanish literary figures. "El árbol rosa", surrounded by a decorative frame, was given pride of place, immediately following Blanca de los Ríos's editorial tribute "Páginas póstumas en honor de Emilia Pardo Bazán". The narrative was never included in any of the author's collections. It is set in Madrid, with Pardo Bazán incorporating, as she often does, well-known and identifiable places in the story: the church of San José (in Calle de Alcalá) and the Parque del Buen Retiro. There is a further detail that links the title of the story "El árbol rosa" with the Retiro: the eponymous picturesque pink-flowering trees in the park are commonly known as *árboles de Judas* [Judas trees], so named for Jesus's betrayer Judas, who was said to have hanged himself from such a tree, after which its white flowers turned bright pink with shame.[4] For readers aware of the tree species in the Retiro, both the allusion in the title and the setting prefigure the likely direction of the plot.

Milagros Alcocer, the female protagonist, is a young middle-class *madrileña* who enjoys more liberty than many of her contemporaries. Her mother has died and, as a result she does not have the strict parental control that would have been the norm for young women such as her at the time. She is reluctant to abuse her relative freedom, limiting herself to attending Mass and browsing various shops as she walks home through nearby streets. She keeps to herself and ignores the male comments that, according to the narrator, all good-looking girls in the city seem to receive.[5]

The story is interspersed with sections of free indirect discourse, and it begins at the point where the male protagonist, Raimundo Corts, follows Milagros to her home and tries to speak with her. She rebuffs him; however, he is waiting outside her house the next day and, despite her evident reluctance and discomfort, he walks with her. As he pressures her to suggest a place to meet, her first thought is "nowhere"; nevertheless, she relents and proposes a public, yet semi-private space that she knows of in El Retiro where there is "un árbol todo color de rosa" [a pink tree] (3: 334).[6] Raimundo

---

4   See, for example, https://www.britannica.com/plant/Judas-tree.

5   Here Pardo Bazán leaves the reader with an unflattering view of the streets of Madrid as places where no woman was able to pass without unwanted male attention.

6   English translations for this story and for "El encaje roto" later in the chapter are by María Cristina Urruela *Torn Lace and Other Stories* (pp. 134-41 and 60-67 respectively).

has apparently already fallen in love and, within minutes of meeting under the tree, Milagros is convinced that she loves him too.

Quesada Novás classifies "El árbol rosa" as a courtship tale. She acknowledges that all courtships are not alike, and not all begin with worthy intentions on both sides (162). This story is a good illustration of her point—Raimundo speaks as if he is an upright man but, as the story progresses, the reader begins to doubt him and by the end of the tale, after Milagros has investigated his story, it has become clear that his intentions were not honorable, and he simply tired of his fruitless efforts to seduce her and moved on.

Pardo Bazán has created a strong female *protagonista* in Milagros, a young woman with sufficient acumen and principles to question what she is told, even if at this point she does not really want to know the truth: "¿Quién era aquel sujeto que así se apoderaba de ella? ¿De dónde procedía, en qué se ocupaba; era, por lo menos, un hombre bueno, honrado?" [Who was this fellow who had captivated her so? Where did he come from, what was he doing? Was he, at the very least, a good man, an honest man?] (3: 334). She bombards Raimundo with questions and he answers them all with apparent sincerity: he is twenty-five, from Lérida, is the manager of a textile factory and in Madrid on business. Milagros's acceptance of his account of himself proves to be naïve. Like Micaelita in "El encaje roto" (in the next section), she endeavors to probe her suitor's character but neither young woman is successful, as both men behave in an apparently appropriate manner, deliberately concealing their baser characteristics of violence and deception. Milagros, in accepting Raimundo's answers as truthful, has set herself up for heartbreak.

From this point on, the couple have different goals for the relationship and the interplay of their two voices in the text leaves the reader in no doubt as to their respective attitudes and objectives. Raimundo wants to continue the liaison away from any public gaze, and he suggests meeting in "sitios más ocultos y menos poéticos" [places that were less poetic and more hidden] (3: 334). Milagros surprises herself with her ability to stand up to him on this matter: "No ... eso no. Aquí me parece que no hago nada censurable. En otra parte ... no. Eso no me lo pidas" [No ... not that. Here it seems to me I'm doing nothing wrong. Somewhere else ... no. Don't ask that of me]. (3: 334-35). It is now evident to the reader that Raimundo is not looking for romance, but seduction. Free direct discourse reveals his thoughts: "Tú transigirás, tú no tendrás remedio; me quieres demasiado para negarte mucho tiempo ya" [You will give in, you have no choice; you love me too much to refuse much longer]. So too are Milagros's mental calculations revealed as she responds:

"¿En qué ha de parar un amor como el mío, sino en boda? ... Si procediese con ligereza, él mismo dejaría de estimarme" [How is a love such as mine to end, if not in marriage? ... If I rush into this, he will lose his respect for me] (3: 335).

Milagros's upbringing serves her well, as the text states unequivocally that her "honradez de burguesa la amparaba" [her bourgeois honor protected her] (3: 335). Living "happily ever after" in Lérida seems an attractive proposition to her, but only as a respectable married woman, and her unwavering stance on this matter produces a battle of wills; she is steadfast in her decision to meet only in public, while Raimundo is longing to see her in secret. The tree at the center of the liaison is at first a welcome, attractive space. For Milagros it is semi-private, but still a community space; conversely, Raimundo increasingly regards it as semi-public, a fact which curtails his actions. Nevertheless, like all trees on the planet, the *árbol rosa* has a life process governed by the changing seasons of the year. When Milagros notices one day that the flowers are fading and falling, she instinctively sees it as a fateful signal that their relationship is also changing. That day they reprise their argument about their meeting place, and he berates her, telling her that she denied him "porque no le quería; se negaba porque era una estatua de yeso" [because she didn't love him, that she said no because she was a plaster statue] (3: 335). And, like María Azucena in "La redada" (again, in the next section), she responds to the man's petulance coolly and rationally, telling him that she is refusing because, from the beginning, she has understood their love as something serious and worthy. She questions him as to whether he agrees, before confronting him with the blunt truth, asking him if he is treating her simply as a distraction while he is in Madrid.

Suddenly Raimundo realizes that he is trapped. His confused reply confirms Milagros's accusation and, after one last unsuccessful effort to entice her into a private assignation, he snaps off a flowering twig and pockets it, presumably as a souvenir of their time together, before leaving. Unbeknownst to Milagros, that is the last time she will see him. That night he sends her a letter saying that he has been called away. Any doubts about Raimundo's character that may have grown in the reader's mind now seem justified.

The text has been scattered with "clues" that he is no respected businessman from Lérida, beginning with the deception and betrayal implied in the popular name of the tree itself. Raimundo, who has betrayed the woman who believed in him, is first depicted as a scruffily dressed young man inspecting a jeweler's shopfront; he himself later admits that he cannot afford to buy from there. He knows to smarten up before he accosts Milagros the next day and forces his company on her. He talks himself up as a hardworking and successful man, allegedly working in Madrid; however, he appears to have all the time in the world to pursue Milagros.

Milagros is depicted as an example of a well brought up, middle-class young woman, with strong moral and religious values. Yet she has a curiosity beyond that expected of a woman in her position, as is demonstrated by the fact that after Raimundo's disappearance she enlists a friend to help her trace him in Lérida, only to discover that nobody has heard of him in that city and, for her, reason eventually prevails over her heart. Quesada Novás observes: "Lo que caracteriza el desencuentro de los personajes de "El árbol rosa" es lo antitético de sus expectativas" [The marked characteristic of the discourses of the couple in "El árbol rosa" is the antithesis of their expectations] (167). Neither Raimundo nor Milagros get what they initially expected from the encounter. Raimundo's objective of a mere "distraction" proves to be too difficult, and he is not interested in marriage, the outcome that so appealed to Milagros.

Pardo Bazán's use of the ambiguity of "querer" that means either "to want" or "to love" in the text is interesting. A romantic interpretation of "él la había querido al mismo punto de verla" [he had fallen in love with her at first sight] leads the reader to believe that Raimundo has fallen hopelessly in love with Milagros. However, the eventual outcome of the story exposes Raimundo's true intentions. Throughout the narrative he has insisted that he and Milagros should move away from the public park to somewhere out of sight. His plucking the "memento" from the tree when he realizes that he has underestimated his quarry indicates to the reader that Raimundo has been fixated on desire rather than love and, for him, it is time to move on to a more compliant young woman.[7]

By contrast, Milagros is presented in the story as a strong, upright and resourceful young woman. Her values are traditional, and she is prepared to challenge a man who tries to coerce her into relaxing them. Even amid disappointment and heartbreak she can act rationally, as her enquiries in Lérida illustrate. The last paragraph of the narrative, almost a postscript, informs the reader that her dream of marriage did eventuate as some years later she marries an uncle, a moneyed returnee from Cuba. As discussed in the next chapter, few of Pardo Bazán's tales about these wealthy individuals depict happy, uncomplicated situations, but this story does not elaborate on Milagros's marriage, although it would be reasonable to assume that it was ar-

---

7   As she describes Raimundo's action of taking the flowering twig from the tree Pardo Bazán plants a covert double entendre in the minds of her readers—if she had used the verb "desflorar" her implication would have been overt.

ranged by her family. One day, accompanied by a small child, probably her own, (but the text does not specifically say so), she returns to the tree in the Retiro, to find it once more covered in blossoms, vibrant and luminous. While Raimundo picked a twig to remind him of the encounter under the tree, Milagros has the tree itself as it was during their "romance", and her memories of the few weeks, long ago, when she imagined that she was truly in love.

Also set in Madrid, "Comedia", the second story, questions gender and class, and their connection to power. It was published in 1904 in *Blanco y Negro*, whose name reflects its culture: the "contraste de la vida (a lo duro y a lo blando)" [the contrasts of life, both the good and the harsh] (Hemeroteca Digital *Blanco y Negro*).[8] The female protagonist, Lorenza, is alone in Madrid, but as the story progresses it becomes evident that, unlike Milagros in the previous story, she has few inner resources (and less cultural capital) to draw upon when she is called to make important decisions. Despite its name, the narrative form is still that of a short story and not a "comedia"; the *comedia* as a theatrical genre refers to the three-act poetic play, written by Lope de Vega (1562–1635) and his followers during the Spanish Golden Age,[9] and constitutes "probably the largest distinctive corpus of national drama in existence" (Wilson 39). Nor is it a story about a *comedia*; rather, it is a story that echoes selected motifs and tropes of the Golden Age dramatic form and, indeed, its temporal structure imitates that of the three-act drama. This temporal structure is created by the broad timeline based on the changing seasons that runs through the narrative. As the story opens, the trees in the plaza are "no muy hojosos" [almost leafless] (3: 352), indicating late autumn; winter afternoons are mentioned in the next paragraph and, in the following paragraph, "vino la primavera" [spring arrived] (3: 353). I demonstrate that these changing seasons divide the text into three "acts" that correspond with

---

8   *Blanco y Negro* has also been described by María Cruz Seoane Couceiro as "una publicación ligera ... y combinará lo literario ... con lo informativo, ofreciendo el aspecto gráfico de la actualidad ... y dirigiéndose a un público burgués y bienpensante" [an entertaining publication ... that combines the literary ... with the informative, offering a realistic view of the world ... tailored to a bourgeois and well-educated public] (308-10).

9   This term is defined by Carlos Fuentes as "*el siglo de oro*, the Age of Gold, the greatest century of Spanish literature and painting—the age of the ... dramatists Lope de Vega and Calderón de la Barca" (169). Another historian, Henryk Ziomek, extends the time frame somewhat, to "almost two centuries of great cultural intensity" (1).

the traditional three acts of the *comedia*: I "Introduction", II "Seduction" and III "Tragic Outcome" (my titles).

There are three main motifs in the Golden Age *comedia* genre. Love is one, but as Margaret Wilson observes, it is a love that seldom looks beyond physical fulfilment. The attraction between the sexes rarely moves beyond the physical, with the characters falling in love at first sight, and after that, desire is their chief spur to action. Beauty in women and the corresponding physical qualities in men inspire this love (42). Honor is a second motif of Golden Age drama.[10] In this era female honor was a preeminently sexual matter. By contrast, for a man, honor was judged by positive actions, with reputations being based on a man asserting himself and controlling women, in Mandrell's words honor "accrues to men but inheres in the comportment of women" (*Honor* 44) and men "make and do", while women "be and exist" (80). First and foremost, the Spanish notion of female honor stressed abstinence from sexual activity. With the loss of her virginity, a girl or woman diminished or extinguished her prospects of marriage and her hopes of a respectable and honorable womanhood.

During the Golden Age, Madrid not only became the theatrical capital of Europe but also the contemporary setting of the *comedia urbana*. Plays, notably those of Calderón, were set in private houses, patios, gardens, parks and plazas within the city (García Santo-Tomás 166). Pardo Bazán echoes this in "Comedia" where the setting of the opening scene follows the *comedia urbana* trope: a garden within a Madrid square, complete with a statue of an unnamed dramatic poet, where Lorenza, a nursery maid, often takes her small charge to play.[11] This square, a public place, is near a theatre and among the passers-by are actors leaving rehearsals, one of whom is the male protagonist of the story.

The reader learns that the female protagonist of "Comedia", Lorenza, is on her own in the world; her mother had died, and she left home when her father remarried a short time later. Here Pardo Bazán introduces a further literary trope, "the conventional omission of the mother in the *comedia* of the Golden age" (Templin 219). Pardo Bazán refers to the male protagonist as a *galán*, and as she did in the previous story, makes use of the ambiguity of a

---

10   The third motif, religion, does not feature in this narrative.

11   The Plaza de Santa Ana in central Madrid is a possible setting for "Comedia". The Teatro Español is situated on the eastern side and in the plaza itself there is a statue of Pedro Calderón de la Barca (1600–1681), one of Spain's prominent Golden Age *comediantes*. For two months during the late 1880s Pardo Bazán herself lived in la Plaza de Santa Ana, 31 (Acosta 265).

Spanish word (3: 353). Not only is *galán* the title given to the second leading man in a theatre troupe, but it is also the name given to a stock character of a *comedia*, a patient, persistent adorer who can be amusing and also a "wicked lover ... and a conqueror of female hearts" (Ziomek 45).

These attributes of Mariner, the male protagonist of the tale, align with the tropes of the classic *comedia* that Ziomek and others have described. Lorenza, however, does not represent the traditional strong female lead in a *comedia*, the dama; rather, she is an abandoned victim of the *galán*. She is similar, in some ways, to Tisbea, a fisherwoman in Tirso de Molina's play about Don Juan de Tenorio, *El Burlador de Sevilla y convidado de piedra* (1625), a character who was also seduced and abandoned. Tisbea, a fisherwoman, however, recognizes the class difference between herself and Don Juan Tenorio, her seducer, as she points out to him: "Soy desigual a tu ser" [I am not your equal] (41).

The narrative begins, as many of Pardo Bazán's narratives in this selection do, with a philosophical discourse in which Pardo Bazán addresses the question often asked of Realist writers: what impels them to write about everyday life? She explains herself by appealing to her readers to consider a question and to answer it for themselves; can one isolate oneself, encased in a rock-crystal urn perhaps,[12] and thus avoid encountering the harsher aspects of our daily lives? Pardo Bazán's challenge probes further: "¡Dolor! ¡Dolor ajeno ... sobre todo! ¿En qué nos atañe?" [Pain! Other people's pain ... in particular! Is that what concerns us?]. It is the answer to this question that "Comedia" invites (3: 352). As the tale concludes, the full extent of the female protagonist's emotional suffering becomes apparent, and the behavior of the male protagonist is shown to be clearly responsible for her plight. However, the attitude of this particular man is not uncommon; despite being already married, he seduces an attractive woman who crosses his path, and he then abandons her with no recriminations or regrets—a further Golden Age Don Juan trope.

Pardo Bazán's views on such licentious behavior were well known, having been delivered publicly at a conference in 1892 and reprinted in *Nuevo Teatro Crítico* a week later: "[Q]ue no haya inmoralidad comparable a la de una moral doble ... y la cuestión sexual ha arrastrado a la humanidad a constituirse una moral doble, monstruoso Jano que por un lado ríe con risa de sátiro y por otro se contrae con hipócrita mueca" [[T]here can be no im-

---

12   The Spanish is "una urna hialina" (3: 352) and refers to a vessel cut from hyaline quartz, more commonly known as rock crystal. The Prado has an example of such a vessel, currently included in their Catalog with the reference O000118.

morality comparable to that of the double standard. ... Sexual matters have disordered society in the creation of a moral double standard, typified by a monstrous Janus, with a lewd satyric smile on one face and a hypocritical grimace on the other] ("Educación" 157-58).

In the narrative Pardo Bazán continues her philosophical introduction with an aphorism: "Si revuela a nuestro alrededor un solo murciélago, nos crispa; si en una gruta pabellonada de sartas de murciélagos se nos aplana encima el enjambre, nos ahoga." [If a single bat flutters around us, we flinch; if an entire swarm envelops us in a in a confined grotto we are completely overwhelmed] (3: 352). Following on from this uncomfortable vision, the narrator addresses the reader, likening the universalization of human suffering to a swarm of bats. This reference to bats would, to many of Pardo Bazán's readers, recall the etchings by Francisco de Goya (1746–1828), *Los Caprichos*, and would find in this mention of bats an allusion to *Capricho 43*, "El sueño de la razón produce monstruos" [The Sleep of Reason Produces Monsters]. This etching depicts a swarm of bats (among other creatures) about to descend on to a sleeping figure. The *Diario de Madrid* reported on February 6 1799 that these art works were: "A series of prints ... etched by Don Francisco Goya [censuring] human errors and vices ... common throughout civilized society, and among vulgar prejudices and frauds rooted in custom, ignorance, or interest" (*Artstor*, anonymous translation for the Carnegie Gallery). Paul Ilie observes that in this etching, with its recognizable animals, "it is the concept of monstrosity itself that Goya explores and portrays". He adds that Goya's aim is to envision the nonrational possibilities of experience and these creatures come into existence during the withdrawal, "the so-called sleep", of reason (35, 38). I suggest here that in Pardo Bazán's allusion to Goya's famous etching she is, once again, calling out licentious male behavior, where irrational carnality, the specific moral failing at the heart of "Comedia", has suppressed reason.

The story itself begins with a succinct description of the female protagonist Lorenza, "[u]na mujer—una sirviente, niñera en casa de modestos empleados" [a young woman employed as a nursemaid by a middle-class couple] (3: 352), thus immediately establishing her situation and lowly status. Malito, Lorenza's charge, is an attractive, cherubic-looking child and, as the actors from a nearby theatre pass by, they often stop and run their fingers through his curls. However, one man, Mariner, has little interest in playing with the child, but he has noticed Lorenza with eyes "embebidos de sensualidad y desilusión" [that take in both her sensuality and her sadness] (3: 352). His verdict: "El chiquillo es divino, pero la niñera no es maleja" [The child is delightful, but his nursemaid is stunning.] (3: 352). "What is your name?" he asks her. And with this forthright, "love at first sight" approach to the girl, he ascertains her situation; she is young, vulnerable and alone in the area.

For Mariner, following the trope of the *galán*, the second "act", Winter, is a time for patience (3: 353). He looks for Lorenza each day and he stops to talk, although they have nothing in common and little to talk about, except Malito. The gulf between them is highlighted by the narrator's rhetorical question: "¿De qué se va a charlar con una pobre sirviente, una lugareña?" [Just what is there to talk about with a poor servant-girl, a local?] (3: 353). Mariner is a male, middle-class actor while Lorenza is a poor, little-educated local woman in service to a middle-class family. The gender and class differences ensure that Mariner's wishes will dominate the affair and ultimately prevail, while, unlike Tisbea, Lorenza appears to be unaware of the likely outcome of the "friendship". Mariner, like Raimundo in the previous story, has had seduction on his mind since he first saw Lorenza and he perseveres, knowing that talking to her, difficult as it is, is a necessary prelude to, in the narrator's words, "una seducción vulgar y regocijada" [a tawdry, but amusing seduction] (3: 353). Time does not improve Lorenza's conversational skills, even when the conversation is solely about her small charge. When Mariner does manage to take her and the child away from the square to a nearby café, he is reduced to humoring her by reciting lines from a play, a "comedia apasionada y romántica" [a passionate and romantic play] (3: 353), simply to keep some dialog and, indeed, the relationship itself, going. And that day, almost inevitably, Mariner achieves his nefarious wish, with Lorenza naïvely "cometiendo la locura mortal de no reservarse el alma." [making the grievous mistake of submitting herself totally] (3: 353).

"Act III", the arrival of Spring, the season of hope and renewal, signals a turning point of the story. Lorenza, who by now envisages an ongoing future with Mariner, confronts him timidly, declares her profound love for him and enquires about their next encounter. Mariner, whose upcoming contract in Catalonia is imminent, responds harshly with the belated truth: "Era casado; tenía ya dos retoños" [I am already married and have two children], before hurrying away (3: 353). This revelation stuns the young woman for several minutes before she feels able to return to her house. Lorenza's life is shattered; however, her final tragic action takes the reader by surprise. Female deaths are common in *comedias*, but the majority of these, forming a subgroup of at least thirty-one plays, are "wife-murders"—honor plays in which a husband kills or conspires to kill his wife (Stroud 91). The suicide of a disdained lover is less common.[13]

The narrative follows Lorenza's movements as she cleans the house, prepares the family's midday meal and gifts her two precious religious medals to Malito. We know her thoughts as she laboriously climbs several flights of stairs, evades the doorman of the building and opens the windows overlooking the central patio; at the last moment she somewhat absurdly worries about her earrings, before she steps out and plunges to her death. Her employers will obviously be shocked and miss her, but they will find someone else to care for Malito, and Mariner, by now in Catalonia, will probably never know about her death. She will be buried alone, with no one to mourn her—which brings the reader back to the beginning of the story and Pardo Bazán's question "¡El [d]olor ajeno, sobre todo! ¿En qué nos atañe?"

At the end of the narrative, it is obvious that this is the tale of a successful seduction and its unforeseen consequences. It emphasizes that casual, almost socially sanctioned seductions of vulnerable women have far-reaching consequences. The fact that many men, in their insulated middle-class homes, do not see the consequences of their self-gratifying actions, does not absolve them from blame. In "Comedia" Pardo Bazán has made widely accepted licentiousness both specific and heart wrenching. Lorenza, who appears in the story as unsophisticated and trusting, has little agency in her life. She, like Milagros in "El árbol rosa", does nothing wrong or immoral by chatting to an attractive man in a public place and, in the end, her downfall and her subsequent unbearable emotional pain are due to her naïvety and subservience. In Lorenza, Pardo Bazán has represented millions of other uneducated working-class women with scant personal agency. Her seducer, following the Golden Age Don Juan model of Tirso de Molina (and personifying Pardo Bazán's image of the married "monstruoso Jano") has triumphed, and is directly responsible for her suicide, the all-too common fate of seduced women that Pardo Bazán also references in her short story "Los escarmentados" (1909) (not included here).

Lorenza is representative of generations of women who have been taken advantage of and deceived by such men. And, with her feminist views concealed inside the philosophical questions that she directs at her readers, Pardo Bazán has informed them that the lives and the pain of women like Lorenza should concern them also. It is a strong message, cleverly delivered.

---

13 The suicide of a disdained lover follows the trope, influenced by Italian literature, that was introduced to Spanish drama at the beginning of the sixteenth century by Juan de Encina (1468–1529) (Wilson 39).

Refundiciones, or re-workings, of iconic Spanish dramas appeared, often centuries after the first works were performed.[14] In "Comedia" Pardo Bazán has provided the reader, not with a *refundición* of a specific narrative, but with an 1100-word prose re-working of the literary genre of the *comedia* itself, while also directly challenging and subverting the traditional popular image of the *galán* from a female perspective.

Lorenza and Mariner provide a complete contrast to the protagonists of "El árbol rosa". Unlike Lorenza and Mariner, Milagros and Raimundo (also something of an actor, it transpires) appear to find conversation easy, but the real difference is that Milagros is adamant that her meetings with Raimundo be public and, although this leads to the collapse of their relationship, she is able, in retrospect, to have some comprehension of the alternative. Lorenza, however, takes Mariner's "bait", leaves the public plaza for a private assignation, and pays the ultimate price. In both stories, however, disparities of class and education intersect with issues of gender. Milagros has been instilled by her family with a strong sense of personal morality and responsibility; she is streetwise and has a confidence in her own ability to stay safe and meet a man such as Raimundo on her own terms. With a character such as Lorenza, Pardo Bazán is able to remind her readers that poverty and ignorance are liabilities for any woman. When women who lack education and financial security encounter a man, who with society's blessing, is intent on seduction, their vulnerability is exposed and their lives and futures are in danger.

"El zapato", "La redada" and "El encaje roto": A Definite "No"

This next group of stories, "El zapato", "La redada" and "El encaje roto", are all Realist narratives that depict privileged women: one is a viscountess, and from the details provided by the texts, it is clear that the other two are from similarly wealthy families. All three women exercise their agency by acting in ways that are outside the prevailing "angel" construct that the society of their time might expect them to conform to. The first two stories are linked by an over-riding jealousy exhibited by the male protagonists, while in the second and third stories—both described by Paredes Núñez as "cuentos psicológicos" [psychologically oriented tales] ("Estudio" 1: 32)—a small, apparently insignificant action on the part of the male protagonist pivots the narrative entirely as each woman is suddenly made aware of the true characteristics of her respective fiancé and, as a result, dramatically ends the relationship.

---

14 Arguably, the best known of these is Zorrilla's *Don Juan Tenorio*, which was premiered in 1884, some two hundred and sixty years after Tirso de Molina's iconic *El burlador de Sevilla y convidado de piedra* (c. 1616).

Pardo Bazán's recourse to stories set in the upper echelons of society, as these three are, has been noted by critics. She was a countess in her own right, familiar with the Galician aristocracy and the upper reaches of Madrid society and, as Pattison comments, she "often assumes the position of an observer who is informing her public about things concerning which they have no first-hand knowledge. She smugly lets us know that she is quite at home in high society and implies that she can write about it with true insight" (3-4).[15] Bieder offers two reasons for what she describes as Pardo Bazán's "continued reliance on wealthy and/or aristocratic settings and characters" ("Plotting" 142). The first is the Spanish reading public's taste for stories about a private and privileged sphere outside their own experience, and the second is that the absence of economic desire and greater freedoms for women among the upper classes creates a world that is both attractive and alien to Pardo Bazán's readers. Indeed, Pardo Bazán herself comments about this aristocratic lifestyle at some length in "The Women of Spain". Bieder adds that this particular setting "frees [her readers] to follow her plot through a gender realignment that they would otherwise resist or reject. By creating this world within conventions of established literary genres, but outside most readers' experience, Pardo Bazán frees herself to undercut traditional plotting without initially alienating her reader" ("Plotting" 142). This trio of stories are all set in this "attractive and alien" world.[16]

Linda M. Willem has observed that within Pardo Bazán's immense corpus of short stories there are individual stories that echo each other and retell the same idea in a different manner (91). The next two stories, "El zapato" and "La redada", illustrate this. Willem's examples compare unframed and framed narratives, but the narrative constructions of these particular stories are less complicated. They were published in popular literary magazines and both stories employ similar, socially well-connected, first-person male narrators. These narrators also share the same self-awareness of their own frailty; an emotionally crippling jealous streak in their makeup that in each case leads to a similar ending. In each of these two stories, Pardo Bazán makes one point, and she does it well.

---

15 Pardo Bazán was even included in a photograph with the Spanish royal family taken in 1912 at a Valencian art gallery (Acosta 320-21).

16 Pardo Bazán also used alien world settings in both Fantastic and Gothic narratives for the same reason. Examples of these are discussed later in this chapter and in Chapter 5.

"El zapato" and "La redada" are two of nine Pardo Bazán "love stories" in which jealousy on the part of the male has destroyed the relationship.[17] Considering jealousy as a significant theme in short stories such as these Quesada Novás notes: "[L]o cierto es que su aparición implica el nacimiento de una etapa en que la violencia se instala en la pareja, en un crescendo continuo que suele desembocar en la destrucción del sentimiento amoroso" [The truth is that its appearance implies the death knell of a relationship. Jealousy causes a continuous crescendo of outrage between a couple that usually ends with the destruction of mutual love] (83-84). From the opening sentences, all-consuming male jealousy underpins "El zapato" and "La redada" and, as the stories unfold, they illustrate exactly Quesada Novás's observations. The female protagonists also act unconventionally as they themselves precipitate the dramatic, public terminations of the respective liaisons. The two women display entirely different personalities, but their defiance of their respective partners' wishes also defies expected bourgeois behavior. The introductions to the stories are similar; soliloquies delivered by a neurotic and bitter ex-fiancé relating the final moments of his relationship with a young woman whose actions or words caused the marriage to be called off. The narratives themselves are short. Nevertheless, they are accessible and, most importantly, they do deliver a powerful feminist statement.

"El zapato" first appeared in 1911 in *La Ilustración Española y Americana*, a prominent bi-monthly Madrid publication in which more than eighty of Pardo Bazán's stories appeared. "El zapato" is a first-person narration, and it is principally a reflection by the narrator on an incident that publicly ended a particularly turbulent engagement somewhat embarrassingly. At the time of the narration, the engagement and its outcome are long past, but the breakup is recalled in vivid detail.

The unnamed male narrator tells his side of the story, opening with a self-pitying response to the somewhat banal aphorism he has heard more than once that "el amor es felicidad" [that love equates with happiness] (3: 424). In this rambling, rhetorical reflection he admits to a major flaw in his character—that love and jealousy have become inextricably intertwined in

---

17   These stories are: "Apólogo", "La careta rosa" (1918), "El guardapelo" (1898), "Heno" (1908), "Humano" (1909), "La puñalada" (1901), "La redada", "El revólver" (1895) and "El zapato". In all but one of these stories listed by Quesada Novás, jealousy is an uncontrollable male affliction that is a source of unhappiness to the man himself as well as to his partner, and these men view themselves as victims of their failed relationships (83). The exception, "El revólver", focusses on a woman's mental suffering at the hands of a jealous husband.

his psyche—and he has been made to appear ridiculous over the years because of this. The tale that he then relates illustrates this point precisely. At the time his main story is set, the narrator is twenty-three and in the process of establishing a career. He and Meli Padilla, the female protagonist, are obviously a well-to-do upper-middle-class young couple. Meli is irked at her fiancé's constant correction of her behavior while he, in turn, is possessive, overly jealous and suspicious of her every move. The relationship is not easy; the narrator laments the fact that "[n]i el demonio, que todo lo añasca, podía haberme buscado novia más inquietadora" [not even the devil, who ruins everything, could have found me a more unsettling fiancée] (3: 424). Meli is angelic looking, but she refuses to conform to his patriarchal expectations and follows her own impulses. He is provoked by her flirting and gossiping, and this leads to constant bickering between them. The narrator is introspective and self-centered, but also surprisingly self-aware, as he describes the depths of his despair over his inability to master Meli.

Meli, in fact, holds the upper hand in the liaison by disobeying and provoking her despairing *novio* who, perceiving her behavior as somewhat malicious, laments: "La idea del suicidio me visitaba, como siguió visitándome después en otros accesos de dolor celoso; pero me lo callaba, porque temía la burla de Meli, que, despiadada, parecía complacerse en mi sufrimiento" [Tormented by fits of jealousy, I contemplated suicide, but I never spoke about this, because I was afraid of Meli's mockery. She was merciless and seemed to take pleasure in my suffering] (3: 424-25). Here the narrator speaks of events long past, but he also suggests that jealousy has affected other later relationships in his life. Similarly, he suggests that Meli has, since then, tried the patience of other men who have courted her, although she later succeeded in marrying well.

The announcement of a charity ball—at which the King and Queen are to be present—will prove to be the beginning of the end of the engagement. The narrator does not want Meli to attend but, if she does insist on going, he does not wish her to dance with anyone. She simply laughs at him, and his jealousy leads him to devising a way to thwart her. The narrator meets Meli as she arrives at the ball. He is stunned by both her beauty and her dress and makes one of the few positive comments about her in the entire text: "¡Qué guapa, la maldita! ¡Cómo la sentaba aquel traje rosa de múltiples volantes, según la moda de entonces, y aquel peinado a la griega, con los dos aros de oro pálido que lo ceñían!" [How stunning the little minx looked in her fashionable pink ruffled dress and with two pale gold hoops encircling her Greek hairstyle. It suited her!] (3: 426). The narrator then diverts Meli to a hidden corner and, with a forced sweetness and amicability, deftly removes and pockets one of her shoes, before walking off with it. Her father is obliged to take her home and the narrator is elated at his apparent victory in this battle of wills.

The following day the protagonist encounters a friend who also attended the ball, and he is informed that the outcome of the events was, in reality, very different from the one that he had imagined. Meli, wearing a different pair of shoes, had returned to the function, and danced with everyone. The truth is evident: Meli has defied him, and his so-called friends are now laughing at him. He dismisses Meli with a nonchalant (but insincere) comment: "¿Contrariarme? ¡Bah! ... A Meli, ¿quién la toma por lo serio?" [Am I cross? Hardly! ... Who takes Meli seriously?] (3: 427). Meli has the advantages of wealth, beauty and social connections and she appears to have used them all for her own gratification. Her nature is shown to have no real substance; in modern parlance, she could be described as somewhat of an "airhead". She does not even appear to accept that as a formally betrothed young woman in her society, it might not be acceptable to still seek male "admirers" or to openly flirt and walk on the arm of another man. However, she will not consent to the narrator's attempted domination.

"El zapato" is a story that questions the boundaries of male control and female submission. In Spanish society of the time an unmarried middle-class woman was controlled by the males in her life. In this story the narrator imagines he will assume control from Meli's father when the couple are betrothed but, in fact, he is unable to exert his influence over her with any success. Her return to the ball (presumably accompanied by a family member) indicates that she was making her own decisions that night. For many young Spanish women, a headstrong action such as Meli's would damage their reputation, as it far exceeds the expected behavior of an obedient middle-class "angel". However, in the eyes of society, Meli appears to have walked away unscathed from the incident, even after publicly humiliating the narrator (in his eyes, anyway) and, with a later marriage, she eventually became the Marquess of Cerezal (3: 424).[18]

There is an inescapable allusion in this story to the fairytale "Cenicienta" with its references to shoes, and a society ball from which the female protagonist flees. However, Pardo Bazán has inverted the figure of the prince.

---

18   This could be seen as an allusion to the Russian dramatist Anton Chekhov's 1904 drama *El cerezal* [*The Cherry Orchard*], a play that pits old customs against a new and progressive way of doing things, an image that both mirrors and gives weight to the female protagonist's actions in "El zapato".

The male protagonist of "El zapato" is churlish rather than charming, and his removal of Meli's shoe (rather than putting it on the heroine) signals the end of a romantic, but turbulent, relationship rather than the beginning of a lifetime of happiness. This allusion echoes Ashley's opinion that the original fairytales both critiqued the patriarchal order and featured heroines who were agents of their own destinies and, in "El zapato", it is evident that Pardo Bazán has fulfilled both of these criteria.

A decade earlier, a similar story, "La redada", had appeared, first published in Pardo Bazán's collection entitled *Historias y cuentos de Galicia*, (1900). As Dario Villanueva and José Manuel González Herrán observe, in comparison with most of the stories in this volume, it owes little to its Galician location: "[L]o gallego no es fundamental en el asunto, limitándose a ser el marco o un mero referente accidental" [Galician references are not fundamental in this story, they are limited to the background or the occasional aside] (9: xii-xiii). Narratorial flashbacks place the main scene in rural Ourense, at a finca bordering the barely disguised rio Támara (Amara). However, the story itself is about something more universal: the jealousy of a man who feels that his fiancée has betrayed him by noticing and admiring another man, and his overpowering desire to control her. As we noted, there are clear similarities between this story and "El zapato": both feature a well-to-do female protagonist and a jealous fiancé who is publicly humiliated. Both stories are also first-person narrations that open with the respective suffering male protagonists, who view themselves as victims, voicing soliloquies that outline the fateful situations that led to their continuing bachelorhoods.

In retrospect, the un-named male protagonist of "La redada" views the incident that led his fiancée María Azucena Guzmán, Viscountess of Fraga, to walk away from the marriage as "insignificante", a "mínimo incidente" [insignificant, a trifle] (2: 92). Self-pitying and melodramatic, he suffers from a deep-seated jealousy "en el fondo, allá en el fondo inescrutable y sombrío del alma" [buried in the shadowy and unfathomable depths of his soul] (2: 92). Love itself has caused this jealousy, he pronounces; during their time together, María Azucena had already recognized this propensity in her future husband and consciously "evitaba toda occasión de agravarlo" [avoided ever aggravating him] (2: 93).

Shortly before their wedding, the couple accept an invitation from María Azucena's uncle to a summer party on his estate. As they arrive, the guests are led to the riverbank to witness traditional trout fishing. It is hot, and the fish shelter in the deeper, colder pools in the river. Nets are laid near the pools and fishermen, shirtless and with their trousers rolled up, enter the water and scare the fish towards the nets. María Azucena is captivated by one young fisherman in particular. He is, tanned and well-muscled, eliciting a verbal response from her: "Parece una estatua de museo. ¡Da gusto verle!" [He's like a museum statue—well worth looking at!] (2: 94) This marks a breaking point for the narrator, who now mentally compares his own scrawny body with that of the well-proportioned fisherman and feels humiliated. Taking María Azucena aside, he reprimands her, barely able to physically contain himself, and, by the time he has spoken his mind, the look on her face reveals that it is all over. María Azucena's reply is quiet and simple: "No podemos casarnos. ... ¡Seríamos tan infelices!" [We can't get married. ... We would be too unhappy together!] (2: 94), and the narrator meekly agrees.

This story, which portrays "una concepción más idílica o idealizada del país, lugar de descanso de cortesanos y veraneantes" [an idyllic and idealized view of the countryside, as a playground for the affluent and for holidaymakers] (Villanueva and González Herrán 9: xii), emphasizes the apparent wealth of the country estate setting. Details abound; the chaperoned outing (with María Azucena's married sister watching their every move), María Azucena's clothing including her hat and Swedish gloves, and the extensive landscaping of the estate. The labor-intensive but obviously effective method of netting trout, destined for the picnic lunch table, is also explained in detail. Within this busy world, carefully constructed along socially accepted lines, Pardo Bazán's female protagonist appears to do and say very little and her adoring utterance praising the athletic and tanned torso of the fisherman would seem out of character for a woman of her standing. Her behavior to this point has been demure and exemplary but, with these words, María Azucena—only days away from being married—has publicly positioned herself outside the model of the "angel wife" who was "supposed to love her husband with a mild, un-selfish, maternal friendship unsullied by sexual passion" (Jagoe 24). Even noticing attractive male bodies was frowned on for women, much less audibly commenting on them. Furthermore, for a Viscountess to be admiring the physique of a fisherman, even if the admiration is couched as an aesthetic appreciation of his body rather than a lustful one, it was a public humiliation for her fiancé. His behavior may have caused the final breakup, but with her challenge to both gender and social boundaries, even allowing for the laxity of these among Spain's upper-class, María Azucena must be held at least partly responsible.

In the couple's final acrimonious interactions, by the conventions of the time, María Azucena's behavior also challenges accepted female conventions. The contrast in the controlled responses of María Azucena to the mental and verbal histrionics of her fiancé speaks volumes. Without needing to expound further, Pardo Bazán challenges one of the gendered stereotypes of her society, the supposed exclusivity of masculine and feminine attributes; that women possess love, they are controlled by passion and dominated by their hearts, while men possess logic, they are controlled by reason and dominated by their minds (Aldaraca "Medical" 404). This quasi-theory had its origins in the (male dominated) medical science of the era, typified by the ideas of men such as Dr F. de P. Campá who in 1876, wrote: "La sensibilidad altamente exquisita de la mujer, es el origen de sus más tiernos afectos, es la base de su carácter moral: la estremada delicadeza de su sistema nervioso, la finura excepcional de sus fibras elementales, es la condición física de su organismo, la razón anatómica de su exquisita sensibilidad" [The highly developed sensitivity of women is the basis of both her emotional and moral characters. Her nervous system is delicate, as is her whole physical makeup. Truly, the entire body of a woman is an example of matchless sensitivity] (qtd. in Aldaraca "Medical" 404). These misogynistic views of a woman's emotional and mental capabilities were both publicly and privately eschewed by Pardo Bazán, as perusals of catalogs of both her personal library and her scientific writings confirm.[19]

"La redada" directly confronts these supposedly limited emotional and reasoning abilities of a woman. From the beginning of the story the male narrator is presented as neurotic and depressed. He is emotional, becoming physically ill with jealousy at the mention of another man and is reminiscent of a toddler throwing a tantrum, unable to contain his feelings and his temper. María Azucena's measured, definite and perceptive response is also atypical of the gendered feminine stereotype. Abandoning subtlety, Pardo Bazán makes her point. Just as the trout had been caught in the nets of the fisherman, terminating their lives, a web of jealousy and emotion has trapped the narrator, controlling him and causing him emotional distress. Self-recrimination and self-pity dominate his thoughts—a most unmanly existence. María Azucena, on the other hand, is like a trout that has spotted the trap—that of marriage to a jealous and unreasonable man—and makes a rapid escape.

"El encaje roto", which achieved front-page prominence when it was published in *El Liberal* in 1897,[20] is one of the most discussed of Pardo Bazán's short stories. It is the third story in this trio united by both their first-person narration and the female protagonists' roles in the public and dramatic ends to the respective betrothals that we have seen in the two previous stories.

---

19   See Hemingway *Making* (165-68) and Bravo-Villasante (309-39).
20   It was also included in *Cuentos de amor* the following year.

Tolliver (*Cigar*), Hoffman ("Torn"), and Walter (*Frames*) have all contributed substantial analyses of the story, while numerous other writers have made reference to it. I include it in this trilogy as I believe it adds a further example of a narrative that is entertaining and arresting, and it subversively challenges societal expectations of female behavior. It also indirectly critiques the accepted practice of chaperoning young women as they meet with suitors. It is difficult for a young woman to ask probing or personal questions to assess a suitor's character when a third party is present, and it is equally awkward for the man to respond. In fact, revelation of one's true self is nigh on impossible. In addition, as we shall see, the narrative faces the reader with a question: from a woman's point of view, is male violence towards women just a "trivial thing"?

"El encaje roto" is a framed narrative and it is generally accepted that it is the only Pardo Bazán story with two acknowledged female-voiced narrators. The gendered adjective *convidada* [guest], the opening word of the story, unequivocally establishes the unnamed embedding narrator as female (1: 331), and her story frames the homodiegetic account given by Micaelita Aránguiz, the embedded narrator. In addition to the use of the word *convivada*, the breathless, enthusiastic and gossipy first sentence (that forms the entire first paragraph), leaves the reader in no doubt as to both the gender and the personality of this narrative voice (Lanser "Feminist" 348).

The story opens with the narrator receiving an invitation to Micaelita's wedding to Bernardo de Meneses, which she is unable to attend. Nevertheless, she appears to be well informed about the scandal that eventuated when Micaelita called a halt to the wedding ceremony and any future relationship with Bernardo, publicly and emphatically by refusing to assent to her vows. The narrator makes it clear to the reader that she is reconstructing the event from both hearsay and her imagination: "Parecíame ver el cuadro, y no podía consolarme de no haberlo contemplado por mis propios ojos" [I could picture it in my mind and was very disappointed not to have witnessed it with my own eyes] (1: 331). Numerous details are described: the guests and their probable attire, Micaelita's family, the bishop, the house and its floral decorations and she even includes the ceremony where Micaelita refuses to affirm her vows. This refusal causes a terrible drama for the upper-class family and guests, adds the narrator. Contributing to the confusion, Micaelita also refuses to explain her action. Hoffman speculates that this may be because Micaelita "has already provoked a scandal [and] she cannot find it in herself to justify her actions. ... Candor is a luxury that the bourgeois angel-woman can ill afford" (Hoffman "Torn" 241).

Marriage in nineteenth-century upper-middle-class Spain was a threshold moment for a young woman, a "transition from being the father's daughter to the husband's wife" (Hoffman "Torn" 238), from being under authority in one man's house to being under authority in another man's house. Weddings were usually elaborate and, as the narrator's account shows, followed a carefully "scripted" narrative, with largely interchangeable minutiae. Walter suggests that the narrator's imagined account emphasizes that "social customs are a form of representation, and for that reason the imagined version of the wedding suffices as the real one" in the mind of the reader (*Frames* 72-73).

The British writer Tessa Hadley (1956–), when asked how much can actually be conveyed through meticulously detailed description (such as the narrator has provided in this story), replied: "I suppose that's the whole premise of ... realist fiction ... that we can get at the general through the particular". She adds that, as the details accumulate on the page, the life in the piece thickens, the details breed, and the story starts to stir (qtd. in Tolliver "Colonialism" 215).[21] I maintain that it is this technique of "thick description" that Pardo Bazán employs in "El encaje roto" to draw the reader into the drama through the profusion of detail surrounding the wedding. After doing so, the reader will now be as mystified as the narrator is about Micaelita's apparently incomprehensible action. In this way, Pardo Bazán has "re-positioned" the reader to finish the story in order to satisfy their curiosity. And, apart from Micaelita's unexpected response, there is nothing in the story so far that challenges the accepted order of society.

The narrative abruptly moves forward three years to a spa where the narrator unexpectedly meets Micaelita, who is there with her mother. A spa, largely patronized by women, can be seen as a place outside the sphere of patriarchal society, a female-oriented setting that opens "a space within the text for the representation of female experience" (Bieder "En-gendering" 480). It was a setting with which Pardo Bazán herself was familiar, as Bieder reports: "Pardo Bazán, accompanied by her mother and daughters, enjoyed joining friends at Galicia's elite spas" ("Family" 39). "No hay cosa que facilite las relaciones como la vida de balneario" [nothing facilitates friendship like resort life], observes the narrator of "El encaje roto" (1: 332), and Pardo Bazán stories that are set in spas—including "Cenizas", "Feminista" and "El revólver"—generally involve the revealing of confidences or the disclosing of long-forgotten events.

---

21 This is not an isolated use of this technique in the stories analyzed here; it is also identified in "Dalinda".

"El encaje roto" follows this trend. As the friendship between the two women deepens, Micaelita proffers an explanation of her mystifying behavior on her wedding day. It centers on a length of expensive heirloom Alençon lace, a gift from Bernardo to wear with her wedding gown. Micaelita is a little irked by Bernardo's repeated emphasis on its monetary value. As she enters the room where the ceremony is to take place, she glances at the delicate design of the lace and interprets it as "una promesa de ventura y que su tejido, tan frágil y a la vez tan resistente, prendía en sutiles mallas dos corazones" [a promise of happiness, and that its weave, so fragile and yet so strong captured two hearts in its tenuous mesh] (1: 333).

In her haste to arrive at the altar, the lace catches on a door fitting; it rips and, as the patterned lace breaks apart, everything that the lace symbolizes for Micaelita breaks irreparably also. As Bernardo hears the lace ripping, his face changes, "contraída y desfigurada por el enojo más vivo; sus pupilas chispeantes, su boca entreabierta ya para proferir la reconvención y la injuria..." [contorted and disfigured by the most vivid rage; his eyes blazing like coals, his mouth already half open to issue a rebuke and an insult] (1: 333). Micaelita is aware of Bernardo's rumored propensity for violence and has spent the entire courtship period endeavoring to find evidence of it, but without success: "Maldecía yo mil veces la sujeción de la mujer soltera, para la cual es imposible seguir los pasos a su novio" [A thousand times I cursed the helplessness of a single woman, for whom it is impossible to trail her fiancé's every move] (1: 332-33). On her way to the altar, Micaelita realizes in a split second that she now has the first real evidence of her bridegroom's tendency to violent rage. Her fears are not unfounded after all, and she knows instantly that life with such a man is not what she wants. As she is called to assent to her vows, the word "no" springs out: "me lo decía a mí propia ... ¡para que lo oyesen todos!" [I was saying it to myself ... so that all could hear!] (1: 333).

Her explanation for the three years of silence that follow the fateful nuptial scene is philosophical: "[L]a gente siempre atribuye los sucesos a causas profundas y trascendentales, sin reparar en que a veces nuestro destino lo fijan las niñerías, las "pequeñeces" más pequeña. ... Pero son pequeñeces que significan algo, y para ciertas personas significan demasiado" [People always attribute profound and transcendental causes to events, not noticing that our fate is sometimes determined by trifles, the most unimportant little things. ... But they're little things that mean something, and for some people they mean too much] (1: 332). Even three years after the event Micaelita is still reticent about the truth, unsure if the malevolence and rage she saw for a moment on Bernardo's face was "too trivial" to be considered a reason for refusing to marry him. Here Pardo Bazán has positioned Micaelita as "everywoman". Spanish societal attitudes and practices were gendered; for generations Spanish women had been taught that a woman's judgment of a situation was considered inferior to that of a man, and Micaelita was only too aware of this.

I suggest that "El encaje roto" confronts the reader with the social reason for Micaelita's silence. The momentary expression on Bernardo's face might be considered by some as trivial, and Micaelita would have been shamed by telling the truth. In this instance, Pardo Bazán's response to the gendered inversion of values is to fictionalize the differences and publish the resulting story on the front page of a popular newspaper.

Micaelita's problem had its origin during the courtship, long before the wedding day itself. Single women of her class and status were chaperoned when they met with a man, a practice advocated by the ubiquitous middle-class conduct manuals. Aware of the rumors circulating about his violent nature, Micaelita found that her efforts to truly test Bernardo's character were futile. His behavior when he was with her was impeccable and in her split-second decision she exerted the only agency that she had during the ceremony. Walking away from the commitment to marriage would certainly have opened her to criticism of the omnipresent *el qué dirán*, but it saved her from a lifetime of domestic misery. Marital violence in Spanish society was all too common, and is at the center of dozens, if not hundreds of Pardo Bazán's stories.[22] Micaelita confirms in her mind, after her revelation, that anger and violence do matter, while public opinion does not. By rejecting marriage to a violent man, she asserts that it is anything but a trivial matter and she takes her life into her own hands.

In "El zapato", "La redada" and "El encaje roto" Pardo Bazán demonstrates that if a young woman notes a flaw in her fiancé's nature, such as jealousy or anger, which she knows would make her life intolerable, it is possible to walk away from a marital commitment. This is not an option open to every woman, but these stories suggest that if a young woman is from a wealthy family or able to support herself, it is a possibility. And, it can be added that, although the reader is not made aware of the parents' perspectives in the tales, they appear to either accept their daughters' decisions or to have little control over them. In publishing these stories, and others that are similarly themed, Pardo Bazán gives voice to the many women in her society who cannot speak for themselves. Here, in two stories, she has used first-person male

---

22 See Noya Taboada's dissertation, *Violencia*, for a comprehensive analysis of this topic.

narrators who are affronted that a woman can not only challenge them but can humiliate them with a public rejection of their troublesome character traits. They appear to realize the condemnation that they are bringing upon themselves even as they foreground the strength and integrity of their respective *novias*. The third story depicts a sympathetic woman who breaks the protagonist's enforced silence with a clear and unequivocal explanation of her fears and inadvertently shames the man for his dissimulation of his faults.

"Los pendientes" and "Posesión": All in the Mind

The stories previously discussed in this chapter were all written in a Realist style, depicting events arising from lust, jealousy or anger. The actions of the two young women faced with philandering men differ, as do the outcomes of the tales, while the three wealthy, formally betrothed, young women all act defiantly in order to break the relationship with their respective fiancés before they are married. They may not all be about everyday occurrences, but the situations are readily identifiable to the reader. However, this last pair of stories "Los pendientes" and "Posesión" are among the strangest and most disturbing of Pardo Bazán's entire output. They depict, respectively, the voluntary bodily disfigurement of one young woman to please the man she had set her heart on ("Los pendientes"), and the relationship of a second young woman with Satan himself ("Posesión"). They are not situations that Pardo Bazán's readers will personally encounter; however, they are arresting narratives that reinforce one of Pardo Bazán's chief concerns, the gendered power imbalance in her society.

These narratives have two important features in common. The first, as with the earlier stories, is that neither woman achieves her objective of a relationship with the man she loves, and the second is that they both employ the common Victorian-era trope of the "double" (Mc Kenna 31). In "Los pendientes" the two female protagonists, Claraluz and Mara, the virgin and the prostitute, have physical, spiritual and emotional attributes that are exact opposites. In "Posesión", the female protagonist, Dorotea, who formerly exhibited the traits of an ideal woman, is transformed both physically and spiritually when she is "possessed" by the Devil. Thus, in many ways she presents two opposing personalities.

"Los pendientes" is a dark, fantastic and magical fairytale.[23] There are two contrasting female protagonists, Claraluz and Mara, who symbolize the two opposed female stereotypes of the late nineteenth century—light and dark-

---

23   Paredes Núñez identifies thirteen of Pardo Bazán's stories as *cuentos de fantasia* (*Cuentos* 4: 473).

ness, the obedient angel and the demon—"emanations of eternity" (Auerbach 63). Claraluz's portrayal can be read as a parody of the *ángel del hogar* construct. She willingly, almost eagerly, gives her eyes to her *novio* Floraldo, to present to his lover, Mara, who has demanded them to wear as earrings. As Claraluz hands the eyes over to Floraldo she warns him that if they cloud over it means that Mara has been unfaithful to him. When the eyes do go cloudy Floraldo knows that Mara has betrayed him, and he kills her.

"Los pendientes" could well be subtitled "A Cautionary Tale for Young Women", as the third-person narrator addresses the implied readers—"dueñas y doncellas honradas" [young women and their guardians] (4: 250)—and proceeds to relate the distressing fate of a protagonist who is only too willing to oblige her suitor. It has Gothic undertones but at its heart it is a Fantastic narrative. The reader is invited to be as much a part of this magical and fantastic world as those being read about. I contend that accepting "Los pendientes" and its inexplicable series of events on their own terms, as an immersive fantasy set in its own world, is key to its analysis.[24]

In "Los pendientes", Pardo Bazán employs this facet of the Fantastic to critique, to the point of parody, the *ángel del hogar* construct at the heart of the patriarchal control of middle-class women in her society. It first appeared in 1909 in *Blanco y Negro* and was later included in Volume 3 of Pardo Bazán's own *Obras Completas*, but it was not included in any of her various themed collections.

The two female protagonists of "Los pendientes", Claraluz and Mara, both objects of Floraldo's desire, personify the age-old struggle between good and evil, the angel and the demon, virtue and vice—a prominent trope in *fin de siècle* women's writing, not only in Spain.[25] Claraluz, whose name translates as "bright light", is "más de ángel que de mujer" [more angel than woman]. She has golden hair, "ojos azules incomparables" [incomparable blue eyes] and is Christian (4: 250).

Mara, her rival (a Hebrew name meaning "bitter"),[26] is referred to by the narrator as "la hija de Satanás" [the daughter of Satan] (4: 250). She is an exotically perfumed, brown-skinned Jewish-gypsy dancer, presented to the reader as the personification of enticement and seduction (4: 250). Her body moves with "ágil y culebrosa gracia" [agility and snake-like gracefulness], alluding to the serpent, the agent of temptation in the Garden of Eden, and she dances "los bailes de infierno" [the devil's dances], driving the "barraganes"

---

24   Caroline Richardson Durham also views "Los pendientes" as a fantastic text.
25   Auerbach dedicates several chapters of her book to these topics.
26   See Exodus, ch. 15 v. 23.

[concubines] of the city into frenzies (4: 250-52). As "Los pendientes" progresses, the self-centered Floraldo will realize that he is unsatisfied by both versions of femininity.

"Los pendientes" presents a bizarre plot but, if considered as an immersive fantasy, it is relatively straightforward. A young, good-looking charmer, Floraldo has a reputation for flitting from woman to woman in the manner of a Don Juan, (a characterization only hinted at and not emphasized). He pursues Claraluz, the first of the two female protagonists and wins her heart, but when he is sure of her lasting affection, he soon tires of her beauty and seeks the company of Mara, who, in every respect, is Claraluz's opposite. Mara, who was "acostumbrada a dádivas" [used to presents] as a payment for her sexual favors, resists Floraldo's advances, despite his offerings of gold, pearls and diamonds (4: 250). However, she does suggest one gift that she will regard favorably, and Floraldo, trembling with lust and fear as he waits for her to voice her request, acquiesces to the demand before he is aware of her intentions. Mara, who knows of his previous relationship, demands that Claraluz's eyes be made into earrings for her to wear. Floraldo voices some concern, but it is short-lived. Self-absorbed, he sees Claraluz as a woman who can be exploited because of her love for him.

Claraluz, for her part, is equally aware of Mara's request and is willing to oblige and to accommodate Floraldo's unseemly haste in obtaining her eyes. However, Claraluz's eyes come with a warning—if Mara is unfaithful to Floraldo he will know, as the earrings will cease to sparkle. Spanish *fin de siècle* society, by and large, operated on a sexual double standard and, much as Claraluz might have wished Floraldo was faithful to her, she knows that infidelity is common. Masculine infidelity, young girls were warned, was only to be expected, as women are "criaturas esencialmente espirituales" [essentially spiritual beings] and their future husbands are "esencialmente carnales" [essentially physical], needing extra-marital liaisons (Salustio). Sinués advocates tenderness, dignity and resignation towards a man indulging in such a relationship, rather than fury (123).

Claraluz's surprising acquiescence to Floraldo's request is a parodic and extreme example of the female submission that was a recognized and accepted part of the society of the time. However, as a stereotype of a perfect young woman, Claraluz acts in the acceptable manner, with emotion rather than reason. Half an hour later Claraluz's eyes have been delivered to Floraldo, and that night Mara is wearing them as earrings, with the eyeballs having apparently been transformed into translucent, magical sapphires. People flock to see the earrings with the "zafiros celestes, cuya lumbre prestaba hermosura y atraía misteriosamente voluntades" [celestial sapphires, whose light lent beauty and that mysteriously attracted followers]; even the queen is covetous of the jewels and wishes to see them (4: 251). Floraldo, overtaken by jealousy at Mara's new-found popularity, kills another of Mara's suitors in a duel, and then discovers that while he was fighting for her honor, the sapphires have turned to glass. Realizing the implication of this transformation, he stabs Mara to death. Floraldo was also unfaithful but, like many men, he sees it as his right; however, he is outraged when a woman is unfaithful to him.[27]

Like Lorenza in "Comedia", Claraluz has little agency. A young middle-class Spanish woman had little to give other than herself and, paradoxically, allowing her virginity to be taken negates even her chance of marriage. Sacrificing her bodily integrity to please a suitor is a radical step and, in this case, I believe, a gross misuse of the little agency that she has.[28] Mara, because of her heritage and occupation, lives beyond the margins of bourgeois society and, in many ways, has more agency. She makes calculated but unwise choices by asking for Claraluz's eyes and then betraying Floraldo. Thus, a "minor" precept that can be drawn from the story is that agency, in itself, is not always the answer for a woman; rather, it is the wisdom to recognize a good and a bad decision and, again, this is overstated to the point of absurdity.

After the opening paragraphs the narrative departs from realism entirely, leaving the reader faced with a myriad of fantastic and implausible events, "a confused topsy-turvy world which lays no claim to re-present absolute meaning or reality" (Jackson 141). Light, with its linked metaphors, vision and eyes, dominates the narrative: the moon and the moon goddess Febe, the way Claraluz herself illuminated her surroundings, her sun-kissed hair, her "ojos de luz" [eyes of light] (4: 251), shining and luminous that became dazzling jewels—shining as sapphires, they sparkled and flashed like stars. However, the reader's attention is fully claimed when Claraluz's eyes are demanded by Mara so that they can be worn as earrings. Despite Floraldo's lie as he asks for them, Claraluz is aware of their destination: "Y mis ojos seguirán brillando como zafiros orientales en las orejas de la que prefieres ahora" [And my eyes will continue to shine in your new love's earlobes] (4: 251). Once the eyes leave Claraluz's body (seemingly bloodlessly), they are

---

27   In *fin de siècle* Spain, the gendered inequities in society included punishment for a crime of passion. The crime that Floraldo has just committed would incur a short-to-medium prison term, but if a woman had committed the same crime she would be imprisoned for life (*Artículo* 438, *Código Penal*) (Scanlon *Polémica* 131).

28   "La dentadura" (1898) is another Pardo Bazán story that also deals with this topic.

transformed into sapphires. Rosemary Jackson writes about bodily transformations, such as this, in Fantasy tales: "[T]he fantastic does not proceed by analogy ... but upon equation (this did happen). ...[I]t insists upon the actuality of the transformation" (84-85), and Pardo Bazán, at this point in the story, needs her readers to accept such a concept, and acknowledge that this inexplicable event happened, for the story to have its full impact.[29] Claraluz supernaturally retains both the knowledge of what her "repurposed eyes" are seeing and her control of them. When Mara is unfaithful to Floraldo, they again transform from translucent jewel to opaque glass.

The moral of this story, I believe, is rooted in its opening dedication to its implied readers, the "dueñas y doncellas honradas". When the tale is told, what are they to make of it? The story, like many others expounding on the perils of courtship, highlights the sexual double standard that so incensed Pardo Bazán. We have noted that Claraluz followed the advice that middle-class young women received about the need for extreme devotion and self-sacrifice and the need for dutiful latitude towards an unfaithful male in a relationship. With Claraluz's dire situation fresh in their minds, "Los pendientes" can be read as a warning to readers about the dangers of a woman's self-sacrifice and acquiescence to the amorous affairs of her *novio*. The narrative foregrounds the reality and suffering caused to a faithful woman by the patriarchally-inspired and supported sexual double standard. By using the conventions of the Fantastic mode, Pardo Bazán goes beyond the bounds of reality and portrays an impossible and unbelievable story in order to transmit this message. She was familiar with the criticism that arose when she challenged boundaries in Realist narratives (see Villanueva and González Herrán 7: 7); the ambiguity that exists in the "interpretation" of fantastic stories such as "Los pendientes" permitted Pardo Bazán some protection from her critics, while still sowing the seeds of doubt in the mind of other readers about the dangers of (literally) blind acquiescence to the males in their lives.[30]

In both "Los pendientes" and "Posesión", the last story to be discussed in this chapter, the female protagonists are entranced with the men who sought them out, and both women make misguided decisions in order to keep these men: Claraluz's, as we have seen, is life-altering, and it indirectly causes the death of another woman, while Dorotea's is fatal. "Posesión" has been also

---

29 Along these same lines, Samuel Taylor Coleridge, in his *Biographia Literaria* (1817), speaks of the need, at times, for the "willing suspension of disbelief for the moment, which constitutes poetic faith" (189).

30 This wordplay on "blind obedience" also translates into Spanish— "obediencia ciega" (*REA* 1458).

described by some critics as belonging to the "fantástico" genre (Ramos 218, Richardson Durham 60), though I believe that this applies to only part of the story. The basis of the tale is, according to Pardo Bazán, factual (*OC* 8: 613), but the phrase "immersive fantasy", discussed in relation to the previous tale, certainly describes the world that the protagonist Dorotea de Guzmán conjures up in her mind as she "journeys" into Satan's kingdom.

"Posesión", an unconventional story of female demonic possession, was first published on 13 May 1895, a month after Pardo Bazán's story "La sed de Cristo" had been published in the same newspaper. Pardo Bazán later included both stories in her collection *Cuentos sacroprofanos* (1899). On Good Friday, 12 April 1895, Pardo Bazán published "La sed de Cristo" in *El Imparcial*. It is a story that re-imagines Mary Magdalene's actions at the crucifixion, culminating with her offering Jesus her own tears to slake his thirst, which arguably attracted more criticism than any other story that Pardo Bazán had written. During the following week, accusations of heresy were thrown at the author and they, together with her lengthy rebuttals, occupied prominent positions in a variety of newspapers, including *La Correspondencia de España* (18 April p.1), *La Época* (17 April p. 2), (20 April p.2), *El Heraldo de Madrid* (12 April p. 2), *La Justicia* (20 April p. 2) and *La Unión Católica* (13 April p.3). The column in *La Justicia* included the wording of a telegram from the Vatican that noted that Pope Leo XIII himself was displeased with Pardo Bazán's story. I contend that "Posesión" needs to be considered in the light of the criticism that Pardo Bazán received about "La sed de Cristo" and that it constitutes a doctrinally correct counterstatement to her multitude of critics.

Four years later, still defending herself over "La sed de Cristo", Pardo Bazán explains in the Prolog of *Cuentos sacroprofanos*, that "Posesión", despite its subject matter, is "perfectamente ortodoxo" [totally orthodox] (*OC* 8: 613); the re-telling of a report she discovered in a book in Salamanca that had been approved by the church authorities. The inspiration for the story itself, she says, originated in the well-known phrase "el diablo es el mono de Dios" [the devil is the ape of God] (*OC* 8: 613-14).[31] The story's orthodox theology was deliberate, in order to avoid becoming "enzarzados por arte de birlibirloque con algún Santo Padre o Doctor de la Iglesia" [engaged in explaining the

---

31   As briefly mentioned in Chapter 1, the subject of women's mystical religious experiences leading to hysteria was investigated by the medical profession, however Smith reports that these experiences followed an orthodox Catholic theology, based on the figure of Jesus. In this story Pardo Bazán, despite her protestations of orthodoxy, has both used and subverted this theory (69-70).

inexplicable with some holy priest or Doctor of the Church], as she had with "La sed de Cristo" (*OC* 8: 614-15). It is evident at the conclusion of "Posesión" that the female protagonist, Dorotea, is about to be doubly punished for her ideas (for that is all they are) with a physical death at the stake and an eternal death as an unrepentant sinner.

A third-person narrator introduces the two protagonists, a nameless Dominican friar and Dorotea, a woman apparently possessed by a demon, subsequently imprisoned and sentenced to death at the stake, a fate scheduled for the following day. The friar's mission is to persuade Dorothea to repent and thus avoid eternal damnation.[32] As her specific fate is mentioned, the reader realizes that the story is set sometime during the Spanish Inquisition, before 1781, the date of the last *auto-da-fé* (Rawlings 136). The Inquisition, which lasted from 1478 until 1834—more than three and a half centuries—was a court of law with supreme authority to root out heresies and restore obedience to the church, reinforcing both the political and ideological interests of the Catholic State (Rawlings 21). Dominican clergy, such as the friar represented in this story, effectively ran the Inquisition in Spain (Young 112). Jewish, Islamic and Protestant heresies, defined as Major Heresies, were the initial foci of the inquisitors but after the 1560s unorthodox beliefs and behavioral practices of Old Christians, referred to as Minor Heresies, were increasingly scrutinized. Ritualistic practices "incorporating elements of ... witchcraft, in which the worship of God was abandoned for that of Satan"—one of the Minor Heresies—would appear to have been Dorotea's crime (Rawlings 114, 129).[33]

Exorcism had always been an authorized part of the Church's activities: "An exorcist speaks with the authority of God to cast out demons. Whether or not this invisible drama really takes place behind the outward words and actions of exorcist and demoniac, the Catholic exorcist's pretensions to authority are grounded not in personal self-assurance but in legal fact" (Young 5). Jules Amédée Barbey d'Aurevilly (1808–1889), a French novelist and short-

---

32 In Pardo Bazán's fiction, the depictions of priests are mixed; some are cruel or insensitive, for example the priests in "Un destripador de antaño" and "La novia fiel" (1894). Others, such as the friar in this story and those in "El aviso" and "La capitana", are just and reasonable.

33 The Spanish Inquisition later adopted a more extreme sceptical stance towards witchcraft, as illustrated by the Spanish Benedictine and Inquisitor Feijóo who, in 1739, wrote a treatise on demoniacs that, whilst acknowledging the reality of possession in the Gospels, concluded that all contemporary demoniacs were frauds (Levack 258-59).

story writer whose work was familiar to Pardo Bazán, wrote: "L'Inquisition savait bien que les crimes spirituels étaient les plus grands, et elle les châtait comme tells. ... Et, de fait, si ces crimes parlent moins au sens, ils parlent plus à la pensée; et la pensée, en fin de compte, est ce qu'il y a de plus profond en nous" [The Inquisition knew well that spiritual crimes were the most grievous and punished them as such. ... And, in fact, if these crimes speak less to the senses, they speak more to thought; and thought, after all, is what is most profound in us] (d'Aurevilly 300; qtd. in Ramos 224).

The narrative setting is Dorotea's cell, and the story opens as she is being questioned by the friar. Her surroundings are miserable, dim and full of cobwebs while Dorotea herself is a pitiful figure, bedraggled, and half-naked. The friar who pleads with Dorotea is just and reasonable, sure of his mission. He is compassionate towards her, speaking with "unción y ternura, encareciendo la amorosa efusión de Cristo" [sincerity and tenderness, emphasizing the outpouring of Christ's love] (1: 394). However, Dorotea has another agenda. She is in her present position following the outcomes of a chain of previous events: her denunciation, her detention in solitary confinement, then a later series of hearings that endeavored to elicit repentance and confession, and lastly a formal trial with an *auto-da-fé* pronouncing judgment. Being burnt at the stake was the most severe punishment that could be imposed. Dorotea has had ample opportunities to confess and repent and has rejected them all. Soft words from a churchman, for her, were a waste of his breath and, as he is speaking, she gains some control of the situation by transfixing him with her gaze: "[C]lavaba en el religioso sus grandes pupilas color de humo, donde, de cuando en cuando brillaba fosfórica chispa" [{S}he fixed her eyes on the friar and, from time to time a phosphorescent spark would blaze out from their wide smoke-colored pupils] (1: 394). Pardo Bazán's description of this gaze, with its references to smoke and sparks, serves as a reminder to the reader of Dorotea's imminent death.[34]

The friar reasons to himself that with the lack of a verbal response, he must goad Dorotea into an argument, as he is sure of his ability to triumph in what has now become a battle of wills. With direct discourse now introduced into the narrative he vividly expounds the terrors of her fate that will,

---

34   The gaze Pardo Bazán describes recalls Foucault's succinct characterisation of the coercive power of such a self-aware gaze: "There is no need for arms, physical violence, material constraints. Just a gaze. An inspecting gaze, a gaze which everyone under its weight will end by interiorising to the point that he is his own overseer, each individual thus exercising this surveillance over, and against, himself" (155) but expounding on this concept is beyond the scope of this work.

he says, continue beyond death, reducing himself to tears with his own argument, and it is these tears that finally elicit a response from Dorotea. She reveals her pride in her allegiance to her "dueño y señor Satanás" [lord and master Satan] (1: 395); he has taken all tears from her and lit his own fire inside her. As the friar suggests that she dedicate this fire to Jesus, Dorotea's malevolent look makes him realize that this woman, a madwoman in the eyes of the Church, has prevailed.

Puzzled, he begs her for an explanation: "Dame una razón, una siquiera. ... Eras hermosa y eres horrible; eras dama principal y pudiente, y eres menos que las mujerzuelas de la calle; eras buena y honrada, y eres ludibrio y vergüenza de tu sexo... ¿En qué moneda te paga el maldito? ¿Qué felicidad ignominiosa te da a cambio de todo lo que sacrificas por él?" [Give me at least one reason. ... You were beautiful and now you are bedraggled; you were a socialite, a wealthy lady, and now you are less than the street beggars; you were good and honest, and now you scoff and are ashamed of your sexuality. ... In what currency does the evil one pay you? What ignominious happiness does he give you in exchange for everything that you sacrifice for him?] (1: 395). With this question, Pardo Bazán has set up the narrative structurally for Dorotea to explain her actions in her own words—an opportunity given to few Pardo Bazán female protagonists.[35] Until this point in the narrative Dorotea, with her unkempt appearance and her sullen responses, has appeared as a victim.[36] Nevertheless, in her own mind, Dorotea has triumphed. Her reasoning is simple: she has no wish to repent as the numerous exorcisms have driven Satan away from her, and her imminent unrepentant death at the stake will reunite her with her love. She is existing in an "immersive fantasy" of her own creation and presents herself as the subject of her own story rather than the object of derision, anger, pity and judgment of the inquisitorial process.

Dorotea agrees that the friar was correct about her early life and adds that she has always yearned for something higher than herself and following her cousin into a convent appeared to be a logical step towards her objec-

---

35   Joyce Tolliver notes that Pardo Bazán "rarely represents female discourse in the first-person in her own work. When she does ... the fact of the narrator's female sex plays a crucial part in the narrative dynamics" (*Cigar* 172). In addition to "Posesión", other similar stories include "Champagne" (1898), "El encaje roto", "El rival" (1902) and "Sor Aparición" (1896).

36   Walter identifies eight different pejorative words that the friar uses to reference Dorotea in this first half of the story: "la rea", "la endemoniada", "la posea", "la sentenciada", "la pecadora", "la pobre oveja", "la esclava del demonio" and "la poseída". Only in exasperation does he address her as Dorotea (395) ("Femme" 182).

tive. However, her story moves beyond Catholic doctrine and then beyond reality as she voices a perceived stumbling block to her ordination: the "sharing" of her new husband, Jesus, with innumerable other nuns. One night a pale, sad, beautiful young man with curly blonde hair and a reddish halo appears to her in her cell. He describes himself to her as "un gran príncipe, arrojado de los reinos de su padre por un instante de rebeldía, y que mientras a su padre todos le ensalzan y pronuncian su nombre con adoración, del hijo rebelde abominan y maldicen" [a great prince, driven from his father's kingdoms because of a moments rebellion, and while everyone extols his father and speaks his name with adoration, his rebellious son is abominated and cursed] (1: 396). Ramos comments that the description of Dorotea's visitor corresponds to the post-romantic imaginary, where the presence of the devil is marked by the heroic air of those who rebel against authority that they perceive as unjust (219). That Satan would appear to Dorotea as an attractive man and, we learn, offer her the one thing that she most desires, an exclusive relationship, illustrates Milner's description of Satan as possessing extreme malleability and an ability to flatter and seduce (qtd. in Ramos 220).

Dorotea's gullibility is exposed as her new-found master takes her on an aerial adventure to his diamond-studded caves, where hordes of his previous "conquests" are gathered, including some of history's most infamous women: "[M]ujeres hermosísimas, cortesanas, reinas o diosas, desde la rubia Venus y la Morena Cleopatra hasta la insaciable Mesalina y la suicida Lucrecia" [T]he most beautiful women, courtesans, queens or goddesses, from the blonde Venus and the dark Cleopatra to the insatiable Messalina and the suicidal Lucrecia] (1: 397).[37] As Dorotea feels a pang of jealousy, Satan assures her of her place in his affections, despite the fact they have agreed to a purely spiritual relationship, and she accepts his words unreservedly. Now deluded, she wishes to die, to be reunited with her "dueño y señor Satanás" (1: 394).

Dorotea, with her fierce gaze, dominates the interview, and when the friar asks for "una razón, una siquiera" [even one reason] (1: 395), she seizes the opportunity to control the conversation and, indeed, the friar himself. Walter points out that Dorotea's narration has replaced the confession sought by the priest, regardless of the consequences, and allows her to gain subjectivity ("Femme" 182). The vehemence of her delivery and the sheer fantasy of her story leave her inquisitor defeated and almost speechless. He withdraws

---

37 Pardo Bazán's allusions to the infamous historical women by name seems out of place here. Dorotea is unlikely to have received a classical education and, if she had, salacious details such as the "insatiable" Messalina's activities would surely have been withheld from a young woman.

from the cell sobbing and doubting his own faith, bitterly asking: "¡Cómo permites, Jesús mío, que te parodie Satanás!" [How, my Jesus, can you allow Satan to parody you?] (1: 397).

Pardo Bazán presents Dorotea's story with little interruption from the friar, and the few comments that he does make are perfectly orthodox (Ramos 220). They leave little room for criticism of the writer on theological grounds, although she has subtly mirrored the language of a Catholic nun's commitment to be a "bride of Christ" and subverted it. There is other "mirroring" in the story too. Dorotea's former self is noted by the friar: "Eras hermosa; ... eras dama principal y pudiente; ... eras buena y honrada" [You used to be beautiful; ... you were an influential wealthy lady ... you were good and honest] and he contrasts this with her present position: "[E]res horrible; eres menos que las mujerzuelas de la calle; eres ludibrio y vergüenza de tu sexo" [now you are appalling; you are less than the street prostitutes; you are a laughing stock and bring shame to your sex] (1: 395), thus recalling the "double" of "Los pendientes".

Pardo Bazán achieved much with "Posesión". A month after the furor over "La sed de Cristo", she faced her theologically minded critics squarely with a second religious story, one with impeccable Catholic credentials, and historical and theological correctness. However, I suggest, like her protagonist Dorotea, Pardo Bazán also won the battle of words that her critics had instigated against her and the parallel tacit battle of wills. Dorotea is on trial for her unorthodox ideas and was "moving through" a system that would silence her for ever. She is expected to submit meekly to the Dominican's request for a confession and so at least die shriven. Instead, she faces the friar and beats him down with her will and her words, leaving him, not her, as the victim (see Smith 69-70). Dorotea is a strong, dominant and articulate woman, challenging the hegemonic values of her society, including those of the clergy, exactly as Pardo Bazán did.

Pardo Bazán had all but been accused of heresy and vilified when she "re-imagined" the crucifixion scene in "La sed de Cristo". Ironically, there is seemingly no public outcry when she imagines the inner workings of Satan's kingdom, and foregrounds one of his devoted and unrepentant followers, who mocks a priest and welcomes the Church's most extreme punishment. The literary crafting of "Posesión" with its subversive, albeit delusional, protagonist who truly models the power of female agency, was therefore both a narrative and personal triumph for Pardo Bazán, vis-à-vis her critics.

"Los pendientes" and "Posesión" may well be viewed as an unlikely pair of stories but in each Pardo Bazán has critiqued the nineteenth-century norm of an ideal woman, submissive in all aspects to prevailing patriarchal and ecclesiastical viewpoints. In these two stories Fantasy and horror styles are used traditionally, however these unsettling forms, in Pardo Bazán's hands, provide a freedom to convey a variety of messages that would be unacceptable in more standard Realist writing.

Conclusion

The narratives discussed in this chapter are diverse. The first five—"El árbol rosa", "Comedia", "El zapato", "La redada" and "El encaje roto"—are written in a Realist style, while "Los pendientes" is a Fantastic tale and "Posesión" is an unsettling, tragic and horrific story that wavers between historical fact and fantasy. In all these stories Pardo Bazán has created diverse protagonists, all young and all, with one exception, defying the social expectations of their respective societies.

Milagros, the protagonist of "El árbol rosa" is the exception. She adheres to her principles and gives herself the chance of future happiness as a married woman, while the three women from moneyed families in "El zapato", "La redada" and "El encaje roto" become aware of character flaws in their fiancés and publicly break their engagements. Marriage, apparently, is not an economic necessity for them and their futures beyond the narrative space can only be guessed at. The protagonists of the remaining three tales all fail themselves in some way and three of the four lose their lives. Lorenza in "Comedia" does not have sufficient emotional or social resources to deal with her seducer's betrayal and rejection, and Pardo Bazán places the blame for her death squarely on the man. Mara, the female antagonist in "Los pendientes" betrays her lover and is stabbed in retribution, while Dorotea has sealed her own fateful destiny before "Posesión" opens. Only Claraluz, the protagonist of "Los pendientes" survives, albeit disfigured, the result of gullible and unreasonable submission to the man she loved. All seven of the female protagonists discussed here looked forward to a long relationship with the men they loved, but none realize their dreams, and their relationships all encounter serious pitfalls.

The next chapter examines three pairs of stories in which the female protagonists are fending for themselves in the world rather than relying on romance. In the first pair of stories, the protagonists are faced with an ultimatum: a career or an imminent marriage and confinement to the domestic sphere. In the second pair of stories, the women, for entirely different reasons, are struggling to survive, enduring constant surveillance and criticism from their neighbors, and the third set features women on their own who seek security in a relationship. Once again, some women make good decisions; others do not. For one of the women, any decision that she makes will have an uncertain outcome. It is a chapter in which few of the story endings are predictable.

3
Ruled by Head or Heart?

> Vivir es constantemente
> decidir lo que vamos a hacer.
>
> [To live is to constantly
> decide what we have to do]
>
> - José Ortega y Gasset
> *¿Qué es filosofía?*

THE CIRCUMSTANCES OF THE female protagonists portrayed in this chapter differ, but all are ultimately alone in the world and forced from necessity to make decisions about their lives and their futures. Six narratives are analyzed, and the stories are discussed in pairs. The first two protagonists are young and needing to make career choices; in the next two stories the women endure uncomfortable circumstances; and in the last pair the women are seeking financial or emotional security of their own choosing. When these differing choices are examined, it becomes apparent that the women in the first of each of the paired stories have made considered and rational decisions about their various actions, while the women in the second tales have been led by their emotions in their decision-making. In these analyses, the wisdom of each decision is considered and it will be seen that the "unangelic", rational decisions may indeed result in better outcomes for the women.

Pardo Bazán's writings attest to the fact that from her earliest years she openly disavowed the accepted patriarchal view of "Woman"—that she is characterized by "love not logic, controlled by passion rather than reason, she is not sense but sensibility, dominated by her heart rather than her head" (Aldaraca "Medical" 404). This is evident in Pardo Bazán's feminist essays and also in many of the stories selected for this book, where the female protagonists choose to ignore societal norms and behave in calculated, logical and well-reasoned ways that are outside the *ángel del hogar* construct.[1] In addition to thematic, narratorial or other similarities, the first story of each pair presented in this chapter features an atypical, unangelic female protagonist whose positive life-changing decisions are based on "unfeminine" reason or logic. In the second narrative of the pair, the protagonists are perhaps harder to classify, but the crucial decisions in their lives are ultimately based on emotion, a more "feminine" approach in the eyes of the patriarchy. In addition, all the female protagonists are alone in the world and supporting themselves (except, perhaps, for Saletita who lives with her widowed mother). The protagonists of the first two and last two stories discussed have marriage (or re-marriage) on their minds, whilst the women in the central pair of stories concentrate on more immediate objectives.

"Apólogo" and "La dama joven", the opening pair of stories, present women who are facing the choice of either marriage or a profession. Both are artistic performers: an operetta singer and an actor. Laura, in "Apólogo", foregoes marriage to an insanely jealous man in a dramatic but reasoned manner in order to retain a professional career, while Concha, *la dama joven* of the second story's title, is a seamstress who is offered a choice between an imminent marriage (to an equally jealous fiancé) or an immediate role as *la dama joven*, a new, young actress, in a travelling theatre troupe. She vacillates over the decision but opts for marriage so as not to disappoint her sister and her priest.

At first glance there appears to be little similarity between the protagonists of the next two stories, "Las cutres" and "Coleccionista". They seem to be linked only by the narratorial viewpoint and a broad societal classification of the female protagonists as "eccentrics". Three sisters, the collective protagonists of "Las cutres", suddenly begin to live as frugal recluses, a dramatic and mystifying change that guarantees that their entire existence becomes the object of gossip in their community. "Coleccionista" opens just after the death of the protagonist Rosario. While she was alive, she had no obvious source of income and spent her days very much in the public arena, scouring the streets picking up anything that caught her eye, valuable or otherwise. Unfortunately, she could not override her impulse to hoard and failed to use any of her gleanings to supply herself with adequate food or clothing, again leading to speculation from her community about both her past and her present habits. However, as the stories progress, the private reasons for

---

1   Examples of such essays include: "Concepción Arenal y sus ideas acerca de la mujer", "La educación del hombre y la de la mujer" and "Sobre los derechos de la mujer".

these women's actions are revealed: the sisters' decisions are based on reason, while Rosario's is based on emotion.

The protagonists of the last pair of stories, Saletita in the story of the same name and Cipriana, a youngish widow in "La mascarón", are both looking for security in their lives. Saletita deliberately and stealthily sets her cap at a wealthy *indiano*, her mother's acquaintance, flirting with him in her mother's presence. Cipriana, who supports herself by keeping a shop, is deceived by a handsome late-night customer and misreads his intentions; she is hoping for an amorous encounter. Sadly, it is not her affections that the customer wants, but rather her savings and her life. Three of these protagonists are led by their logical decision-making, while the other trio follow their hearts.

"Apólogo" and "La dama joven": Life-defining Choices

The analysis of the opening pair of stories, "Apólogo" and "La dama joven" does not deal with the public nature of the protagonist's professions per se, but rather the choices that the women make as they consider their futures. The texts include tropes, allusions, intertexts and subversions—literary devices that abound in Pardo Bazán's short stories—that merit further comment, and my analyses of these add a depth and complexity to the narratives that may not be obvious from surface readings. "Apólogo" raises the topic of atavism that was hotly debated in Spanish literary circles during the 1890s, and "La dama joven" incorporates an intertextual reference to *Consuelo* (already mentioned), while the entire text parodies the traditional Spanish *folletín* genre.

Laura, the female protagonist of "Apólogo", acts with unusual logic and reason when faced with a life-threatening crisis. She is a professional singer with an established career that she has no intention of relinquishing for marriage. Unfortunately, Laura's *novio* is consumed by her public success, and the fact that she is on stage, with other men enjoying her performances, proves too much for him and his behavior becomes irrational. Laura realizes this and, when it is obvious the relationship is about to erupt into violence and her personal safety is threatened, she escapes to safety overseas, thus avoiding assassination. Laura's defiance of her partner's wishes in relation to her employment challenges acceptable middle-class behavior and the reader is left to presume that she will have followed her own desires. It has taken a dramatic attempt on her life to free her from Spain's oppressive gendered restrictions.

"Apólogo" illustrates Quesada Novás's observations about the motif of jealousy in Pardo Bazán's short fiction, discussed in the analyses of "El zapato" and "La redada" in the previous chapter. In all three of these stories an amorous relationship is underpinned by the all-consuming jealousy of a male who wishes to control his female partner. "Apólogo" is a serious story, portraying a male protagonist with a deep-seated violent jealousy of any potential rivals and a desire for complete control over his *novia's* actions. It was first published in 1898 in *Blanco y Negro* and republished later that same year by Pardo Bazán in her *Cuentos de amor*. Although it appears in *Cuentos de amor*, it is far from being a conventional love story; in fact, it is closer to being a psychological thriller. Indeed, Pérez makes this very point about Pardo Bazán's so-called "love stories" arguing that her "tales of courtship treat deception or disappointment in love, abandonment or broken engagements, abusive or jealous suitors, and the discovery of defects in the beloved so disillusioning that some epiphanies result in ... such drastic escapes as emigration" ("Winners" 348).

The two protagonists are Vicente Zegrí, a soldier, and Laura, a successful operetta singer. As the story opens, the omniscient third-person narrator emphasizes the famous (albeit distant) Arabic antecedents of Vicente Alcántara Zegrí, the male protagonist, and follows this with the statement that "por atavismo y tradiciones de raza, llevaba en la sangre el virus corrosivo de los celos" [{the ideology of} atavism asserts that because of his racial origins, he carried the destructive virus of jealousy in his blood] (1: 337). The narrative portrays a man so psychologically disturbed by jealousy of his successful *novia* that he attempts to murder her.

With the insertion of "atavismo" into the text, it is implied that Zegrí's actions are pre-ordained by his ancestry. "Apólogo" is far from being a lone occurrence of Pardo Bazán's opinions on atavism, although she rarely used the word itself. It features in her travel writings of the late 1880s, where, in *Por Francia*, she relegates various non-European cultures to "at best 'mucho elemento exótico' [exotic elements] and, at worst, 'nada más que gorillas [sic] y macacos'" [nothing more than gorillas or apes] (Ordóñez 23). It is discernible in several of her travel books, short stories and novels, with the most obvious examples, written between 1898 and 1901, focusing on Blacks, Moors, Jews or Asian peoples.

It is irrefutable that in some of Pardo Bazán's Naturalistic works her use of atavistic descriptions is explicit. A typical (if lengthy) example can be found in *Insolación* (1889) where Gabriel Pardo (a character whose Naturalistic views have been expressed in Pardo Bazán's previous novels) opines about the personality of Diego Pacheco, an Andalusian of obviously mixed ethnic heritage (64): "Ese andaluz es ... [p]erezoso, ignorante, sensual, sin energía ni vigor, juguete de las pasiones, incapaz de trabajar y de servir a su patria, mujeriego, pendenciero, escéptico a fuerza de indolencia y egoísmo, inútil para fundar una familia, célula ociosa en el organismo social. ... Así anda ello" [That Andalusian is ... lazy, ignorant, sensual, without any energy or vigor, a plaything of passions, incapable of working and serving his country, a womanizer, quarrelsome, cynical and because of his indolence and selfishness he is uncommitted to family life, he is an idle cell in the social organism. ... That's how it goes] (66-67). Such sentiments are deterministic, as is the reference to Andalusian *atavismo* in "Apólogo", a return to Pardo Bazán's Naturalism of the 1880s, where physical and natural impulses, rather than morality or ethics, determine a person's behavior.

The first two paragraphs of "Apólogo" set up a tension between the two protagonists. The contrast between them could hardly be greater. Laura, an operetta singer, is introduced with florid descriptions of her appearance and achievements: "La natural hermosura de la cantante parecía mayor realzada por atavío caprichoso y original, al reflejo de las candilejas, que jugueteaban en la tostada venturina de sus ondeantes y sueltos cabellos, flotantes hasta más abajo de la rodilla" [The singer's natural beauty was enhanced by her ornate and imaginative costumes, while reflections of the footlights sparkled like brown aventurine crystals in her loose wavy, almost knee-length hair] (1: 337).[2] Her early years of success on the stage have already brought her recognition, publicity, flowers, gifts and an adoring public. She is encouraged by this, and her dream is that one day she will be truly famous. From among her male admirers, she chooses one as her *novio*—Zegrí, an army officer, "que no poseía más que su espada y un apellido" [who owned nothing apart from his sword and an exotic surname] (1: 337). No further reasons for her choice are given, but presumably he is dashing and handsome. Laura's background and origins are not mentioned in the text, but her occupation as a singer in a seemingly successful operetta company indicates that she is both literate and has had some musical training. Zegrí's description portrays him in a Naturalistic fashion, as a man of Moorish descent, an "other", whose actions will be driven by hereditary, rather than rational impulses and whose behavior in this relationship is already determined. The third-person omniscient narrator intervenes at the beginning of the story with his personal opinion: If Laura, a well-known artist, who is almost considered "public property" does

---

2   In popular folklore, two attributes of brown aventurine crystals are emotional stability and mental clarity, two of Laura's qualities that are exhibited later in the narrative (see, for example, https://jewelandcrystalguide.com/what-colors-are-aventurine/)

marry Zegrí, her choice to enter into the relationship will be "muy perjudicial a su tranquilidad y dicha" [very detrimental to her peace of mind and well-being] and predestined to fail (1: 337). And, as the narrator predicts, the relationship does become difficult. Zegrí experiences increasing discomfort as he suppresses his jealousy until he finally confronts Laura.

The central section of the narrative consists of direct speech interspersed with narratorial comments about Laura, a narratological technique that, from the reader's perspective, controls the pace of the verbal exchanges. The reader is positioned as eavesdropper on the couple's conversation, and in this dialog their true characters are revealed. Zegrí, in an emotional outburst, divulges the intensity of his jealous torment: "Cuando te aplauden, siento impulsos de prender fuego al teatro—cuando se te llena de necios y de osados el camerino, se me ocurre sacar la espada y entrar pegando tajos a diestro y siniestro" [When people applaud you, I feel like setting fire to the theatre—when a bunch of imbeciles dare to invade your dressing room I think about drawing my sword and entering it, slashing to the left and to the right] (1: 338). As Laura processes the impact of this confession, she has the presence of mind to remain cool and enquire "-¿Y qué has pensado hacer? ... [D]ímelo sin reparo y te contestaré con franqueza" [And what are your future plans? ... [T]ell me now and I will be honest with you] (1: 338). Zegrí, assuming they would marry and also that Laura would give up her career, answers her with a poorly-phrased marriage proposal: "Desde el momento en que Vicente Zegrí se llame tu marido, a tu marido pertenecerás, y él solo él podrá contemplar tus hechizos, oír tu canto y ver desatada esta cabellera" [From the moment that I, Vicente Zegrí, become your husband, you will belong to me, and I alone will be able to succumb to your spells, hear your music and see your hair unfurled] (1: 338). He underscores this statement with a physical attack on Laura, pulling her hair violently.

Despite the assault, Laura has the presence of mind to appear unmoved and relates a seemingly random traditional Russian *apólogo*, a fable which conveys a moral truth, to the disturbed man.[3] It concerns the fate of the architect who was commissioned by Ivan the Terrible, the first Russian czar, to design St Basil's cathedral in Moscow. The building pleased the czar who, seemingly innocently, enquired of the architect if he thought that he could construct an even grander edifice. Upon replying that he could, he is promptly blinded by the czar to prevent this ever happening.

If it was Laura's intention to discern the mental state and likely intentions of her (by now former) *novio*, Zegrí's reaction to the story provides all

---

3   See <wordreference.com> for a definition of "apólogo".

the answers she needs. He appears on the verge of an epileptic fit: "Ligera espuma asomó al canto de su boca y por sus venas serpeó el frío sutil del aura epiléptica" [He began to foam at the edge of his mouth and a subtle cold, characteristic of an epileptic aura, snaked through his veins] (1: 339).[4] His eventual reply to Laura is ominous and settles any questions about his state of mind and his intentions: "Ese rey hizo mal. Sacar los ojos es acción propia de un verdugo. Si quería inutilizar al arquitecto, debió matarle" [What the king did was wrong. Gouging out his eyes is an executioner's act. If he wanted to incapacitate the architect, he should have killed him] (1: 339). He then squeezes her violently, causing her to scream, before he flees.

The narrator details the depth of Zegrí's depressive and emotional state during the following twenty-four hours. Pardo Bazán's prose describing Zegrí's thoughts and actions during this time is particularly poetic and lyrical with a "recurrent use of nouns, verbs and adjectives in groups of three", typical of Pardo Bazán's later writing (Sánchez 312): "Su alma pedía sangre, hierro y fuego, violencia, destrozo y aniquilamiento; el instinto anárquico, que tantas veces acompaña al amor, se alzaba, rugiente y desatado, como racha de huracán" [His innermost being called for blood, fire and irons, violence, destruction and annihilation; a turbulent impulse, which so often accompanies love, rose up, roaring and unleashed, like a howling hurricane] (1: 340). Zegrí's pathological jealousy of Laura's public persona has utterly engrossed him resulting in his love for her being transformed into hatred—a hatred which "clamaba por saciarse y gozarse en la destrucción" [demanded to destroy Laura and offer satisfaction in her destruction] (1: 340).[5] At the theatre the next day, Zegrí is in the audience, pistol at hand, intent upon shooting her. However, he becomes agitated when Laura fails to appear on cue and he enquires about her absence before realizing that she has second-guessed his

---

4   Pardo Bazán was recognized by her contemporaries, such as Enrique Díez Canedo, a poet and literary critic, for her "thirst for encyclopaedic knowledge" (Hilton "Centenary" 345), as this medically correct reference to epilepsy illustrates. Louis Maisonneuve (1745–1826) was the first researcher to describe the so-called sensitive aura of sympathetic epilepsy, about a century before this story was written, and Pardo Bazán was clearly familiar with his findings.

5   *Fin de siècle* Spanish justice sided with men who carried out an action, such as the one Zegrí is plotting. Scanlon describes a historical legal case prosecuted under Article 438 of the *Código Civil*. A husband had murdered his wife "en el paroxismo de la pasión y de los celos" [in a frenzy of passion and jealousy] and was exonerated by the judge, who described the act as "un gesto gallardo y simpático en un país que conservaba el espirítu calderoniano" [a gallant and charming gesture that follows the spirit of Calderon's dramatic tragedies] (*Polémica* 139-140).

intentions: "Aquella misma mañana, la cantante había rescindido su contrato, perdiendo lo que quiso el empresario, y partido en dirección a San Petersburgo" [That morning, in spite of her employers wishes, Laura had terminated her contract, and left for Saint Petersburg] (1: 340).

In the central exchange, using distinct masculine and feminine voices, Pardo Bazán has exposed the innate characteristics of the two protagonists. From a patriarchal viewpoint, she has almost completely reversed the traditional gender roles. Laura's voice and traits largely conform to the societal male expectations—she is direct, decisive, strong in both word and tone, and rational. Zegrí's voice and actions, on the other hand, conform to societal female expectations; he behaves in a way that is emotional, immature, and unpredictable (Lanser "Feminist" 348-49). Laura's lifestyle also eschews the accepted *ángel del hogar* mold. She has a successful professional career played out almost entirely in the public rather than the private sphere. There is nothing of the expected meek and hysterical woman about her; in fact, she is portrayed as being exactly the opposite, a woman who appears to have propitiously resisted patriarchal mores and created her own feminist script. Zegrí, for his part, is so consumed by jealousy that any manliness he may have possessed has deserted him and his portrayal in the latter section of the narrative exhibits a disconcerting number of emotional and barely rational actions. Following the atavistic introductory remarks, this feminized behavior appears to be attributed to his Moorish heritage.[6]

---

6   The Moors had been part of Spanish society since 711 (see Fuentes 51-77), and after the fall of Granada in 1492 Spaniards with a Moorish heritage, the Moriscos, had a complex and often difficult relationship with their Old Christian compatriots (see Fuchs, *Exotic Nation*). However, there is one aspect of this topic that is particularly pertinent to "Apólogo"—the perceived feminisation of Moorish males, an attitude highlighted in the legend of "The Moor's Last Sigh." This relates the flight of the defeated Moorish leader Boabdil Muhammad XII (1460-1532) from Granada in 1492. Elizabeth Drayson describes one detail surrounding the legend: "[W]hen the Moorish king reached his house ... he began to weep for what he had lost. Upon which his mother told him that as he had been unable to defend his kingdom like a man, he did well to weep for it like a woman" (306). It is a legend that has never waned in Spanish society, and it was given renewed impetus in 1895 when the historical landscape artist Francisco Pradilla Ortiz (1848-1921), at that time the Director of the Museo del Prado in Madrid, painted *El suspiro del moro*, depicting Boabdil's exit from Granada. Pardo Bazán admired Pradilla's work (Faus 2:97) and, with her fondness for attending art exhibitions (Zárate 129-145), it is very likely that she was aware of the painting, and its associated legend, one which undermines Moorish masculinity. There is a second facet of Spanish cultural history that sub-

"Apólogo" is a disturbing and unsettling story, and Pardo Bazán certainly achieved her aim of crafting a narrative that illustrates the corrosive effects of jealousy on a person and their relationships. However, it is difficult for the reader, and particularly the modern reader, to determine if this is in fact related to ancestry. Male jealousy also surfaces in the next story, "La dama joven", but here Pardo Bazán avoids any racial aspersions and portrays this jealousy as merely a defect of human nature. Published in its entirety in 1885, in Barcelona, "La dama joven" was the titular story in Pardo Bazán's first collection, *La dama joven y otros cuentos* although today it is usually considered a *novela*. It was republished in instalments in the *Folletín* section of *La Época* in July 1893. Despite its obvious length, Pardo Bazán made no distinction, in either the title of the volume or in the prolog, between the first two narratives, "La dama joven" and "Bucólica" (also now considered a *novela*), and the other, shorter *cuentos*.

"La dama joven" has received some critical attention. Bravo-Villasante offers an interesting interpretation of the story. She considers "La dama joven" to be autobiographical since it was published at the time Pardo Bazán separated from her husband. Bravo-Villasante speculates: "[C]omo aquella protagonista de la novela [Pardo Bazán] quería aplausos, gloria literaria ... y como la protagonista, tiene que escoger entre un destino brillante aunque, al parecer, peligroso, y una vida oscura" [Just like the protagonist of the story {Pardo Bazán} wished for acclaim and literary fame ... and, like the protagonist, she has to choose between a brilliant, although apparently precarious, destiny, and a life as an unknown] (100). She observes that the *novio* of the tale is a hindrance to the protagonist's dreams, and that would still be the case when they were married. She adds that Pardo Bazán herself "no quiere ser como la dama joven [y] escapa hacía el mundo, hacia el destino ancho, grande, hermoso, apasionada por su cara literatura" [she does not want to be like her protagonist [and] passionate about her sweeping literary dreams she makes her own escape into the world, towards her own great future] (100). Pardo Bazán's 2019 biographer, Burdiel, also comments briefly on "La dama joven" and agrees with Bravo-Villasante about the seemingly autobiographical nature of the text, although she does mention the obvious socioeconomic differences between the author and her protagonist (187-88).

---

verts the masculinity of Moors: the traditional festival of "Moros y Cristianos" that has survived through the centuries and is still held annually in many Spanish towns and villages. In some celebrations, a female figure, La Mahoma, replaces the male figurine representing Muhammed (Harris 52, 56).

By contrast, Charnon-Deutsch's criticism concentrates on the text, rather than the author, viewing it as perhaps "Pardo Bazán's most representative example of environmental determinism" outside *Viaje de novios* (*Strategies* 86-87). Her analysis ascribes a major role to the direction of the priest, a strong and insidious force, "a 'jesuita sagaz'" [a shrewd Jesuit] (7: 17), who sees marriage as the only option for Concha and whose every word is taken to heart by Dolores. Charnon-Deutsch concludes that Concha's submission to marriage is the result of manipulation by forces beyond her power or will (*Strategies* 87-88). David Henn's brief comments on "La dama joven" focus instead on the "presentation of the attitudes and existence of the urban Galician proletariat" and the foregrounding of Dolores's concern that Concha marry a man from her own social stratum (10, 18).

However, in my opinion, two recent critics, Julia Biggane (*In a Liminal Space: the Novellas of Emilia Pardo Bazán*) and Margot Versteeg ("'A Most Promising Girl': Gender and Artistic Future in Emilia Pardo Bazán's 'La dama joven'"), have provided the most thorough and compelling analyses of the story, with Versteeg addressing the text as a parody of a *folletín*, or *novela por entregas*.[7] Stephanie Sieburth mentions that a significant number of nineteenth-century Hispanic novelists, following Cervantes, introduced popular genres, such as the *folletín*, into their texts in order to parody either their artificial conventions or facile moralizing (100).[8] An examination of the tropes of this particular style will reveal that in "La dama joven", Pardo Bazán has indeed adopted and parodied the style of the *folletín*.

A *folletín*, as we noted earlier was essentially a fragmented novel, published in instalments in the popular press, but over time, "*folletín*" has come to describe a literary stereotype—a melodramatic novel associated with popular and mostly female readership (71, 65), considered to be paraliterature, without aesthetic value and viewed as falling outside the canon of the nine-

---

7   Biggane's title encapsulates the dilemma of categorising a narrative of this length which, in terms of word-count, exists in the "liminal space" between the short story and the novel. Such narratives, part of Spanish literary tradition since Miguel de Cervantes's *Novelas ejemplares* (1613), have been variously described as *novelas breves, novelas cortas* or *cuentos largos,* and Biggane notes that the "Spanish designation of prose-fiction genres remains inconsistent and anachronistic even today" (10). However, later *novelas breves* (post 1907) published in popular weekly mass-market magazines were categorized more strictly, with length and thematic restrictions (11). N. Friedman, writing about dilemmas such as this, pragmatically states: "To haggle over the borderlines is almost always fruitless, and that is one very good reason for not even trying" ("Short" 101). I agree, and I have followed this advice.

8   Ronald B. Richardson's *Narrative Madness* offers numerous examples.

teenth-century novel (Martí-López 66). The *folletín*, and all it represents, does not exist in a vacuum; rather it is a product of the social and political systems of its day—the mid-nineteenth century. Sieburth holds that it can be read as the fantasy of the middle-class about the workings of society and, therefore, to question the *folletín*'s conventions is to question the regime in which it flourishes (100).

The *folletín*, with its "cualidad inocente [e] infantil" [virtues of innocence and simplicity] and its characteristics of order, truth, pure love and justice (which, perhaps, protect the longings and dreams of its readership), exists in stark contrast to the Spanish nineteenth-century Realist novel (Andreu 59-60). Realist novels, described by Martí-López as "mature male writing for a grown-up and select male audience" (66), reject the sentimentalism, romanticism and arguably old-fashioned ideals of the *folletinista* and replace them with "una visión más 'real' de la vida" [a more 'real' vision of life] (Andreu 60). Nevertheless, as Sieburth notes, the dominant views about women's behavior elucidated in the various conduct manuals of the time were incorporated, without parody, into Realist discourse (117).

By 1885 Pardo Bazán had established herself as a writer, having published four novels, an acclaimed study of the life of Saint Francis of Assisi (1882) and *La cuestión palpitante* (1882).[9] Her reputation was hard-won and, at this point in her career, if "La dama joven" had simply been a traditional, sentimental *folletín*, as its opening pages with their recognizable tropes suggest, Pardo Bazán would have left herself open to censure from her many, mostly male, critics. A critical analysis of "La dama joven" reveals that it is an unsentimental Realist text and, although it concludes with the obligatory imminent marriage, the future happiness of the protagonist is not wholeheartedly assured. The traditional, patriarchally acceptable path of marriage, motherhood and domestic confinement is questioned, as the protagonist seriously considers, and almost accepts, a public profession as an actor in a theatre troupe. In this narrative, Pardo Bazán breaks with the *folletín*'s conventions of what constitutes a happy ending, and, by extension, she challenges the societal structures responsible for them.

This contemporaneous story is set in Marineda, (Pardo Bazán's fictional representation of the Galician city La Coruña), where seamstresses Concha and her older sister Dolores live and work. The narrative opens in the third person; however, extensive passages of direct speech throughout the text per-

---

9   These novels are *Pascual López, Un viaje de novios, La Tribuna* and *El Cisne de Vilamorta,* although her major works *Los pazos de Ulloa* and *La madre naturaleza* were still in the future.

mit the reader to achieve a greater understanding of the characters. Dolores and Concha's past is related in some detail: their mother died when Concha was a year old. Dolores, despite her own seduction during Carnival festivities and her subsequent abandonment, her pregnancy as a young single woman, and the later tragic loss of her own child, has raised her sister. Even now, as adults, she is still protective, longing "borrar el pasado y proteger a Concha" [to ignore the past and to protect Concha] (7: 16).[10]

Dolores's relationship with her parish priest, a purely spiritual one, is emphasized. She had been desperate for help after her child died and he had organized charitable aid for the two penniless girls: food, medical help for an ailing Concha and sewing orders for Dolores. However, at times his ongoing concern irks Dolores, particularly when he reprimands her for allowing Concha to develop a love for the theatre. Nevertheless, Dolores immediately turns to him for advice when Concha receives an unexpected marriage proposal, and she eagerly carries out his instructions to safeguard her sister's chastity and to ensure that the marriage does take place.

In the first few pages of this trope-laden tale, Pardo Bazán has provided the reader with a number of time-honored conventions and topics of nineteenth-century popular fiction: "poverty, orphanhood, charity and the Church, love, honor, marriage, chastity and happiness" (Gold 107).[11] She has drawn two of the characters, Dolores and the priest in some detail, while the protagonist, Concha, has only been presented passively—introduced as a helpless, motherless infant, and later as an obedient young girl, accompanying her sister as she works as a seamstress in various houses. Concha becomes a compliant teenager who prefers visiting the theatre and participating in amateur dramatic productions to interacting with unsuitable and predatory *novios*. She is compared in the text, in a typically sensual *folletinesque* way, to a graceful sculpture with white unblemished arms, compact breasts like flower buds, an oval fair-skinned face with blue, candid eyes and thick, wavy, dark-blonde bobbed hair. An uncomplicated marriage with an honest, hard-working handsome young man, such as Ramón, who sent the proposal, will complete the set of *folletín* tropes.

The stock character of the "virtuous priest" is only partially accurate. The initial impression is of a compassionate man, willing to help the orphaned and destitute teenager Dolores and her infant sister, but his character alters and becomes manipulative as he attempts to influence Dolores in her

---

10   Paredes Núñez omits "La dama joven" in *Cuentos completos*, therefore all referencing to the text will be from *OC*, volume 7.

11   In the original 1895 publication, the illustrations reinforced this impression.

guidance of the teenaged Concha. He fully subscribes to the prevailing patriarchal view of women "submitting, yielding and obeying" (Pardo Bazán "Women" 886), chiding Dolores for permitting Concha to spend time at the theatre, even instructing her to make her sister wear a cilice to curb her enthusiasms, an order which appalls Dolores. Later, he even suggests to Dolores that she encourage Ramón and Concha to spend time alone together in order to break down the young woman's resistance to a timely marriage.

Concha's character is developed after her encounter with Ramón, and her decisions become the focus of the story. Ramón is a disquieting character; self-absorbed, manipulative and, once again, intensely jealous. He has decided that it is time that he was married. He has seen Concha at the theatre and been struck by her beauty, but although he has never spoken to her, he has decided that Concha will be his wife; he composes a flowery marriage proposal and sends it to her. Dolores is delighted; a "good" marriage is all she wants for her sister. Concha, who has accepted an all-consuming role in *Consuelo* at the local theatre, is not so ecstatic, responding: "¡Casarse! ¡Bah! Claro que se casaría: ¿pero qué prisa corría eso? El caso era lo que se le preparaba para mañana" [Get married! Hardly likely! Of course I will get married sometime, but is this not rather too quick? My priority is preparing for tomorrow] (7: 19). As their relationship develops, Ramón becomes irritated at Dolores's constant chaperoning, and he forces his presence on Concha as she walks to the theatre for a rehearsal. During the encounter he inadvertently reveals much of his true nature. He displays his anger when Concha informs him that she is not permitted to walk with him in public, and he retorts that Dolores need never know. Ramón's rage at Concha's reluctance to be alone with him frightens her, and she acquiesces, in order to placate him.

Concha is just beginning to relent and secretly enjoy being accompanied by a good-looking *novio* when she becomes aware of the deep rancor and resentment simmering inside him. He refuses to shield her from an urchin's deliberate shove and suddenly his fury pours out. It becomes clear that he resents her very presence on the stage, beautifully costumed and admired by the men in the audience. She is the object of gossip and, he adds, "mil desvergüenzas" [utter shamelessness] (7: 26). He gives her a warning: "[N]o te digo nada, Dios me libre, haz lo que quieras; pero tengo que advertirte una cosita. ... [c]uando nos casemos ... yo no consiento que vuelvas a representar, aunque se empeñe Dios del cielo... ¿Te has enterado? ... En fin, vé acostumbrándote a la idea" [God help me! I'm not telling you anything, do what you want to. But I have to warn you about one small thing. ... When we get married ... I won't allow to you to perform again, even if God in his heaven insists—do you hear what I'm saying? ... Anyway, get used to the idea] (7: 26).

These words echo those of Zegrí, in "Apólogo" quoted earlier. The storyline of "La dama joven" underlines the fact that Concha is a young woman who lives "sólo en lo presente, o al menos en lo futuro inmediato" [only in the present or, at the most, in the immediate future] (7: 19), and she has neither the composure nor the maturity that Laura possesses, nor her ability to take command of the situation. Concha appears not to realize the full import of Ramón's belligerent manner and his dictatorial words and, besides, foremost on her mind that day is the imminent rehearsal of Lopez de Ayala's *Consuelo*, where she is the leading actor.

Ramón, now totally in control of the conversation, changes his approach, calming Concha and attempting to kiss her. His second attempt is successful, and she experiences "una ola de caliente sangre que henchía sus venas" [a wave of hot blood surging through her veins] (7: 27), leaving her perturbed for some time. In retrospect, this will be the turning point of the relationship. Even as Ramón succeeds in kissing Concha, he has no compunction in delivering one last warning to her, as though he already "owns" her; she must keep the neckline of her dress at a decent level onstage or he will leave her forever. Ramón is filled with joy at his seeming success with the reluctant Concha, while she is left "aturdida y cabizbaja" [dazed and crestfallen] by the turn taken during the short walk (7: 27). Biggane notes that it is not the narrator who judges Ramón's personality or motivations, rather that Ramón characterizes himself through his own speech acts, and it is left to the reader to decide if he is "touchingly possessive" or a boorish chauvinist (21).

The second half of the story is centered on the theatre, both the physical theatre in Marineda's *Casino Industriales*, and theatre as an abstract concept, a shorthand for the life and working environs of the people associated with a production. Indeed, Pardo Bazán uses Adelardo Lopez de Ayala's *Consuelo*, (1878) an *alta comedia*, or drawing-room melodrama, as an intertext. The *alta comedia* was a drama that represented the clashing of powerful political forces, that allowed audiences "to feel the surge of controversy and polemic characteristic of the times" (Dougherty 211). In *Consuelo* a failed marriage was the pretext for dramatizing "the battle between good and evil, conscience and duty, man and the angels ... and at stake was a woman's ambition to rise in the social hierarchy by means of marriage" (Dougherty 212). The female protagonist, Consuelo, opts for a financial speculator and social prestige over an honorable suitor, a decision which is followed by punishment for her ambition.

In "La dama joven" the protagonist Concha also chooses between two options, with the same two possible outcomes for her: if she chooses the theatre, she has the promise of the social prestige that comes with being an actor of renown or, alternatively, a dutiful marriage to a boorish woodworker who resents her passion. When Concha is offered a theatrical contract, a future as an actor suddenly appears both possible and attractive: "Ella podía ser actriz... es decir, dominar aquel arte apenas entrevisto, ponerse en comunicación todas las noches con el público, volver a escuchar aquellos embriagadores aplausos, viajar a ciudades grandes, para ella nunca vistas. ... Un destino ancho, grande, hermoso" [She *could* be an actress, that is to say, master that barely glimpsed art, communicate every night with the public, listen again and again to intoxicating applause, travel to major cities that she had never seen. ... A great and wonderful destiny awaited her] (7: 49). She is also aware though, that life in this particular troupe could be hard, with rumors circulating of unpaid wages and physical hardships.

During the performance of *Consuelo*, with Ramón in the audience, Concha deliberately edges the neckline of her dress downwards to expose her cleavage. In this we see that Concha is a young woman who can act for herself when she chooses; however, in the larger scheme of things, her rebelliousness is over relatively trivial incidents. She is ill-equipped to make a reasoned, independent, decision on a particularly important choice that is imminent, a choice that paralleled Consuelo's in the role she had just played, and one that will determine the rest of her life. The culmination of the tale concerns the moment when Concha must decide between the churlish and patriarchal Ramón, who nevertheless knows how to incite her passion, or a possible independent career as an actor.

Versteeg describes the acting profession as one that "challenged the neat divide between public and private spaces" and when a woman used it as an escape from homebound domestic life, she exhibited an onstage persona at odds with the middle-class idealized woman, eschewing passivity, modesty virtue and asexuality (131). Concha has already experienced the difficulties of negotiating these two spaces, as Ramón twice threatens to leave her if she appears on stage in a dress with a low neckline, once before a rehearsal and the second time between the acts of the actual performance. Ironically, this second threat produces a level of resentment in Concha that inspires her to openly defy him and to refuse Dolores's offer of a shawl that would decently cover her up: "[Ramón] [e]s un tonto; bien sabía lo del escote, y no tenía para qué darme ahora este mal rato. ... Y con un dedo impaciente, bajó el tul que rodeaba la línea del escote, como si quisiese aumentar el crimen" [Ramón is a fool; I did know his views about the cleavage, and there was no reason for him to harass me at this point. ... And impatiently, she pushed the tulle that surrounded the neckline even lower, as if she wanted to accentuate the crime] (7: 41). Even more ironically, it is her galvanized performance in that scene that captivates both the audience and Juan Estrella, a troupe owner, who now has no hesitation in offering her a contract as an ingénue.

Dolores is with Concha when she hears about the contract and tries to reason with Gormaz, the play's director, and Estrella, telling them that it would be impossible for Concha to accept it as she is about to marry. The men reprimand Dolores, and she literally runs to the priest once again for advice. She is upset, almost bitter, that Concha wants to make up her own mind, and willingly follows the priest's latest directive to permit Concha and Ramón to be alone together, in the hope that Concha will realize what pleasures she would miss out on if she were to become an actor. Concha's fateful decision is made under pressure as Gormaz and Estrella arrive at her house to get their answer, only to find the two young people in an embrace.

Concha's downfall is that she is constantly distracted by the immediate to the detriment of the important. She has always been overly protected by Dolores, out of sisterly love (and a certain shame on Dolores's part, related to her own experiences). Dolores has always tried to moderate Concha's behavior and in turn Dolores herself seeks out and is influenced by the parish priest's constant advice to her, most of which she follows. Pardo Bazán portrays Ramón as a churlish and selfish man who, with his premeditated assault on Concha's modesty and principles, asserts a certain dominance over her, leaving her at a second person's mercy. In addition, Concha's new role in the theatre leaves her open to both advice and criticism from the director, Gormaz, who encourages and coaches her in *Consuelo*, and also from Estrella, who needs to know if she will accept his contract. Thus, pressure is directly and indirectly applied to Concha by everybody in her immediate circle and, as a result, she cannot please everyone. Dolores arrives, and at the critical moment of decision Concha becomes passive and takes the path of least resistance reverting to her childhood mantra: "[l]o que quiera mi hermana" [whatever it is that my sister wishes] (7: 57)—she will marry. Gormaz and Estrella have the last word:

> "¡Bah!" murmuró Gormaz "¡Y quién sabe si la acierta, hijo! A veces en la oscuridad se vive más sosegado... Acaso ese novio, que parece un buen muchacho, le dará una felicidad que la gloria no le daría". "¿Ese?" exclamó Estrella, cortando con los dientes la punta del puro. "Lo que le dará

ese bárbaro será un chiquillo por año... y si se descuida, un pie de paliza" ["Bah!" Gormaz murmured "And who knows if he is a good choice! Sometimes as nobodies you can live more peacefully. Perhaps that fiancé, who seems like a decent chap, will give her a happiness that she would not get from fame." "Him?" exclaimed Estrella, cutting off the end of his cigar with his teeth. "What that barbarian will give her will be a baby a year, and if she is neglectful, a good thrashing"]. (7: 58)

Every critic of the story agrees that the ending is ambiguous, giving no indication of the direction that Concha's future will take. Charnon-Deutsch views it as an inevitable ending for a Naturalistic story (*Strategies* 88), while Versteeg sees it as echoing the finale of *Consuelo*, with Pardo Bazán punishing Concha for her choice; for not being able to think beyond her immediate future. She adds that for Concha, marriage to Ramón will become a "metaphorical death in life" (137). Nevertheless, as the narrative closes, the reader is aware that for Concha, neither choice is perfect. She is aware of the precarious financial position that an actor in a traveling troupe may be in but is probably unaware of Estrella's reputation as a Don Juan. The reader knows that he wished to enlist her in his troupe to profit from her looks, possibly personally.

Pardo Bazán wrote "La dama joven" in the style of a *folletín*; however, she parodied the established *folletín* text by the "imitative use of the words, style attitude, tone and ideas of an author in such a way as to make them ridiculous, generating a subtle balance between the accepted style and a deliberate distortion of its characteristics" (Cuddon 640). The end result is a largely unromantic Realist text, one that I believe owes much to Pardo Bazán's fellow Realist writer Pérez Galdós's *Tormento*, published the previous year. *Tormento*'s protagonist is a *folletinista*, and the novel has been described as a "conscious parodying of the popular genre" (Martí-López 79). Michael Nimetz writes that Pérez Galdós "championed the Realistic novel against the *novela por entregas*", which he set out to ridicule in *Tormento* (70). *Tormento*'s structure, with its suspense points, builds tension and mystery, with the parody itself being focused on the characterization and theme. Pardo Bazán had admired Pérez Galdós's writing for some years (*Cuestión* 171) and by the time she was penning "La dama joven", the two writers were in the habit of meeting and discussing their respective literary works (Acosta 265). Pardo Bazán was at the beginning of her literary career, with perhaps a dozen short stories and four novels already published and was widely regarded (and frequently criticized) as a Naturalistic writer. By using *Tormento* as a model, she demonstrated that she was able to shift from Naturalism, which she was initially connected to, to Realism. By incorporating a parody of a *folletín*, a style that idealized submissive, obedient women into a Realist story, she was able to demonstrate her versatility with different genres that would be so evident later in her career.

In Laura and Concha, the working-class protagonists of these two narratives, Pardo Bazán has drawn two very different women both facing, arguably, the most important decision of their lives. Laura believed that stage-work and marriage could be compatible, while Concha wished to work first and marry later, but they are both delivered the same ultimatum by their *novios*: an imminent marriage and no further public appearances. Aldaraca states that by the nineteenth century there was a tendency for the bourgeoisie to impose its ideology on the rest of society and, in the process of fabricating their ángel image, the propagandists fall victim to their own illusion of an egalitarian society (*Hogar* 64). The two male protagonists in this pair of stories, one an army officer, with a sword and seemingly little else, and the other a self-employed cabinetmaker each have the same wish—to marry an angelic-looking woman, wearing an extravagant stage costume, has caught their eye. Pardo Bazán has contrasted the female protagonists in these tales as one of the newer prevailing *fin de siècle* female stereotypes: the still-emerging, (and decidedly un-angelic) *Nueva Mujer Moderna* with the traditional *ángel del hogar* (Nash 31-32). Laura, the *nueva mujer*, is independent, emotionally stable and decisive with an established professional career; and she has a cool-headed wisdom that enables her to survive, even if it means leaving Spain. Concha, on the other hand, has made few decisions on her own behalf and appears unable to realize the future import of marriage to a man with a jealous and erratic temperament. As the stories culminate, the women make their stand. Laura dramatically rejects her suitor—like the trio of defiant fiancées in the previous chapter, she has the advantage of financial independence. Concha, who has fewer financial resources, chooses marriage, rejecting the chance of a possible career. In these stories, Pardo Bazán has portrayed women who do have options, however dire some may appear; the next two stories show how difficult life can be for women whose options are taken from them in one way or another.

"Las cutres" and "Coleccionista": Nonstandard Behavior

The often-quoted line from T. S Eliot's philosophical "Little Gidding" "[t]he end is where we start from" (49), is very pertinent when studying the narrative structures of "Coleccionista" and "Las cutres", the next pair of stories to be considered—both can only be fully understood when their respective endings are revealed. The narratives depict seemingly eccentric female protagonists: in "Las cutres", three apparently miserly and reclusive sisters, Paulina, Marcela and Rosario, and in "Coleccionista", a scavenger, coincidentally also named Rosario. In addition to the protagonists' eccentricities, there are three other similarities that connect these texts. Firstly, both employ a character observer-narrator other than the protagonist who tells the tale. Norman Friedman names this device "I as Witness" ("Point" 1174), and in this context it is the narrators who speak for and relay the collective thoughts of the respective neighborhoods. The protagonists themselves do not speak. Friedman explains that the "garrulous omniscient author, who tells the story as he perceives it" is eliminated and replaced by a character narrator who imparts intensity, vividness and coherence to the text, providing an immediate rendering of the story ("Point" 1163, 1170). The second similarity is that both story endings contain additional information that provide an unexpected rationale for the behavior of the respective women protagonists. In "Las cutres", the narrator, after decades of observing the details of the protagonists' lives, eventually guesses the truth behind the unusual actions of these women and reveals it to the reader. And, in "Coleccionista", the narrator reveals the unusual contents of Rosario's home. McKenna, speaking of "Las cutres", but implicitly including other similarly structured stories, states that in the light of an ending such as this, the reader reinterprets the narrated events to reveal "alternative endings within the narrative content of the stories themselves" (100).

The third similarity in the narratives is the communities' respective attitudes towards the seemingly eccentric behavior of the women protagonists. Odd behavior patterns, particularly in women, were frowned upon by the gossips of Spanish society and led to their every movement being noted and discussed by those around them.[12] John Beard Haviland states that it is the nonstandard behavior that activates this "collective busybody", with the oddness of a person's behavior stimulating community chatter about what is odd in it (160). Patricia Meyer Spacks suggests that being a gossiper "applies with particular force to the experience of a class largely deprived of social power and fulfilling limited function in the public world" (33)—in other words, even the lowliest villager can gain a sense of importance by passing on the latest "heresay". Thus, accepting the axiom "knowledge is power", it follows that this informally gained knowledge about other people is a type of power over

---

12   This community talk, *el qué dirán,* has been discussed in some detail in Chapter 1.

them, and the gossiper, in effect, "takes partial possession of other people's lives" (Meyer Spacks 30).

In both "Las cutres" and "Coleccionista" this phenomenon can be observed. The stories are each relayed first-hand by an eyewitness, in "Las cutres" it is a male voice and in "Coleccionista" a gender-neutral narrator is employed, and in neither story is there any clarification in the text as to the reason for the narrators' preoccupation with the lives of the protagonists, other than curiosity. In each story, the unexpected revelation late in the text provides an entirely different perspective on the related events and casts the protagonists' apparently irrational actions in a more reasonable light. These revelations lead to the discovery of a previously unsuspected narrative theme. In "Las cutres", the centuries-old issue of gendered honor expectations is revealed to be the driving factor behind the unusual actions of the women; while in "Coleccionista" the private museums that were popular with middle-class nineteenth-century Spaniards (and fictionalized at length by Pérez Galdós) come into focus. In both narratives the women seem able to ignore the neighborhood gossip and speculation about their lives and carry on with their apparently eccentric personal missions regardless.

Both narrators largely conform to the definition, coined by Henry James, of a "ficelle"; that is, a subordinate character—"the reader's friend ... a direct aid to lucidity" (322)—who throws light on the meaning and significance of the situations and events in the tales (Prince 30). The stories each span several decades and, with Pardo Bazán employing single narrators who have observed each one of their respective protagonists over so many years, she has successfully created a "sense of passing time" in the reader's mind (Wharton 35). While the first-person pronoun is used overtly in "Las cutres", it is used sparely in "Coleccionista" towards the end of the story. It is only a single verb usage in the second to last paragraph of "Coleccionista", "[y] *eché* la última ojeada al cadáver de la mujer" [I took] one final glance at the woman's body (1: 235; my emphasis), that reveals the fact that this story is a first-person account. This sudden disclosure of a first-person narrator is a traditional framing structure indicating the imposition of the narrator's own views which are external to the story. Boris Uspensky explains that this literary technique provides, for the reader, a final transition from an internal view in the tale to the external view belonging to the everyday world (146).

"Las cutres", which appeared in 1910 in *Blanco y Negro*, foregrounds three spinster sisters, known locally as "las cutres", a pejorative nickname reserved for stingy, shabby, and vulgar women. After the sudden death of their unnamed mother, they cut themselves off from society and live in miserly poverty for twenty-five years, attracting curiosity and contempt from their neighbors. In this story, Pardo Bazán confronts two gendered patriarchal norms, the primacy of male inheritance and, more importantly, female honor; by the end of the story, it is evident that the women have made a conscious decision to sacrifice their otherwise normal lives to defend their mother's honor. The narrative also emphasizes the insidious damage that community gossip can cause in the lives of innocent people. The key to understanding "Las cutres" is disclosed mid-way through the text, and the story needs to be read in its entirety for the related events to be assembled in their correct order. Doing so gives the reader an understanding of the women's behavior, and it is only in retrospect that Pardo Bazán's treatment of the various historic, feminist and social issues depicted in this story becomes apparent.

The narrative opens philosophically, similarly to other stories included in this collection, considering, in the abstract, the vagaries of ugliness, beauty and love (3: 366). The narrator, who speaks from a personal perspective, turns his thoughts towards the sisters, Paulina, Marcela and Rosario (only once mentioned by name in the story), who live in his town.[13] They were brought up in a conventional middle-class household by their widowed mother who is described as a beautiful and virtuous widow, a woman of honor. Nevertheless, since her death, the sisters have formed, in the eyes of the townsfolk, including the narrator, an unconventional collective female entity. Day after day for more than twenty years, living in their family home in increasing poverty, the sisters are "sometida a la tiranía del sórdido interés" [dominated by their neighbours' sordid interest in their lives] (3: 366).

During this time, the narrator has been part of this collective group of gossipmongers who have taken a particular interest in the comings and goings of the three women. However, he stands apart when he voices his conclusion that pain, resignation and melancholy—"sentimientos todos nobles" [all noble sentiments] (3: 366)—are responsible for their lifestyle and demeanor. This conclusion notwithstanding, the role that the narrator has given himself warrants some comment. Much depends on his reliability, (and also the readers' acceptance of it) otherwise the story itself fails to make sense. He has an undeniable (and unexplained) interest in the three women's

---

13 In the Spanish language, gendered adjectives with either -o or -a word endings indicate masculine or feminine respectively. In this text, "me declaró *apto*" (3: 367; my emphasis) makes it clear to the reader that the narrator is male and, in addition, his closing words demonstrate an undeniably masculine action, the tipping of a hat: "Y cuando paso ... de la casita [de] las tres valientes, me descubro" [And when I pass by the house where those three selfless ladies live I tip my hat] (3: 368).

lives and can also be viewed as a meticulous conveyer of gossip about them, yet at times, as we have noted, he also defends the sisters in public.

Half-way through the story, the women begin to live according to their class again; they refurbish their house and once more employ a maid and a cook. However, a young, personable and educated man suddenly appears in their home and, once more, gossip flourishes: "[L]as hermanas dijeron 'nuestro sobrino', pero la maledicencia sugirió '¡su hijo!'" [The sisters referred to him as 'our nephew', but the gossips suggested he was 'your son'] (3: 367). It is only with the appearance of this mysterious young man that the narrator's years of wondering yield the answer he has been seeking. He believes that the young man is the sisters' half-brother, their widowed mother's illegitimate son and, also that the sisters "habían salvado, a costa de la propia, la honra de su madre" [had saved, to their own detriment, their mother's honor] (3: 368). With this comment comes a further unspoken suspicion: that the supposedly honorable mother's sudden death was the result of the boy's birth, as the sisters' miserly lifestyle begins at that point.

This is the key to "Las cutres"; the tale is, primarily, a confrontation with and a challenge to the Spanish female honor code. Sarah L. White points out that "[t]he figures of the chaste Christian mother—the anchor of society—and the subversive sexual siren delimit the spheres of female identity in much of Spanish history [and a] female out of control was not only disorderly; she was dishonorable" (233). Both clerical and public opinion decree that there is no middle-ground, and for many centuries Spanish society has punished guilty women in some way for transgressing this inflexible honor code.[14] Honor in a woman, as we have seen in Chapter 1, is based almost solely on an apparent absence of disgraceful behavior or illicit sexual activity and that understanding had been part of Spanish society for centuries. Scott K. Taylor puts it simply: "[A] woman's honor rests solely on chastity, and particularly on the outward show of chastity" (164). The mother had certainly given the appearance of living a chaste life during her widowhood. Nevertheless, even though "nadie se recató para cortejar y galantear a la madre en presencia de las muchachas" [nobody was imprudent enough to court or flirt with the mother in the girls' presence], there was, presumably, at least one man who succeeded in winning her favors, if the narrator's version of the story is cor-

---

14   This punishment is commonly portrayed in Golden Age drama, where women who have only given an appearance of transgression, as well as actual transgressors, are severely and publicly punished. Calderón's *El médico de su honra* illustrates this point with the female protagonist, doña Mencía, being unjustly put to death on a wrongful suspicion of unfaithfulness.

rect—although his guess remains hidden for the next twenty-five years (3: 366). The narrator's analysis exposes the mysterious youth's origins, and the truth about the last few months of his mother's life is indirectly exposed to the reader. In addition, the narrator has surmised that the mother's dying wish is that her daughters protect her honor.

The sisters' faithful execution of this credible request is responsible for their poverty-stricken and reclusive lifestyle that had, in effect, been an act of love and respect for their mother. The price for her infraction is paid by her daughters, whom she unintentionally condemns to exclusion from society. They conceal the child's existence by paying for him to be raised elsewhere and, over the years, they are forced to liquidate every asset they can muster to provide for this remote upbringing and education. Their marriage possibilities are destroyed as they become increasingly impoverished, and the social discourse around them becomes more and more negative over the years.

Anything valuable or of sentimental value that the sisters might have inherited from their mother, such as her jewelry, or even her clothing, is sold to raise money. Paid help for the house is unaffordable, furniture is sold, as are farm animals from their small holding, while their diet, consisting mainly of home-grown pulses, resembles that of the poorest laborers in the country. Their mother's honor may have been maintained, but the price is almost a living death for her daughters. Furthermore, when the half-brother is of age and well educated, he is welcomed back to the sisters' house as their nephew. The young man is "tan simpático [y] tan amigo de divertirse" [so popular and fun-loving] that he soon finds a young woman to marry who appears unconcerned about his mysterious background (3: 368). However, her family insist that possession of the family home be a condition of the marriage contract, leaving the three sisters in penury again. Penniless once more, they move to the family farmlet and carry on living in the same impoverished state that they endured before their half-brother's homecoming. Gendered inheritance patterns prevail.

Pardo Bazán condemned the gendered inequality regarding sexual infidelity multiple times in her short stories and essays, sometimes obliquely, as we will see in the next chapter, and sometimes confronting the problem more directly in narratives such as "Comedia" and "Los escarmentados".[15] "Las cutres" is situated between these two extremes, as the reader is given no information about the circumstances surrounding the conception of the boy.

---

15   The seduced and abandoned pregnant protagonist is walking through a storm to obtain help with the impending birth when she is rescued by a misogynistic doctor.

The widowed mother appears to have been left to continue with the pregnancy and subsequent birth alone except for her daughters, and the father of the child is never mentioned. In "Las cutres", Pardo Bazán has illustrated the consequences of this false and destructive gendered standard imposed by Spain's patriarchal society. Only the mother's death saved her from public dishonor and its attendant societal retributions.

Any unmarried woman in Spain can be referred to as a *soltera*, a word without obvious negative connotations but, in "Las cutres", Pardo Bazán has drawn on the disparaging trope of the *solterona*, or old maid, a woman seemingly single for life and adapting to that status in her personality. Nina Auerbach describes the common Western European perception of the old maid as one who is "[g]rotesque, out of nature, her very name reducing itself to a snicker" (109); in this tale their status has been diminished to the point that their very names have been forgotten.

"Las cutres" is a tale of contradictions, with outward appearances neither denoting character nor indicating true social standing. The deceased mother appears to have been an admired paragon of beauty and chastity (albeit somewhat vain and frivolous), while after her death, her less attractive daughters are jeered at and despised. The first half of the story presents the reader with the well-known literary tropes of an "angel" and three unloved "old maids". The inverse tropes are revealed as the tale concludes: the "virtuous woman" proves to be the "fallen woman", and the "old maids" (*solteronas*) prove to be "noble, self-sacrificial offspring defending a parent's honor".[16] As the mother is transformed from a model of virtue to a "fallen woman", in the eyes of the reader, the narrator's deduction reverses the impression of the sisters as mean and unfriendly recluses. They too are transformed, in Auerbach's words, from old maids to sacrificial angels to a surrogate family (111).

The ending of the story, when stripped of the profusion of narratorial detail, reveals a reasonably straightforward and logical story about female honor and family loyalty. McKenna, too, agrees with this conclusion: "Seen from the vantage point of the Spanish honor code the sisters' behavior no longer appears to be so extreme" (116). In "Las cutres", the readers, once they realize the implications of honor in the text, may be quick to judge the mother. They may condemn her for placing her daughters in the invidious position that they find themselves in in their community, but it must be remembered that there is no mention of the father of the boy. Spain's honor

---

16 The tropes of the virtuous and the fallen woman were familiar to Spanish society from Church teachings, where the virtuous womanhood of the Virgin Mary is compared and contrasted to the reputedly fallen Mary Magdalene.

tradition, popularized by Tirso de Molina's hero, subtly praised Don Juans for seductions, while shaming their victims. Pardo Bazán's personal and overt response, effectively condemning this "traditional" right to seduce and then ostracize, discussed in the next chapter, is once again fictionalized and disseminated in this story.

"Coleccionista" was published in 1912, (two years after "Las cutres"), in the widely circulated *La Ilustración Española y Americana*. The story is centered around the activities of a marginalized elderly *madrileña*, Rosario, who lives alone and collects all manner of mislaid valuables, trinkets and rubbish off the streets, earning her the derogatory nickname of *la Urraca*, the Magpie.[17] The narrative begins immediately after Rosario's death, which is signaled to her neighbors by her failure to make her usual early-morning milk purchase. The narrator's background information about Rosario includes an explanation about her understandable but somewhat demeaning nickname, the well-known—but unsubstantiated—fact that she had in the past been employed, and an account of her predatory habits during the last thirty-five years of her life. All these snippets of information, true or otherwise, tell the reader as much about the neighbors' (and the narrator's) curiosity as about the late woman herself. One might think that Madrid is large enough to afford a person such as Rosario some anonymity, but every area of her acquisitive life appears to have been observed and remarked on by scrutinizing onlookers.

The narrative style, although Realist, is reminiscent of that of a *costumbrista* story, being an almost sentimental, impersonal, apparently third-person eyewitness account, in many ways similar to the stories contained in the 1851 collection entitled *Los españoles pintados por sí mismos* (Gil y Carrasco). However, the last few sentences of "Coleccionista" reveal that it is in fact a first-person narration. The narrator recounts Rosaria's nondescript clothing and her daily watchfulness at places around Madrid frequented by wealthy people, where she would swoop on any fallen valuable, such as a shawl or a purse, and scoop it up the instant that it touched the ground. Although she kept much of what she found, she also showed some discernment as she regularly discarded objects from her collection: "[S]acaba diariamente la basura a la calle envuelta en un periódico y oculta bajo el indefinible mantón color de tierra" [She took newspaper-wrapped trash out to the street each day, hidden

---

17 The magpie is attracted by bright objects which it can steal. The word "magpie" is used in similes or comparisons to refer to a person who compulsively collects things, especially objects of little use or value. See https://www.oxfordreference.com/.

under her shabby earth-colored shawl] (1: 234). The extent of this discrimination becomes evident as the tale concludes.

Ricardo Senabre, in his review of Pardo Bazán's *Obras completas 12*, considers "Coleccionista" a narrative in which Rosario's actions "dejan entrever hondos problemas psicológicos que la autora procura no desvelar, dejando que el lector complete por sí mismo las ricas implicaciones del relato" [reveal deep psychological problems that the author tries to suppress, leaving the reader to complete the complex implications of the story for themselves]. The curiosity and judgment of Rosario's neighbors, including the narrator, who all enter her house with the police after her death, is emphasized. The surprising discoveries for the reader are, firstly, that the police and some neighbors find a sparsely furnished, but neat and tidy house and, secondly, the puzzling fact that a spare room, rather than being an unsanitary jumble of street-litter, is found to filled with hundreds of wooden cigar boxes. On inspection, these boxes contain selections of Rosario's treasures, acquired over many years, carefully and minutely classified and stored, with the narrator exclaiming: "[Y]o no podía dudarlo: la Urraca coleccionaba" [There was no doubt about it: the Magpie *was* a collector] (1: 235).

This unexpected discovery invites the reader to consider "Coleccionista" both as a psychological study of an obsessive-compulsive hoarder and as a narrative that borders on a parody of the various nineteenth-century novels about middle-class collectors.[18] Pérez Galdós's *Novelas españolas con-*

---

18   The "centenares de cajitas de tabacos" [hundreds of cigar boxes] (1: 234) in the house also invites the question of where Rosario would have obtained them. Cristina Maria Percoco, one of the very few critics who have covered this story suggests that the presence of these boxes hints that Rosario, at some point, may have been a cigar factory worker (218). This suggestion is possible, given Pardo Bazán's interest in this industry, but it is problematic when the management and working conditions in the tobacco factories are examined. Beginning in 1755 in Spain, the tobacco industry, was a state monopoly with tight control of both the production and the workforce, which by the *fin de siècle* was almost all female (Capel Martínez 132, 34). Cigar manufacture consists of three separate processes: stripping, making, and packing; the latter a more skilled procedure which Edith Abbott describes as a "trade by itself" (2). Packers obviously had access to empty cigar boxes, but the lowest grade of worker, sweepers, would also have some access to them. Sweepers worked after hours, just before the factory was sealed for the night by two men. Every tobacco worker was subject to a high degree of scrutiny, with their work hours, and the materials they handled recorded and, in addition, compulsory personal searches, carried out "without hurry" as they left the premises. Theft was specifically prohibited, but any breaches of protocol were considered serious, and a range of punishments was

temporáneas (1881–87) are typical of the nineteenth-century fiction that features museums, both public and private, as a focal point of the narratives. According to Hazel Gold, Pérez Galdós reaches "the very bottom of the scale, the complete degeneration of the museum" in *La de Bringas* (1884). In this novel, members of the Bringas family constantly sort and rearrange their possessions, which for the daughter include "apricot pits, bone and metal buttons, artificial flowers, postage stamps, whistles, screws, old gloves, and so on" (137). Soledad Pérez Mateo also singles out "Coleccionista" and *La de Bringas* as being representative of the banality of the private museums housed in modest dwellings.

Accumulations such as these result in the discrediting of logic of the museum as a place of ordered and purposeful display of art and history; they designate not the world, but rather the being and social ranks of their possessors (Gold 138-39). And, just as Pardo Bazán encapsulated the tropes of Golden Age drama into her short story "Comedia", or the *folletín* into "La dama joven", she has embedded into "Coleccionista" the nineteenth-century novelistic theme of the compulsive desire to own objects and curate them in private collections. "Coleccionista" takes the concept of a museum even below "the bottom of the scale" that was imagined by Pérez Galdós in *La de Bringas*—in Rosario's museum every exhibit was scavenged from the street. Her carefully curated street-findings include:

> [G]uantes ... pedazos de encaje ... peines, jabones, pañuelos ... flores artificiales, objetos de cotillón, desdorados y marchitos; portamonedas de plata, piel y cartón vil; devocionarios, libritos de memorias, peinas de estrás, agujas de sombreros, frascos de esencias y de medicinas, ... cartas de amor, letras sin cobrar ... billetes de Banco [y] ¡un collar de perlas!
> [[G]loves ... bits of lace ... combs, soaps, handkerchiefs ... artificial flowers, party decorations, faded and withered; silver, leather and ugly cardboard purses; prayer books, autograph books, rhinestone combs, hat pins, bottles of tonics and medicines, ... love letters, uncollected bills ... bank notes [and] a pearl necklace!]. (1: 234)

Rosario had known where best to watch for pickings and exactly who to watch: well-dressed middle-aged ladies, her *marquesas*; elderly, white haired women whom she called duchesses; and those she nicknamed countesses,

---

specified (Capel Martínez 137-145). There is no definitive answer to questions that arise about the origins of the cigar boxes, but following Pardo Bazán's hints about Rosario's working life, a placement in a tobacco factory does appear feasible.

the women in their thirties. As they came and went from various venues and entered and got out of their cars and carriages, they frequently lost valuable items: "bolsos, saquillos, tarjeteros, abanicos, pañuelos y otras menudencias" [handbags, evening bags, card holders, fans, handkerchiefs and so on] (1: 233). These luxury articles, once they had been pounced on by Rosario, were never returned to their owners. The implication in the narrative is that, although they are treasured by Rosario, they would hardly be missed by their rightful owners.

For Rosario these were indeed treasures that exceeded the dreams of a working-class woman, treasures that enabled her to experience "emociones de intensidad violentísima al recontar y clasificar el botín" [intense, even violent, emotions as she counted and classified her "treasure"] (1: 235). Pérez Mateo asserts that, in the literary world, at least, collections such as Rosario's, offer their own gratifications, substitutes for real-life affection and love, for solitary people like *la Uracca*. Rosario appears to be almost destitute, describing herself as she is begging as an "abuelica de más de setenta años" [a seventy-something year old grandmother], before correcting herself slightly, "pobre abuelica" [poor grandmother] (1: 232); however, as Senabre noted, Pardo Bazán has drawn a more complex protagonist than is initially apparent. Her overriding compulsion to snatch and hoard, like a magpie—"la gustosa locura del coleccionismo, el goce egoísta y callado de reunir lo que nadie ve y lo que de nada nos ha de servir" [her pleasure, verging on madness of collecting, her selfish and private enjoyment of gathering things nobody missed that were ultimately of no use to her]—has dominated her life (1: 235). In 1893, Pérez Galdós, who had a longstanding interest in Spain's collectors, described the compulsion to collect, as far as "los pobres" [the poor] are concerned, as a diversion that usually keeps them out of trouble ("El Coleccionista" 197-98). With her story, Pardo Bazán presents an exception to this statement. For her protagonist, Rosario, the relentless collecting was an outward manifestation of a psychological compulsion to hoard that, rather than improving her life materially, led to physical debilitation and quite possibly an untimely death.

Public scrutiny of Rosario's clean and tidy home challenges the community views that she was no more than a pathetic scavenger, but it is the discovery of her "museum" that offers a more rational explanation of her life. She is driven by her impulse to collect, to keep her findings and not part with even the banknotes that would have given her the means to live comfortably. Her attachment to her collection overrode her reason. Paulina, Marcela and Rosario, "Las cutres" in the previous story, also attracted attention to themselves with their unusual lifestyle; however, the revelation that uncovered their behavior indicates that their lives were ultimately driven by logic and reason. If, as discussed at the beginning of the chapter, emotion is a "feminine" trait and logic is a "masculine" trait, neither set of protagonists fits this criterion. Rosario, in "Coleccionista", may have been driven by her passions, but she hardly exhibited a normal feminine lifestyle, while the asceticism of the three sisters was instigated by filial affection and loyalty. In these two stories both sets of protagonists challenge the patriarchal view that the "ideal woman" acts from emotion and not from reason.

"Saletita" and "El mascarón": Searching for Security

As we have seen in previous stories, the nineteenth-century Spanish woman sought financial security above all, and reliance on a man, through marriage, was the accepted path to this end. However, as with any generalization, there will always be cases that fall outside the ideal situation. Saletita and Cipriana, the respective protagonists of "Saletita" and "El mascarón", offer two contrasting examples of women eager to better their current situations. Saletita appears to be largely dependent on her widowed mother Maura, while Cipriana, in her 40s and already widowed, feels that life is passing her by as she works all hours in her shop with only her young nephew for company.

Both women experience a sudden, unforeseen meeting with a man who arouses their interest; neither man would fit the stereotype of "ideal husband" material, but the women each have their reasons for encouraging the encounter. Saletita, driven by monetary logic, and having time on her side to plan, devises a slow and reasoned course of action. She smoothly, shamelessly and purposely brushes her mother aside as she works towards her objective of marrying a rich *indiano*, more than old enough to be her father. Her short-term aim is to inherit his fortune when he dies and, at the end of the story, she appears to be on the verge of achieving this. Cipriana, a shopkeeper, on the other hand, driven by loneliness and perhaps self-pity, makes a split-second decision to allow a young and handsome customer, who has entered her shop for the first time, to embrace her. Her impetuous action proves to be misguided as, rather than taking her out for a social evening, he hustles her out of sight and, with calm deliberation, murders her before robbing the premises. Cipriana's impulsive emotional response to her customer, driven by her enforced solitude and the fact that she is almost hypnotized by desire, is a mistake that, had she been observant rather than excited, she might have been able to avoid.

Pardo Bazán's "Saletita", centers on Pánfilo Trigueros who, more than twenty years earlier, had emigrated from Galicia to Latin America to better himself. Now wealthy, he has returned to his hometown where he is taken advantage of by a scheming mother and her daughter. It is one of a handful of stories that Pardo Bazán wrote about the relatively few successful returnees to Spain and the varying responses from their families and communities.[19] "Vampiro" (1901) has a similar theme to "Saletita", that of a septuagenarian *indiano* who marries a teenaged girl. "Vampiro"'s narrative ventures into *lo fantástico* (Romero López 67-70), while "Saletita", written in the Realist style, has an entirely credible storyline.

During the *fin de siècle*, the tenor of literary representation of the *indiano* changed from that of the wealthy prodigal sons of the old Restoration Spain, who sowed suspicion with their visions of modernity that encroached on traditional rural values, to a representation of the prodigiously money-laden sons, ready to build a new modern Spain (Conlon 1). Pardo Bazán's stories, while perhaps closer to the former model, do not readily fit into either of these categories. Rather, the majority depict scenes of chaotic inter-personal and inter-family relationships, many of them driven by greed or envy.

The original publication details of "Saletita" are straightforward. In 1898 it appeared in "El Gato Negro" (the only Pardo Bazán story that was published in this magazine), two years later it was included in the collection *Historias y cuentos de Galicia* and it was then re-published in *Lecciones de Literatura* (1922).[20] "Saletita" opens with Pánfilo Trigueros returning to

---

19   "Barbastro" (1898) tells of a man who covets some Galician land and marries the owner, an *atroz mujer*, in order to secure it for himself; in "Contra treta" (1912), the *indiano* is murdered for his money. In "El tetraca en la aldea" (1892), the husband returns from Uruguay to find three additional children and improvements to his house and in "El vidrio roto" (1907), the returnee from South America finds that the money he has sent home has not been used to improve the family home as he had intended.

20   However, "Saletita" reappeared, word-for-word in the Catholic, Carlist magazine *La Hormiga de Oro* on 19 March 1921 (82-85), two months before Pardo Bazán's death, re-titled as "Le falló el cálculo" and signed by C Pérez Bordas. Hemeroteca Digital describes *La Hormiga de Oro* (circulation 30,000 [1900]), as being set up to counter the liberal influences of publications such as *La Ilustración española y americana*, *Blanco y Negro* and *La Esfera*. These three magazines alone accounted for more than half (252) of Pardo Bazán's published stories (Paredes Núñez *CC* 4: 451-56). On 7 August 1890, *La Hormiga de Oro* had insulted Pardo Bazán by describing her, among other things, as "la ilustre y descarrilada escritora" [the well-known but un-hinged lady writer] (Buriel 443) and, presumably, the presence of the re-titled and re-authored manuscript in this unexpected publication was Pardo Bazán's private, yet very public, revenge.

Marineda and visiting doña Maura, who had scorned his suit years before.[21] The local gossip has preceded him however, and Maura is already aware of his arrival and the rumor that he has deposited a million pesetas with the local bank. Nevertheless, she is not prepared for his appearance, well-dressed but shaky, toothless and drooling, and supported by an ornate gold-headed cane. He is still bearing the decades-long rancor of being rejected by Maura: "De aquí me echasteis por desnudo ..., y vuelvo vestido y calzado y con gabán de pieles" [You dismissed me when I went barefoot and dressed in tattered clothes ... and I return with shoes on my feet and a fur coat] (2: 90). With the million pesetas uppermost in her mind Maura, undeterred by his reminder of her past decision, sits him down in her shop and enquires directly about the truth of the rumor.

As the conversation (which forms the first half of the story) progresses, Pardo Bazán exposes the base motives of her protagonists. Trigueros is vain—"el más tenaz y constante de los sentimientos humanos" [the most tenacious and constant human feeling]—and proud of his financial success as he confirms the deposit: "[E]l millón de pesetas precisamente, no; pero, vamos, se le acercaba, se le acercaba..." [Not precisely the exact million pesetas; but near enough, near enough] (2: 90). Overcome with greed, Maura realizes "¡[q]ué existencia ancha, fácil, deliciosa, representaban esos cuatro millones de reales!" [what a wonderful lifestyle one could live with those four million reales!] (2: 91). Maura, widowed and the owner of a haberdashery shop with few customers, has known better times and is now struggling to survive. Making a sudden effort to appear more enticing, she sits up straight and hides her feet, shod in homemade patchwork slippers. Their conversation is interrupted by the arrival of Saletita, Maura's nicely dressed, angelic-looking daughter who, once she is introduced, has only one immediate topic of conversation (as did her mother), as she asks pointedly: "¿Es usted ese tan rico, tan riquísimo? ¡Ay! ¡Quién me diera ser usted!" [Are you as rich as they say? Oh! What would I give to be you!] (2: 91).

Ricardo Piglia's view that a short story always tells two stories is, in this instance, valid for "Saletita". Piglia asserts that "the classic short story ... narrates Story One in the foreground, and constructs Story Two in secret. A visible story hides a secret tale, narrated in an elliptical and fragmentary manner. The effect of surprise is produced when the end of the secret story appears on the surface" (24). He adds that both stories are told differently, with the same events entering simultaneously into two antagonistic narrative logics.

---

21   Three possible meanings of the name Pánfilo are "simple", "gullible" and "stupid" (*Collins* 721).

Applying this premise to "Saletita", the first half of the narrative establishes a basis for "Story One", where two young lovers, Maura and Trigueros, meet again as mature adults and are still attracted to each other, but for reasons more prosaic than love. The secret, unexpected and, in this case, less socially unacceptable Story Two begins with Saletita's entrance and her instinctive grasping attitude towards Trigueros's money. Story One would be predictable: something of Maura and Trigueros's old relationship would re-kindle and they could be happy together. The town gossips have already assumed that this will be the outcome of the reunion. Story Two has darker undertones: Saletita's naivety and enthusiasm make Trigueros smile, and the reader is presented with Maura's sudden decision to push her daughter towards the old man with the command: "Déle un beso que es una chiquilla" [She's a girl, give her a kiss] (2: 91). Not only does Trigueros obey, but it is the beginning of his unspoken infatuation with Saletita, and his daily visits to the house as "el viejo se encandilaba y se deshacía en babas mirando a la chiquilla" [the elderly man was mesmerized by the girl and went to pieces when he just looked at her] (2: 92).

Maura appears to observe the now double-pronged charade with consternation. She has indeed succeeded in using nineteen-year-old Saletita as bait, "hooking" Trigueros (and his money), while deliberately encouraging the gossipers with their talk about her own romance with him. However, Maura is increasingly concerned that Saletita does not realize the implications of her flirtatious involvement with the broken down man and wonders how to broach it with her. She recoils at the thought of Saletita being married to a decrepit old man of "setenta y cinco [años] achacosos, hediondos, envueltos ya en la atmósfera de la tumba" [seventy-five, ill, smelly and appearing ready for the grave] (2: 92). However, driven by greed, she tells herself that Trigueros does need a wife "[p]ara cuidarle, para servirle las medicinas, para dirigir su casa, para ..., para heredarle, en suma ..., sí, para recoger aquel fortunón, que no cayese en manos indiferentes, extrañas ..." [to look after him, to give him his medicines, to run his household, to ... to inherit his money, in short, yes, to collect his fortune, so that it would not fall into the hands of some stranger] (2: 92), with the fortune obviously mattering most.

Maura, in fact, does not truly know her daughter, and neither does the reader, as Maura's character is the only one of the three that Pardo Bazán has meaningfully developed. The reader is aware of Trigueros's physique, facial peculiarities and his flattery of Saletita, but almost nothing of his character or personality has been revealed. And even less has been shown about Saletita, who sits with her mother and Trigueros in the house, appearing naïve in her response to the man's attentions. Maura is astute enough to realize that Trigueros has lost interest in her and, as she gathers herself to explain the implications of Trigueros's attitude to Saletita, Story One concludes.

Story Two has not been voiced directly, but a re-examination of the text reveals "fragments" of the story that will be revealed in the conclusion. Maura clumsily tries to explain that to Saletita that she is sure that Trigueros is seeking a bride and swears that she would happily spare Saletita the repulsive experience and be the "victim" herself. In her response Saletita is now revealed as a scheming and vindictive femme fatale who is consumed by greed for Trigueros's money: "Desde el primer día conté con él… Si usted me lo quita, ¿Ve estas uñas? ¡Pues no le digo más!" [I worked this out from the first day I talked with him. If you take him away from me, do you see these fingernails? Well, I don't need to say anymore!] (2: 92).

Susan Walter, citing Erika Bornay, highlights some psychological traits of the paradigmatic femme fatale—her capacity to dominate, a coldness, a reluctance to let anything stop her and, when needed, an animalistic sexuality and controlling nature ("Femme" 178). Arguably, Saletita demonstrates each one of these traits, including her cat-like response as she threatens to scratch her mother. Walter, referring to other texts, adds that it seems that "Pardo Bazán relies on her readers' familiarity with the femme fatale figure from the male literary tradition, while, at the same time, she creates unique representations of [her] female characters, which highlight how their rejection of certain patriarchal social norms allows them to claim autonomous positions as subjects" ("Femme" 179). In threatening her mother in this way, Saletita inverts the relationship with her mother, who is now both dominated and manipulated. Saletita shows herself as the *mujer fuerte* in this story, rather than her mother. Despite the absence of an explicit text relating Story Two, Pardo Bazán has left no doubt in her readers' minds as to Saletita's mindset and the eventual outcome of this tale.

Both women have made active decisions to acquire the vulnerable and aptly named Pánfilo Trigueros's money. If Maura had simply decided to entice Trigueros into marriage with companionship, her motive would be obvious but understandable. However, avarice has driven her to use Saletita to entice Trigueros to their home. Saletita's actions, in both tempting Trigueros and deceiving her mother, are shameful. The reader has a clear impression that Maura, a widowed lower middle-class shopkeeper and her nicely dressed daughter, lived within their society's norms, of necessity needing to make their own decisions; however, their joint manipulation and outwitting of Trigueros would change this. Saletita, as a femme fatale, has made a decision that pushes her mother aside and to enrich herself personally and, by so doing, she has set herself (and her mother) up to be the subject of her society's judgment.

Saletita is exposed as cold-hearted, deceptive and greedy, and deserving of any condemnation directed at her from the gossipers. Maura, surely, will back away and meekly watch her daughter inherit Trigueros's money. Saletita, with her carefully considered moves, will have done nothing illegal. Her calculating forethought contrasts with the emotional actions of Cipriana, the protagonist of "El mascarón", who in a few seconds of ill-considered judgment loses everything.

"El mascarón" is one of about a dozen Pardo Bazán stories that relate to Carnival in some way, deploying the anonymity provided by the masks and capes worn by the participants to create narratorial tension.[22] While many of Pardo Bazán's Carnival stories are relatively light-hearted, concerned with amorous encounters or playful revenge, "El mascarón" stands apart, relating the cold-blooded murder and robbery of a lonely and vulnerable widow by a masked man. The only publication of the story was in the annual Carnaval edition of the Madrid-based weekly magazine *La Esfera* on February 19, 1915.[23]

In Christian Europe, Carnival, a time of public festivities, is celebrated the week before Ash Wednesday, the day that marks the beginning of the Lenten period of abstinence.[24] These festivities, combined with the customary attire of the revellers—an enveloping cloak and a mask—led to social and sexual laxities. It is a festival with a long history, as Michael Holquist explains: "Carnival must not be confused with mere holiday. The sanction for carnival derives ultimately not from a calendar prescribed by church or state, but from a force that pre-exists priests and kings, and to whose superior power they are actually deferring when they appear to be licensing carnival" (xviii). Pardo Bazán was an early critic of Carnival, and "El mascarón" ad-

---

22 Pardo Bazán's Carnival stories include: "Aventura" (1899), "Ceniza" (1897), "La careta rosa" (1918), "La charca" (1919), "Los dominós de encaje" (pub. 1994), "El dominó verde" (1895), "El escapulario" (1915), "La máscara" (1897), and "Travesura" (1918).

23 Jean-Michel Desvois states that *La Esfera*, was an expensive, luxury magazine, with excellent illustrations and engravings and high-quality print (343-44).

24 The name, Carnival, derives from the Latin *carne levamen*, literally "flesh put away".

dresses many of the points expressed about the festival by later twentieth-century critics.[25]

Later scholars, such as Bakhtin, analyzed European Carnival festivities and their unique effect on societal behavior. In *Rabelais and His World*, Bakhtin described Carnival festivities as arising from a thousand-year-old development of the pageants of culture, linked externally to the feasts of the Church.[26] He writes: "Carnival is not a spectacle seen by the people; they live in it, and everyone participates because its very idea embraces all the people. While carnival lasts, there is no other life outside it. During carnival time life is subject only to its laws, that is, the laws of its own freedom" (7-8). These laws liberated people from norms of etiquette and decency, with free and familiar contact among people usually divided by the social barriers of caste, property, profession and age (10).

Expressing similar sentiments, and referencing "El mascarón" in particular, Paredes Núñez writes: "Cuentos como éste constituyen un testimonio de este tipo de sucesos en los días de Carnaval, donde el bullicio, el confusionismo, el anonimato del disfraz y el general desconcierto, eran circunstancia propicia para el robo, la venganza y el crimen" [Stories such as this represent the times during Carnival, where noise, confusion, the anonymity provided by the costumes and the general mayhem provided propitious circumstances for robbery, revenge and crime] (4: 356). Other scholars voice comparable sentiments. Leonardo Sancho Dobles remarks that: "[G]racias a la trasgresión que permite el carnaval, las diferencias entre los hombres se desvanecen, las clases sociales se borran y se olvidan por un momento, o bien se ironizan los aspectos cotidianos como la muerte, el trabajo, el poder, las diferencias y la abstinencia" [The permissive atmosphere that prevails during carnival permits the inequalities between men to vanish, social classes to be erased and forgotten for a moment, while daily events such as death, work, power, and abstinence are made fun of] (66). From an ethnographer's perspective, David D. Gilmore states that in Spain, Carnaval is, above all, a license for the expression of powerful feelings and impulses normally kept in check by the country's repressive moral code, and it is also a time in which

---

25 In "La dama joven", discussed earlier in this chapter, Pardo Bazán indirectly critiques the moral laxity of Carnival as she describes Dolores's experience, one that changed the course of her life: "En Carnaval asistía a tres seguidos. ... Unos amoríos breves, la seducción, la deshonra, el desengaño" [I went to three Carnivals. ... A few brief love affairs, a seduction, dishonour, and disappointment] (7: 15).

26 *Rabelais and His World* was completed in 1940 but was not published until 1965.

participants experience and negotiate the conflicts and contradictions that trouble them deeply and that demand some sort of psychological release (Carnaval 3). This point will become pertinent shortly, as the female protagonist's thoughts and actions in the story are examined.

The narrative reflects Pardo Bazán's publicized distaste for the excesses that are sanctioned during the festival: "El Carnaval es, por su esencia misma, insensatez, desorden, involuntaria infracción de todas las reglas sociales. Es el momento en que el capricho, la espontaneidad, la mofa, la ironía despreciadora de etiquetas y formulismos, se abren paso rompiendo la valla que les oponen, durante el resto del año" [Carnival is, by its very essence, foolishness, disorder, an uncontrolled violation of society's rules. It is the moment in which whims, spontaneity, mockery and a contemptibility for norms and formalities all break down the social barriers that restrain them during the rest of the year] ("Ex momo" 146).

"El mascarón" is a further example of Pardo Bazán 's multivocal titles. In Europe the mask is associated with Carnival and was, according to Mikhail Bakhtin (1895-1975), originally connected with "the joy of change and reincarnation ... and with the merry negation of uniformity and similarity", but it can also be associated with "the violation of natural boundaries and mockery" (39-40). Furthermore, in its Romantic form the mask acquires other meanings; it "hides something, keeps a secret, deceives ... [it] acquires a somber hue" (Bakhtin 40); it is the attributes of this more Romantically inspired mask that Pardo Bazán alludes to in this narrative. In "El mascarón", the male protagonist—the masked man—wears it to disguise his identity. However, there are also other interpretations of the word that can be drawn from the text. Some things are "masked" and are not as they appear to be. Cipriana, alone in her shop, is in an emotional state when a late customer enters, but she manages to mask her feelings and present herself as a guileless, middle-aged woman. The Carnival attire worn by her customer masks the fact that he is carrying offensive weapons and tools and, even with his mask removed, the real reason for his visit—burglary—is masked by his initial (seemingly) seductive actions towards Cipriana. "El mascarón" is, indeed, a multi-purpose title.

The story itself, set in urban Madrid, is presented by a somewhat judgmental third-person narrator. It opens on the Monday evening during Carnival with Cipriana, a haberdasher, alone in her shop, which appears to be well-stocked and profitable and which she runs with the help of her nephew. Some items, such as shawls, fans, masks and gloves, are in great demand during Carnival week and the probability of unexpected late-night customers explains Cipriana's wish to remain open beyond eleven o'clock at night. Even that evening, "hasta las once y las doce estaban viniendo chulillas del barrio, modistas y ribeteadoras, a llevarse aquellos trapos castizos" [until eleven or twelve, the *chulas* from the neighborhood, the seamstresses and trimmers, were picking up traditional accessories] (4: 35). It also explains the normalcy of a masked man entering her shop at half past twelve to purchase gloves.

"El mascarón" is written in the Realist style, portraying the "fragmented, flawed world" of everyday life" (Slattery 55). Pardo Bazán extends this depiction of commonplace experience to the inclusion of local inflections in the direct speech of her protagonists. As Cipriana discusses the early closing of the shop with her nephew she requests: "[D]eja la puerta encajá, pa que si pasa alguna de esas, sepa que velo ... [y] listo... pa llegar más antes" [Leave the door unlocked, so that if anyone passes by, I'll know they are there... [and] I'll be able... to get there in time (4: 35). This use of "pa que", local, lower-class speech, subtly signals to the reader that "El mascarón" is a story with characters drawn from a class that, in all probability, they know little about. For the readers, Carnival will be a time of formal masked balls, such as the one featured in another of Pardo Bazán's carnivalesque stories, "El escapulario", where the participants have the means to transport themselves through the city safely. They have no first-hand knowledge of the perils of festival-time for women on their own in working-class neighborhoods, and with this narrative and its grisly outcome, Pardo Bazán reminds them that other women lead less fortunate lives.

Cipriana's unnamed nephew is out on the town, making the most of the festivities, while she, from choice, has kept her premises open and is sitting alone. Madrid appears to be caught up in one great party, typified by "las calles regadas de confeti, [y] los chiquillos vestidos de demonios verdes, azotando a los transeúntes con el rabo" [streets strewn with confetti, [and] young children dressed as green demons, whipping passers-by with their tails] (4: 35). Cipriana's wistfulness at being alone on nights such as this is communicated to the reader. She sits in a poorly lit corner, pondering the vagaries of Madrid's electricity network, with all the brightness and excitement taking place outside her door. Despondency and nostalgia envelop her "como impertinentes moscas" [like a swarm of persistent flies] and she falls into self-pity: "¿Por qué no había ella de divertirse? ¿Por qué no había de volver a casarse? No era ningún vejestorio, apenas cuarenta, carnes lozanas, firme 'dentaúra' y mata de pelo gruesa y reluciente. Un marido le daría sombra, la ayudaría al negocio." [Why didn>t she have any fun? Why shouldn't she get married again? She was no old woman, she was barely forty, with a firm body, good teeth and masses of thick, shiny hair. A husband would give her protection, he would help her with her business] (4: 36). Her mental state illustrates Gilmore's statement that the relaxation of moral restraints during Carnival week allows troubling conflicts, contradiction, and desires to emerge. For Cipriana, it is her pent-up desire that surfaces and demands release and, as it is Carnival, a release without consequences.

Cipriana promises herself to step out more in the future, daydreaming about sparkly earrings and her own transport, when a late customer arrives, wearing a dirty mask and a bedspread tied into a makeshift cape. His request is for gloves and, as Cipriana turns her back to find them, he removes his mask. Cipriana then faces a "guapo mozo, 'un tipazo'" [a personable man, a "looker"] (4: 36). The sight of this handsome man and her unexpected proximity to him, (as she obeys his request to fit the gloves on his hands), suddenly releases the suppressed longing that she has been harboring.

As they converse, the man is seemingly open about his home city, Cádiz, and like Raimundo in "El árbol rosa", he offers her a plausible reason for being in Madrid. He quickly establishes that Cipriana is on her own before he initiates an apparent seduction. The narrator could not be clearer about the customer's intentions: "Los ojos del mascarón, insolentes de galantería, de nacarada córnea, húmedos de vida, bebían el rostro de la mujer. ¡Besaban ya aquellos atrevidos ojos!" [The eyes of the masked man, arrogant and fearless with pearly corneas, drank in the woman's face. He had already kissed her with those daring eyes!] (4: 36). While the brief conversation continues Cipriana is completely taken in by his talk of the rigors of business in his trade, cabinetmaking. Here, the narrator, voices a personal criticism of Cipriana's judgment: "En otro momento acaso se hubiese fijado la señá Cipriana en que las yemas que estaba calzando no tenían callo alguno, y aunque fuertes, eran de holgazán. Pero la adormecían los ojos del cliente, enviándole su fluido, y, semirrendida, consintió en el mariposeo de unos labios sobre su mejilla sofocada" [Any another time Cipriana might have noticed that the fingers she was holding were uncalloused, and although they were strong, they appeared lazy. But her customer's eyes numbed her, confusing her, and, half surrendered, she consented to the touch of his lips on her blushing cheek] (4: 37). Almost hypnotized by his gaze, Cipriana's emotional vulnerability is now her downfall. She allows the man to move behind the shop counter, thus losing any control of the situation. Suddenly, she finds herself locked inside her own premises, hustled behind the shop area and pushed onto her own bed.

The mock cape has concealed the customer's tools of his true trade. He uses his knife to stab Cipriana to death before producing lock-breaking instruments, opening and ransacking drawers, taking unbanked money from the bedroom. He empties the till before re-masking, leaving the premises, and quickly disposing of the fateful gloves in the nearest drain. Pardo Bazán's cryptic closing sentence references Cipriana's erroneous emotional judgment, clouded by desire: "[E]l mascarón, en quien creyó ver el Amor, era la Muerte" [The masked man in whom she thought she saw Love was in fact Death] (4: 37).

For Pardo Bazán's original readers, the subscribers to *La Esfera*, the man's appearance and his later actions will come as no surprise, as the story's publication page has, at its center, an illustration of this tale, drawn by Varela de Seijas, "one of the most important illustrators of the period" (Cuesta 349 n43). It depicts the customer as a stereotypical, suspicious-looking Berber-like figure, while Cipriana is drawn as a rather stout and unattractive middle-aged woman, far from the self-image that the character has articulated. Three of the seducers and so-called villains mentioned in this study are indeed presented in the respective texts as having shortcomings which are somehow attributed to their origins, both geographical and ethnic. Raimundo, the would-be seducer in "El árbol rosa" is from Lérida, and in "Apólogo" the protagonist is Andalusian and has an Arabic surname, Zegrí, which, is said to account for his jealous nature, while the murderer in this tale is from Cádiz. In addition, the stereotypical illustration in *La Esfera* is that of a villain, slanting the reader towards a negative view of the man before reading the story. As has been discussed, while atavism is an overt theme in "Apólogo", it is merely implied in both "El árbol rosa" and "El mascarón". Although Pardo Bazán may have only been hinting at a cultural basis for the man's violence, the editors of *La Esfera* have contracted an artist who has made any atavistic assumptions in "El mascarón" explicit.

"El mascarón" personalizes both the defenselessness of a lone woman during Carnival and the freedom that a guaranteed anonymity affords to those with sinister intentions. It is the one week in the year when even the Church appears powerless. Pardo Bazán, as we have seen, was aware of the consequences of this freedom, as were the numerous later scholars, as previously stated. In this story Pardo Bazán challenges her upper-middle-class readers, who were unlikely to ever need to visit shops such as the one described in this story, to consider the "dark underside" of the Carnival celebrations for single, vulnerable women. Both Saletita and Cipriana were seeking long term security in their lives. Logic, timing and cunning appear to have granted Saletita her wish, although the true ending of the tale is never revealed. Cipriana's rush of emotion, on the other hand, sadly means that her perfectly understandable desire to re-marry will never be fulfilled.

Conclusion

The six stories discussed in this chapter, although written over a time span of thirty years, demonstrate a consistency in Pardo Bazán's feminist messaging, and they also illustrate two facets of her message. The first is that women can and should be able to act in their own interests. Laura, in "Apólogo", displays reason and ingenuity in dramatically and successfully avoiding her death at the hands of her deranged *novio*; Paulina, Marcela and Rosario in "Las cutres", forgoing individual futures, voluntarily exile themselves from their own community for twenty-five years to uphold their mother's honor; while Saletita outwits her mother as she works towards a marriage with a wealthy older man.

The second part of Pardo Bazán's wider message is that the women who do permit themselves to be driven by emotion rather than reason, face less positive outcomes: Concha's decision to marry a jealous and patriarchally-minded man was made under pressure. Her sister may be happy, and the priest who influenced her certainly is, but Concha's future happiness appears uncertain; Pardo Bazán has surely left this question open. Rosario is unwilling, due to her emotional state, to use her findings to supply herself with the basic necessities of food and clothing, and Cipriana's few seconds of longing for male company costs her her life.

In this chapter Pardo Bazán's female protagonists all make their own decisions and follow them through. In "Las cutres", "Coleccionista" and "El mascarón" the narratives reveal the conclusions, and it is left to the reader to imagine the ongoing story in the other three. None of these women, however, conform to the patriarchal ángel model, and none are the "mirrors of all perfection" imagined by Spanish menfolk ("Women" 779). As the discussion of these stories has shown, Pardo Bazán demonstrated an earnest concern for women who were, in many ways, on the fringes of urban society: the single, independent operetta star, an orphaned seamstress, the seemingly eccentric misers and street scavengers and the insignificant widowed shopkeepers and their offspring. All used their agency and made life-changing decisions. Some appeared to better their futures; others, although they made their decisions knowingly, had adverse outcomes.

The next chapter, focusing on six of Pardo Bazán's Don Juan narratives will also engage with a variety of female protagonists who meet widely differing fates: two do not survive, another is saved by her naivety, while others are portrayed as strong and resourceful women who both shame and trick their would-be seducers. There is, nevertheless, one constant in these tales. None of the Don Juans, for all their previous "experience", is successful in the seduction of their intended victim, thus confirming Pardo Bazán's effort to provide some degree of awareness and agency to her female characters, even within the limits of a restrictive society and literary tools available to her.

4
Don Juan's Downfall

> Sevilla a voces me llama el burlador, y el mayor gusto
> que en mí puede haber es burlar una mujer y dejalla sin honor.
>
> [Seville calls me the deceiver, and my greatest pleasure
> is to seduce a woman and leave her without honor.]
>
> - Tirso de Molina
> *El burlador*

The Spanish literary prototype of Don Juan Tenorio, the embodiment of the serial womanizer, was created by the Golden Age dramatist Tirso de Molina (Fray Gabriel Téllez) (1579–1648)[1] and his play, *El burlador de Sevilla y convidado de piedra*, was first performed around 1630.[2] The continuing success of this production ensured that the Don Juan figure, together with the numerous tropes that the play established, inspired successive generations of writers, both in Spain and throughout the rest of

---

1 Mercedes Formica has stated that the real-life inspiration for Don Juan was Don Juan de Austria (1547–78), a half-brother to the Spanish King Felipe II (qtd. in Leggott 52). (See Mercedes Fórmica, *La hija de don Juan de Austria: Ana de Jésus en el proceso al pastelero de Madrigal*. Occidente, 1973). Pardo Bazán, however, published an article in *La Nación* (24 March 1909) in which she asserted that it was Alfonso X's (1221–1284) medieval lyrics, recorded in the *Cantigas de Santa María*, which gave rise to the seventeenth-century Don Juan legend (Zárate 98).

2 This play portrays four of Don Juan's seductions. The first, in Naples, is that of the Duchess Isabela, and the second, in Tarragona, is of the fisher-girl Tisbea. In Seville, Doña Ana, who has been sent to a convent, also appears to have been seduced, and the final victim is Aminta, a bride. However, Don Juan's wrongdoing is complemented by a sense of propriety, by a foreshadowing of retribution and divine justice (Edward H. Friedman 61).

Western Europe.³ However, in Pardo Bazán's hands, the popular perception of Don Juan as a swaggering libertine is often challenged, as we will see in the following analyses. It is James A. Parr's view that *El burlador de Sevilla* was at the heart of the *Comedia Nueva* canon, inspiring ongoing critical commentary, as well as being the foundational text for all subsequent versions of Tirso de Molina's archetypal character (185). Well-known European interpretations of the figure of Don Juan are found in *Dom Juan ou le Festin de pierre* (1665) by Molière (1622–1673) in France and *Don Giovanni Tenorio* (1735) by the Italian, Goldoni (1707–1793). Two famous musical versions are *Don Giovanni* (1787) by the Austrian Wolfgang Amadeus Mozart (1756–1791), and *Il trovatore* (1853) by the Italian Giuseppe Verdi (1813–1901). Lord Byron's (1788–1824) epic poem "Don Juan" (1821) is arguably the most famous English version of the story. The versions most pertinent to the current discussion, however, are those of a trio of Spanish Romantic poets who, in the early 1800s, created their own interpretations of Tirso de Molina's *El burlador*: José de Espronceda (1808–1842) with the epic poem "El estudiante de Salamanca" (1836–39) and Antonio García Gutiérrez (1813–1884) and José Zorrilla (1817–1893) with their respective dramas *El trovador* (1836) and *Don Juan Tenorio* (1844). Pardo Bazán appears to have been familiar with these pan-European works, referencing some of them in various stories, while both real-life and fictional Don Juans often modelled their behavior on various literary "heroes" from this canon.

The Don Juan theme is notable for its adaptability across different literary periods and movements, with the character of Don Juan represented as, among other things, a Catholic believer for Tirso's Catholic Renaissance Spain or a seeker after the ideal woman for countless Romantics (Singer 5-6). Mandrell explains, at some length, this constant *refundición* of the Don Juan theme in Spanish literature, arguing that it is "literally a rewriting in which aspects of one literary text are reworked so as to admit the claims of both inclusion and originality within another text, which is to say the *refundición* supposedly contains its precursor—the elements of plot and character—even as it stands apart from the earlier text" (Honor 90).

The behavior of literary Don Juans generally follows a common pattern. Either alone, or aided and abetted by male friends, they select an apparently unattainable and initially unwilling *víctima*, chase her, court her and in so

---

3   In the twentieth century, arguments arose concerning the authenticity of the authorship of this play. These arguments are discussed at length in Parr's *Don Quixote, Don Juan and Related Subjects* and the matter is resolved in favor of Tirso de Molina (138-59).

doing, wear her down with persistence, and if necessary, promises of a future together. Zorrilla, in the poetic drama *Don Juan de Tenorio*, encapsulates this conduct:

> Partid los días del año...
> uno para enamorlas,
> otro para conseguirlas,
> dos para substituirlas
> y una hora para olvidarlas (ll. 683-89)
> [Allocate the days of the year/ one to fall in love with them,/ another to take them,/ two to replace them/ and an hour to forget them].

Some Don Juans, however, believe their attractiveness to be so irresistible and their powers of seduction so great that even completely unattainable victims are within their reach, including nuns, married women and other women of principle. As the Don Juan figure was repeatedly recreated over time, these same plot elements or tropes were recombined according to the writer's whim. Don Juans were represented as being well aware of the destruction their chosen lifestyle wreaked on their female victims. Espronceda, who was himself a shameless womanizer, made this clear when his protagonist, Don Félix, admits his awareness of his destructive power in "El Estudiante de Salamanca":

> Corazón gastado, mofa
> de la mujer que corteja,
> y, hoy despreciándola, deja
> la que ayer se le rindió.
> Ni el porvenir temió nunca,
> ni recuerda en lo pasado
> la mujer que ha abandonado
> ni el dinero que perdió (1: ll. 108-15)
> [His empty heart mocks/ the woman he courts,/ spurning today yesterday's fancy./ ...He spares no thought for the future,/ for jilted women/ or for riches lost]. Translated by Salvador Ortiz-Carboneres

The majority of Don Juan's victims (the traditional way of referring to these abused women) are single and vulnerable—serving girls, seamstresses or cleaners, often young country women who have arrived in the towns or cities seeking employment, and in this situation, they lack the direct protection offered by a father or a husband. These women are, because of Don Juan's actions, dishonored and disgraced in the eyes of Spanish society.

The figure of Don Juan and the Spanish concept of honor are inextricably intertwined. Seduction, Mandrell argues, reinforces the aims of patriarchal society by appropriating and elaborating on Don Juan and his story. Donjuanesque dramas restate and refocus several dominant cultural truths and the figure itself embodies the validity of the status quo, that sexual conquest reinforces masculinity. The Spanish Don Juan tradition of men seducing and dishonoring a series of women has a long and socially sanctioned history. Mandrell notes that the literary Don Juan's seductions are, however, only one facet of the overall picture; the reader is often also made aware of the general social chaos stemming from this individual's desires and actions (Honor 60). Self-interested and self-absorbed Don Juans, inspired by the Romantics with their arrogant attitude to life, were a danger to any attractive young woman they happened to notice, and they were well aware of the long-term grief that their actions would cause. It is these romantic Don Juans who feature in many of Pardo Bazán's stories about the figure.

In the Spanish psyche, Roberta Johnson argues, Don Juan conjured up an image of a positive national symbol of masculine energy and links it to the glorious traditions of the past. However, the majority of female critics, including Pardo Bazán, saw Don Juan, the inveterate seducer, as a serious threat to women's precarious position in bourgeois society when the "angel of the house" archetype, with its emphasis on chaste young women, was the favored model of female behavior (Gender 122). However, by the mid-eighteenth-century, romantic writing had developed and evolved to include writing which appealed to the imagination and feelings, as the romantic writers looked beyond surface reality to the immanent ideal (Furst *Romanticism* 40).

Don Juan's behavior, which had always been modelled on Romantic precepts, had been a target of criticism since Tirso de Molina's work was first performed but, in general, early critics avoided belittling Don Juan himself to protect their own reputations. The romantic glorification of Don Juan changed that stance, with opposing critics approaching the figure from both a moral and an anti-romantic perspective. When women writers entered this arena, starting with George Sand's novel *Lélia* (1833), they tended to criticize Don Juan's selfish and cavalier treatment of women and at the same time often expressed anti-romantic sentiments (Leo Weinstein 130-31, 133-34).

Even though the majority of Pardo Bazán works were Realist, she was very familiar with earlier writing styles including romanticism, which reached Spain in the early nineteenth century (but, due to Spain's political and social climate, was not fully taken up until later). Where George Sand overtly criticized Don Juan, Pardo Bazán, half a century later, was more indirect in her criticism of the figure. Pardo Bazán was jealous of her own reputation as a serious writer and understood overt criticism would antagonize sections of her male readership. It is in her short fiction that this indirect criticism is particularly apparent. Pardo Bazán wrote twenty-four "Don Juan" short stories (Quesada Novás 127), and she was among the first Spanish female critics to censure the Don Juan figure.[4]

Several of the Pardo Bazán stories discussed in this chapter depict protagonists who subscribe to the self-centered and self-indulgent lifestyle of many of the Romantic poets. In common with other women writers, Pardo Bazán challenged the poetics of romanticism, as well as mocking the Romantics' style, thereby creating an anti-romantic discourse in order to mock both Don Juan's pretentious behavior and his callous attitude towards women. This anti-Romanticism resulted in a critical belittling of Don Juan's actions and, furthermore, highlighted the plight of his victims.

Dismissive of male Romantic authors, Pardo Bazán used her detailed knowledge of the genre and its followers to subtly undermine them in various ways. One way of achieving this was to use either parody or satire. Satire is particularly evident in the final paragraph of "La última ilusión de Don Juan" (1893), a widely studied tale not included in this work, where the narrator responds to Don Juan's anguish as he realizes that his cousin will marry an ideal fiancé, a rich and honest man. His last dream, that of marrying her himself, after ten years of "eternal self-sacrifice" spent seducing hundreds of other women, will never be fulfilled. He, not his cousin who appeared to be looking forward to a secure future, was, of the two, the true dreamer.

Pardo Bazán sometimes undermined the traditions of Romantic writing by creating a stronger opposing female figure who was able to counter and overshadow the Don Juan. In "Sor Aparición" (1896) (another well-known tale not included here) the protagonist's seducer, Camargo (a barely disguised Espronceda), is shamed in the eyes of his society by his victim's decades of public penance for both her sin and that of her seducer—although he probably does not care (Paredes Núñez 1: 486n1). Another example, in-

---

4 Other notable Spanish female critics of the Don Juan figure included: Carmen de Burgos, Sofía Casanova, Concha Espina, María Martínez Sierra and Blanca de los Ríos. Several of their works depicted Don Juan domesticated, while others portrayed a feminine Doña Juana (Gottleib 32-36, Johnson *Gender* 134). This later feminine manifestation of the Don Juan legend was a tendency that Pardo Bazán did not subscribe to.

cluded later in this chapter is Dalinda, who in the story of the same name, pushes her would-be seducer off an upper-level balcony as he tries to force his way into her room, thereby injuring him badly, and by implication, ending his philandering exploits.

As Weinstein observes, during the mid-nineteenth century a different, "more vitriolic" line of attack on the Don Juan figure developed, depicting Don Juan at the end of his life as a decrepit and unattractive old man, rather than the glamorous, dashing, profligate younger version (134). Otto Rank describes this development as a devaluation of the figure that arose as the subject matter itself grew older. It involves not only humanizing the hero but reaching a point of involuntary ridicule and then descending into caricature (111). Pardo Bazán embraced this particular perspective and used it to great effect as a further censure of the Don Juan figure in the two opening stories of this chapter, "Cenizas" and "Remordimiento".

When outlining the so-called achievements of various Don Juans, Pardo Bazán often narrates their various exploits in an apparently sympathetic manner that appears to view the protagonist as heroic and his actions meritorious. However, each story discussed here allows for an alternative feminist reading, where the plight of one woman is emphasized against a background of hundreds of victims. This device enables Pardo Bazán to expose to her readers the vast number of women whose lives she believes to have been adversely affected by such seducers. In addition, it is notable that when these six stories are considered as a group, the reader becomes aware that, as in most of Pardo Bazán's donjuanesque tales, her literary Don Juans have failed in some way to achieve their ends.

There are numerous tropes in the Don Juan plays of both Tirso de Molina and Zorrilla which later writers made use of in their adaptations of the story. As there are obviously too many tropes for a comprehensive exposition of each of them in a single short story, Pardo Bazán necessarily selected only a few for any specific narrative. One traditional trope though, that of Don Juan's final redemption, is almost absent in Pardo Bazán's treatment of the theme, due, one suspects, to her personal contempt for amoral, philandering men, as discussed in Chapter 2, and mentioned very forcefully in her essay "La educación del hombre y de la mujer" where she likens such men to the two-faced Janus: one face focused on their victim, the other on their own families. My findings are that even when the Don Juan's behavior can be looked on as morally acceptable and there is a reasonably satisfactory outcome from a victim's point of view, as is the case in "El aviso", in Pardo Bazán's stories he almost always acts for reasons other than genuine remorse or repentance. "El cinco de copas" however, stands apart from other stories on this matter. The epilog informs the reader that the protagonist, Agustín, has become a friar, and presumably has repented of his misdeeds before his ordination.

In contrast to the opportunistic seducers portrayed in some previous narratives, the stories in this chapter explicitly mention previous victims of each of the Don Juans; however, the focus of the stories is on the attempted seduction and ultimate fate of one particular young woman. This emphasis on one figure serves as an example and gives greater weight to the dozens or even hundreds of other women referred to as "background information" and reminds the reader that each conquest alluded to represents a life changed forever. Each story is no more than a few pages in length and the brevity of the texts allows no opportunity for the reader to put these once conquered and now discarded women from their mind; they stand as shadows, or ghosts behind the main narrative. The attitudes of the female characters themselves in these stories vary. One, a nun, in "Cenizas", appears eager for an illicit assignation, while female protagonists in "Remordimiento" and "El aviso", accept marriages arranged for them by the men in their lives. Rosario, a fifteen-year-old intended victim in "El cinco del copas", seemingly has no understanding of the ramifications of a seduction and is apparently saved only by divine intervention. Rosa, in "El pajarraco", who is very aware of her would-be seducer's history, arranges a very visible revenge for the womanizer, and Dalinda, in the eponymous story, acting in self-defense, forcibly repulses an unwanted entry to her bedroom by the Don Juan. Nevertheless, in all these stories the victims themselves are silent. No female victim, from the many hundreds alluded to, offers her own opinion or viewpoint of the events. Only one protagonist, Dalinda, is even given a voice, being allowed to explain her background at the beginning of the story and speaking in her own defense at the end. However, any private interactions with her would-be seducer are not recorded.

The narratives are again arranged in pairs. In the first pair, "Cenizas" and "Remordimiento", the Don Juans are portrayed as aged men, almost senile. Both have long-standing notoriety as seducers; the first man apparently indiscriminate in his choice of victims, while the second preferred to seduce women of a certain "class". The second pair of stories "El aviso" and "El cinco de copas" are connected by Pardo Bazán's use of the literary trope *deus ex machina*. In the final pair, "Dalinda" and "El pajarraco", the careers of both Don Juans are ended dramatically because of the female protagonists' actions.

"Cenizas" and "Remordimiento": Decrepit and Detestable
Both "Cenizas" and "Remordimiento" are framed stories whose framing (or embedding) narrators provide impassioned and romanticized introductory remarks, while the internal (or embedded) narrators are both sympathetic to the Don Juan "philosophy" of life. The narratorial interactions in each story have the effect of positioning the reader as an eavesdropper on a private conversation. However, in these two stories the role of the narrators differs. The framing narrator of "Cenizas" provides an extended introduction and some closing remarks, while remaining silent as the dramatic central story is related in its entirety. In "Remordimiento", the two narrators interact throughout the narrative, offering contrasting opinions, and also contrasting worldviews.

In "Cenizas" and "Remordimiento" Pardo Bazán's re-interpretation of the figure emphasizes one specific anti-Romantic critical strategy, that of once-successful Don Juans portrayed as old men whose characters appear to have no redeeming features. The catalog of ruined lives described in both stories is similar, although Vizconde Tresmes, the protagonist of "Remordimiento", certainly seduced more affluent women than Juanito Morán in "Cenizas" whose "mil amorosas aventuras" [thousand amorous escapades] (4: 133) were chiefly with laundresses, dressmakers, and lower-class women. In addition, the texts both draw attention to the female victim's point of view and can be read as feminist condemnations of the destructiveness of the men's actions on the women they seduce and, by extension, on society.

"Cenizas", which appeared in 1902 in *Blanco y Negro*, is one of the relatively few stories that was not re-published in one of Pardo Bazán's collections. The narrative offers an excellent example of what Ernest Hemingway, in 1932, called the "wow at the end", achieved, in Armine Kotin Mortimer's words, by "the careful embedding of a second story in the first" (Mortimer 276). The first story, which accounts for almost half of the text, gives context to the second, principal story. The narrative is set in a forest near Doctor Veiga's spa, where Veiga and the first-person framing narrator are walking, arm in arm. It is twilight and the eerie forested setting itself promises a story with, the narrator claims, "[u]n soplo suave y fresco salía del río. La hora era propicia a las confidencias" [a soft breeze coming from the river that made the hour conducive to sharing confidences] (4: 134), thus connecting with the reader who is carried along with the hope of a secret revelation. A somewhat unsteady elderly man crosses their path, seeming, to the narrator, to be one of life's "leftovers", the type who appear at spas hoping to prolong their lives and are only still above ground "con permiso del sepultero" [by the dispensation of the gravedigger] (4: 134). They are astonished when the elderly man greets Veiga, who instantly recognizes him and excitedly exclaims, echoing the narrator's sentiments, "¡[e]l pasado que sale de su sepulcro! ¡Al famoso Juanito Morán!" [he has returned from death's door! The illustrious Juanito Morán!] (4: 134).

Veiga takes over the narration with his own story centred on a seduction and relates the story of a seduction Morán had carried out decades before, a tale selected from a thousand similar tales, he adds, while the narrator listens intently. It is a shocking drama, cloaked for years in silence, concerning a young and reputedly beautiful nun, a niece of the Marquis of Ulloa.[5] The incident occurs in the Galician village of Montañosa, where Veiga and Morán have both lived.[6] Veiga appeared to know Morán well; Morán was a man, he says, who explicitly wished to be compared to El trovador or Don Juan Tenorio, two of Spain's best known literary Don Juan figures. With these few sentences, Pardo Bazán has emphasized the *fin de siècle* patriarchal worldview of men such as Veiga, with his excited and admiring references to the "famous Juanito Morán" and his literary heroes. The status of their anonymous victims, who were deliberately seduced and discarded with no care or concern for their altered futures, is immaterial. The fate of the women—a lifetime of social ostracism—is in the service of a man's (often dubious) reputation. The women's stories are interchangeable, while seducers such as Morán are viewed by other men as admirable role models.

Coincidentally, the narrator is familiar with both the story and the village of Montañosa itself but is puzzled by the discrepancy between the donjuanesque hero-figure in the tale of a nun who fell to her death in the Plaza de Muerte and Morán, the decrepit old man they have just sighted. At this point the narrator launches into a daydream, clearly inspired by Gothic and Romantic tropes, reminiscent of Espronceda's "Estudiante de Salamanca". In the narrator's imagination, the young Morán is transformed into a dashing, cloaked figure in the plaza, surrounded by ancient buildings, including the

---

[5] The family of Ulloa is in itself a reference to characters in Tirso de Molina and Zorrilla's dramas and also to Pardo Bazán's own Naturalistic-gothic novel, *Los pazos de Ulloa* (1886).

[6] In "Doña Emilia en Compostela", José Manuel González Herrán identifies the fictional town of Montañosa as being, without doubt, modelled on the Galician city of Santiago de Compostela. The convent of San Juvencio in the story is, in reality, the Monasterio de San Pelayo de Antealtares, and the central Plaza de la Muerte is the Praza da Quintana, or Quintana dos Mortos (where a medieval graveyard was later paved over). He also states that the story of the nun narrated in "Cenizas" is adapted from a well-known local legend (135).

cathedral and adjacent convent protected by a high moss-covered wall. The chimes of the cathedral clock echo around the square, marking out eternity and, as the peals ring in the mist "diríase que los muertos yacentes bajo las losas de la plaza y que le dan nombre se revuelven en la húmeda tierra y entrechocan sus huesos gimiendo de inmensa fatiga" [it would seem that the dead lying under the flagstones of the square (and which give it its name) turn themselves around in the damp earth, clashing their bones and groaning with endless fatigue] (4: 134). The daydream demonstrates the narrator's susceptibility to romantic and gothic tales and imagery and, with its allusions to death, offers a grim portent of the tragic outcome of the story.

Veiga remarks that adolescent girls adored Morán and women blushed as he passed. The town is divided; he is revered by some, including the then fifteen-year-old Veiga, and reviled by others, such as schoolteachers and the authorities in general. Tired of "la monotonía de la eterna seducción de modistillas, fregonas y señoritas de medio pelo" [the monotony of seducing an endless line-up of needlewomen, cleaners and other lower-class women] (4: 135), Morán seeks a new challenge, repeating one of Don Juan's "traditional" conquests and, to that end, "rondaba el convento y frecuentaba con insólita piedad la iglesia" [haunting the convent and attending church with an unaccustomed piety] (4: 135). People whisper about his new-found religiosity, guessing Morán's motives, however "nadie se preocupó seriamente, como no nos preocupamos de los revuelos de un milano en derredor de inexpugnable palomar" [no one was seriously concerned, comparing Morán's actions to that of a kite fluttering around an impregnable dovecote] (4: 135).

Then Veiga himself, who at this point confesses to following Morán around, notices the many hours that Morán spends parading in front of the convent looking upwards, his eyes fixed on one particular grille. They are both rewarded when a nun's pale face appears behind the cloister grille and seems to exchange glances with Morán before giving a quick wave of her "paper-white" hand. This phrase, with its metafictional connotations, reminds the reader that this is, in fact, a fictional tale about a quest for a fictional quarry—an ideal and perfect woman, a figment of the collective Romantic imagination. Indeed, the story, with a nun as the female protagonist, is itself drawn from literature with its echoes of Morán's idol, Zorrilla's Don Juan Tenorio. When the exchange of gazes and the cursory wave are repeated on another occasion, Veiga takes a vicarious pleasure in the discovery of their secret, as happy in fact as if he were the lucky seducer. Not only is he unwittingly projecting his own sexual fantasies about women—pale-faced, fragile and eager to be seduced—but he also appears to have subscribed to the fictional myth of the seduction of a romanticized yet unattainable ideal woman.

Early the next morning Veiga notices a cluster of churchgoers in the plaza and is horrified to see the center of their attention is the inert and bloodied body of the nun at the base of the cloister wall. Tied around her waist is an improvised rope, made of strips of knotted sheets, that has obviously broken as she attempted to climb down from her quarters to meet Morán. Veiga's first instinct is to see just what this young woman had looked like, expecting that she would be as beautiful as he had imagined, the incarnation of the elusive but fictional Romantic ideal. However, he is extremely disillusioned: "Ni era fea ni bonita: como cien mujeres que andan por ahí" [She was neither pretty nor ugly: rather she was indistinguishable from any one of the hundreds of girls who wander around every day] (4: 136).

The authorities know exactly whom they need to question about the incident and seek Morán, but in vain, as he has fled before daybreak towards Portugal, on his way to Brazil. Two shocking facts thus confront the reader—the nun's sudden brutal, apparently accidental death and Morán's degenerate actions. Mandrell observes that none of Tirso de Molina's Don Juan's seductions are merely sexual indulgence; each is aggravated by circumstances which make seduction heinous (*Honor* 59). These sentiments are also pertinent to "Cenizas". Here Morán has not only attempted to seduce a nun, but he also abandons her as she is dying, and flees. Veiga's expressed admiration for Morán and his conquests, together with the complete absence of any expression of remorse or shame concerning the women whose lives Morán has destroyed, seemingly reinforces the patriarchal idealization of the Don Juan figure. However, the juxtaposition of the death and Morán's subsequent flight reveal Morán's true nature.

The text illustrates the way in which Pardo Bazán subverts the patriarchal ideology of the traditional Don Juan story by using the events of the narrative itself to critique the Romantic idealization of the character. Morán may be commended by some for his manliness and the bravado of his many conquests but for others and, I would suggest, the majority of female readers, the narrative ending tells quite a different story. The extent of Morán's self-centeredness and baseness is revealed as appalling, as he left the young woman to die when he fled. This Don Juan has been exposed as the shallow, heartless lecher that he is. Moreover, he has not succeeded with this seduction.

The framing narrator closes the story with a wry comment about ashes, "¡[v]ejez, vejez; cenizas yertas!" [old age, old age; dry ashes!], a link to the title of the story, which can be interpreted in a number of ways (4: 136). One possible interpretation is that in old age, the fires of passion in men like Morán die, leaving only a cold residue; however, it could also suggest that the decrepit old man himself is now burnt-out and depleted, a remnant of his former self. I would add that there is an ironic alternative: ashes traditionally symbolize repentance in the Catholic tradition. "Cenizas", following this line of thinking, renders the title ironic, as there is no sign of repentance on Morán's part for a life of self-seeking pleasures.

"Remordimiento", the story that follows, depicts a second Don Juan, Tresmes, as a tragic, aged man who, in earlier days, exhibited the same cavalier attitude towards his multiple victims as Morán. There is one difference, however. Morán spent his days (and nights) parading through the streets and seducing any woman who would listen to him, while Tresmes, a nobleman, seeks out more refined women to seduce. Both stories are framed, although the dialog between the two narrators in "Remordimiento" is more complex than the verbal interchanges in "Cenizas".

"Remordimiento" was published four times, with three of these in Pardo Bazán's own publications. The first was in 1892 in *El Imparcial*, one of Madrid's leading newspapers of the time, whose circulation included Europe and the Americas, and Pardo Bazán re-published it the following year, 1893, in *Nuevo Teatro Crítico* before including it in her 1894 collection *Cuentos nuevos*. It made a fourth appearance in the second edition of Pardo Bazán's *Cuentos de amor* (1911), a choice that perhaps reinforces the "pessimistic view of love" she so often expressed (Feeny "Pessimistic" 7-14). In many ways, this framed story is a daring exposé of the Don Juan figure as the protagonist himself, narrating the central tale, is given a voice. It unflatteringly illustrates the notorious character of this particular Don Juan, the Vizconde de Tresmes, as he discloses his personal philosophy. He appears here not only as a "confirmed bachelor" but as a hard-hearted mercenary, and a self-important libertine. He exemplifies the Don Juan trope of seeking a challenge and enjoying a chase and he is also ultimately responsible for his niece's premature death. The character Tresmes appears in several of Pardo Bazán's tales as a man-about-town—a man of leisure who is fond of women—however it is in "Remordimiento" that his worst traits are exposed.[7] For the Spanish nine-

---

7   "Adriana" (1896), "Apuesta" (1910), "Desde afuera" (1897), "Drago" (1911), "Los hilos" (1899), "El rival" (1902)" and "Un parecido" (1897) all feature Vizconde de Tresmes as a protagonist. In some of these tales he is portrayed as a Don Juan-type figure, while in others he simply appears as a man with time on his hands and a fondness for flirting with women (Paredes Núñez *CC* 4: 422).

teenth-century readership, the female framing narrator, who has established a friendship with an infamous Don Juan and discusses his affairs with him, is also an audacious figure, one who has entered a forbidden world outside the prevailing *ángel del hogar* construct.

The gender of the framing narrator of "Remordimiento" has a somewhat puzzling history. It is an important issue, as the gender of a narrator is often pertinent to the interpretation of a text, and even more so in "Remordimiento", which is so intently focused on relationships and the balance of power between the sexes. The narrator's gender is normally obvious, but occasionally, as in "Cenizas" and "Feminista", Pardo Bazán appears to deliberately leave the framing narrator's gender ambiguous. However, in "Remordimiento" the answer to the question about gender depends on the edition of the narrative.[8] The original 1892 publication shows the gender of the framing narrator as feminine, and in this analysis, I follow that edition.

The unnamed embedding narrator becomes the narratee who acts as an internal audience for the central story, the embedded narrative, related by Tresmes. The embedding narrator is well acquainted with the background and Donjuanesque reputation of the aging Vizconde Tresmes, "un famoso calaverón" [a well-known debaucher] (8: 71), however, she has only met him

---

8 True gender-neutral narrators such as the one in "Feminista" (3: 106-09) are devoid of linguistic gender markers. Bieder suggests that in Spanish "the erasure of a narrator's gender requires careful attention to suppress cultural and linguistic gender markers" and that it is a "principal ploy in [Pardo Bazán's] strategy of authorisation" ("Plotting" 141). "Remordimiento" has two instances of these markers—"perplejo/a" and "entusiasmado/a"—, and it is the use of one set or other of these words which identify the framing narrator as either male or female. In both the original publication of the story and in the re-publication in *Nuevo Teatro Crítico* "perpleja" and "entusiasmada" are used, thereby indicating a female narrator. This did not change when the story was included by Pardo Bazán in the 1894 collection *Cuentos nuevos* (1st ed.). This is the edition used by the editors of *Obras completas*, (8: 69-75), 2004, and it is the one I have chosen to discuss. Meanwhile, Pardo Bazán personally compiled *Cuentos de amor* in 1898 without including "Remordimiento". However, when this collection was revised in 1911 (either by Pardo Bazán herself or the editor), "Remordimiento" was included and the gender markers of the two words in question were altered to become masculine, presumably a deliberate decision. Typographical errors in the texts are not unknown (as the introductions in *Obras Completas* demonstrate), however it defies credibility that both gender markers in this story would suffer this fate. Paredes Núñez, in his 1990 *Cuentos completos*, reproduced the 1911 edition of *Cuentos de amor*, including the masculine gender markers in "Remordimiento" (1: 349, 350).

as an old man. They have struck up a friendship—"[g]ustaba el vizconde de charlar conmigo" [the Vizconde liked to converse with me], she says (8: 72). As they begin their conversation, she recalls in great detail, his reputation as a womanizer who squandered his family's fortune. The narrator refers to him as a "perdulario", a "calvatrueno" and a "terrible traga corazones" [a spendthrift and a madcap, with an appalling reputation as a heartbreaker] (8: 71) and seemingly fond of high-born victims, mentioning two in particular: a duchess who ended up in an asylum and a princess who lost her inheritance, both as a result of their liaisons with him (8: 71). The narrator views him critically, seeing (in her imagination) a refined and artistic man: "Las noble facciones de su rostro recordaban las del Wolfgang Goethe ... en la época del famoso viaje a Italia" [His aristocratic facial features recalled those of Wolfgang Goethe ... when he took his famous trip to Italy] (8: 72).[9] Exhibiting the same ability as the embedding narrator of "Cenizas" to create a romanticized daydream whilst simultaneously holding a conversation, the narrator mentally reconstructs an image of an aristocratic, young, handsome and virile Tresmes:

> [A]quella boca un tanto carnosa; aquella nariz de vara delgada, de griega pureza en su hechura; aquellas cejas negrísimas, sutiles, de arco gentil, que acentúan la expresión de los vivos y profundos ojos; aquellas mejillas pálidas, duras, de grandes planos, como talladas en mármol, ... aquel cuello largo, que destaca de los bien derribados hombros la altiva cabeza ... en su musculosa esbeltez, algo recogida como de gimnasta, la robustez de acero del hombre a quien los excesos ni rinden ni consumen [That rather thick mouth and the slender narrowed nose bring to mind a traditional Greek face; the black, subtle gently arching eyebrows accentuate the expression of lively and deep eyes; the pale, chiseled cheeks, like carved marble, ... the long neck, standing out from well-sloping shoulders, a haughty head ... in its muscular slenderness reminiscent of a gymnast, the steely robustness of a man who has neither yielded to his excesses nor been consumed by them]. (8: 72)

Here Pardo Bazán's descriptive language appears overly grandiose, objectively yet imaginatively noting every feature of this Romantic hero. In fact, the description is so excessive and the narrator's mental picture so idealized

---

9   An examination of Goethe's biography fails to reveal any behaviour remotely similar to the catalog of shame featured in Tresmes's life, and it appears that the narrator is merely captivated by his romantic appearance.

(and patently false) that it becomes another facet of this narrative that could be considered as anti-Romantic parody.[10] This "female gaze" of the narrator is in itself unusual, being a reversal of the more socially acceptable "male gaze", defined in the Cambridge dictionary as "the fact of showing or watching events or looking at women from a man's point of view". It is the opposite here and provides a subtle reinforcement of the gender reversal that Pardo Bazán has attributed to this embedding narrator, portraying her as a strong woman, challenging and questioning a man who appears to be her social superior, and whose behavior pattern was hardly an acceptable topic of conversation for a sheltered middle-class *ángel del hogar*.

Pardo Bazán's use of an extended introduction in this narrative may be viewed as a manipulation of the reader, ensuring that they have a certain opinion of Tresmes before his own voice is heard as the "second story" in the text. Despite the elderly Don Juan's obvious physical attractiveness, the narrator's early litany of his selfish debauchery, both physical and moral, is polarizing. It is probable that readers will have by this early stage already decided if Tresmes's actions are commendable or reprehensible. As the narrator questions Tresmes about his life, despite being entranced by his physical appearance, she is revolted by his "absoluta carencia de sentido moral, el cinismo frío, visible bajo la delicada corteza del lenguaje" [total lack of moral sense and his cold cynicism, discernable despite his carefully chosen words (8: 72). At this point she confronts him directly about the effects of his womanizing as she demands to know just how many husbands, how many brothers and how many fathers (not to mention the victims themselves) will have been consumed in the hell fires of shame because of him.

Tresmes is quick to justify his actions, cynically explaining that the women in question were ready to be seduced, and he was the one who was "best qualified" to do so: "Y lo que yo, por escrúpulos más o menos justificados, desperdiciase, otro lo recogería, quizá con menos arte, tino y miramiento que yo. La pavía madura cuelga de la rama y va por instantes a desprenderse del tallo. El que pasa y la coge suavemente le ahorra el sonrojo de caer al suelo, de mancharse, de ser pisada [If I, because of moral scruples, passed on a an opportunity for seduction then some other man would take it. He may have less finesse, skill and consideration than I do. A mature fruit hangs from its branch and is eventually going to fall. If a passerby gently picks that fruit, it is saved from the indignity of falling to the ground, of getting dirty, of

---

10   There are also non-fiction examples of Pardo Bazán's equally grandiose descriptions of men she held in high regard. One is found in *Retratos y apuntes literarios* where she lauds the recently deceased Juan Valera (1824–1905) (219-221).

being stepped on] (8: 73). His interrogator is both perplexed and intrigued by this brazen self-justification, then enquiring if he has any regrets. This is a question, comments Feeny, that "reveals Pardo Bazán at her artful best as she moves to reinforce the irony embodied in the title. For by painting the Vizconde in the darkest of colors ... she has managed to plant some small seed of doubt in her reader's mind: Can any man be so evil?" Feeny adds that the reader now expects some indication of the remorse alluded to in the title ("Illusion" 69).

By way of response, Tresmes relates the central embedded story involving his unnamed niece, for whom he was responsible. She is in love with him and wishes to marry him (a relationship permissible in Spain only with a papal dispensation which, with his upper-class connections, he would no doubt have been able to procure [see Walter Alison Phillips]).[11] Tresmes has, however, sworn himself to bachelorhood and refuses her "offer" of marriage. After much agonizing, she asks him if she could be his mistress. Showing the only shred of decency in the entire narrative, he again declines her and seeks out a prospective husband who is both young and good-looking and, using his influence, forces the marriage. Unfortunately for the couple and the young woman in particular, the self-absorbed Don Juan realizes after her marriage, when she is no longer available to him, that he does want her as a mistress after all and pursues her, behavior typical of a Don Juan. He treats her callously, even though she is also his ward.

To her credit, his married niece spurns his advances, despite the fact she is in love with him. However, within a year of her marriage she falls ill and, with her dying breath, tells Tresmes that she still loves him. In answer to the framing narrator's initial question, Tresmes states that his one regret in life was declining his niece's offer to be his mistress because, in doing so, he had acted in a way that was against his nature. The reader is perhaps mystified about his reasoning, as having a ward as a mistress, in society's eyes, was surely a step too far, even for a Don Juan. Pardo Bazán's use of irony is masterful as Tresmes informs his interrogator that his role has never been to lead anyone along the path of either duty or virtue.

With the pressing questions and frank opinions of the framing narrator, the embedded story itself is given context. The differing worldviews of the nar-

---

11 This is a typical example of the relationship that Patricia Menon calls the Mentor-Lover. She raises questions of sexual love and its links to the power, judgment and moral authority of the mentor. It was a popular trope in nineteenth-century literature, used by authors such as Jane Austen, Charlotte Brontë and George Eliot.

rators demonstrate that even when an action may appear to be one thing, the dialog reveals that the truth is the exact opposite. And yet, even expected "truths" are mis-placed. Walter notes the narrators' disparity of opinions as the marriage is discussed: a generous action, according to the female framing narrator, who echoes the social mores of the time. Tresmes himself describes forcing the marriage as a detestable action (*Frames* 138)—not, it must be noted, for the fact that it removes all agency from his niece, but from his "romantic" self-centered point of view as, in society's eyes, it places her out of reach as his victim but, at the same time, makes her desirable. Without the leading question about remorse, this would have been a simple, sad story of a ward's misguided, unrequited love, and her uncle and guardian could have been viewed as a man doing his best to act honorably. However, when Tresmes's callous and self-serving behavior is both described and admitted proudly, the dynamics change with the niece viewed as yet another Don Juan victim lacking agency in a patriarchal world. Tresmes does refer to honor, not that of his niece, but his own; how would he appear to his family? It is personal loss of honor in their eyes that halts his possible relationship with the young woman.

In "Remordimiento" Pardo Bazán presents the reader with the melodramatic fates of Tresmes's various victims, as well as the sad central story of his niece. As in "Cenizas", she highlights the unprincipled depravity of an elderly Don Juan who still thinks only about himself, proud of his life-long lack of decency, discarding morals except, regrettably in his view, on one occasion, and rejecting any murmurings from his conscience. Both stories have powerful and unexpected endings. Pardo Bazán has deployed an anti-Romantic discourse by undermining the figures of the handsome, dashing and virile Don Juans described by Veiga in "Cenizas" and in "Remordimiento" by the female narrator herself. They are both imbued with pathos and ridicule, and their licentious corruption has been exposed. They are presented as aged men who have lived lives of self-interest and debauchery, with the incidents related in the body of the narratives exemplifying the worst traits of these two protagonists.

Some readers might admire this type of behavior, particularly those who identify with Tresmes's self-imposed bachelorhood and admire him for refusing a socially unacceptable marriage, but, for many others, the closing sections of both stories would show the Don Juans as despicable characters. Morán's wooing of a cloistered nun, an alleged legendary beauty, is shameless in itself. Fleeing from the consequences of his attempted seduction marks the depths of his depravity and highlights his baseness. With Tresmes's final admission in the closing sentence of "Remordimiento" that he regretted nothing except for once taking a morally correct path, Pardo Bazán again leaves a very negative impression of the character in the mind of the reader.

There is irony in both titles. In "Remordimiento", the "remorse" in the tale is for an ethical action, subverting the accepted definition of remorse as sorrow for an immoral action. "Cenizas" is used as a perceptive, oblique afterthought in the last line of the text. An obvious interpretation relates to the fires of passion and lust burning out with age, leaving only ashes. However, the more subtle Catholic interpretation, that of ashes symbolizing contrition, provides a link with "Remordimiento"—with both protagonists being self-centered amoral Don Juans who seek pleasure with no regard for either the consequences of their actions or their victims' fates, and with no remorse.

"El aviso" and "El cinco de copas": Saved by miracles?

"El aviso" (1897) and "El cinco de copas" (1893) both present quasi-religious themes, with seemingly miraculous visions in churches deterring the respective Don Juans from their ways. The protagonist of "El aviso" is halted minutes from carrying out a carefully planned seduction and later marries his intended victim (thus sparing her from social ostracism). The marriage is most likely because of the obligations of a covenant of military honor, discovered late in the story. In "El cinco de copas", a fifteen-year-old girl, the potential victim, may be disappointed that her seducer fails to meet her, but she has unknowingly been spared a lifetime of humiliation. The Don Juan himself, frightened by an apparently supernatural experience in a chapel forgoes the seduction, later becoming a Franciscan friar.

The literary device of *deus ex machina,* employed in both stories, is exemplified by divine intervention and it saves the respective women from further shame. However, it is a device seen by some critics as a clumsy and lazy method of rescuing the author and his characters from a hopelessly involved situation (Abel 128).[12] This may well apply in the case of these two narratives; however, I suggest that Pardo Bazán, whose Christian beliefs are well-documented, uses this device to illustrate that these men, who are so confident of themselves and their powers of seduction, are in reality flouting the Catholic concept of morality and need to be brought to heel.

"El aviso", first published in 1897 in *Blanco y Negro* and republished two years later in *Cuentos sacroprofanos,* illustrates the late nineteenth-century

---

12 *Deus ex machina,* ('god out of the machine') is the introduction of any unanticipated intervener who resolves a difficult situation in any literary genre. The term originated in ancient Greek drama, named for the convention of the gods appearing in the sky by means of a crane (Greek: *mēchanē*) (Cuddon 237, Lother).

Spanish honor system as applied to males, with covenants of honor between men being paramount, while women were expected to be passive and to accept the males' actions as the duties of honor were fulfilled. I will argue that the male protagonist of "El aviso" is driven by honor and a sense of obligation to a fellow soldier, rather than remorse for his planned imminent seduction. In "The Semantics of Honor", Brian Dutton addresses the question of a man earning honor as a soldier thus: "A man sallied forth to *ganar precio*, to make himself *de precio, de valor* to society and his king. This social worth was achieved and earned by his own efforts, by the demonstration of his physical strength and military courage" (12). Furthermore, Timothy Mitchell notes that historically the prestige one earned in battle was automatically transmitted to blood descendants (173). The significance of this point will become obvious to the reader as the storyline is revealed.

"El aviso" is a Realist story, with the text in the form of a private conversation between Baltar, the priest, who delivers the monologic central story which dominates the narrative, and two or more listeners, one of whom is a hidden character-narrator (indicated as gender-neutral by the Spanish pronouns and verb forms) who acts as an interlocutor.[13] The narrative opens with a parable-like theological statement by Baltar concerning man's judgment of a person and divine mercy. If, on an earthly level, he says, even grains of wheat that have lain dormant for centuries in the pyramids can sprout, then we must allow for divine acts and miracles to occur in people's lives as well. It is, he continues, such a story that he is about to tell. His opening words, with the promise of an almost secretive and miraculous tale, draw in both the listener and the reader in a similar manner to Pardo Bazán's introductory sentences in "Cenizas".

The protagonist, whom Baltar refers to as Román (not his correct name, thus adding to the air of mystery that has already developed), like so many men in his society, appears to be a sincere Catholic, fulfilling all the obligations of the church. However, in Baltar's eyes, Román has completely ignored the law of God in the matter of his relationships with women. Baltar is surprisingly outspoken as he articulates his strong feelings on this topic: "Suprimir la responsabilidad; desatar el apetito; transformar el mundo civilizado en bosque donde el cazador acecha la caza, ¿qué es sino retroceder al estado de barbarie?" [Eliminate chance; whet the appetite; transform the civilized world into a forest where the hunter stalks the game, what is this

---

13   Baltar addresses his audience with "Voy a referirles a ustedes" [I will refer to you (pl)] and "¡El granito de trigo! exclamamos" [The grain of wheat! we exclaimed] (1: 400, 403).

but regressing to the state of barbarism?] (1: 400). In addition, the cleric makes a connection between moral degradation and physical degeneration: "Este error es comunísimo, y no contribuye poco a sostener la anemia y la miseria fisiológica de las generaciones actuales. La pureza de costumbres es un tónico, y el pueblo que sabe conservarla, conserva también la virilidad y la salud" [[Moral depravity] is common, and contributes to the lethargy and afflictions of the current generation. Chastity is a tonic, and people who do preserve it, also retain their virility and health] (1: 400). It is possible that here Pardo Bazán is referring to the degenerative effects of venereal disease. If this were the case, then this is a strong and somewhat unusual condemnation of a Don Juan's lifestyle and, arguably, a topic that few women of the time would have been willing to discuss publicly.

Baltar, the embedded narrator, is expressing his perspective in this anti-donjuanesque (and, by extension, anti-romantic) tirade. In this impassioned speech Pardo Bazán has offered the clearest overt condemnation of don-juanesque behavior in this chapter.[14] Pardo Bazán, herself a Catholic, was mindful of the Church's normally lax attitude to the sexual double standard, which from her perspective was contrary to the messages about it imparted in Scripture. I believe that Baltar's remarks in "El aviso" can be interpreted as an example of Phelan's mask narration, which he defines as a situation where a character narrator is a reliable spokesperson for the implied author and serves as a means for conveying their views (Phelan 216).

About a third of the way through the narrative, Baltar turns to the tale he has promised his interlocuters. Román, the Don Juan, was a soldier whose life was saved during a battle by the heroic actions of General Andueta.[15] The General had rescued him, arranged hospitalization and, when he had recovered, provided him with sufficient money to live fairly comfortably in a guest house in Madrid; in short, he had treated Román like a son. At the time of the narrative, there are only two occupants in this guest house: Román and

---

14   The priest in Pardo Bazán's short story "La novia fiel" (1894) illustrates a more common clerical attitude to extra-marital sexual activity in *fin de siècle* Spain. When the female protagonist confronts this priest with details of her fiancé's infidelity, he chastises her for her attitude and explains to her that "[l]os hombres.... por desgracia... mientras está soltero habrá tenido esos entretenimientos..." [That's men, unfortunately. While he's been single, he's probably enjoyed these diversions]. (1: 307).

15   The fact that the protagonists in the tale were from Pamplona suggests that the war mentioned in the text was the Third Carlist War (1872–1876), fought largely in the Basque region of Spain.

María Mestre, a quiet young woman from Pamplona who appears to be in mourning. Román quickly sees an opportunity for seduction. He is not deterred either by the fact that he has no romantic feelings for María or that she is grieving. For her part, while María appears to be happy to have company, someone to talk with and the safety of a male companion for evening walks, she spurns his sexual advances. Román persists with his attentions, and one evening he decides that he will have his way with her.

As he walks the streets that afternoon Román feels uneasy and agitated. "Hacía un calor bochornoso; el celaje madrileño estaba color de plomo y púrpura, como el del célebre boceto de Goya, y la tempestad amagaba con rápidas exhalaciones, que por momentos rasgaban con luz sulfúrea las nubes" [The air was muggy and hot; the Madrid sky was a leaden purple, like the one in Goya's famous sketch, and a storm threatened, with sudden gusts which, at times, tore the clouds diffusing a yellowish light] (1: 402). Pardo Bazán's Realist prose is intense and descriptive, building suspense in the reader, alluding to a fresco that, undoubtably, some would have been familiar with. A service is underway as Román enters Baltar's church, lit by hundreds of candles; the narrator poses a question—did Román arrive there by instinct or because he reasoned that an act of devotion beforehand would mitigate the sin he was about to commit? He looks towards the altar and sees the holy bread in the opened tabernacle. He is horrified to see that it is not white, but an intense blood red.[16] Here Pardo Bazán covers her options concerning miracles, as Baltar says that it may just have been a trick of the light. Román flees in confused terror but the sky outside is red too—"como una hoguera" [like a bonfire]—and, as a result, he returns to the church and remains there, kneeling and sobbing until it closes (1: 402). Baltar's listeners, and possibly the reader at this point, are envisaging a repentant Román. However, this Don Juan is not easily deterred, even by divine warnings.

Surprisingly, for Román, María is not alone when he returns home. A young man, apparently her brother, is with her and he presents Román with a letter from General Andueta, written shortly before his death, adding that he and María are the General's children but that they use their mother's surname, Mestre. The closing sentence of the letter concerning Andueta's perceived relationship with Román stops him in his tracks. The brother explains: "Escribió esta carta muy poco antes de morir, para recomendarme

---

16   Pardo Bazán used this same narrative device in her novel *Pascual López* (1879) that of having the protagonist frightened by an apparently supernatural vision (including the phrase "rojo de sangre"), followed by a rational explanation (*Pascual* 184). In "El aviso", however, the explanation is provided only as a possibility.

a usted..., porque decía que era usted su mejor amigo, su otro hijo, y que era usted muy bueno..., ¡muy bueno!" [He wrote this letter just before he died, to recommend me to you. He said that you were his best friend, his other son, and that you were a very good man, very good!] (1: 403). The male bond of loyalty and honor, Román knows, must be adhered to and, as Andueta's honor has now passed to his children, this now affects Román as his "other son". Román very soon realizes that he would be betraying María's father if he carried through with his plan to seduce his daughter that evening (and, in addition, he would now have her brother to contend with). He acts with some integrity by moving lodgings that night and formally courting María for several months before marrying her. In Baltar's opinion, he appears content with his future as a husband. However, marriage and its subsequent "domestication" can be seen as a failure for a Don Juan (Quesada Novás 143), and it appears to put an end to Román's womanizing.

Throughout this whole encounter, María, behaves meekly. She makes it as clear as she can that she is happy with a simple friendship with Román but seems powerless to resist his constant sexual advances. When her father's name is revealed, her fate is ultimately determined by the tacit understanding of honorable obligations between men and, in particular, the historical bonds of honor between fighting men (Mitchell 173). The priest-narrator has ignored this factor entirely as he extols the Catholic virtues and repentance, as he sees it, of the protagonist, Román. Baltar's listeners are sure they have ascribed the correct motive to Román's actions, referring back (in keeping with the Realist narration) to the miraculously sprouting grains of ancient Egyptian wheat, and comparing this equally unlikely event with Román's repentance. I maintain, however, that it was not repentance that leads to the "matrimonio ejemplar" [exemplary marriage] (1: 403) but rather, the social pressure on Román to maintain his bond of honor with the late General Andueta. The fortuitous chain of events, divinely inspired or otherwise, that leads to this marriage saves María from the shame of seduction and subsequent abandonment that had almost certainly been the fate of Román's previous victims.

Pardo Bazán has again given a story an enigmatic title. Here the reader expects that the vision in the church, "el aviso", to be the climax of the story. However, Pardo Bazán carries the narrative beyond this with the unexpected revelation about María's father and, as Baltar comments, "El aviso" has now become a self-warning as María is no longer available to Román as a victim. Nevertheless, the text has left unanswered questions in the reader's mind. María's brother went to the boarding house to deliver a letter to Román: was it simply coincidence that his sister was living there also, or had she told him Román was also there? If so, had she told him about Román's unwelcome behavior? The reader will never know.

Acts of God, or *deus ex machina*, were traditionally employed to create a favorable outcome for a narrative whose plot provided no way out for the author, but here Pardo Bazán uses it as a red herring, a literary device that will distract the reader from her apparent intention to reflect on the question of honor. I suggest that one reason for this is to reinforce her views about the prevailing lack of spirituality and morality of late nineteenth-century Spanish men. In her opinion, they were more concerned about the consequences of disrupting gendered societal social pressures than they were about religious values. In their patriarchal worldview, honor, not religious belief, was paramount.

In a similar manner to the previous story, "El cinco de copas", which first appeared in 1893, also turns on an apparent miracle, although the supernatural, almost sacrilegious event described here is far more dramatic. The narrative first appeared in Pardo Bazán's self-published *Nuevo Teatro Crítico*, which, in Varela Jácome's opinion, provided her with the opportunity to publish, without editorial censure, material such as this which arguably crossed moral boundaries of the time (164). The "cinco de copas" of the title refers to a fresco on the ceiling of a Franciscan chapel, a minimalist design composed of five reddish blotches representing the traditional crucifixion wounds of Christ, which at the end of the story, mysteriously drip blood on and around the protagonist Agustín—once again a serial philanderer. However, as with many other Pardo Bazán story titles, the narrative allows for a second interpretation of the fresco that Agustín creates in his mind, that of a playing card. The five of *copas* (or hearts), predicts sorrow, loss, despair and disappointment.[17] Agustín's intended victim, Rosario, a friend's fifteen-year-old daughter, has a lucky, perhaps divinely ordained escape, as the protagonist, frightened by his experience, fails as a Don Juan and forgoes the seduction.

At first the narrative appears to be in Pardo Bazán's preferred style of third-person omniscient narration. However, the final sentences reveal that the identity of the story's narrator is an unnamed person, an observer-nar-

---

17   Pardo Bazán was well aware of the art of fortune telling using playing cards, as two scenes from *Los pazos de Ulloa* illustrate. In the first, Sabel watched by Julián, tells a fortune with playing cards; the narrator interprets the meanings of specific cards, uncannily applying them to Julián's life. Later that night, Julián dreams of grotesque visions morphing into playing cards, which again, the narrator interprets (137-140, 145-49).

rator, who has become aware of the tale and some years later visits Agustín who is now a sombre friar. The narrator questions him: "Padre, ¿se acuerda del Cinco de Copas?" [Father, do you remember the Five of Hearts?] (1: 141). James Phelan defines observer narration as being voiced by a character narrator who is not a protagonist (217), while Gerald Prince refers to this style of storytelling as "narrator-witness" (66). Iria Lopez Teijeiro offers three pertinent points about this voice. The first, that it is they are re-telling the story from a limited perspective and therefore unable to see everything or to know what a character is thinking; the second, that they are considered reliable witnesses; the third that they rarely make value judgments (102). All three of these criteria appear to be applicable to "El cinco de copas".

"El Cinco de Copas" is set in Málaga.[18] The narrative is Realist; however, the protagonist, Agustín, at the start of the story, is a romantic aesthete. He is a law student who pens Romantic poetry and spends his time partying, in *devaneos* [amorous dalliances], reading and sleeping. However, he feels unsatisfied with this life and is, apparently fruitlessly, searching for something more. He is drawn to churches, where he stands "absorto ante los ricos altares, complaciéndose en los primores de la talla y las bellezas de la escultura, y sintiendo esa especial nostalgia reveladora de que el espíritu oculta aspiraciones no satisfechas y busca algo sin darse cuenta de lo que es" [captivated before the rich altars, enjoying the delicacies of the carvings and the beauty of the sculptures, and feeling that inexplicable longing of the spirit that is hiding unsatisfied aspirations and searching for something without realizing just what it is] (1: 138).

Two very different churches attract and refresh him. One is an ornate Renaissance era basilica where he becomes distracted in his search for life's meaning by a statue of Mary Magdalene "vestida sólo de un pedazo de estera y de sus ondeantes y regios cabellos" [dressed only in a woven mat and with her hair flowing and regal], and he unashamedly undresses the statue with his eyes (1: 138). In complete contrast, his other refuge is a secluded Franciscan chapel with a rough, daubed ceiling fresco representing Christ's crucifixion wounds. He views this somewhat primitive fresco, which offends

---

18   Together, the "La cruz del Humilladero", a starting point for the Camino Mozárabe, and the narrative mention of "los peregrinos" (1: 140), indicate that the setting is Málaga, while other place names appear to be fictitious. There is a further link to the city with the description of the Magdalene statue in the basilica (1: 138,) where the narrator appears to be describing the famous sculpture "Magdalena penitente ni penitente" by Pedro de Mena (1628–88), who lived much of his life in Málaga.

his sense of beauty, with "aversión atractiva" [fascinated horror] (1: 139) and derisively refers to it as "el cinco de copas". He and his friends gain a perverse gratification from mocking and deriding both the chapel and its worshippers whenever they drop by.

A short stay with family friends has unexpected repercussions for Agustín when he catches sight of Rosario, their daughter, skimpily dressed. Startled, she screams and flees in shame, but Agustín is transfixed by the sight he has just seen, "mezclando en su desenfrenada imaginación la inerte escultura de la Magdalena y la escultura viva de la doncella" [merging in his wild imagination the inert sculpture of Mary Magdalene and the living sculped body of the young girl] (1: 139). Overriding his conscience, for the next four months he pursues Rosario. In her innocence, she is unaware of exactly where Agustín's attentions are headed, or what the consequences of their fulfilment might be on her life. She arranges a tryst for a particular week, with only her elderly, deaf maid as a chaperone.

Agustín neither sleeps nor eats as he waits to meet Rosario. The day before the assignation, he decides on a walk, followed by an involuntary nap, and wakes at twilight. He realizes he is within sight of the Franciscan chapel and once again he is drawn to it. The narrative at this point takes a decidedly gothic turn. As Agustín recalls the fresco in his mind, a friar crosses his path, re-appearing as he reaches the chapel, and signals to Agustín to enter. The sight of the chapel fresco with its rough representation of the crucifixion wounds, inexplicably brings Rosario with "su inocencia, y su frescura de azucena en capullo" [her innocence, and her youthfulness, like an azucena lily in bud] back to his mind (1: 140). Simultaneously, the wounds of the fresco begin to moisten and open, first throbbing and then disgorging drops of blood, like rubies, around Agustín. A final, dense drop lands on his forehead. The Catholic symbolism here is striking with the forehead being the traditional site of anointing with oil, water or ashes, depending on the circumstances.

Pardo Bazán's use of *deus ex machina* at this point in the story is powerful and brings the narrative itself to an abrupt, unresolved conclusion. Rosario is not mentioned again, and the reader must presume that the longed-for seduction of the innocent victim is never consummated. However, I suggest that Agustín's frenzy during the five-day wait for his seduction of Rosario offers a subtle undermining of the seeming miracle, in that Pardo Bazán has tacitly offered her readers the possibility that after five days without sleep or food, Agustín may be hallucinating.[19] The observer-narration may provide,

---

19   Pardo Bazán had a well-documented lifelong interest in both the sciences and human behaviour (see Faus chapter XXXI), and her description of Agustín's be-

as in this case, a temporal ellipsis in the narrative which enables readers to formulate a logical ending to the tale for themselves (Phelan 198). The narrator is not omniscient, as the facts of the story and the knowledge that each character possesses, have been related by Agustín. Considering the fantasies that blend his erotic thoughts about the Magdalen statue with a titillating glimpse of a partially robed Rosario, his four-month pursuit of the naïve girl appears to be almost obsessive, a typical Don Juan trait, with the challenge being as compelling as the seduction itself.

Three facts of this planned seduction place Agustín, a man enamored of romanticism and its concepts of honor, squarely in a dishonorable light. Firstly, the fact that he is fully aware of the carnal ignorance of his intended victim—"[n]o tanto se requería para vencer a la criatura inexperta, que ignoraba toda la extensión del mal" [it would not take much to seduce the naïve teenaged girl, who was quite oblivious of the misfortune that was about to eventuate] (1: 139); secondly, the fact that he knows that he will relish taking full advantage of her inexperience. Third is his callous betrayal of his friends, the young woman's parents, who are seemingly unaware of his true background or of his immediate intentions.[20] In "El cinco de copas" Pardo Bazán has created a portrait of a particularly distasteful self-absorbed young man. Although he has an inkling that there may be more to life than his hedonistic lifestyle provides, his lust for sculpted wooden church saints and beautiful but naïve adolescents dominates his thoughts and actions.

However, the two-sentence postscript following the body of the narrative informs the reader of Agustín's subsequent fate. Long ago, explains the narrator, he "took the cloth", renouncing his romantic poetry and music, his seductions, his joviality and his love of cards, a trait that has significance in the interpretation of the title. He is now Father Agustín, who has risen to the position of gatekeeper at the priory. Ironically, as gatekeeper, he is the person responsible for ensuring that the Franciscan community remains untainted by the outside world. There is also further irony in the contrast between Agustín's formerly selfish life as a self-styled romantic and the harsh everyday realities of his later life as a friar.

---

haviour certainly correlates with recent research reported in *Frontiers in Psychiatry*, "Severe Sleep Deprivation Causes Hallucinations and a Gradual Progression Toward Psychosis with Increasing Time Awake" by Flavie Waters, et al. Blom (https://www.ncbi.nlm.nih.gov/pmc/articles/PMC6048360/).

20   This scenario has similarities with Pardo Bazán's "Sor Aparición", in which Camargo outwits both his victim Irene and her parents (1: 295-98).

The sorrow, loss, despair and disappointment predicted by the *cinco de copas* playing card may have materialized for Agustín in the chapel that evening some years before as he decided to abandon his tryst with Rosario, but the reader is left wondering if perhaps some of these attributes have remained with the somber friar in the gatehouse. In "El cinco de copas" Pardo Bazán has crafted a compelling story with the events building towards the final dramatic scene in the chapel, before presenting the reader with the unexpected epilogue and the realization that Agustín, one of her most reprehensible literary Don Juans has, presumably, repented.

"El aviso" and "El cinco de copas" are linked chiefly by the use of the device of *deus ex machina* to control the Don Juan plot at the end; however, they show other similarities. The two framed stories both follow the familiar pattern of the focus being apparently on the Don Juan while the intended victim is foregrounded, but silent and largely passive. Additionally, the history of inveterate womanizing by the protagonist is stressed in both the narratives. There are two other obvious links that are particular to these two stories. The first is that the young women who escape the fate of Don Juan's victims are particularly vulnerable: María, through her lack of any immediate support from family or friends, and Rosario through childlike ignorance. In "El aviso" the supposed miracle permits acceptability concerning the failure of the Don Juan to realize his intentions. It is only because of the "miraculous" events recounted in the respective narratives that the young women are apparently both saved from the social ignominy befalling most of the women who encounter a Don Juan. However, a less obvious and more subversive reading of "El aviso" reveals that near the start of the tale there are underlying references to the obligation of male honor, perhaps the true reason that finally led to the protagonist's abandonment of his quest for a conquest (1: 401).

"Dalinda" and "El pajarraco": The tables are turned

"Dalinda" and "El pajarraco", the final pairing of stories discussed in this chapter feature Don Juans whose years of seducing women are brought to an end when they, rather than their victims, are publicly disgraced. The first is badly injured as he attempts a seduction, while the second is outwitted and shamed by his intended victim. They are both Realist narratives, a style that contrasts with the worldview of the Don Juan protagonists themselves who, like Agustín in the previous story, are driven by their romantic self-delusions and fantasies regarding their own importance. Reality hits both Don Juans hard.

In the Galician tale "Dalinda", the Don Juan's attempt at seduction ends in misfortune resulting from the potential victim's actions. Mariano, the male protagonist is badly injured as he falls from a balcony and it is Dalinda, his intended quarry, who sends him tumbling to the ground. The story was first published in *El Imparcial* and later in Pardo Bazán's Galician collection *Cuentos del terruño* (1907). Darío Villanueva and José Manuel González Herrán assert that the stories in this latter volume were inspired by the earlier works of Ramon Valle-Inclán, a fellow Galician author, and that the prototype for "Dalinda" was based on Valle-Inclán's image of "la delicada doncella campesina, "rosa mystica" que parece extraída de leyendas medievales" [the fragile country maiden, "the mystic rose" who was typified in medieval legends] (10: xvi). They also note that, following Valle-Inclán, Pardo Bazán also uses direct speech in these stories, where any use of regional dialect is finely balanced with the need for the text to be comprehensible to readers in the rest of Spain (10: xvi). Faus supports Villanueva and González Herrán's opinion regarding Pardo Bazán's inspiration for her Galician tales, mentioning specifically Valle-Inclán's "Sonata de otoño", with its naturalistic leanings, and its "magia del pasado y sentimiento rural" [magic of the past and its rural sentimentality] (275, 376).

"Dalinda" does not have a convoluted plot; rather, it follows a straightforward and uncomplicated linear narrative timeline. The reader is carried from one relatively mundane, everyday scene to another, except for an ellipsis surrounding the final, surprising event. A linear story, by definition, is without the temporal variations and the complexity of voices and often opposing worldviews, which are the features of framed narratives in general, and which have the effect of drawing the reader into the story. This style of narrative uses different literary techniques to catch the reader's imagination, one of which, thick description, can be identified here. This writing "goes beyond surface appearances to include the context, detail, emotion and webs of social relationships. It presents the significance of an observation, event or behavior and includes voices, feelings, actions and meanings" (Ponterotto). All are characteristics which can be identified in the first half of "Dalinda".

Set in the fictitious Galician town of Cebre,[21] the narrative, is related by a third-person omniscient narrator, interspersed with direct speech and, while a straightforward reading of the text offers a typical Pardo Bazán Don

---

21 This setting is also used in "La capitana", which has internal references to both Galicia itself and to Montañosa (Santiago de Compostela), the fictional town of "Cenizas". Cebre may have been more familiar to Pardo Bazán's readers as the town adjacent to the manor in *Los pazos de Ulloa*.

Juan tale, further study discloses various sub-texts. Perhaps the most important is Pardo Bazán's use of Mariano's own words and attitudes to expose his character as selfish, callous and shallow, thereby subverting, once again, the Don Juan figure. An urban-rural subplot also emerges as numerous textual comparisons are made between Mariano, a sophisticated *madrileño*, and his Galician hosts, whose manners and lifestyle he treats at times with disdain. And once again, the Spanish code of honor and loyalty amongst men is instrumental in Don Juan's potential victim's fate.

The text introduces a traditional Don Juan trope not encountered in other stories so far—the friends who are aware of and, to some extent complicit, in Don Juan's seduction plans. Other tropes, featured in previous stories, also feature in the text. In addition, this is the only Don Juan tale where the female protagonist's own voice is heard directly. The opening setting is an inn, where a sumptuous lunch is being served. The text rapidly establishes the status of three diners and their relationships: Camilo Ramidor, the local *mayorazgo*, his brother Juanito and Mariano, a friend from their student days, who has arrived from Madrid for the hunting season. An urban-rural dichotomy permeates the text, beginning with the contrast in appearances of the men. Mariano is smartly dressed, with new, clean leather leggings, while his hosts are still in their normal, begrimed, working clothes. A sack of partridges, destined for the inn's kitchen, contrasts apparently differing views of hunting itself. Rural men, such as the Ramidors hunt to provide food, while for men like Mariano, it is seen as a wealthy man's sport, where appearances matter.

Their waitress is attractive: "una niña casi, vestida de luto pobre, dividido en dos trenzas el hermoso pelo rubio; finita de facciones y con boca de capullo de rosa, menuda y turgente, hinchada de vida" [scarcely past childhood, in simple mourning dress with two simple plaits holding her pretty blonde hair. Her facial features were fine and her rosebud, mouth, tiny yet full, appeared full of life] (2: 328). As Juanito reaches out and catches her by the waist, she blushes and recoils. Mariano leaps to her defense, chiding his friend for his impulsive reaction and, somewhat pretentiously, proceeds to defend her: "¡Es una criatura! Déjala en paz. ¿Cómo te llamas, hija mía? Contesta, que yo he de tratarte con el mayor respeto" [She's just a child! Leave her in peace! What's your name, miss? I will treat your answer with the greatest respect] (2: 328). The reader may detect a second urban-rural divide here: as the story progresses Mariano's duplicity in uttering the last remark will be exposed. The girl, on the verge of tears, outlines her situation to Mariano: "Dalinda me llamo, señor, [e]ntré ayer, señor; porque soy huérfana de padre y madre, y ahora se me murió mi tío, el señor cura de Doas, que si viviera él, no sirviera yo más que a Dios" [My name is Dalinda sir, and I started yesterday. I am an orphan, my father, mother, and now my uncle, the priest of Doas, have all died. When I lived with my uncle, I was planning to serve God and enter the convent], a reply which should have been sufficient to elicit both sympathy and consideration from Mariano (2: 328). Nonetheless, at this point Mariano begins his pursuit of the young woman, offering her a generous tip, which she refuses. The brothers, having obviously previously witnessed their friend's ways with attractive young women, jokingly confront Mariano, telling him he is a hypocrite, as they know that Dalinda's protection and well-being are not uppermost in his mind. This comment acts as a pointer to the reader of the likely direction of the narrative.

The brothers, as hosts, now face a dilemma. They are respectful of their guest but realize the implications of his intentions. By jesting in this manner, they temper their growing unease. Mariano, unable to accept even the mildest rebuke, offends his companions by retorting: "Encontráis una muchacha, y con tal que podáis estrujarla y ella no chille, tan contentos. Que ella sea así o de otro modo, no os importa. Os basta un cacho de carne con ojos" [You two, you find a girl, and as long as you can squeeze her and she doesn't squeal, you are happy. Whether she is this girl or that girl, it doesn't matter to you. You treat her like a piece of meat with eyes as long as you get what you want] (2: 329). As the conversation continues, Mariano reveals the true baseness of his thoughts. Becoming consumed by passion, he appears to be unable to comprehend Dalinda's emotional pain following her uncle's death and he also ignores the fact that Dalinda is little more than a child. Unfortunately for her, it is the thought of being the destroyer of her innocence that now animates and drives Mariano: "[M]e parece una figura de retablo ... ¡La sobrina de un cura! Una azucena mística, intacta" [In my eyes she is like an altarpiece statue. ... A priest's niece! An Easter lily, mystical and virginal] (2: 329). A priest's niece is, apparently, near enough to the traditional donjuanesque seduction of a nun to excite Mariano, and he pleads with his friends to help him seduce the young woman. Yet another Don Juan trope can be observed here: the Ramidors' ready acquiescence to Mariano's request creates a pact between the men which, from that moment, the brothers are honor-bound to keep. The reader will realize the implications of this pact and, with the outcome of the story seeming obvious, will either agree with the solidarity of the three men or will lose any sympathy that they may have had for the brothers' dilemma of being caught between politeness to their guest and compassion for Dalinda.

Mariano's mind is now set, and as he departs, he gives Dalinda a pendant "un capricho de oro y turquesas [que] se lo había regalado a Mariano, una novia, una señorita con la cual estuvo a pique de casarse" [a dainty gold and turquoise piece [that] had given been given to Mariano by a young lady with whom he was on the verge of marrying] (2: 329). Mariano appears to travel, and even hunt, well-prepared for any possible seduction attempt. Dalinda, for her part, unaware of the provenance of the pendant, is childlike as she accepts it: "[C]on movimiento infantil, casto y apasionado, besó la joyuela al recibirla" [unaffectedly and passionately kissing the gift as she received it] (2: 329). And, as they promised, the brothers help Mariano in his quest by hunting near Cebre to facilitate his meetings with Dalinda. Now, Camilo and Juanito find themselves torn between their friendship with Mariano and their discomfort with his behavior towards Dalinda, while they laugh and mock him behind his back for his apparent failure to immediately seduce his targeted woman.

The use throughout the text of the word *forastero*, outsider or stranger, to describe Mariano, emphasizes his "otherness" in rural Galician society. If his actions cause distress, he can just depart, leaving Camilo and Juanito to weather any consequences. However, Dalinda's steadfast refusal of Mariano's affections frustrates the would-be seducer. She appears to him both mystical and "más... más... más difícil" [very, very, very difficult] (2: 330). She presents an unaccustomed challenge and, driven by both his desire and his friends' scornful attitudes, he attempts to force an outcome. He informs the brothers that to prove his success, they will see him at the window of Dalinda's room at midnight. A temporal ellipsis in the text forces the reader to imagine the seduction scene, as it is not recorded. Mariano apparently reaches the unprotected upper balcony, echoing the "leyendas medievales" [medieval legends], in which a knight climbs a tower to rescue a princess. Here, however, Pardo Bazán has provided an anti-Romantic travesty: Dalinda at this point is in need of protection, not salvation. She sees only a man outside her window and in self-defense, pushes him away.

The text picks up the story as Camilo and Juanito arrive and see Mariano unconscious on the ground, badly injured. Dalinda rushes downstairs, sobbing, arriving at Mariano's side a few seconds later. The men, shocked to see their friend lying motionless, turn on Dalinda: "Pero ¿cómo ha sido?" preguntó Camilo a Dalinda. "¡Yo misma le tiré por el balcón abajo!" respondió ella, sollozante. "¿Sabes lo que hiciste?" gritaron, amenazadores, los dos hidalgos" ["What have you just done?" Camilo asked Dalinda. Sobbing, she responded "I pushed him off my balcony!" "Do you know what you did?" the brothers shouted threateningly] (2: 330). Dalinda defends herself staunchly: "¡Hice bien!" exclamó la niña, enderezándose y relampagueando indignación" ["I did what I had to do!" the girl indignantly replied as she straightened up] (2: 330).

Dalinda nurses Mariano back to health, although he is permanently lamed. He offers her a reward but she asks only for a dowry so she can enter the convent. Here, Pardo Bazán makes an important point. If Dalinda had capitulated to Mariano's requests, she would have destroyed both her honor and any hopes that she held for her future as a respectable member of society. But paradoxically, protecting her honor and standing up for herself has also destroyed any possibility of a future quiet, peaceful life in Cebre. The pact that Camilo, the *mayorazgo*, and Juanito made with Mariano ensures that their loyalty ultimately stays with him. Dalinda, in their eyes, has behaved badly, and her safety is now immaterial to them. The moment Mariano set eyes on Dalinda, the *azucena*, her fate was sealed. If she acceded to his demands or if she resisted, either way, her life would be irreconcilably changed. Still, by instinctively pushing Mariano to the ground, Dalinda has secured her future. She had earlier expressed her wish to serve God, but her uncle's death left her without shelter or support. Mariano's offer of recompense for nursing him secures the dowry money for the convent life she had wished for.

This storyline concludes with yet another Don Juan failing to realize a seduction. The ubiquitous Spanish honor system is shown to create male loyalty pacts that can transcend social and regional status and can blur principled judgments. With the incorporation of numerous Don Juan tropes into this relatively short narrative [22] Pardo Bazán is presenting an almost parodic interpretation of the figure and, by so doing, successfully creates an anti-Romantic sub-text. Pardo Bazán's text on one level reinforces a typical narrative of Don Juan's ingenuity; but, at a deeper level, the character is portrayed as egoistic, insensitive and callous. The final irony of

---

22 The most obvious tropes mentioned are smooth talk and flattery, while publicly disparaging Juanito's attempts at seduction; considering the niece of a priest a particular and stimulating challenge; seeking an elusive ideal (and virginal) woman; likening Dalinda to a Madonna statue and a Madonna lily; courting Dalinda with a desirable gift; and seeking the help of supportive friends. The balancing of the libertine lifestyle with retribution mentioned earlier (E. H. Friedman 61) can be argued as tropes also. There is no repentance mentioned in the text, however Mariano, in retrospect, surely regretted his attempt at this particular seduction.

the tale is that his destructive lifestyle has been curbed by the actions of an honorable woman and he himself has been damaged physically.

Following "Dalinda", the Don Juan in "El pajarraco" also ends his womanizing days unexpectedly and (in his eyes) humiliated, with the tale being published, seemingly ironically, in Pardo Bazán's *Cuentos trágicos* (1912). The narrative is longer and more loosely constructed than the others discussed in this chapter and, as with the majority of Pardo Bazán's works, its narrator is omniscient. The story opens as the narrator philosophically reflects on the mysterious nature of a Don Juan's charm: "Así como es misteriosa la vena en el juego, lo es la vena en amor. Los seductores no reúnen infaliblemente dotes que expliquen su buena sombra. Siempre que dice la voz pública: "Ese tiene con las mujeres partido loco", nos preguntamos: ¿Por qué? Y a menudo no damos con la respuesta" [Just as the plot of a play is mysterious, so is the path of love. Seducers always have a way with women that explains their conquests. Whenever public opinion says: That rake manages to drive every woman crazy, and we ask ourselves: Why? And often we don't have an answer] (3: 166). The second paragraph, in the same vein, finally arrives at the point that even in small towns there are men "que en opinión general ejercen la fascinación, y padres y maridos los miran de reojo" [who, it is generally agreed, captivate women, and fathers and husbands who look at these men askance] (3: 166).

As the protagonist Laurencio Deza is introduced as the "twenty-something" pajarraco of this story, the reader is made aware of his sense of self-importance and his rejection of morality: "Jamás discutía principios de moral. Procedía como si no existiesen" [Never discuss moral principles. Proceed as if they do not exist] (3: 166). He struts the streets hoping to glimpse a girl watching him through a window, thinking to himself "¿Soy costal de paja, niña?" [Hey girl, I'm worth looking at, aren't I?] (3: 166), as the narrator expounds on his smooth-talk, elegance and wit.

Norman Friedman explains that omniscient narrators may editorialize and condense, thus enabling brevity of textual episodes, and they have opportunities to analyze motives and the states of mind of the characters ("Short" 116-7). All of these points are exemplified in "El pajarraco" as the true focus of the story emerges—the friendship between three prominent families of the town and Deza's lofty ambition to seduce a woman from each of these families. He has already succeeded with two of these women, Cecilita Mardura, the daughter of the haberdasher and Obdulia Encina, the wife of the bookseller, in whose shop the three families socialize together each day. He intends his next victim to be Rosa la Gallinera, the wife of Ulpiano Paredes, an owner of a poultry farm where chickens are raised to a marketable size, slain, and then sold dressed for the table. Deza's activities with Obdulia and Cecilita have already been whispered about and laughed at; in this town, *el qué dirán*, Spanish society's communal moralistic watchdog, constantly observes and comments on Deza's every move. However, for these two women, such gossip appears to be the only consequence of their actions.

The text condenses years of Deza's brazen activities as it prepares the reader for the details of his next seduction. The question of whether he can be successful in seducing the third woman of the group is on every busybody's mind—and lips—and the answer is soon apparent. One day, Rosa is seen wearing fashionable and seemingly expensive dresses and jewelry and, later, when her husband is away, she appears in a feathered hat "no de gallina, sino de legítimo avestruz" [not chicken feathers, but real ostrich ones], setting the whole town alight with gossip (3: 167). The narration moves into reported speech as Cecilita and Obdulia confront Paredes, who, preoccupied with his own dreams and plans is apparently unaware of the situation, and the gossip becomes more heated. Rosa and her husband seem oblivious to the fact that she is becoming the center of the town's attention.

Deza's downfall is, in fact, inevitable from this point and any apparent delight Rosa may take in being in Deza's company and accepting his gifts is merely a cover for a larger plan. An elaborate revenge for Cecilita and Obdulia's seductions is being plotted by the three couples in question to avoid the same fate for Rosa. Their plan involves a sustained role play with Rosa accepting Deza's gifts, Cecilita and Obdulia openly criticizing her, and her husband's supposed absence explained away as being "especulaciones en gran escala, negocios bancarios. Hablábase de emisión de acciones, de capitales dedicados a una fabricación vasta, de papel y serrería" [banking business and large-scale financial speculation. There was talk of raising capital and issuing shares in extensive manufacturing ventures involving sawmills and paper] (3: 167). Rosa will also have to endure the harsh and critical gossip about her actions, particularly when Paredes is rumored to be on a business trip, leaving her apparently alone in the house and Deza is believed to be visiting her each night: "Es bruto cuando no ve lo de su mujer...", iba a contestar el murmurador de Casino; pero, advertido por un guiño expresivo de alguien, se limitó a decir, con diplomática reserva. ... La gente sufre a veces por prudencia..., hasta que un día u otro ... ["It's stupid when he doesn't see what's going on with his wife" opined a gossiper from Casino. Encina was going to answer; but, warned by an expressive wink, he curbed his tongue with diplomatic reserve. ... "People sometimes put up with things out of prudence—until the day comes ..."] (3: 168).

An observant reader will, however, notice subtle textual indications that perhaps this turn of events is not as it seems. The textual wink indicates that somebody knows more than is apparent, with Encina's cryptic comment hinting at a future threat for somebody.

The narrative appears rather slow-paced and meandering as, by this stage, the reader is more than halfway through the story. In "Dialogues", Susan Lohafer contends, however, that delaying a resolution by the insertion of non-narrative material creates variations in pace that are an especially useful technique for creating not only dynamic effects but also clues to meaning (Winther 244). Peter F. Neumeyer also refers to non-narrative text with seemingly endless "scene-setting in which 'nothing happens" as a deliberate authorial device, which, he notes, was lampooned by Mark Twain as "weather" (10). In "El pajarraco", it builds the reader's expectations for a resolution. Further narratorial comments (including, literally, a description of the weather) indicate that a particularly hard winter has descended, and wrap-around capes have suddenly become both fashionable and necessary, as well as being a "disfraz protector de secretas aventuras" [a disguise for secretive adventures], adding to the reader's knowledge of the complex setting (3: 168).

The freezing winter contributes to Deza's downfall. As he makes his way to Rosa's house after nightfall, he attempts to avoid detection by winding his way through back streets. Disconcertingly, three other people seem to dog his path, and dark, amorphous shapes appear and promptly disappear in front of him, unsettling (and outwitting) him. For the reader, this creates suspense and foreshadows future events. Deza is a Don Juan so fixated on his chase that normal reasoning and caution desert him. At Rosa's window he pleads with her, night after night, to open her outside door. The reader's interest is well awakened, and they are about to be rewarded with one of Pardo Bazán's most memorable endings to a story.

A trap is carefully prepared for the *pajarraco* and he walks willingly into it on the night that Rosa finally invites him into the barn. As he goes towards her, he notes, in passing, the piles of feathers from the plucked poultry and then he reaches out to embrace his victim. However, before he truly has hold of her, Paredes strikes him violently in the face. Rosa seems unsurprised and is ordered home by her husband, before Paredes and his two friends, Encina and Mardura, disrobe Deza and beat him savagely. In a complete contrast with the slow-paced, descriptive opening pages of the story, Pardo Bazán now picks up the narrative tempo. The verbs are active, and the phrases are short, giving a sense of urgency to the proceedings: "Con una brocha enorme, pintaron a grandes brochazos el cuerpo inerte, untándolo de miel mezclada con pez. Y hecho esto, tomaron al fascinador, uno por los pies y dos por los sobacos, y llevándole bajo el cobertizo, le revolcaron en la pluma, hasta que lo emplumaron todo, de alto abajo" [With a large brush, they painted the inert body in broad strokes, smearing it with a mixture of honey mixed with fish. And when this was completed, they carried the philanderer under the shed where they rolled him around in chicken feathers until he was coated from head to toe] (3: 169). Then the men push him into the street where he is jeered at as he heads home. In a fitting twist to one of Pardo Bazán's Don Juan tales, it is disclosed that it was Rosa who suggested both Deza's ambush and his final public mockery and humiliation. Pardo Bazán uses the impersonal and anonymous "se dijese" [it was said] (3: 170) to describe the circulation of her name. Both Rosa and her husband appear to have used the public gossip chain to their advantage, and likely minimized any further damage to Rosa's reputation. Rosa's responsibility for Deza's downfall with her apparently willing response to Deza, followed by her suggestion of his humiliation in the barn, is in many respects a daring action from a married woman, whatever her social class.

Throughout the text, the narrator makes subtle (and not-so-subtle) reference to Paredes's social standing; that he was a chicken farmer, a lower-class occupation, rather than a shopkeeper like his middle-class friends. When the rumors about Paredes extending his successful business interests to include papermills and sawmills (which may or may not have been true), the criticism was a "voz unánime de la envidia" [unanimous voice of envy] (3: 167). The chicken farmer "jamás llegaría a señor, ni perdería su facha ordinaria y tosca, sus manazas peludas, sus orejas coloradas y su faz ruda, en que los dientes sin limpiar, verdosos, infundían repugnancia" [would never become a lord, nor would he lose his common, coarse appearance, with big hairy hands, red ears and a rough face, in which uncleaned, greenish teeth inspired disgust] (3: 167). However, it is Paredes who takes Rosa's idea and manages the complex and lengthy scheme through to its successful conclusion. Pardo Bazán thus juxtaposes the popular idea that social class and good looks define ability with the fact that it is the unkempt Paredes, with his natural ability, rather than his middle-class companions, who has triumphed in a battle of wits with this particular Don Juan.

In "El pajarraco" Rosa's intentions display a daring gender role reversal. The Don Juan takes delight in shamelessly seducing and humiliating a large number of women, with his actions being generally accepted by the patriarchal society. However, it is shameful if the man is assaulted and humiliated, even indirectly, by a woman. As we saw earlier, a woman's honor resided in her passivity, in her chaste being and existing, while making and doing (and here we can substitute assaulting and humiliating) were masculine prerogatives (Mandrell *Honor* 279-80) In this story, Rosa, who makes the audacious suggestion that a man be stripped naked as part of his punishment, has the protection of her husband.[23]

As already seen, Pardo Bazán often used ambiguous titles for her stories. Sometimes they provided clues as to her motives in penning these tales but, other times, as in "El pajarraco", the title provided a double meaning for the names of the characters themselves. In this context the title draws the reader to the meaning of "womanizer" or "rogue", but it is also a word for a big, ugly bird. And, as Deza runs through the frozen streets after his treatment at the men's hands, he hears laughter from people on a balcony and the words "¡Vaya un pajarraco! ¡Buena gallina para el puchero! ... ¡Hu, hu, el pajarraco!" [There goes the serial womanizer! What a lovely hen for the pot!] (3: 170). With the "hu hu" sounding very like a cuckoo's call, it adds the additional implication of a bird that surreptitiously takes over another's nest. And a wordplay on "gallina" also being a coward. Deza has been tricked by the chicken farmer, "dressed for the table" and humiliated by the townsfolk. The predator has become the victim and, with this event, Pardo Bazán has truly cut this Don Juan figure down to size. After a month of recovery, Deza cannot leave the town fast enough and never manages to shake off the ignominy of the episode, being known as "el pajarraco" wherever he goes. Pardo Bazán can never resist a literary reference either, as the narrator ironically likens Deza to Byron (who created his own poetic and Romantic Don Juan) living with melancholy and misfortune. The final revelation of this rather rambling, but ultimately satisfying tale, reveals that Deza considered a permanent escape, perhaps to America, or

---

23 Pardo Bazán, however was not the first nineteenth-century Spanish writer to use the trope of familial retribution for a Don Juan's pursual of a victim in a short story. Some four decades previously Pérez Galdós published "El don Juan" (29 Mar. 1868, *La Nación*, pp. 2-3), in which a Don Juan, with an attitude and self-confidence not unlike Deza's pursues his self-styled "*victima* number 1,003". Despite being knocked unconscious by her husband with massive religious tomes and deposited in a nearby trash bin, this Don Juan persists with his chase. The *victima* herself arranges their next meeting, but in his fervor, he fails to notice that the woman escorting him to the house is not his "intended" but a wizened, blind, ninety-year-old. He is then set upon by the entire family, led by the *victima* and her husband and again left unconscious. His ultimate fate, he reveals, is that he is incarcerated in an asylum.

even suicide. However, "halló otro refugio, otro género de muerte. ... Se casó..." [he found another refuge, another version of death—he married!] (3: 170). Perhaps ironically equating marriage with death was in Pardo Bazán's mind when she published this humorous story in *Cuentos trágicos*? In both "Dalinda" and "El pajarraco" Pardo Bazán has created strong and apparently principled female protagonists whose actions have ended the "careers" of two typical Don Juanesque figures.

Conclusion

As we have seen, the six stories analyzed in this chapter all illustrate that these so-called romancers, often abetted by their friends, are as much a peril to Pardo Bazán's single women as the fickle and jealous fiancés of the previous chapters. When Pardo Bazán's Don Juan narratives are considered as a group, despite being highly individual in many ways, they are all quite formulaic. One female protagonist, the potential victim, is individualized and the reader is made aware of a multitude of previous victims of the Don Juan. However, these tales were written over a period of twenty years between 1892 ("Remordimiento") and 1912 ("El pajarraco"). They were published in a variety of newspapers and magazines, so this pattern would not necessarily be noticed by the average reader of the time. It is their juxtaposition in this book that brings to the fore Pardo Bazán's consistent message. Each story conveys a picture of a distasteful, selfish male protagonist whose history of seduction is recounted, set against a prominent (but largely silent) female protagonist, Don Juan's intended victim of the story in question.

In each of the six narratives that I have discussed Pardo Bazán has been able to subvert an apparently male-centered story to create a feminist subtext which alludes, either directly or indirectly, to the mostly calamitous effects that seduction has on the subsequent lives of the various victims. These stories also present another, somewhat unexpected, common feature—that of the foiled Don Juan who for one reason or another, fails to achieve his planned seduction. The fates of the intended victims are diverse: a nun falls to her death ("Cenizas") and a niece of the Don Juan dies of a broken heart ("Remordimiento"); a young woman is saved from seduction by the social force of the Spanish honor code ("El aviso"), while another is kept safe when the Don Juan fails to appear at the arranged time ("El cinco de copas"); the lack of male protection means that successfully challenging a Don Juan restricts one young woman's future as much as a seduction would ("Dalinda"), while the protection of a man means that the final potential victim survives the encounter with Don Juan with her reputation more or less intact ("El pajarraco").

Parallels exist between the two innocents Rosario and Dalinda, who are both viewed as statues and as objects, when a similar metaphor, the Madonna lily, *la azucena*, crosses both Agustín and Mariano's minds. However, their fates are different. The grieving María in "El aviso" and Dalinda can also be compared, as they are both likely to find meaning and fulfilment in their lives, despite their fates being determined by the actions of a Don Juan. The proposed seduction of Dalinda, a priest's niece, is reminiscent of the traditional Donjuanesque challenge of the seduction of a nun, which Morán, the protagonist of "Cenizas", also attempts—with the nun, somewhat surprisingly, appearing eager for the assignation and ultimately dying for it.

Analyses of the individual stories also reveal, in many cases, a more subtle, textual level of criticism of the figure of Don Juan himself. These range from the portrayal of the figure in the first pair of stories as a pathetic, irrelevant old man, glorified for his past conquests while social and religious forces bring the next two Don Juans back to reality. In the final two stories discussed in this chapter, the female protagonists out-maneuver the Don Juans, by causing them physical or emotional harm, thereby avoiding the planned seductions. The final story, "El pajarraco", portrays a further public humiliation of a Don Juan. It is perhaps unsurprising that Pardo Bazán's obvious distaste for the figure, and all that he represented in terms of women's lives being irrevocably altered by his actions, never wavered in her various portrayals of the image over the two decades that these stories cover.

Six literary portrayals of Don Juans have been examined, each subscribing to Deza's ethos of acting as if moral principles did not exist: it is precisely this lack of morality that Pardo Bazán challenged in her stories. And, more importantly for this work, by publishing in the popular press, she provided an opportunity for a wide range of readers to be confronted with the extent of the misery, shame and suffering the Don Juans inflicted, not only on her fictional protagonists, but on countless real-life late nineteenth-century Spanish women.

The final analytical chapter of this work moves from a thematic to a regional focus—the Spanish province of Galicia, where Pardo Bazán spent much of her early life. As we discussed in Chapter 1, she set over a hundred of her short stories in Galicia and stories in Chapter 5 will feature distinctive figures, folklore and lifestyles of the area. Two of the tales concern nineteenth-century female legendary figures, a saint and a bandit, two women are millers, one is a delivery woman and another an agricultural worker. The stories are grouped in trios, with the first three stories portraying hardworking, respectable women. However, Pardo Bazán's emphasis on portraying verisimilitude is evident in the second trio of stories, where the realities of a darker and more violent side of Galician rural life are exposed.

5
Galician Tales

> No, I've never been to Galicia,
> Galicia is the land of Others.
>
> -José de Sousa Saramago
> *The Stone Raft*

IN PARDO BAZÁN'S TIME Galicia was a province of singular cultural and demographic hardship, a "región afligida por un tremendo atraso económico y desangrada por la emigración, con una burguesía minúscula, una nobleza absentista, un analfabetismo galopante y un caciquismo endémico" [a región suffering from economic underdevelopment and bled dry from emigration. There are few middle-class citizens, even fewer nobility, widespread illiteracy and overarching feudalistic land tenures] (Pereiro Muro 71). Pardo Bazán incorporated the realities of these shortcomings into her storylines, effectively providing the reader with what amounts to a social history of *fin de siècle* Galician life, emphasizing the unconventional roles that often fell to the women of the region. As Hills writes: "No se idealiza el campo mismo; de hecho, se alaba la superioridad de la mujer en presencia de condiciones miserables" [{Pardo Bazán} does not idealize the countryside itself, but she does underline the superiority of the women who face its miserable conditions] (178).

The majority of Pardo Bazán's Galician short stories were first published in newspapers or journals, and subsequently re-published in one of four Pardo Bazán collections dedicated to the region: *Cuentos de Marineda* (1892), *Historias y cuentos de Galicia* (1900), *Cuentos del terruño* and *Cuentos de la tierra* (both 1922). Paredes Núñez's assessment of these Galician narratives is positive. He considers that they illustrate the beauty of the countryside, the diversity of the people, their customs and their beliefs. However, he continues, while some critics such as García Sabell and González López are of the opinion that Pardo Bazán's Galician works exhibit true literary greatness, unnamed "others" differed on the grounds that she used "el castellano, en lugar de la lengua vernácula, como vehículo de sus obras" [Castellano rather than the vernacular to convey her ideas](*Realidad* 8-9), a matter that was discussed in Chapter 1.[1]

Despite the polemics surrounding Pardo Bazán's linguistic choice and her subject matter, she was particularly knowledgeable about the traditions and folklore of the province and took an active part in Galicia's cultural sphere. This led to the founding of the *Sociedad del Folklore Gallega* in 1884, with Pardo Bazán installed as the inaugural president and holding meetings in her own home. The Society published a substantial collection of Galician traditions before its disestablishment in 1895. Somewhat cynically, Pattison notes that it "soon became moribund, probably because of personal resentments towards her" (50). However, it could be argued that eleven years was a reasonable length of time for the Society to accomplish many of its objectives, primarily the systematic recording of Galician folklore and traditions.

Pardo Bazán viewed Galicians as "una raza", a people standing apart from the rest of Spain (López Quintáns 48). She repeatedly raises the question of race in both her fiction and non-fiction works and, as we have noted, is ready to ascribe any regional differences in the various provinces of Spain to their ethnic provenance.[2] In "The Women of Spain" (1889), whose intended readership was originally one outside Spain itself, Pardo Bazán ranges through characteristics of Spanish women in different Spanish regions but surprisingly she says little about Galicia beyond the abject poverty of the agricultural workers, and their "susceptibility to the tender passion" leading to an inevitably large number children being born out of wedlock (904).[3] In her 1884 *costumbrista* essay, "La gallega", Pardo Bazán, returning to the subject of racial origins, expounds at length on the women of Galicia, setting them apart ethnically from the rest of Spain. They are, she says, descended from Celts, Greeks, Phoenicians, Romans and Germanics, with the "noble" Celtic race, originating in Britain and Ireland, now predominating. Several of Pardo Bazán's Galician stories incorporate references to Celtic traits in the

---

1   Paredes Núñez uses "otros" without further clarification (9).

2   This has already been noted in "Apólogo" and alluded to in "El mascarón", where Andalusian (and, by inference, Arabic) ancestry is considered to be the source of a jealous or a violent nature.

3   Three stories discussed later in this chapter, "El molino", "La hoz" and "Un destripador de antaño", describe various relationships between young unmarried people attending social events at their local mill.

protagonists or the settings; examples are Minia, the victim in "Un destripador", who is described as *roxa*, or redheaded, a perceived Celtic feature (2: 6), and place names such as Karnar, where karn is a word "de puro origen céltico" [of pure Celtic origin] (2: 81).

Helena Miguélez-Carballeira asserts that the historical facts of Celtic settlement are undisputed, but it was not until the nineteenth century (following José Verea y Aguiar's 1838 *Historia de Galicia*) that Galician historians would use Celtic history as a basis for the construction of a Galician national identity (9). This fact, she argues, must, and did, involve a transformation from the traditional beliefs about the valiant, violent and bellicose culture of the ancient Celts to the nostalgic and sentimental Celt of post-1838 literature (9-10). This "trope of Galician sentimentality", reinforced by the *Rexurdimento* and Murgía's writings, has given rise to the assumption that "Galicians are a nostalgic people, living in communion with their landscape or yearning for their province if away from it" (Miguélez-Carballeira 15, 2). Pardo Bazán's non-fictional views of Galician women do tend towards the sentimental (as seen in "The Women of Spain" and "La gallega", for example), as do some of her short stories; nevertheless, there are also many Realist and Naturalist representations of Galician female-incited violence, examples of which are included in this chapter.

Galicia's geography and climate differentiate it from the rest of Spain. The Atlantic Ocean borders the north and west of the province where numerous and often remote fishing villages and the trans-Atlantic passenger ports of La Coruña and Vigo are situated. Mountain ranges create natural borders on the other two sides, with Asturias, Castile and León to the east and Portugal to the south—a haven for some of Pardo Bazán's criminal protagonists (see "Cenizas" 4: 136). The climate is temperate, the rainfall abundant and agriculture, largely on small, rented plots, used to be the dominant occupation for both men and women (Shubert *Social* 77-78).

There was a rational reason for the large numbers of Galician female agricultural workers in the nineteenth century: necessity (Pardo Bazán "Women" 904) or, more specifically, a lack of manpower due to emigration. Both voluntary and economic, migration to Latin America had been a part of Spanish society since the sixteenth century, with a preponderance of middle-class emigres—administrators, clergy and businessmen being the norm (Guia 297). However, after the mid-nineteenth century, when most of Spain's Latin American colonies gained independence, the numbers of Spanish emigrants increased dramatically. Rural laborers predominated, and Galicians were over-represented in comparison with the rest of Spain (Guia 287). This is illustrated by Blanca Sánchez-Alonso's figures which show that between 1880 and 1914 alone more than 3 million mainly male Spaniards emigrated, a third of whom were Galician, although Galicia only had 10% of Spain's population (730, 745). Paredes Núñez quotes an even higher figure; between 40 and 70% of Spanish emigrants to America were from Galicia (*Realidad* 131). This fact was publicly recognized by Castro who dedicated her fifth book, *Follas novas* (1880), to "As viudas dos vivos e as viudas dos mortos" [The widows of the living and the widows of the dead] in recognition of the numbers of Galician women having to manage their lives, livelihood, and families single-handedly, effectively as widows (235).

The reason for this exodus of Galician workers was both economic and social: it was "por falta de patatas, por falta de pan, por falta de libertad" [for lack of potatoes, bread and freedom] (Paredes Núñez *Realidad* 128). Paredes Núñez elaborates further on the conditions of a society with poor governance, tied by historical and political circumstances to an endless Middle Ages, a society lacking the minimum foundations to develop its industrialization process (*Realidad* 129). It is unsurprising then, that when a number of successful, wealthy migrants did return to Spain, hearsay and exaggerations about an easy and financially rewarding life in the Americas circulated amongst the rural poor. A literary example of this patent untruth is portrayed in Pardo Bazán's "Las medias rojas" (1914), where the protagonist sincerely believes that in Latin America "el oro rueda por las calles y no hay sino bajarse para cogerlo" [Gold coins roll through the streets and all you have to do is bend down and catch them] (3: 196). Sometimes emigration was a means to avoid unpleasant obligations such as a military conscription ballot, as we will see in the next story.

Pardo Bazán herself was horrified at the level of deprivation that male emigration caused in rural Galicia and in 1907 expressed her feelings publicly about a lack of governmental action preventing the further loss of manpower.[4] The desperate poverty of the Galician *campesinos* underpins the majority of Pardo Bazán's Galician works. It was caused partly by the land governance traditions of hired workers on large estates or subsistence farmers on small, often inadequate, rented plots of land and partly by emigration. Emigration can also be said to account for the instances of the *mujeres fuertes* in her Galician short stories—women who, through necessity, were forced to fulfil both traditional female roles and many of the male roles in their societies. Their difficult world is far removed from the lives of Pardo Bazán's largely middle-class readership.

4   *La Ilustración Artística*, no. 1305, Jan 1, 1907.

Paredes Núñez compares Pardo Bazán's Galician writings to a multicolored altarpiece that depicts a humble farm laborer toiling in an unforgiving landscape. She has given her readers a vivid contemporaneous document of rural *fin de siècle* Galician life and lifestyles: the peasants' daily struggle for existence with its misery and poverty, their problems and worries. Galician socio-economic structures, politics, provincial culture, and the mental and spiritual world of folktales and legends, with its coalescence of reality and fantasy, are all woven into Pardo Bazán's stories (*Realidad* 143-146). Her writing is stripped of romantic idealism and takes a more direct approach. Of note is her often sensitive and compassionate treatment of the *campesina gallega*: self-sacrificing, strong women, bent and prematurely aged from the rough and difficult farm work. Paredes Núñez concludes: "Podemos decir ... que estos cuentos, independiente de su valor estético, cumplen perfectamente ... su misión de testigos elocuentes de la Galicia rural de una época" [We can safely say ... that these stories, regardless of their aesthetic value, perfectly fulfill ... their mission as powerful witnesses of rural Galicia at a particular period (*Realidad* 145).

The six stories discussed in this chapter highlight various aspects of Galicia's unique culture. The Galician language, rural lifestyles and deeply entrenched local myths and legends are incorporated into the stories and all foreground women who deliberately step outside their respective class or society's behavioral norms. The chapter reveals the range of literary styles that Pardo Bazán used to convey a particular impression in a specific story, and it investigates the over-arching theme of female agency present in these narratives. It examines both examples of Galician women who used this agency to better their own lives and the lives of those around them, and examples of Galician women who deliberately caused harm to others.

In three stories, the female protagonists are good women. The protagonist of "El molino" is protective of her fiancé and scornful of his jealous tormentors. In "El aire cativo", which considers the power of the myth surrounding salamanders, the protagonist is an independent woman, and the third story, "La santa de Karnar", based on the legendary tale of a real-life holy woman, is a longer, more complex tale, with several strong female protagonists all working together to help a young invalid.

Nevertheless, it is impossible to ignore darker, violent themes in many of Pardo Bazán's Galician stories. Misery, superstition, hunger, violence, envy, brutality, ambition and evil—a somewhat disturbing panoply of actions and emotions—permeate the narratives, which, in Pardo Bazán's appraisal, reflect the true nature of the province (Villanueva and González Herrán 10:

xxx). The protagonist of "La capitana" has chosen to lead an aggressive band of rural thieves; "La hoz" takes the reader up to the instant before one woman murders another woman; and "Un destripador de antaño", a re-working of a Galician legend, focusses on the circumstances of a brutal killing of an orphaned girl by her aunt, who is responsible for planning both the murder and the subsequent desecration of the girl's body.

"El Molino", "El aire cativo" and "La santa de Karnar": *Gallegas respetables*

"El Molino" and "El aire cativo" are written in a lighter style than the other stories analyzed in this chapter and illustrate Pardo Bazán's ability to communicate various aspects of the everyday lives of unmarried *campesinos*, while "La santa de Karnar" is a more serious tale centered on a recently deceased local recluse. All three incorporate a variety of myths, customs and legends that were a natural part of rural Galician life. In these stories Pardo Bazán illustrates the immense influence that an orally transmitted legend can have on a *campesino* when they believe that the events described in a legend have affected them personally.

"El molino" touches on several aspects of rural Galician life. Foremost is the miller, Mariniña, a fictional embodiment of "la bella molinera", a character prominent in Galician folklore (Sotelo Vázquez 299); male emigration to the Americas, *enchoyadas* and *loitas* at social evenings spent at the local mill, and the legend of *La Santa Compaña* are also incorporated into the narrative. "El aire cativo" offers two rural insights: the archaic agricultural practices that still existed in the province and the superstition surrounding salamanders. Indeed, the male protagonist believes that he is dying because he has been poisoned by one of these creatures. Both texts also incorporate their respective community's ubiquitous *el qué dirán* and, like most of Pardo Bazán's Galician tales, Galician words, implying authenticity of observation, are used throughout the texts. In this pair of stories Pardo Bazán has also offered a cultural gender reversal, where the female protagonist of each is an independent, rational working woman who regards the particular legend she encounters as mere superstition (taking a masculine stance) and acts accordingly. "El aire cativo", however, adds a twist at the end. In "La santa de Karnar", two countrywomen direct an ailing girl to the local legendary "saint", locally believed to possess healing powers, although other protagonists hold diverging views.

"El molino", a *costumbrista* narrative, was selected by *La Ilustración Artística* for inclusion in number 940, published on January 1, 1900, a commemorative edition, that celebrated both the New Year and the new century and was re-published a year later by Pardo Bazán in *Cuentos dramáticos*. *La Ilustración Artística* (1882—1916) was, according to its self-promotion, "siempre ... á la altura de los mejores periódicos de su índole" [always ... one of the better publications of its style].[5] This commemorative edition contained stories by prominent writers from Spain, South America, Morocco and Japan, each illustrated by a noted artist, creating a publication that was intended to be "verdaderamente notable" [truly outstanding] (*Artística* 940 p. 2).

The "cuadro de costumbres gallegas" sub-heading of "El molino" allows Pardo Bazán to incorporate numerous italicized Galician words, Galician legends and local customs into this relatively short and fast-moving text, including the legend of *La Santa Compaña* and a traditional *loita*, a wrestling duel used to settle a grievance. Mariniña, a miller, the female protagonist, is a *campesina* and a *mujer fuerte*. She is an independent single businesswoman, decisive, astute, apparently unsuperstitious, physically strong, loyal and fair; the antithesis of an *ángel del hogar*.

Mariniña is broad-hipped and curvaceous (the original publication adds an imaginative illustration of her character in Galician dress—lace bonnet, patterned shawl, long skirt and white frilled apron). She awakens desire in several local youths, who are jealous of her relationship with her *novio* Chinto. *El qué dirán*, the community gossip, resurfaces in this narrative: Chinto, in the collective mind of "everyone in the parish", is considered effeminate. He is slight, shy, polite, softly spoken and almost saintly looking; nevertheless, he is constantly at the mill, helping Mariniña, who is besotted with him. The entire town appears to have an opinion about Mariniña and Chinto's relationship. In particular, the focus is on his reluctance to commit to Mariniña, because of his unmanly fear of military service, coupled with the fact that if he should be conscripted, he would "largarse a la América del Sur en el primer barco que del puerto de Marineda saliese..." [take off for South America on the next ship leaving Marineda] (2: 188). Here, casually, Pardo Bazán refers to the widespread Galician problem noted earlier—male emigration to America as an easy (if sometimes short-sighted) solution for an immediate difficulty.

---

5   *La Ilustración Artística* promoted itself as having a "weekly run of 26,000 copies circulating among the moneyed classes and 'la Buena Sociedad'" ... in Spain and America (Charnon-Deutsch "Fictions" 290). Pardo Bazán published fewer than twenty stories in this magazine, however the majority of these were in Christmas, New Year or Easter editions.

The narrative introduces aspects of a typical vibrant rural Galician social life that, year-round, centered on many of the province's mills, particularly in the evenings. It describes, in particular, the traditional improvised poetry contests, *enchoyadas,* lively gallant dialogues, of finesse and disdain, satire and mischief (2: 188).[6]

However, throughout the descriptions of the communal festivities, the reader detects an unmistakable animosity towards Chinto from a group of young men envious of his place in Mariniña's heart. One misty, wintry night, the words of ridicule switch to deliberate actions. Three of these men dress in ghost-like sheets with pots on their heads and, carrying candles (a parody of *La Santa Compaña*), plan to waylay Chinto in the forest, but he fails to appear "on cue". At daybreak Mariniña and Chinto, also disguised as two groaning ghosts, surprise and terrify the three men. Two of them, suddenly fearful, trip as they try to escape, while the third is stopped by an accurately thrown stone. They instinctively fall to their knees and begin to confess their sins. Their identities are exposed and, when the village learns of this exploit, they are publicly ridiculed.

La Santa Compaña is a widely known Galician legend stemming from traditional Galician funereal tradition. This includes a belief that there is a transitional, collective, liminal space between the living and the dead, where individual identity ceases to exist: "no longer life, not yet death" (Nora 12). The souls forming the processions known as *La Santa Compaña*, mimicked by the men in the story, are from this transitional space.[7] The villagers expect Chinto to panic when he sees them and possibly die of fear. Mariniña, however, going against the traditional feminine stereotype, is not supersti-

---

6 *Enchoyadas,* or *regueifas,* are oral improvisations of eight syllable couplets, thrown at speed between two competitors. They were popular around La Coruña, where this story was set. See https://www.mintzola.eus/en/europa-bat-batean/participants/expressions/regueifa.

7 Pardo Bazán's short story "La compaña" (1901) relates the legend: "Es una legión de muertos que, dejando sus sepulturas, llevando cada cual en la descarnada mano un cirio, cruzan la montaña, allá a lo lejos, visibles sólo por la vaga blancura de los sudarios y por el pálido reflejo del cirio desfalleciente. ... Si no se muere en el acto la vida se le secará para siempre a modo de hierba que cortó la fouce. ... ¡Infeliz del que ve la 'Compaña'!" [It is a procession of the dead who, leaving their graves, carrying a candle in their fleshless hands, cross the distant mountain. The procession is visible only by the vague whiteness of the shrouds and by the pale reflection of the fading candles. ... If you do not die instantly, your life will dry up forever like harvested grass. ... He who sees the 'Company' is doomed!] (2: 176).

tious. She is somehow aware of the young men's plans and turns their plot against them, showing them to be unmanly and cowardly.

One man seeks revenge for this public humiliation. He appears one night at the crowded mill and kneeling, challenges Mariniña to a *loita*. Mariniña takes up the challenge and not only triumphs in the contest, but also publicly shames the man by rubbing his face on the floury floor before washing him down outside. She then informs him that if she does marry, it will be to Chinto. The narrative closes with Mariniña in control, obtaining the man's word that he and his accomplices will leave Chinto alone in future.

In Mariniña, Pardo Bazán has created an unconventional protagonist— a successful businesswoman who is resourceful and fearless, deliberately facing down groups of young men intent on injury, and physically able to match their strength. It is she who is the physical protector of her intended spouse, reversing the gender stereotypes. Another of Mariniña's unconventionalities is her sensuousness. An *ángel del hogar* is chaste, bearing children out of duty rather than desire; however, Mariniña, "se bababa de gusto, se moría, en fin de amor por el mozo delicado y aniñado" [is drooling with pleasure and almost dying of love for this delicate and boyish young man] (2: 188), and is driven crazy by the silky smooth chest that she has discovered under Chinto's shirt.[8] Thus "El molino" validates this unorthodox woman who eschews the bourgeois gendered societal conventions of the reader and, in fact has overturned traditional gender roles, becoming the protector of her man.[9]

Pardo Bazán challenges the widespread belief that all Galicians conform to stereotypes by portraying Mariniña as strong and capable, a seemingly likeable, loyal and independent woman. She is faithful to her *novio* and, furthermore, manages a business that provides a focal point for the community. Jiménez points out that *costumbrismo*, an uncritical genre, may not always represent the whole truth of the community it portrays (60). However, in this story, Pardo Bazán uses this facet of the style to her advantage in order to foreground Mariniña as an ideal *mujer fuerte* and, in her portrayal, debunks some of the commonly held prejudices and stereotypes relating to Galicians.

By contrast, the self-sufficient female protagonist of "El aire cativo" is determined to stay single. Like Mariniña, she is employed in a traditionally masculine occupation, that of an armed delivery woman. The story centers

---

8   A hairy chest is a traditional sign of virility; here Mariniña likes Chinto for characteristics that are the inverse of societal expectations.

9   Two other Pardo Bazán Galician tales with similarly strong, unconventional female protagonists—"La mayorazga de Bougas" (1886) and "La capitana" also confront traditional Spanish gender conventions.

on a Galician legend about the salamander, a creature shunned by superstitious Galicians, but one that appears to hold no fear for this protagonist. In *Sociedad del Folklore Gallega* it is recorded that "de que quien coge en la mano una salmántiga, salamandra, alcanza fortaleza e invulnerabilidad, magia contaminante por la potencia mágica de este bactracio" [that whoever picks up a salamander achieves strength and invulnerability, transmitted by the magical power of the amphibian] (Taboada Chivite 207). However, the truth, firmly established in European myth and folklore and known since ancient times is that, far from making a person who handles a salamander invulnerable, the toxic white fluid secreted from the creature's skin affects a handler. This amphibian is considered among the most harmful of animals if they are held (Lüddecke 1).[10] As its title suggests, "El aire cativo" takes the legend a step further, adding a questionable assumption—that the salamander exudes poison and that this will fatally infect the surrounding atmosphere.[11]

"El aire cativo" was first published in the literary magazine *Caras y Caretas* (Argentina) in 1919 and re-published in the collection *Cuentos de la tierra* (May 1922) that commemorated the first anniversary of Pardo Bazán's death. Despite the editor's fanfare about the significance of the publication it was, effectively, Volume 43 of the series *Obras Completas de la Condesa de Pardo Bazán* that she started in 1891 (Villanueva and González Herrán 10: xxvii). El aire cativo is a simpler tale than many others but, considering the extraordinary number of stories that Pardo Bazán produced and given the time constraints that she imposed on herself for writing many of them, it is not surprising that some stories are slighter than others.[12]

The narrative is in the third person, interspersed with direct speech. The two protagonists are Camila de Berte, a delivery woman, and Felipe da Fonte, an agricultural laborer whose daily routine farmwork, in itself, highlights the social plight of countless Galician peasants. Camila is a self-assured emancipated *mujer fuerte* which, in the eyes of the townspeople, sets her apart from many other young women. Early in the narrative, the familiar motif of *el qué dirán* is discerned: "según voz pública, no tenía voluntad de casarse, porque los hijos dan muchos trabajos" [public opinion was that she had decided not to get married, because bringing up children would involve too much work]

---

10 Pardo Bazán alludes to this in "La santa de Karnar," where sickness in a cow is thought to have resulted from an encounter with a salamander.

11 In Galicia, *cativo* is used as a synonym for "malo" (*DLE* 441).

12 She would go to a small room that she had fitted up as a study and sit down before her typewriter and produce, before lunch, at least one short story and a chronicle (Hilton "Centenary" 346).

(3: 301), and the narrator adds that Camila has seen so many distressing things in various marriages that being married does not appear to be an attractive proposition for her anyway. Detesting field work, she has sought out a livelihood that appeals to her—as a service woman for her aunt's inn, delivering orders and picking up new stock. With a basket on her head, or a small horse-drawn cart, she traverses the countryside alone, and it is rumored that she is armed. Even in rural Galicia where women working as laborers or managers of farms and businesses is normal, Camila's views and chosen lifestyle seem, to the gossipers, to be rather too manly and radical.

Felipe, who is physically strong but inherently fearful and superstitious, is attracted to Camila. He works as a laborer, carrying out a menial, rudimentary agricultural task. It is May and seeds are about to germinate below the surface of the soil. It is his job to pound the surface with a mallet to encourage this process. Spain's agricultural development and mechanization at that time lagged behind the rest of Western Europe (Shubert *Social* 15) and Galicia, in most respects, was behind the rest of Spain, condemning generations of men and women to lowly tasks such as the one described here.

Felipe is terrified of reptiles, even lizards, and when a fire salamander appears in a boggy corner of the field his instinct is to hold his breath and flee, as he is aware of the local reputation of the animal. It is not the jewel-like skin of the salamander that bothers Felipe, as he would never actually handle any amphibian, as much as the air surrounding it; he knows, from an oft-repeated legend, that the surrounding air itself holds the creature's poison. Reason prevails, and having run a seemingly safe distance, Felipe hurls a large rock at the animal, narrowly missing Camila whose arrival he had not noticed. In keeping with her character, she is quite unafraid of the salamander but curious to see it, and she commands Felipe to lift the rock. Obediently he does her bidding. As they discuss the supposedly "poisoned air", Felipe realizes that she is mocking him as she leaves to continue her delivery round.

Pardo Bazán has created an image in the reader's mind of a frightened, superstitious young man that is reinforced by the rest of the tale. Once again Pardo Bazán has reversed the traditional gender roles, beyond even Galicia's flexible norms. Camila is the rational, capable figure curious about the supposedly dangerous salamander, while Felipe is terrified of common country animals and, furthermore, is obedient and ultimately submissive to the woman he encounters. If Camila had not passed by at that moment Felipe would not have dared to approach the salamander again and, as the story progresses, it is evident that she is indirectly responsible for his expected demise, which is seemingly triggered by the incident.

"Todos en aldea" [absolutely everybody] (3: 303), the ubiquitous nameless and faceless Greek chorus, hears of Felipe's encounter with the salamander and attributes his apparently inevitable decline and, as the tale concludes, his imminent death, to the poisoned air that he had been exposed to. He has been portrayed as an unmasculine, credulous youth, while Camila, at this point of the narrative, presents as a true *mujer fuerte*: rational and self-assured, the only person in the town who disregards the legend.

Camila appears at Felipe's bedside with medicine, even offering, out of pity, a glass of liquor from her inn's supplies. In a scene reminiscent of "El principe rana" [The Frog Prince], a Spanish children's fairytale, Felipe, who believes that he is dying from his encounter with a salamander, then pleads for a kiss from Camila, his unrequited love. But there is no fairytale ending here. As in "El zapato", with its echoes of "Cenicienta", Pardo Bazán has offered a few pertinent details that enable the reader to recall the familiar "El principe rana" and then subverts the narrative, jolting it from sentimentality to a troublesome reality. Here, the seemingly emancipated heroine Camila is unexpectedly exposed as fallible, as she declines Felipe's invitation saying doubtfully: "Sabe Dios si el aire cativo se pega..." [Only God knows if the poisoned air really is dangerous...] (3: 304).

When the narrative ends, Felipe is still alive and Pardo Bazán, as she so often does in scenes such as this, leaves the question of his impending death open. Was the air poisoned by the salamander's presence, or is his evident suffering psychological? With Felipe's dramatic decline, self-induced or otherwise, alongside the surprise of Camila's emotional fallibility, Pardo Bazán has provided a complex conclusion to a seemingly simple tale. She underscores the influence that the various Galician legends have on the populace and here illustrates that even the strongest of Galician *mujeres fuertes* can be frightened by regional superstitions. With this story, Pardo Bazán has indicated to Latin America and to the rest of Spain that there *are* progressive women in Galicia, but she has also critiqued her province by illustrating the pervasive and detrimental presence of widespread superstitions and the deleterious effects that these can have, particularly on the *campesinos*.

By contrast, "La santa de Karnar" the last story this in this trilogy, features not just one "good" woman, but several. It moves away from superstition as such and is based on a recently deceased Galician woman whose life had, in Pardo Bazán's time, become legendary. At its heart, it is a tale where Pardo Bazán presents two seemingly diametrically opposed issues in which she had a lifelong interest—religious faith and scientific reason.[13] Saints and sainthood were a central theme in much of her prose writing, with one of her earliest publications being the acclaimed two-volume work *San Francisco de Asís. Siglo XIII* (Acosta 190). Pardo Bazán had a personal interest in the saint and in 1881 had joined the Third Order of Franciscans who, she felt, acknowledged and upheld women's rights (Hilton "Doña" 4-5). She remained a member of this Order for the rest of her life—and beyond—as she was interred wearing the Franciscan habit (Faus 506).

Maurice Hemingway recognizes that the figure of the saint in general had such a powerful impact on Pardo Bazán because "he is both a spiritual aristocrat and a rebel against materialism and pragmatism" ("Religious" 381). However, a critical examination of Pardo Bazán's prose reveals that the universal masculine favored by Hemingway obscures the fact that many of Pardo Bazán's hagiographic interpretations were of female saints (Ezama Gil 240). A closer inspection of these works reveals an unexpected gender split between the different prose genres. The saints depicted in Pardo Bazán's short stories are predominantly male biblical saints or martyrs, with few recognized women saints represented, apart from the Virgin Mary and Mary Magdalene (4: 377-424).[14] The saint characterized in "La santa de Karnar", despite her local reputation, has never been accepted by the Church, while in two other Pardo Bazán stories the supposed saintliness of Clotilde in "Bajo la losa" (1909) and tía Rafaela in "Por dentro" (1907), is revealed as fictitious in the stories themselves.

Pardo Bazán did, however, research and publish biographies of several recognized European and North African Catholic saints, and in 1925 her daughter, Carmen, collected and compiled thirteen of these essays and published them as *Cuadros religiosos*. While some figures, such as Teresa de Jesús and Teresa Reina were well known, many others, such as Olivia de Palermo, Pulqueria, an empress of the Byzantine Empire, Casilda, the daughter of a Muslim king of Toledo, and Catalina of Alexandria, whose life Pardo Bazán fictionalized as Lina in *Dulce dueño* (1911), are less familiar. From this, it may be deduced that Pardo Bazán's respect for the reputations of these real-life women was too deep to treat them as fictional protagonists (with Catalina of Alexandria being an obvious exception).

---

13   Pardo Bazán presented her scientifically based opinions in numerous essays. Fourteen of these essays are summarized and several others are referenced in Zárate (159-65).

14   "La penitencia de Dora" (1897) parallels the life of Santa Teodora Alejandrina (1: 417).

"La santa de Karnar" was first published in Pardo Bazán's own journal, *Nuevo Teatro Crítico*, in April 1891, and reprinted in *Historias y cuentos de Galicia*, (1900), a collection dominated by local *sucedidos* (Villanueva and González Herrán 9: xii). The saint in the story is an unmistakable representation of Josefa de la Torre (1773–1848) who lived at Gonzar, near Santiago de Compostela, and apparently spent the last sixteen years of her life secluded, without food, surviving only on a daily communion wafer. (Paredes Núñez *CC* 4: 418). She was viewed as a holy woman within her rural Galician parish and as a scientific curiosity by the rest of the country. Her life, particularly her latter years when she lived as a hermit, has been well documented.[15]

An example of Pardo Bazán's "imaginative Catholicism" (DuPont 48), the story is structured around the dichotomy between faith and rationality that had preoccupied Pardo Bazán since her exploration of Naturalism in the early 1880s. In "The Women of Spain" she observed that faith was considered as an intrinsically feminine characteristic, writing that while Spanish men had a right, "greatly assisted by the law", to choose their spiritual beliefs, to be deist, atheist, sceptic or materialist, their wives, daughters, sisters and mothers must be "nothing else than Catholics pure and simple. ... All this is so well known and common that nobody pays any attention to it" (885). Both sides of this argument are offered in "La santa de Karnar", as female voices present faith and a male voice presents rationality; the female narrator is torn between her adult mind's wish for reason and her emotional childhood response to a personal miracle. As will be seen later in the analysis of "Un destripador de antaño", Pardo Bazán uses her longer short stories to offer the reader serious philosophical and sociological questions to ponder.

The story is framed and is one of the very few Pardo Bazán short stories with an embedded narrative female voice. Tolliver has noted that in Pardo Bazán's short stories this voice is always framed by a second narrator, who is also the narratee (*Cigar* 90).[16] Here the framing is minimal; the unnamed,[17] gender-neutral framing narrator's only verbal participation in the text is in

---

15 Josefa de la Torre died in 1848 after sixteen years of living as a hermit. An internal textual reference in "La santa de Karnar" sets the story in 1847, a year before she died (2: 78).

16 Tolliver's *Cigar Smoke and Violet Water* provides an analysis of Pardo Bazán's limited use of the feminine voice in her fictional work (90-91).

17 The doctor, Lazcano, is one of only two protagonists in the text who is named. The other is the elderly, blind woman, referred to by the daughters as "señora María". Other protagonists are referred to by their position, e, g, *mayordomo* or *mayordoma*, or by family relationships.

the first sentence where they announce their presence: "De niña—*me dijo* la anciana señora—era yo muy poquita cosa" [As a girl—the elderly lady *told me*—I was just a bit of a thing] (2: 77) (my emphasis). However, the embedded narrator herself often addresses the narratee directly, for example: "[Y]a ve usted si soy vieja" [this will show you how old I am] (2: 77) ... "[m]ire usted si ha pasado tiempo" [{j}ust see how much time has passed] (2: 80) ... "el Rosario, como usted sabe" [rosary prayers, as you know] (2: 80). This contrasts with other framed stories that have been considered—"Cenizas" and "Remordimiento" in particular—where the framing narrator supplies background information and narrative settings which explain the circumstances leading to the central narration. And, in addition, the two narrators usually interact. However, the absence of an elaborate introduction in this text removes all emphasis from the framing narrator and permits an exclusive focus on the central story.

Pardo Bazán has incorporated a thought-provoking local figure, Josefa de la Torre, into a fictional tale that also includes undisputed facts about her life, the second writer to do so.[18] At the end of "La santa de Karnar" the reader is left with an unanswered question: was Josefa a saint or a fraud? The fictional protagonists of the story are unable to agree, just as real-life contemporaneous medical opinions differed (see Logú y Zelada). Even today, there is a continued interest in Josefa's life as the truth of her story continues to be probed (see Romar García and González Pérez).

The *anciana señora* delivers a first-person autodiagetic monolog, relating an incident in her life during 1847, when she was twelve and speaks, with few exceptions, from the viewpoint of her twelve-year-old self. Nevertheless, there are opinions which she appears to have unconsciously adopted during the intervening years, some of which will be discussed shortly. Despite her introduction as an *anciana* (this is a very inexact term in Pardo Bazán's stories, often being an assessment relative to the age of the assessor),[19] she

---

18   The first was Benito Vicetto (1824–1878), a Galician playwright, historian and novelist who penned "Cristina. Páginas de un diario" (1852), that related fictitious diary entries of two pilgrims to Santiago. It details their time in Gonzar and their impressions of Josefa, "La enferma de Gonzar" (Sánchez Cantón 329). Sánchez Cantón reproduces the relevant text from "Cristina", together with an excerpt from Pardo Bazán's story. He does not discuss the two texts but merely notes that they are from different epochs and written in different styles (330-35).

19   In "Cuaresmal" (1899), the protagonist, accused of being old, describes herself as "cincuenta y..., y pico" [fifty something], which although not exact, by today's standards is hardly ancient, while Cipriana, in "El mascarón", at "apenas cuarenta"

appears to have total recall of the events from decades before, which she describes. Hence the reader is presented with a first-hand account of the events, presumably at the request of the framing narrator. It is based on memory, rather than one that is recording the present, which creates a sense of ambiguity for the reader. Dolores Troncoso Durán comments that the narrator can communicate some uncertainty as to the truth of her impressions, while simultaneously reproducing the exact words and gestures that she heard (or believed she heard) or observed decades earlier. It is a literary technique that gives the reader an overall impression of a trustworthy narrator and serves to illustrate Pardo Bazán's mastery of the art of narration (311).

However, James Phelan considers young narrators recalling adult conversations and situations to be unreliable. He does not assert that these narrators are being untruthful, or are of doubtful character or motives, but rather that they are unable to fully understand the true meaning and the wider implications of some of their statements about the things that they observe (67). I too argue that this assertion applies to some statements in this text, when the adult narrator reports events experienced and witnessed as a seemingly frail and sheltered twelve-year old in words that seem beyond a pre-teen's understanding. Some of her observations are age-appropriate—for example noting the doctor's pigtail: "Lazcano, el de la coleta" [Lazcano, the man with the pigtail] (2: 84)—while others she would have formed later: "Lazcano ... se hizo más célebre todavía que por estas cosas por haber persistido en el uso de la coleta, cuando ya no la gastaba alma viviente" [Lazcano ... made himself even more famous by persisting in wearing a pigtail when no other living soul was still wearing one] (2: 77). Since so much time has passed, she openly admits to re-interpreting some of her impressions when she states: "Esto lo discurro yo ahora" [On reflection, I now think...] (2: 83). Furthermore, for her twelve years she seems remarkably well acquainted with Murillo's artistic techniques and the facial features of sculptures of San Bruno.[20] Nevertheless,

---

[scarcely forty], considers herself young (4: 36). Assuming that "La santa de Karnar" was written about 1890, the fictional narrator would have been about 55.

20   This reference to Murillo can be seen as a homage to Franciscans. In the second volume of her treatise on San Francisco, Pardo Bazán writes: "Entre las artistas españolas á quienes se comunicó la inspiración franciscana, citemos solo uno, Murillo. ... Nuestro incomparable Bartolomé Esteban Murillo, nuestro gran artista cristiano" [Of all our Spanish artists who acknowledged St Francis as an inspiration we mention one in particular, ... the incomparable Bartolomé Esteban Murillo, Spain's great Christian artist] (164).

even keeping these discrepancies in mind, the narrator delivers a clear, seemingly honest recollection of a life-changing experience.

Forceful women dominate the text. The narrator is the younger of two sisters cared for by their mother. They appear to be a well-to-do middle-class family in Santiago de Compostela and are also owners of a surprisingly dilapidated managed estate, the description of which echoes gothic tropes, near the mountain town of Karnar, managed by a steward. In the narrator's opinion the steward's mother, a blind elderly lady, is notable for her determination, strength of character and personal piety, as is Karnar's reclusive unnamed female saint, the eventual focus of the tale. The doctor, Lazcano, whose appearance in the narrative flanks the main tale, is the only man who has any influence on the family; other males, including a kindly rural priest, serve to support the women, providing accommodation, transport and farm oversight.

The narrator, at the age of twelve, is frail and emaciated due to an undiagnosed condition but, in Lazcano's opinion, she is not dying. However, his prescribed remedy, considering that it is winter, is brutal: "Lo que necesita la rapaza es una docena de azotes..., y aldea, y leche de vaca..., y se acabó" [What this girl needs is a dozen lashes ... and the country, and cow's milk ... and that's that] (2: 78). Her mother, sensible and decisive, appears to ignore the spanking but is willing to follow the advice about time in the country, and arranges for the journey. Fortunately, they have a family holding in the mountains near Karnar, accessible by carriage and horseback. While their Santiago home appears comfortable, the mountain estate is in disrepair, and the narrator's memories, (delivered in *costumbrista* style) provide minute details of the dwelling, its occupants and the various visitors to the family, all seemingly reinforcing the validity of her recollection.

The story turns on the narrator's interactions with María, a fiercely determined blind elderly woman, the estate steward's mother. Refusing to be limited by her disability, María navigates her way freely through the house and the surrounding fields. It is her intense, forceful and very personal manner of prayer that first attracts the narrator's attention:

> Nunca he oído rezar así, con aquel tono ... pero la ciega, al pronunciar las oraciones, revelaba un alma y un fuego, que hacían llenarse de lágrimas los ojos. Al concluir el Rosario y empezar la retahíla de padrenuestros, me cogía de la mano, desplegando sobrehumana fuerza, me obligaba, venciendo mi extenuación y debilidad, a arrodillarme a su lado, y con acento de súplica ardentísima, casi colérica, exclamaba: A Jesucristo

nuestro Señor y a la santa de Karnar, para que se dime de sanar luego a la señoritiña [I've never heard praying like that, in that tone ... but when the blind woman said her prayers, she revealed a fiery soul that brought tears to my eyes. When she completed the rosary and began the string of Our Father's, she'd take me by the hand, exerting superhuman strength, and making me overcome my exhaustion and weakness, she forced me to kneel down beside her; and with an accent of the most ardent supplication, almost wrathful, she'd exclaim: To Jesus Christ our Lord and to the Holy Lady of Karnar, so she may deign to cure the young mistress soon!]. (2: 80)

Here, in this largely female household, Pardo Bazán depicts the rosary prayers as a daily devotion cutting across social classes (DuPont 53). When pressed by the narrator's sister about this unknown saint at Karnar who is mentioned each evening, the old woman shares her belief that the saint—not a statue, as might be supposed but a living woman—is a channel of God's healing. She believes that the narrator should visit her. Once again, the narrator's mother acts on behalf of her ailing daughter, this time by questioning the steward's wife about the saint. The *mayordoma* reiterates her mother-in-law's claims and adds, somewhat incongruously, that a farm cow has been cured through the saint's intercession. When yet another sudden crisis overtakes the narrator, the mother, as a last resort, resolves to take her daughter to the saint, arranging a horseback journey for the pair to Karnar, this time unexpectedly accompanied by María, who insists on walking beside them, to witness the miracle that she believes will occur.

The Karnar parish priest, used to visitors, offers beds to the mother and daughter but not to María, who curls up in a corner of their bedroom, listening to their conversation. When the daughter voices her reluctance about confessing to the local priest at early morning mass before going to see the saint, the old woman waits until both the girl and her mother are asleep, scoops up the girl and, carries her in the dark along a mountain path to visit the holy woman.

Gothic imagery reappears as the pair reach their destination. The saint, who the priest has explained earlier, subsists solely on a daily communion wafer, is skeletal and bedridden, described by the narrator as "en toda la fuerza de la palabra: una visión del mundo sobrenatural" [in every sense of the word: a vision of the supernatural world] (2: 83). Then, as her attendants draw her clothes back, her naked, emaciated, almost transparent torso is revealed.²¹ Surprisingly, the narrator finds the saint beautiful and is inspired by a desire to kiss her. The girl stands, suddenly feeling invigorated as she walks across the room and kisses the woman's forehead. As the saint whispers "Dios te sane, hija mía" [May God cure you, my girl] (2: 84) the girl is seized by ecstasy and can feel her body healing.²²

The narrative then jumps back to Santiago, presumably, though it is not explicitly stated, to the family home where Lazcano learns about the unusual details surrounding his patient's return to health. Here, the doctor is a representative of both the medical opinions of the day and Spanish patriarchal authority. Women, at times, for him are mere objects; he has reputedly kicked mothers in childbirth and, in this tale, ordered that a small and sickly girl be spanked. He expects a women's acquiescence and obedience and, as a rational, educated man, cannot admit a feminine view of Catholicism with its associated "irrational" miracles. Lacanzo is aware of the saint at Karnar, (quoting, almost verbatim, the saint's story recorded in Logú y Zelada [14]) and, as a medical man, is skeptical of her story, as were many real-life doctors (see Logú y Zelada). As he chides the mother for her part in her daughter's recovery, he adds that he too would like to carry out a medical investigation on this saint but is reluctant to do so, following Father Feijóo's conclusion that it is troublesome to determine the truth of a miracle.²³ The narrator's mother, knowing that her daughter has recovered, is no longer intimidated by the doctor. Defending both herself and her daughter, she confronts him with a simple question: is my daughter better or not? The answer is evident. The doctor is forced to agree that she is, but he has no answer as to how she

---

21   The imagery of the body of a female saint (here, a living body) as a relic, "digno de adoración" ["worthy of adoration"] (Ezama Gil 245), recurs in several other Pardo Bazán short stories, for example, "Baja la losa" "La penetencia de Dora" (1897), and "Por dentro" (1907).

22   A discourse analysis of "La santa de Karnar" offers similarities to "La novia fiel". In Tolliver's analysis of this latter story, she demonstrates that passive verbs are used in relation to the female protagonist, Amelia, indicating a complete lack of agency on Amelia's part until the crucial moment of self-revelation in the narrative is reached, after which, active verbs, indicating Amelia's own agency, are used ("Knowledge" 916-17).

23   "Examen de milagros" (Feijóo 524-7) is the essay in which Feijóo discusses the theological problem of miracles. Christine Bridges-Esser summarizes Feijóo's conclusions: "[T]he only true miracles are those that can be proven, and that unproven miracles lead to superstitious practices. That is to say, one should not give a natural explanation to a miraculous event, nor classify an event as a miracle that can be explained as a logical intervention of Nature".

has been cured. The girl can keep her childish arguments, he tells the mother, his mind is made up. It is an abrupt conclusion, leaving the reader to determine for themselves the veracity of the narrator's story.

Pardo Bazán may have bookended the story with Lazcano's typically masculine views, thus apparently normalizing them, but she has more than balanced them with the various portrayals of the six women in the story—the narrator, her mother, to a lesser extent her sister, the *mayordoma*, her mother-in-law María and the reclusive saint. We have mentioned the narrator's apparent trustworthiness and discussed her changing views on some aspects of her story, but the reader knows nothing about her personal life after the visit to the saint or the circumstances in which she tells her story. The entire narrative is a single voice, with Pardo Bazán using one woman's words to personalize, to a greater or lesser degree, each of the other characters.

The mother's character develops in the narrative, with her care and concern for her ailing daughter evident from the outset. There are two crucial decisions that she makes for her daughter. The first is to take the doctor's advice about the country (and in so doing she favors the younger girl's health above the marital prospects of the older girl), a hard decision perhaps for a single mother, and the second is to visit the saint. The mother's behavior demonstrates a balance of rationality and faith, offering a vision of a modern Catholic woman, perhaps not unlike Pardo Bazán herself. Her decisiveness, organizational ability and her firmness with her elder daughter become apparent, while her unorthodox decision to make the journey to Karnar, her quiet faith that holds to the possibility of a miracle and her new-found ability to counter the inflexibility of Lazcano all indicate depth of character. She demonstrates that she is a woman of decision, authority and independence. The elder daughter, a typical older teenager, is reluctant to interrupt her own social plans and later, being bored with the quiet atmosphere of the country residence, is happy to make conversation with the older woman, which leads, indirectly, to the journey to Karnar. With only scant mentions in the text, however, the personality of this young woman is not actually revealed. The *mayordoma*, busy with several children and numerous household tasks, offers her enthusiastic endorsement of the local saint. Yet, when pressed for facts about the everyday miracles she has spoken about, she sidesteps the question with a story which to her urban listeners appears almost comical. Her character is conveyed to a middle-class reader as that of a stereotypical Galician country woman—loyal, hardworking and credulous.

However, it is in the character development of María that Pardo Bazán's command of the monolog is seen, surprising the reader with the woman's personality, worldview and unpredictable actions. She is at the center of the story. Pardo Bazán portrays her in a positive manner—forceful, industrious, self-reliant, determined and sure of her faith—as "a monument to an open, alternative spirituality associated with women, popular culture, and rural/regional articulations of the divine" (DuPont 48-9). Denise DuPont also observes that "'La santa de Karnar' is particularly rich in the imagery of rosaries, Eucharist, and Catholic feminism" (48), all of which center largely on María. The narrator may be intrigued by the intense fervor of María's rosary prayers but, as she is obviously a devout Catholic, it is her unorthodox female-centered rejection of confession and priestly absolution, revealed at Karnar, that is unexpected. The Karnar priest and the mother are both assuming that the visitors will confess and say Mass before visiting the saint, and the mother is surprised by the narrator's reluctance. María forcefully intervenes on the narrator's behalf: "¡El cura no! ¡Señora mi ama...; deje solos a la santa y a Dios del cielo! ¡La santa..., y nada más!" [Not the priest! My lady mistress ... let the Holy Woman and God in heaven act alone! The Holy Woman ... and nothing else!] (2: 83). Taken literally, this appears to be outside strict Roman teaching, but DuPont asserts that the reader will not view María as proto-protestant but simply see her as distancing herself from the male church hierarchy. She possesses an alternate belief system in a local saint whose "claim to holiness rests on a particularly female experience of sainthood as manifested by way of the body and its incorporation of the Eucharist" (DuPont 54).[24]

Pardo Bazán, seemingly deferring to Feijóo's conclusions, avoids making a definitive statement about the unvoiced question at the story's end: is it childish or unsophisticated to accept a miracle? The narrator's ailment is never explained, but with fevers and episodes of unconsciousness it does appear as more than a psychological problem.[25] In this story Pardo Bazán faces

---

24   María also has her own opinions on agnostic doctors: "La salud la da Dios del cielo. Sin Dios del cielo, los médicos son ... Y para recalcar la frase no concluida, la ciega se volvió y escupió en el suelo despreciativamente" [Health is given by God in heaven. Without God in Heaven, doctors are ... And to underline the sentence left incomplete, the blind woman turned around and spat on the floor with contempt] (2: 81).

25   Pardo Bazán may have been referencing female hysteria, a socially constructed condition, popularized initially in France, and later in Spain in the 1880s, by Jean-Marie Charcot. The symptoms are wide ranging, but they do include loss of appetite and mood changes with laughing or crying. However, it is generally referred to within the realm of female sexuality, where, as Aldaraca notes, a diagnosis operates "in the realm of ideology to exercise control ... by those who define the category" ("Medical"

squarely two of the prevailing dichotomies of her day. Firstly, the urban/rural tension divide (that pervades this chapter) and secondly, and perhaps more importantly, the confrontation between a rational, scientific worldview, aligned with masculinity, with one in which folklore and religious beliefs are traditionally linked to ignorance and femininity. The narrator, having considered the episode over the years, looks back on the old countrywoman's faith, seemingly driven by her rosary prayers, as "religiosidad rara y de persona ignorante" [{an} unusual religiosity, characteristic of an ignorant person] (2: 83), from which it is implied that she, a middle-class woman, favors a less passionate expression of faith. Nevertheless, the overall tone of Pardo Bazán's narrative does nothing to diminish either this older woman's femicentric yet still profoundly Catholic faith, or the respect that the rural people afforded to the reclusive saint.

Details from the text of "La santa de Karnar" show that Pardo Bazán was familiar with both Feijóo's "Exámen de Milagros" and the work of Logú y Zelada and, by creating a doctor who is skeptical about a miraculous cure, she provides a foil to Vicetto's "Cristina", whose protagonist proclaims the saint to be a worker of miracles (Sánchez Cantón 329).[26] Ermitas Penas Varela classifies "La santa de Karnar" as an example of *lo fantástico puro* [sheer fantastic], where the miraculous does not have a clear explanation and, in this case, two of the protagonists differ in their explanation of events, an inconsistency which for the reader leaves the question of supernatural open. That is true; it is a question that has long been considered, as Shakespeare noted in Hamlet: "There are more things in heaven and earth, Horatio/ Than are dreamt of in your philosophy" (1: 5, ll. 187-88). However, I argue that Pardo Bazán's portrayal of strong, confident and credible women protagonists in this story may persuade the reader that their professed first-hand opinions of miracles wrought by the saint, albeit fictional, are valid. Conversely, the doctor's rationality may be interpreted as blindly stubborn, with his refusal to accept the evidence of both the healthy girl and the seemingly sensible mother.

402, 411). In this story the protagonist is twelve years old, surely this is too young to be diagnosed as "hysteric".

26   The life and death of Josefa de la Torre in Gonzar were widely reported in several newspapers and various medical journals throughout Spain including *El correo nacional Madrid* (Apr 13, 1838, p.4), *Semanario pintoresco español* (Apr 22, 1838, no. 108, p. 2) and the *Boletín de medicina, cirugía y farmacia* (Oct 20, 1844); however, no article conclusively claimed that Josefa wrought miracles.

Here Pardo Bazán, aware of the double standard of religious observance ingrained in her society, personifies Lazcano as the typical unbelieving Spanish man described in "The Women of Spain" (885). Nevertheless, as a self-proclaimed and lifelong Catholic,[27] Pardo Bazán was acquainted with reports of miracles that appear to defy rational explanation. Using a solitary voice, she presents a story that invites an answer: faith or reason? She offers a multi-faceted text that provides arguments for both sides. The surface text that apparently identifies with Lazcano's patriarchal worldview is compatible with that of Pardo Bazán's implied male readers but, in addition, there is an undeniable feminist sub-text that recognizes and affirms both the role and the faith of strong Galician women. They are all far from respectable bourgeois *ángeles del hogar* (although two are middle-class) and the traditional patriarchal influence of the Catholic Church is noticeably absent in their lives.

In the three stories examined thus far in this chapter, "El molino", "El aire cativo" and "La santa de Karnar" the various female protagonists have been "good" women, certainly acting in their own interests, but also mindful of those around them. However, the next three, "La capitana", "La hoz" and "Un destripador de antaño" demonstrate shifts, both in the female protagonists' outlooks, with each story foregrounding a protagonist who ultimately considers only herself, and a marked shift in the level of female violence that is either described or implied in all three narratives. In "La capitana", the female protagonist is the leader of a gang of efficient and successful roadside bandits, an uncommon occupation for a woman even in Galicia; while in "La hoz" the savage intentions of the female protagonist are communicated to the reader. Although the narrative concludes at the point where murder is about to be committed, possible endings can be played out in the reader's mind. In "Un destripador de antaño", the female protagonist is driven by greed to murder her young niece. These narratives underline Pardo Bazán's broad and arguably realistic representation of many facets of Galician society as the three stories, examined in sequence, portray a downward progression of the baser elements of that society, culminating in the Gothic horrors of the final story.

"La capitana", "La hoz" and "Un destripador de antaño": *Gallegas criminales*

"La capitana" was first published in 1902 in both Spain (*Blanco y Negro*) and Cuba (*Galicia*) and was later included in *Cuentos del terruño*. Villanueva and

---

27 "[S]oy católica apostólica romana" [I am an orthodox Roman Catholic] (*Cuestión* 352), Hilton ("Doña" 6).

González Herrán mention that the stories included in the latter collection are more intense than many other Galician stories, illustrating the brutality, ugliness and violence in the lives of rural Galicians. They cite as an example the ending of "La capitana", a quasi-fictional tale, where a female bandit throttles and almost kills a priest (10: xiv).

Pablo Cancelo López asserts that banditry—assault and robbery—by its very nature, causes harm, and in Galicia (unlike Andalucia) bandits never use the proceeds of their robberies to help the less fortunate in their communities. The *bandolera*, arguably among the most radical examples of a *mujer fuerte*, has been a mythical figure in Spain for centuries (Patiño Eirín 900). However, the existence of one nineteenth-century female bandit whose nefarious activities were known throughout Galicia has been authenticated. She is Pepona, the protagonist of this story, nicknamed Pepa a Loba, the Wolf-lady, as a result of an incident in her youth. José Antonio Adell documents the recognized facts from her life: her illegitimate birth in 1833 at Couso in Pontevedra, being orphaned at twelve years old and subsequently raised to adulthood by her aunt, who treated her harshly. An unfortunate event a few years later resulted in her being wrongly jailed for murder. During this period the noted Spanish writer and social activist Concepción Arenal spent time visiting female prisoners and encountered Pepona. A letter that Arenal sent to Jesús de Monasterio, dated 5 Jan. 1864, described her conversation with Pepona, and this particular documentation has been used by recent biographers as proof both of Pepona's existence and her story (Reigosa 122, 139). Pepona escaped from prison by assaulting the chaplain and absconding in his clothes and her first act in the community was to murder the man who had framed her. She subsequently went on to lead a successful group of *bandidos*, based at Cebreiro, who garnered a reputation in the province for cruelty. Later, romance and motherhood slowed her belligerent lifestyle, and accounts of her death vary from a natural and peaceful passing to a strange, somewhat suspicious report of a sudden demise and prompt burial (Reigosa 16-211, 17-18).

Pepa a Loba's story has been rewritten by different authors over the last century or so; the most notable is Carlos G. Reigosa's meticulously researched book *Pepa a Loba* (2006),[28] which draws from the collective memories of the various Galician communities where Pepona and her men were active. Several books dedicated to Galician legends have an entry for her story and, of these, Adell appears to have penned the most authoritative contribu-

---

28   Reigosa describes his work as a novel, although it is based on amply documented facts.

tion. A graphic novel based on her exploits also exists, there is a Facebook page in her name, and various Pepa a Loba cafes and restaurants can be found throughout Galicia.

Pardo Bazán used the figure of the bandit several times in her Galician stories (Patiño Eirín 899). One tale, in particular, "Vitorio" (1894), uses the same dynamic confrontation of the bandit and the cleric as "La capitana", with both stories skillfully blending documented facts and fiction. "La capitana" also introduces intertextual references to Pardo Bazán's own work in the character of the cleric, whose pistols were a gift from the Marquis of Ulloa, a character from her novel *Los pazos de Ulloa*. Indeed, Villanueva and González Herrán suggest that the cleric himself resembles the chaplain in that novel (10: xiv).

"La capitana" is a straightforward story with an unexpected twist at the end as the strong woman is undone by her least likely opponent. The narrative opens with a gender-neutral first-person narration that focusses on Pepona, whom the narrator had encountered as she scoped local fairs and festivals seeking out prospective victims for her *bandidos* to assault. The tone of the narration is that of a typical *costumbrista* tale, from the perspective of a Galician, a learned person who is somewhat patronizing and at times verges on moralizing. This is illustrated by the pronouncements on the traditional, subservient role of a woman, even in the criminal underworld. Such women who exist on the edges of acceptable society, the narrator states, are usually: "[m]anceba, encubridora y espía de ladrones; esperándolos al acecho para avisarlos, o a domicilio para esconderlos; ayudándolos y hasta acompañándolos" [concubines, harborers of fugitives, and thieves' spies; they've been on the lookout to warn men and at home to hide them; and they've even aided and consorted with them] (2: 343).[29] However, they explain that Pepona is above this, asserting her agency and, as an active participant, she is the one who organizes the *bandidos* and gives them their orders.

By comparison with female Andalusian bandits who are flamboyantly dressed and carry arms (which they obviously use), Pepona could be mistaken for a humble housekeeper. A goad is the only weapon she carries, as she wishes to avoid injuries that would involve serious consequences. Again, the narrator, who appears to have an extensive knowledge of the Andalusian bandits, informs the reader that these men also target the upper classes, while Pepona and her men target small businessmen and peasants. As the subject of the clergy is introduced in the narrative, the widespread suspicion

---

29 English translations of "La capitana" are by Robert M. Fedorchek.

is voiced that they are clandestine hoarders of wealth and therefore deserve punishment.

The narrative style changes at this point as the first-person narration (with its single point of view on the subject) gives way to an omniscient third-person account which will relate Pepona's demise as a bandit. It begins with an emphasis on her seemingly mysterious hatred of the clergy, and the non-factual statement that they may have given her the Pepa a Loba nickname. The text focusses on the local clergy, "la gente tonsurada" (2: 344), (referring to their distinctive hairstyle) in general, and a new, young and naïve priest in particular who is remarkably confident about his ability to physically overcome any woman, even the legendary bandit. This self-confidence sets him at odds with his clerical companions. Unlike these men, he has no fear of traveling at night, armed with his pistols and a tobacco knife. The final section of the narrative describes his unexpected encounter with Pepona, where Pardo Bazán ventures away from a credible historical account into fiction, thus making the "rhetoric of the retelling" of the figure of the bandit her own (Pérez "Subversion" 38).

As the priest rides home one night, against the advice of his fellow clerics, he becomes increasingly unnerved as he discovers that Pepona is also on the road. At first, he mistakes the tall, muscular figure for a beggar, and is surprised when hailed by a rude hand gesture. A fast and furious encounter follows: the priest, offended by the gesture and now frightened, pulls a gun, the sight of which sends the "wolf woman" running. The priest now appears to recognize his opponent, hunts her down, and she wrestles with him, almost throttling him. The Realist prose describing this sequence leaves little to the imagination of the reader: "El pinar, el cielo, el aire, cambiaron de color para el pobre abad. Primero lo vio todo rojo, luego, grandes círculos cárdenos y violáceos vibraron ante sus ojos, que se salían de las órbitas" [Pine grove, sky, and air all changed color for the hapless cleric. First, he saw everything red, then big purple and violet rings danced in front of his eyes, which were popping out of their sockets] (2: 346). Somehow, the semi-conscious cleric located his knife and stabbed Pepona as she gloated over her victory.

The narrative ending has similarities with a traditional fairytale. Pepona recovers, but "su ánimo quedó quebrantado, su prestigio enflaquecido, deshecha su leyenda" [her spirit was broken, her prestige undermined, and her legend destroyed] (2: 346). A new police superintendent and his men turn on Pepona and her *bandidos* with an impact that quashes their activities. Following that incident peace reigns, and all the priests are able to travel safely at night to their residences. One can imagine readers quietly adding "y todos vivieron felices para siempre..." [and they all lived happily ever after].

The lifestyles of Galician *mujeres fuertes* often breached the lenient gender behavioral patterns of the province, but a female leader of a male bandit gang is arguably one of the most extreme examples. The story gives no indication of the difficult life that Pepona had negotiated before being presented as the central protagonist of this story, as an established *bandido* leader with an organized, finely judged *modus operandi*. Her imprisonment in the 1860s was noted by Arenal, and the real-life Pepona's upbringing was sad, harsh and difficult, but far from unusual for the times. Nevertheless, Pardo Bazán chooses to omit this background and thus avoids using her backstory in a didactic manner. Pardo Bazán herself was unsympathetic to the unjust activities of Galician bandits; indeed, in a newspaper article she described one, Mahmed Casanova, as merely a common criminal (Patiño Eirín 905).

Pepona is not treated sympathetically in this story, and Pardo Bazán's antipathy toward opportunist robbery could well be the reason. Pepona is introduced to the reader in a paradoxical manner: "Aquellos que consideran a la mujer un ser débil y vinculan en el sexo masculino el valor y las dotes de mando, debieran haber conocido a la célebre Pepona" [Those who consider women frail creatures and equate bravery and leadership with the masculine sex should have become acquainted with the renowned Pepona] (2: 343). Her imposing physical presence has been mentioned and, as the story progresses, this image is reinforced. However, in a few short sentences Pardo Bazán overturns this and re-writes her as a hunted and frightened prey. As a gun points in Pepona's direction, her facial expression changes: "[S]e pintó una especie de terror animal, el espanto del lobo cogido en la trampa" [on her face a kind of animal terror was depicted—the fright of the wolf caught in the trap] (2: 345-46). Animal-like, her instinct is not to fight, but to flee. A misjudgment in her moment of victory after the ensuing physical confrontation almost costs her her life. This final scene, in contrast to the body of the text, is purely fictional and serves to leave the reader with an image of a chastened Pepona, a woman who has finally been censured for her violent and immoral lifestyle.

"La capitana" was first published in *Blanco y Negro*. The narrative style and graphic content of "La capitana" is in accordance with the magazine's criteria (that were noted in Chapter 2), with Pardo Bazán's depictions of various Galician rural lifestyles including the timid priests, and local customs, such as the town fairs, the holiday fair of August 15th and the detailing of the inn's menu—"excelente vino viejo y un cocido monumental de chorizo, jamón y oreja" [an outstanding old wine and a monumental stew of pork sausage, ham, and pig's ear] (2: 345).

The figure of Pepona herself, a woman who chose the lifestyle of a *bandida*, forging a life at the margins of her society, behaving like a man and answerable to nobody, is in stark contrast to a bourgeois *ángel del hogar*, unable to act meaningfully for herself. The literary images presented in "La capitana" all offer a challenge to the sophisticated worldview held by the majority of Pardo Bazán's urban readers. Additionally, the tale's ending, with its graphic description of the *cura* being throttled and the unexpected irony of the *marimacho* [manly woman] being conquered by "una madamita de cura mozo" [a dandy of a young priest] (2: 346) would satisfy the voyeurism of the readers seeking an "aspecto gráfico de la actualidad" [a graphic description of reality]. Ultimately, the magazine's readers are left with the reassuring thought that even in Galicia, a province with a reputation for crime and lawlessness, societal good may, in the end, prevail over wickedness, and even the most barbaric of women can be restrained.

The narrative also offers similarities with other stories discussed in this chapter (such as the recognizable "santa de Karnar"), here providing a popular, readable account of a recent legendary Galician woman who deliberately and violently breaks the law of the land. Likewise, in the following stories, a different Pepona, the protagonist of "Un destripador de antaño", and María Silveria, the protagonist of "La hoz" by implication, also commit criminal acts. In common with "El aire cativo", the ending of "La capitana" unexpectedly destroys the myth of the invincible woman that both the figures of Pepona and Camila have built up in the reader's mind. With these stories, Pardo Bazán demonstrates that life for a *mujer fuerte* in Galicia with its traditional, superstitious and ultimately male-dominated society could take sudden and unexpected turns, with life-changing outcomes, as is vividly illustrated in the next narrative, "La hoz".

Paredes Núñez's "Indice Alfabético" (4: 432) states that "La hoz" first appeared in 1922 in Pardo Bazán's *Cuentos de la tierra*, a posthumous collection of fifty, largely rural, Galician stories, but it was published over fifteen years earlier, in 1907, in the Buenos Aires literary magazine *Caras y Caretas*. Set in a coastal Galician village near Marineda, the narrative centers on three women, all of whom have a different relationship with the male protagonist—his mother, his girlfriend and his ostentatious new female acquaintance. "La hoz" is a Realist narrative, depicting experiences, activities and emotions objectively, with little authorial intervention. The open ending, however, pivots into Naturalism, with the implication of an impending brutal and bloody murder, subtly hinted at both in the title and throughout the narrative. At the end the reader is forced to choose between imagined occurrences, the first, and most compelling, being that María Silveria attacks her rival and probably murders her. This scenario provides coherence and connection to the disturbing narrative. Another possibility is that the bloodshed is somehow avoided, but either way, there will be a violent scene. Montserrat Ribao Pereira suggests that it is because of the unsavory ending that it was accepted by *Caras y Caretas*, as Argentinian readers of the time particularly sought out stories about women "enloquecidas por el amor propio herido" [driven mad by love] (63).

Alfonso Rey points out that in many stories included in *Cuentos de la tierra*, there is scarcely any action, and a plot is almost non-existent; it is the clash of the various protagonists with their distinct perspectives that shape the narrative (26-27), and I maintain that this is true for "La hoz". Pardo Bazán develops the story with dialog, monolog, indirect speech, and colloquial language, creating a psychological study that exposes the protagonists from within, revealing their motives and thus creating a heightening tension as each protagonist is introduced and the conflict is developed (Rey 25). The carefully crafted narrative introduces the mother, Casildona, who ponders her past, and her cosseting and idolization of her only child, Avelino. Her immediate focus is on him as he is again late for the mid-day meal; she is fully aware of the reason: "Allá estaría en el playazo de Areal, bañándose y ayudando a bañarse a la forastera de la ropa maja" [He would be at the beach at Areal swimming, along with the "outsider" who wore pretty clothes] (3: 290). As she endeavors to rationalize his behavior, a miscellany of barely coherent memories surface: her devotion to Avelino, who in her eyes can do no wrong, and his idle drunkard of a father, a man of good parentage, a "hidalgo de Dordasí" [a gentleman from Dordasí] (3: 291). In reality, Avelino's father was a serial philanderer whom she forced into marriage with threats of violence when she realized that she was carrying Avelino. Later, after the birth, he expected her to support everyone else by toiling as a farm laborer, "la bestia de cargar" [a beast of burden] (3: 291). The narratorial comment that "un confuso instinto de jerarquía social se alzaba en el espíritu de Casildona" [confused sentiments concerning social hierarchy arose in Casildona's mind] (3: 291) explains her unrealistic hopes for Avelino's future as she places him in an office position where he is "sentado a la sombra, lavadas las manos" [working in the shade, with the opportunity to wash his hands] (3: 291), as befits his supposedly superior social status. The cleanliness of Avelino's workday surroundings provides a contrast to his home, described repeatedly with references to its bare, dusty brown earth.

Casildona suspects, as the townsfolk have insinuated, that Avelino has not been detained at work but is at the beach, swimming naked with his employer's mistress: "la de la sombrilla encarnada y los zapatos de moñete, colorados también" [the woman with the red umbrella and the expensive red shoes] (3: 290). In this sentence Pardo Bazán introduces the overarching motif of the tale—the color red, in the sunshade and the shoes, that presages the implied conclusion. María Jesús Fariña Busto observes that "[e]s destacable el gusto de Pardo Bazán por el uso de objetos que actúan como detonantes de la situación nuclear de una trama", illustrating this by referencing Pardo Bazán's violent story, "Las medias rojas", where red stockings are a symbol heralding violence and bloodshed (576). In "La hoz" the word "red" is emphasized throughout the story with multiple references to "zapatos colorados", "medias coloradas", "la sombrilla ... roja", "los pies ... encarnados ... dos capullos de amapola", "la de los zapatos bermejos" [red shoes, red stockings, a red umbrella, feet shod in red shoes, like poppy buds, the woman with the reddish shoes] (3: 292-94). As Fariña Busto suggests, such a symbolic emphasis, like that in "Las medias rojas", indicates that the ending of "La hoz" will in all probability also be bloody.

After Casildona's introductory reminiscences, Pardo Bazán's narrative is linear, with each literary scene self-contained while building on the previous scenes. María Silveria, a third female protagonist, appears in the yard with a large basket on her head, filled with freshly cut hay and a scythe, (the "hoz" of the title), hastily thrown on the top. The reader learns that she is an acquaintance of Avelino, thus introducing the possibility of a problematic "love triangle". The reason she gives for her unexpected arrival—that her load is heavy, and she is sweating—is quickly seen as a pretext and Casildona, aware of the rumors about Avelino, is less than welcoming. Nevertheless, María Silveria holds the upper hand, with news that stuns a disbelieving Casildona. Not only is there another woman in Avelino's life, one who wears red shoes and stockings, but he has also been dismissed from his job. This was bound to happen, she says, because of his inappropriate relationship with that woman: "Ni se escondían; en la playa se juntaban, escandalizando. Una poca vergüenza se juntar allí, a bañarse sin ropa." [They did not even hide; there they were, on the beach It's scandalous and shameful to be there together, swimming naked] (3: 292).

The degree to which Casildona defers to Avelino becomes apparent as she warns María Silveria not to discuss any of this with him and, as she speaks, another scenario opens, with the arrival of the previously mentioned lovers. Avelino is obviously infatuated with the woman who is described by the narrator as *raida* [seedy], older than he is, not particularly pretty and with dyed hair (292). Avelino, however, is only looking at her small, elegant feet, shod in red high-heeled shoes. And, almost in shame, Casildona and María Silveria, "la abandonada celosa" [the abandoned, jealous friend] (3: 292), both compare these tiny feet, like small poppy buds, with their own: "descalzas ... deformados, atezados, recios, se confundían con el terruño pardusco de la corraliza, en cuyo ángulo, al calor del sol, hedía el estercolero" [unshod ... deformed, tanned and strong, blending in with the brownish earth of the courtyard, in corner of which, in the heat of the sun, was a stinking dunghill] (3: 292). The surprise arrival leaves Casildona stunned, while a brood of newborn chicks peck at the incomer's red shoes and the household hen rushes to protect her babies from this interloper—just as Casildona wishes to protect her son.

María Silveria, still in the yard just outside the house and unable to leave without being seen, sits behind her basket and unavoidably eavesdrops on the couple's interactions with Casildona. Avelino, "niño mimado y hombre un poco más afinado" [the spoiled child and now only a slightly more refined man] (3: 293), has Casildona under his thumb. He demands a meal, before informing his mother that the woman has come to stay as she has been ordered out of her lover's house, a man whom Avelino will kill if he appears (thus imitating his own mother's murderous impulse towards his father as she forced him into marriage). Continuing incoherently, he informs his mother at this point that if he cannot obtain new employment in Marineda, the next day, he will simply leave for America, presumably leaving the woman with Casildona. Here Pardo Bazán reiterates the Galician reality that men have the option, largely denied to women, of solving immediate problems by sailing to America and leaving those left behind to deal with the consequences.

When Avelino finally sees María Silveria she is behind her basket, crying in misery. Unsurprisingly, she is bitter and sarcastic when asked why she is there: "Ver cómo pasan los hombres que perdieron la vergüenza de la cara. Eso es lo que hago aquí, Avelino de azúcar" [I'm looking to see what the face of a shameful man looks like — that's what I'm doing here—Sugar] (3: 294). The narrative now focusses on María Silveria helplessly shaking her fist at the retreating Avelino, burning with rage and despair. She insults him again, as he passes by a second time, with a glass of water for the woman: "Anda, anda a servir a la de los zapatos rojos. Que te pise el alma con ellos, a ver si tienes alma, Avelino de azúcar... ¿Te acuerdas del molino de Pepe Rey? ¿Te acuerdas lo que parolamos?" [Quick, quick, serve the lady with the red shoes. Let her tread on your soul with them and we'll see if you have a soul—Sugar—do you remember Pepe Rey's mill? Do you remember what we talked about?] (3: 294). The reference to the mill, a place where village social evenings often ended amorously for couples, is a second Galician trope that indicates that María Silveria obviously feels that she and Avelino had an understanding about the seriousness of their relationship. A relationship that the interloper has now shattered and, as Quesada Novás suggests, the relationship was clearer perhaps in her mind than Avelino's (108). Picking up her reference to the red shoes, Avelino simply brushes her off and tells her to get her own shoes if that will make her happy, while making sure that not a drop of water spills from the glass that he is carrying. Here, with the story finely balanced, the Spanish proverb "la gota que derramó el vaso" [the drop that caused the glass of water to overflow] comes to mind. María Silveria, who is depicted "como gato montés o tejón salvaje acosado por cazadores" [like an untamed cat or a wild badger harassed by hunters] (3: 294), reaches breaking point. Avelino's comments, that final *gota,* determine their respective fates.

Pardo Bazán uses indirect free speech to transmit María Silveria's train of thought to the reader.[30] As she looks heavenward, protesting the injustice of the situation, her reasoning falters. Before God, she believes that she has never wronged anyone, and a woman who uses red shoes to deliberately entice another's boyfriend has sinned grievously, and with that conclusion, she has her answer. With her experience and skill in reaping grass with a scythe, one swing would be enough to deal to "la mala hierba" [the unwanted weed].

In *Crafting the Female Subject: Narrative Innovation in the Short Fiction of Emilia Pardo Bazán,* McKenna writes at length about closure in Pardo Bazán's short stories and considers that a shocking, defiant closing narrative gesture, carried out by a woman, challenges the accepted culturally constructed notion of gender and also rewrites the traditional feminine stereotype. These defiant endings, McKenna explains, rely on dialogic exchange and depend on the dynamic interplay between author, text and reader to provide an alternative ending positioned within the story/plot itself (100). In "La hoz", it is María Silveria who, out of desperation and jealousy, takes an audacious and shocking action, placing her at the forefront of the reader's consciousness as the narrative closes. McKenna suggests that with a closure such as

---

30   Cuddon defines this as a presentation of thoughts which seem to combine the characters sentiments with those of the narrator. Ambiguity is created when the author's hand in the passage is not clearly marked out from the voice of the character (330).

this, "Pardo Bazán has re-inscribed a conventional short story narrative in a way that forces the reader to construct a logical conclusion to the story" (7).

By the end of the story, María Silveria could be considered the villain. However, she feels deceived by the public, risqué behavior of Avelino with a woman who is unlikely even to be aware of María Silveria's existence. And in addition, Casildona, knowing that María Silveria was nearby, yielded ingratiatingly to the commands from her son. The circumstances that lead to the assumed tragedy, caused by the interactions of the mother, Avelino and his companion, reveal a new reality for María Silveria. Overwhelmed by this new knowledge she sees only one way forward and makes her decision accordingly. She walks from the yard towards the house with her scythe hidden under her apron.

The logical ending, engineered by Pardo Bazán's narrative strategy and imagined by most readers, abruptly shifts the text from Realist to Naturalist writing. This story follows the pattern of Pardo Bazán's typical Naturalistic narrations described by Charnon-Deutsch—a series of actions are depicted which lead up to an act of extreme violence. It is these actions that determine the outcome of the story, rather than the innate tendencies of the protagonist, and this appears to hold true for "La hoz". María Silveria, in making her fateful decision to act, has also followed the point that was noted earlier, that "free-will, or the exercise of it, is an essential feature of Pardo Bazán's form of Naturalism, and no matter how adverse the environmental circumstances, characters always act with free will" (Charnon-Deutsch *Strategies* 85). For the reader, "La hoz"'s Naturalism stops short of murder, but in the last story of the chapter, "Un destripador de antaño", Naturalistic impulses culminating in a brutal murder are at the heart of the plot; it is regarded as one of Pardo Bazán's most violent tales.

This final story of the trio, "Un destripador de antaño" is, at heart, a Gothic horror story, whose title foretells its outcome; it is the only narrative in this selection to employ this style. In it, Pardo Bazán re-works a cautionary Galician legend about a destripador, a story that she recalled from tales told years before, intended to frighten children. Her story first appeared in 1890 in *La España Moderna*, a magazine that had already published many of Pardo Bazán's feminist essays. Many of her works, including this narrative, show a "personal sensibility impossible to detangle from her preoccupation with the rights of women" (Aldana Reyes 118) and, in this light, "Un destripador de antaño" with its feminist sub-text, was well suited for circulation in this magazine. Two years later the story was included in Pardo Bazán's *Historias y cuentos de Galicia*.

In *fin de siècle* Spain *destripadores*, or *destripadoras* as in this tale, (murderers who disemboweled their victims), were both legendary figures, and an unwelcome presence in coeval European society, with Jack the Ripper's widely publicized acts having terrorized London only months earlier. In 1910 Pardo Bazán published an article in *La Ilustración Artística* about the life, confession and death of one such Spanish offender; just one of many, as she informs her readers (no. 831, p.770). Pardo Bazán's article is one of several pertaining to rural Galician barbarism in *La Ilustración Artística* and confirms the public's voyeuristic appetite for tales of such crimes (Paredes Núñez *Realidad* 250-53).

In "Un destripador de antaño" the *curandero*, dispensing from his underground lair, is a central figure. In 1631 Tirso de Molina, in *La Gallega Mari-Hernández*, proclaimed that "Galicia es tan fértil en dar brujas como nabos" [Galicia is as plentiful in witches as it is in turnips], and little changed during the next couple of centuries. Witches, *curanderos*, shamans and other practitioners of folk magic, a universal phenomenon, are common in regions pervaded by ancient myths and legends. (Taboada Chivite 209). Spanish *curanderos*, (abundant, if Tirso de Molina is to be believed), with their mystical potions and unguents, hinder societal progress and, in Paredes Núñez's opinion, this is particularly evident in Galicia (*Realidad* 223). However, Paredes Núñez considers Pardo Bazán to be unexpectedly ambivalent in her dealings with this topic. Normally, he argues, she speaks for progress and science, and she works hard to teach and spread this message, yet she gives apparent credence to superstition in several of her Galician stories such as "El aire cativo" and "La caja de oro" (1894). Other tales, however, such as "Un destripador de antaño", highlight the dangers associated with the practice of *curanderismo* (Paredes Núñez *Realidad* 223, 227), as does a later tale, "Curado" (1903). In the latter story the *curandero* himself ensures the victim's death before being gifted the body by the grieving family, with a tacit understanding that the roles of *curandero* and destripador are intertwined, and that the body may be used for nefarious purposes.

We earlier noted Kilgour's point that the Gothic, rather than depicting character, creates a feeling or effect in the reader by placing them amidst a state of thrilling suspense and uncertainty" (6). "Un destripador de antaño" creates just such a tension from the beginning of the text, but I would add that this story does also achieve significant character development of several of the main protagonists.

"Un destripador de antaño" (1890) is a complex four-section Gothic narrative preceded by an introduction, which discloses that the tale is based on the legend of the destripador who "[v]olvió a aparecérseme, como fantasmagórica creación de Hoffmann" [appeared to me again, like a ghostly creation of Hoffmann] (2: 5).[31] It also references Victor Hugo's protagonist Quasimodo,[32] and newspaper entries, perhaps calling to Pardo Bazán's contemporaneous reader's mind Jack the Ripper. These references confirm that this story will be "a Galician version on a Gothic theme" (Six 105), filled with superstition, terror and mysticism. With the narrator's command—"Entrad conmigo valerosamente en la zona de sombra del alma" [Be brave! Come with me into the soul's shadow] (2: 5)—the reader is prepared for a ghoulish tale. The sinister introduction acts as a frame for the impersonal third-person embedded narrative that follows (H. Porter Abbott 234) and with this literary device Pardo Bazán distances herself in the eyes of the reader from the embedded story and its, by now expected, graphic subject.

The narrative, set in the early 1800s, opens unassumingly, with a typically *costumbrista* view of a Galician village, Tornelos,[33] its mill with its "pobre casuca de los molineros" [miller's meager hut] (2: 6), and an idyllic description of the teenaged, auburn haired Minia, a central protagonist in the tale, sitting in a field quietly watching over contented cattle. However, this peaceful pastoral setting proves to be a ploy to lull the reader into a false sense of normalcy before the shock that will come as the tale progresses from this "quaintly antiquated rural superstition into a horror story" (Six 167). The reader encounters customary Gothic tropes throughout the narrative: a wicked stepmother, forests, wolves, fog and thunderstorms. Several lesser-known tropes are also present: a subterranean alchemist in his *rebotica*, complete with a rumored *trapela* above a pit, a secret underground workshop where supposedly proscribed ointments are prepared, and secrets which haunt characters psychologically. Pardo Bazán has also left open the possibility that the earthly laws of conventional reality and the supernatural connect when Minia is murdered and enveloped by her saintly doppelgänger. Abigail Lee Six, in her analysis of the story, discusses a trope in the text where the principal characters are confronted with gross violence, "explicitly

---

31   The Hoffmann reference also reinforces Montague Summers's later observation that "a huge majority [sic] of terror-Gothic stories owe their influence to German sources" (31).

32   Victor Hugo, *Le Bossu de Notre Dame* (1831).

33   Tornelos is fictional; however, the Galician town of Brión, 13 kms east of Santiago de Compostela, is a likely setting. The wax covered skeleton of Santa Minia, complete with a replica of the throat wound which caused her death, is situated in the parish church of Brión.

shattering the assumed norms ... of everyday life with wildly shocking, and even revolting, consequences" (3) and, as the narrative concludes, a further Gothic trope, that of the morally corrupt priest (expounded on by Diane Long Hoeveler 98-146), is also introduced.

The four numbered sections of the story can be likened to acts in a drama, with each having a discrete setting and theme. The first section introduces the rural miller, Pepona, and her family. She is the main female protagonist, and her decisions, made in desperation, have extreme consequences both for herself and for her family. The second, which foregrounds the Gothic horror aspects of the tale, is largely rural and relates a series of events that take place during a drought; the third section, (set in the *rebotica* of the reputed *curandero* Don Custodio in Santiago de la Compostela), consists mainly of a personal conversation between Custodio and Canon Llorente that offers a strikingly different perspective on the information that the reader has been given thus far. The brief final section details the fates of three of the protagonists and offers a further damning insight into the character of a fourth.

In the first section Minia, a miller's daughter, is introduced sympathetically as a pretty, red-haired, waif-like teenager, named for and closely resembling the figure of the local saint, Minia.[34] The *costumbrista* narrator observes that, if she were glimpsed during the day as she watched the cattle in the meadow, she would be the centerpiece of a typically idyllic pastoral scene. Orphaned in infancy, she lives with her uncle, Juan Ramón and his girlfriend Pepona, together with their own two children. The couple had quickly appropriated the mill when Minia's parents died; however, Ramón, a heavy drinker proves to be averse to steady employment and looks for casual work which, unfortunately, fails to adequately support either his imbibing or his family. Pepona who appears unafraid of hard work, becomes both the miller and the family gardener.

Minia's status as a Cinderella-style figure in this family is tragic. Seen as a liability, she is given the most menial tasks, sleeps on sacks by the fire and is almost starved. She stoically suffers the consequences of her uncle's frequent drunken and violent rages and her one solace in life comes from an affinity with her namesake saint, Minia, a teenaged Roman martyr, whose wax-en-

---

34 Known details of the Roman Saint Herminia (Minia) largely correspond with those given in the text, namely her resting place, appearance and attire, and the direct cause of her teenaged martyrdom, a severed throat. One inconsistency, however, is that this fictional story is set sometime between 1801–05 but Minia's body did not arrive in Brión until 1848. See https://www.atlasobscura.com/places/the-shrine-of-santa-minia-brion-spain.

cased bones lie at the front of the parish church and whom she visits on patronal festivals, returning "ensimismada y absorta" [absorbed and entranced] (2: 7). Each evening, she prays to Saint Minia that the saint would remove her from her miserable existence and take her to heaven, even dreaming one night that the saint is by her side and kills her callous aunt and uncle. The extent of the trauma caused to Minia by her stepparents is brutally described as the section closes. The previous, serene, pastoral scene is an illusion with Minia being an "infeliz niña golpeada y hambrienta, medio idiota ya a fuerza de desamores y crueldades" [unhappy child, beaten, starved and brain-damaged because of the hate and cruelty that she had endured (2: 10). She has now become "la victima propicitoria" [the scapegoat] (2: 10) for all the ills of the destitute family. With the closure of this first section Pardo Bazán indicates to the reader that the rest of her tale will not be a gentle *costumbrista* narrative, but rather a Naturalist portrayal of Galician rural life.

Pepona works hard to make up for Ramón's misuse of the family's income, but a year of drought, with no corn or wheat harvested, brings the family's financial problems to a head. Ramón, in desperation, even contemplates robbing the parish alms box or searching the priest's residence for gold. A Galician *campesino* seldom owns land and the landlords are rarely lenient when rent is overdue (Paredes Núñez *Realidad* 100). With no money for rent and eviction from the mill looming, it falls to Pepona to set out for Santiago de Compostela to meet the landowners and plead for leniency. A chance meeting with Jacoba, an apparently equally poor neighbor, on the journey provides both women an opportunity for conversation and gossip as they undertake the long journey to and from Compostela.

Their conversation takes an unexpected and ominous turn as they discuss Jacoba's mission. She is to visit Don Custodio's locally feared *botica* to purchase a miraculous unguent for her husband. She assumes that Pepona is also aware of the rumors circulating about the pharmacy, and the origins of the ointment in particular which, in Jacoba's opinion, is God's remedy for a myriad of serious afflictions in the community. As Jacoba shows Pepona the precious gold dubloon she will use for the purchase, a fortune for a poor rural family, Pepona is overwhelmed, being "deslumbrada por la vista del doblón y sintiendo en el alma una oleada tal de codicia que la sofocaba casi" [dazzled by the sight of the gold coin and feeling a covetousness rising from her inmost soul so strongly that it almost choked her] (2: 13).

Pepona fails to resolve her debts with the landowner, and on her despondent return journey Jacoba enlightens her about Custodio's business. They had both visited "la temerosa madriguera" [the sinister lair] (2: 13) of Custodio, and Jacoba mentions its *trapela* [trapdoor] through which two young red-headed girls, Custodio's maids, are rumored to have disappeared. Custodio is a *destripador*, Jacoba informs Pepona, and the body fat of the missing young women is used for the costly remedy.[35] At this point in the narrative Minia's fate is sealed.

On the return journey night falls as the women are passing through a forest. Church bells peal faintly in the distance and a ghostly mist rises from the river and, as they converse, they recall a child who had been devoured by wolves. When Pepona finally arrives home, she attempts to talk with the barely sober Ramón. By now it is midnight but Minia, still not asleep, is aware of their furious whispering, when suddenly Pepona orders her to the stable area. Half-awake half-asleep, she prayed her nightly prayer: "Santa Minia querida, llévame pronto al Cielo; pronto, pronto..." [Beloved Saint Minia, take me soon to heaven, soon, soon] (2: 16). At this point the reader is told that Minia may have really been sleeping, or she may have fallen into "ese estado mixto propicio a las visiones, a las revelaciones psicológicas y hasta a las revoluciones físicas" [that trance-like state which leads to visions, revelations and even physical changes] (2: 16).

In this state the effigy of the fourth-century saint, prone in her glass case in the church appears to Minia, but "no era la Santa; era ella misma, la pobre rapaza huérfana de todo amparo, quien estaba allí tendida en la urna de cristal, entre los cirios, en la iglesia" [it was not the saint: it was herself, the poor young girl, bereft of all protection, who was stretched out there in church, in the glass case surrounded by candles] (2: 16): Her appearance is now identical to that of the saint, with a crown of roses on her head and she is wearing the same green brocade tunic and holding a palm frond in her cold, white hands. Her neck bears the same bleeding wound as the saint's. One last sigh escapes her lips then: "puso los ojos en blanco, se estremeció..., y quedóse completamente inerte. Su última impresión confusa fue que ya había llegado al cielo, en compañía de la Patrona" [her eyes went blank, she shuddered ... and was motionless. Her last confused impression was that she had arrived in heaven, accompanied by her Patron Saint] (2: 16). With this dramatic scene the arcadian section of the narrative closes. Minia's fate is hinted at—not explained but surely guessed.

The introduction references Hoffmann, and I delineate the evidence in Pardo Bazán's text to show that the murder scene evinces one of Hoffmann's prevalent Gothic tropes, that of the doppelgänger. Andrew J. Webber introduces doppelgängers as a "complicated conflict between realism and fantasy

---

35   See Boyer, p. 247 n. 1 for a discussion on this subject.

... [where] the 'real' is duplicated as phantasm in such a way as to defy distinction. ... The doppelgänger embodies a dislocation in time, always coming after its proper event ... it resists categorical literary-historical identification. [It resists] temporal change by stepping out of time and then stepping back in as revenant" (9-10). Throughout the story, Minia's likeness to the effigy of the saint and the girl's affinity to Saint Minia has been repeatedly mentioned and I postulate that the events surrounding Minia's death follow Webber's characterization. However, as in two previous stories, "El aviso" and "El cinco de copas", Pardo Bazán has provided ambiguity; in this case it is possible that, in the blurred state between wakefulness and sleep, Minia was perhaps simply dreaming.

A surface reading of the plot so far suggests an obvious conclusion, but the third section reveals that the truth is more complicated and, I suggest, open to interpretation. The setting is Custodio's *botica* (with the text pointedly noting the absence of a *trapela*) and consists of a conversation between Custodio and a further protagonist, Don Lucas Llorente, a canon of the nearby cathedral. This conversation is at the heart of the story, explaining the origins of the pharmacy's expensive miraculous ointment, revealing unexpected facets of the two mens' characters and reinforcing the inferior social status of *campesinos* that led to Pepona's actions. An examination of the relationship between the two men discloses a further Gothic device, the "controller" and the "controlled".

Llorente is Custodio's "constante amigo e íntimo confidente" [loyal friend and intimate confidante] (2: 16), however the friendship appears to be very one-sided. Custodio is portrayed as open, emotional and almost naïve, while Llorente is described as "la quinta esencia del misterio" [the epitome of mystery] with a personal motto: "Que nadie sepa cosa alguna de ti." [Let no one know anything at all about you] (2: 16). Surely, in this context, "la quinta esencia del misterio" is a play on words, with the "fifth essence" being the medieval alchemist's objective [Moran 11]). (2: 16). Custodio voices disappointment at Llorente's previous advice to him concerning his past behavior, including his maids' mysterious departures (the reader could be forgiven at this point for thinking that their leaving may have been due to unexpected pregnancies). And, importantly, we learn it was Llorente who emboldened him to enrich himself with his remedy: "Que crean que usted fabrica sus ungüentos con grasa de difunto ... [c]úrense las enfermedades, y crean los imbéciles que es por arte de birlibirloque ...[e]s y será eternamente un hatajo de babiecas, una recua de jumentos" [Let them go on believing that you make your ointment out of human fats ... cure their illnesses and let the imbeciles believe you do it by magic ... they're a lot of simpletons and they always will be, a herd of asses] (2: 17).

The *boticario* recounts that Pepona, now revealed as a *destripadora*, had covertly visited Custodio to sell cadaver fat from her virginal red-headed niece. Thunder rolls as he plaintively asks Llorente: "¿Comprende la mancha que sobre mí ha caído? Soy el terror de las aldeas, el espanto de las muchachas y el ser más aborrecible y más cochino que puede concebir la imaginación" [Do you understand the stigma that surrounds me? I am seen as the ogre of the villages, the murderer of young girls and the most loathsome and nasty creature that an imagination can conjure up] (2: 18). Llorente laughs, and cajoles him as if he were a child, until he realizes that Custodio has told Pepona that there was no such ointment. Llorente reassures him that the girl will not be dead and so, trusting his purported friend, Custodio sets out to rescue Minia, only to discover her mutilated body in the forest where Pepona had abandoned it to the wolves.

Jacoba and Pepona's visit to the *botica* left the reader with an image of a taciturn but confident Custodio; however, this conversation reveals the influence and control that Llorente has on him, and his weakness is exposed. Control is a common motif in Gothic tales[36]. This argument is that in Custodio, Llorente, who is both a morally corrupt priest and a manipulator, discovered a willing tool who was able to inflict psychological terror and financial duress on the section of society for which the latter appeared to have an almost pathological hatred—the *campesinos*.

Churchmen appear in two stories in this work, Llorente, discussed here, and Baltar, in "El aviso", and both deliver radical statements. Baltar's is against philanderers, and Llorente reveals his utter contempt for the majority of the population that he supposedly pastors and serves. As discussed above, the use of Gothic tropes is a literary strategy that enables a writer to deliver uncomfortable information to their readers and still "keep responsibility for the content at a safe distance from his own standing" (Six 66). I assert that Pardo Bazán used this trope to make a certain point about men and, in particular, priests such as Llorente.

The final section of the text illustrates both the gender and class imbalances in Spain's legal system at that time. All three women in this story are ultimately victims. Minia's status is undeniable. Everything she has, or is entitled to, is taken from her by Pepona and Ramón, who treat her as a slave and

---

36   Two notable examples are Hoffmann's "Der Sandmann" with Coppola's control of his automaton, Olimpia, a work that was familiar to Pardo Bazán, and a later example is Richard Marsh's *The Beetle* (1897).

deny her dignity, respect, freedom and agency, a situation that culminates in her murder and bodily desecration in order to satisfy Pepona's desperation for money. Jacoba too is a victim of both superstition and Custodio's greed. She believes the rumor about the ingredients of the nostrum, and she is reluctant to visit the *botica*, even on the orders of her threatening husband. She knows that her purchase is wrong, (as does her husband), and she crosses herself as she leaves, in fear of God's wrath. She is fearful, too, of her own priest, who will publicly chide her if he learns of this purchase. Jacoba, and many other of Custodio's customers, are victims of his greed and the canon's derision.

Pepona is more complex: a *mujer fuerte*, both a victim and a villain. Despite her strengths as a hard worker and businesswoman, her faults and actions—greed, child abuse, murder and desecration—condemn her. However, her desperation at the near subsistence standard of living of many of Galicia's *campesinos*, is exacerbated by the avarice of a pitiless land-owning class. Pepona is eventually hung for her crimes, while Ramón is merely imprisoned. Custodio, drawn into the legal proceedings, finds that the more he protests his innocence, the less he is believed by country people. Llorente's words, which close the story, underline the priest's own faults: "que veía confirmadas sus doctrinas acerca de la estupidez universal e irremediable" [that he saw his belief confirmed; that stupidity is universal and irremediable] (2: 21).

The reader is left with this misanthropic and unpriestly sentiment. Earlier, following Paredes Núñez, I indicated that Pardo Bazán expected her readership to be civilized, cultured and polite, and her stories present the Galician *campesinos* as primitive and ignorant, offering a contrast between civilization and barbarism. However, in this tale, the bourgeois protagonists, Llorente, the schemer, and Custodio, his passive follower, may well have been polite and cultured, but their actions in deliberately creating and disseminating dangerous falsehoods, and accepting exorbitant amounts of money under false pretenses, are not the mark of civilized men. I contend that they are represented as ultimately being responsible for Minia's death.

Pepona is put to death as punishment for a crime that she did indeed commit, but once again Pardo Bazán has created a female protagonist whose fate is determined, albeit indirectly, by educated bourgeois males. She is a female victim of her society, with her reactions guided by her instincts and not by personal, religious or societal morals. By using the Gothic mode, Pardo Bazán has been able to articulate an unpalatable vision of the different classes of Galician society that would not be acceptable to her readers if they were presented in a Realist manner (Aldana Reyes 113, 118).

Paredes Núñez asserts that when writing about Galicia, Pardo Bazán provides the reader with an appraisal of her province that is realistic and, at times, cool and impartial. He also comments that Spanish city dwellers tend to see themselves as civilized, cultured and well-mannered, while regarding countryfolk as primitive, ignorant and almost savages (Realidad 248). As "Un destripador de antaño" unfolds, the story reinforces not only this worldview, but it also uncovers the duplicity, hypocrisy and greed of two urban, middle-class residents: a pharmacist, widely considered by the *campesinos* to be a *curandero*, and a cathedral canon. As the two realms, rural and urban, are examined, Pardo Bazán exposes the shortcomings of both. They may differ but, perhaps surprisingly, the faults of the seemingly civilized urban men are in many ways as reprehensible as those of their rural neighbors. As the story was read by educated, well-mannered *madrileños*, it would have reinforced the popular opinion at that time that all Galicians, both rural and urban, were barbaric and mercenary.[37]

Conclusion

In these six narratives Pardo Bazán used the short story form to portray realities of Galician life. She foregrounds the prominent role that the women, none of whom conform to the middle-class *ángel del hogar* stereotype, played in this society, through either deliberate choice ("El aire cativo" and "La capitana") or necessity ("Un destripador de antaño"). "El molino" and "El aire cativo" offer the reader an overview of widely believed Galician myths and legends, the social life that mills can create in a community, the often-spurious reasons for emigration from the province and the primitive and arduous agricultural practices. In addition, these two stories depict confident self-sufficient *mujeres fuertes* who each challenge gendered behavior patterns. Strong and independent Galician women, both rural and urban, also dominate "La santa de Karnar" against the backdrop of a more universal consideration of the faith/reason dichotomy.

These protagonists with their opinions and self-reliance (with only threats of harm towards others) live law-abiding lives. Nevertheless, Galician women could be as violent as their menfolk and the second trio of stories discussed here demonstrate increasingly violent behavior patterns, from highway assault ("La capitana") and unrequited love culminating in jealousy and a probable murder ("La hoz"), to cold-blooded murder driven by both greed and despair ("Un destripador de antaño"). Pardo Bazán does not re-

---

37   See Xesús Alonso Montero's *Galicia vista por los no gallegos* (1974) for numerous literary examples of Galician stereotypes from the 15th century onwards.

frain from confronting the consequences of the actions of these women. I maintain that all the Galician stories in this chapter provide an honest depiction of nineteenth-century Galicia, a depiction similar to that held by Medeiros's informant, as he covertly whispered: "Pardo Bazán was the one who best described rural Galicia" (109). None of the Galician female protagonists resembled the protagonists of the preceding chapters. Rather, their behavior resulted from, and reflected, the challenges that they faced as a result of the unique social and economic pressures of Pardo Bazán's Galicia.

Conclusion

> It isn't what we say or think that defines us,
> but what we do.
>
> - Jane Austen
> *Sense and Sensibility*

The twenty-five Pardo Bazán stories discussed in this volume were written over a period of thirty-six years, the earliest being "La dama joven" published in 1884 and the last, "El árbol rosa" in 1921, a few weeks before Pardo Bazán's death. Among these stories are examples from almost every Spanish literary style, the narrative settings are both rural and urban and, among the female protagonists, every social class is represented. These widely read and broadly acceptable narratives all feature at least one female protagonist who faces challenges that echoed the real-life situations faced by women as they responded to specific gendered inequities in nineteenth-century Spanish society. Four, drawn from the many inequities of that society, have been the focus of this analysis: the Spanish code of honor, the *ángel del hogar* construct, the sexual double standard and *el qué dirán*, the first three of which Pardo Bazán addressed directly in her 1889 essay "The Women of Spain".

These inequities affected all Spanish women to a greater or lesser degree, but for middle-class women, the bourgeoisie, whom Pardo Bazán emphasized in "The Women of Spain", the *ángel del hogar* construct defined their lives and restricted every aspect of their existence. This is particularly relevant in the analyses of the stories in Chapters 2 and 3 where representations of middle-class women predominate. Portrayals of both male and female honor codes occur throughout the stories and their unexpected presence and significance in two of the stories, "El aviso" and "Las cutres", adds an unexpected twist to the outcomes. The sixteenth- and seventeenth-century clerical origins of the honor code included an emphasis on the seclusion of young women, a factor that was still incorporated in the *ángel del hogar* model in *fin de siècle* Spain. One aspect of this seclusion concerned the chaperoning of young couples, and, in Pardo Bazán's courtship stories, we noted some of the difficulties that arose for women resulting from this practice.

The third gendered inequity, the sexual double standard, led to promiscuous behavior in both single and married men being widely accepted, and the deleterious effects that such men had on women's lives can be observed in almost half of the stories analyzed here. At first glance, the fourth inequity, *el qué diran*, appears to be non-gendered. However, in these stories, apart from negative comments directed at persistent Don Juans, Pardo Bazán's representations in this selection of narratives reveal community criticism, speculation and gossip particularly directed towards women, and especially single women who do not conform to neighborhood behavioral expectations. Ongoing neighborhood gossip is foregrounded in a pair of stories discussed in Chapter 3 and is prominent in most of the Galician tales. Here, urban and rural women of any age and class who are identified as victims by their communities are targeted by "everybody", but "nobody in particular", thus leaving them with no easy way in which to defend themselves.

As we noted in the opening chapter, from about 1890 onwards, Pardo Bazán's absolute rejection of these historic and widespread gendered mores translated into direct action. When her ambitious, carefully planned and personally funded *Biblioteca de la mujer* became a reality in 1892, she signaled that she was serious about disseminating her feminist ideas. Nevertheless, a print run of 3,000 copies of each book in the series, with only the first of the nine titles selling well, meant that the exercise would inevitably fail to meet her expectations. The project's early demise demonstrated that the Spanish public would not readily accept Pardo Bazán's frank feminist presentations that challenged the very fabric of patriarchal society, and she reluctantly accepted this reality. Her literary magazine *Nuevo Teatro Crítico*, launched a year earlier, was not a financial success either. However, this venture firmly established her credentials in the Spanish literary world as a notable literary critic and, with the inclusion of more than thirty of her short stories in various editions, it also promoted her as a serious practitioner of the short story.

Pardo Bazán's short story writing had, in fact, commenced decades earlier with the publication in 1866 of "Un matrimonio del siglo XIX", although she wrote few narratives in this genre during the next two decades. From the 1880s onwards Pardo Bazán's stories, including many that fictionalized her society's patriarchal mores and their deleterious effects on women, appeared in widely circulated newspapers and literary journals, most with substantial readerships and, in the 1890s, in her own publications. The success that these short stories achieved, including those directly or indirectly advocating for gendered equality, contrasted notably with the above-mentioned limited success of the more direct promulgation of her feminist ideas through her essays and through the commercial feminist publications that formed her Biblioteca. From the 1890s onwards, her short story output increased markedly, and in retrospect, her short stories can now arguably be seen to have been her most effective channel of dissemination for her feminist ideas.

The short stories that are analyzed in this book, apart from the few taken either from Spanish history or from the depths of Pardo Bazán's fertile imagination, do undoubtably reflect the lives of a variety of fictional women from all social classes in late nineteenth- and early twentieth-century Spanish society. In "The Women of Spain", Pardo Bazán emphasized that the *fin de siècle* Spanish man wished for a model wife "still the same as she was a hundred years ago". However, Pardo Bazán was a realist and refuted this notion in her stories, where she has depicted contemporary protagonists who differ greatly from the imaginary angelic image in Spanish men's minds. Each of these stories has provided at least one largely proactive female protagonist who confronts personal and contemporaneous societal challenges in their lives. All these women exert their agency in one way or another. Some rise to overcome a particular gender-related challenge, while others fail to do so. Identifying the way Pardo Bazán was able to subvert a seemingly patriarchally acceptable narrative to convey a subversive feminist message to her contemporary readers has formed a major part of these analyses.

Pardo Bazán's "art" as a storyteller enabled her to delineate many gendered inequities in her fictionalization of contemporaneous Spanish society. In hindsight, she is known as a Realist writer, despite her early Naturalistic novels and *La cuestión palpitante*, that in the early 1880s brought her to the forefront of Spain's literary world. Nevertheless, Pardo Bazán had a deep understanding and command of every major literary style, and her ability to shape and slant familiar established Spanish literary conventions to create subversive feminist sub-texts that can be seen in these twenty-five narratives. Most stories can, however, be described as Realist, an obvious and appropriate style to depict the everyday lives of the majority of the female protagonists portrayed in this work.

This observation notwithstanding, in eight of these Realist stories, Pardo Bazán subverted the accepted narratorial convention by substituting a first-person narrator for the customary third-person omniscient voice. In five narratives, "El zapato", "La redada" "El encaje roto", "El aviso" and "La santa de

Karnar", the substitution is overt, with the narrator being introduced at the start of the narrative, while character narrators in "Las cutres", "Coleccionista" and "El cinco de copas" only reveal themselves during the tale. Character narrators impart a personal aspect to the story, although sometimes, as in "El aviso", their knowledge is limited, and they are unable to ascertain all the ramifications of the events that they relate. The character narrators of both "El zapato" and "La redada" are disillusioned men who open the tales. Their self-pitying words provide sufficient information about their mental anguish for a reader to decide that their respective fiancée's responses to these men appear perfectly logical. The remaining Realist stories employ the more usual third-person narration with its implied masculine voice.

Two of these narratives demonstrate Pardo Bazán's ability to subvert even the masculine voice. In "El aviso" and "Un destripador de antaño" the priests, authoritative figures in society, voice radical social views. The former damns philandering men who, in his opinion, cause social mayhem and spread diseases, and the latter, a cathedral canon, voices his utter contempt for Galician *campesinos*, making a mockery of the church's professed concern for the poor and downtrodden who predominate in the province and, by extension, in the church congregations. In the first of these diatribes Pardo Bazán has put her own opinions into words with the figure of the priest being her mouthpiece and, in the second, she voiced negative views on the attitudes of those who controlled Galician land and its *campesinos* who were forced into subsistence farming. Here, a cathedral canon damns himself with his own words. Although these opinions may have been true, they would have been too uncompromising for Pardo Bazán to voice them explicitly in a speech or an essay.

In some of the narratives, Pardo Bazán has either subverted or tweaked a literary style or genre for her own purposes, often providing an unexpected twist. "Comedia" is ostensibly a short, Realist story, but proves to be an apparent reworking of a Golden Age *comedia*, a three act, trope-laden drama. Tropes from this genre that Pardo Bazán incorporated into "Comedia" include: an innocent heroine; a *galán*, both in his real life as an actor and in his seduction of the heroine; the division of the text to represent the three acts; and an unexpected tragic outcome, nevertheless one foreshadowed by the retribution tropes of the theatrical style itself. The *costumbrismo* style of "El molino" provides an example of a subversion of a traditional style. Pardo Bazán used *costumbrismo* sparingly in her writing and, in her hands, a *costumbrista* narrator normally portrayed the scene before him benevolently, recording events with little comment. These texts were unthreatening, fair-minded, easy to read and sometimes verging on moralistic. Pardo Bazán was aware that by using this style for "El molino" she could present an idyllic view of rural Galicia that would be acceptable for a commemorative version of *La Ilustración Artística*. However, even while working within the traditional restrictions of *costumbrista* writing, Pardo Bazán subverted the narrative by presenting a gender-reversal in the figures of the two protagonists, portraying a strong, physical, forceful female miller and her *novio*, a timid, peace-loving unconfrontational male protagonist. This was a strong message indeed for Spain in 1900, but acceptable when disguised in a gentle, "feel-good" story.

Pardo Bazán takes another path as she portrays the female protagonist in "Un destripador de antaño". Rather than glossing over the very real hardships that nineteenth-century Galician women faced, as she did in "El molino", "Un destripador de antaño" confronts familial abuse, deception and a murder followed by bodily desecration, all against a background of oppressive class discrimination. The level of violence depicted in this narrative would have been unacceptable to many readers in a Realist, or even a Naturalist narrative, but couched in a Gothic tale, following the example of Hoffmann himself, the story was ensured a wide readership in 1880s Spain. In "La capitana", which features an intertext with Pardo Bazán's widely read Naturalist novel *Los pazos de Ulloa*, violence is again made more acceptable to Pardo Bazán's readership by incorporating it into the actions of a local Galician legendary figure, Pepa a Loba. Brutality and murder can be seen in "Los pendientes", an arresting and fantastic parody that underlines the cost to a woman of unconditional submission to a man, where the "blind love" of the female protagonist has left her literally blinded.

The traditional happy-ever-after ending of the *folletín* "La dama joven" is left in doubt, while the Galician tales "El molino", "Un destripador de antaño", "El aire cativo" "La hoz" and "La capitana" all present female protagonists whose occupations, as millers, armed delivery women, manual laborers and female bandit leaders, are normally associated with males. In these particular representations of Galician women, they are certainly emancipated from the home but, like the Galician women Pardo Bazán observed and reported on in "The Women of Spain", these fictional women are arguably driven to their occupations by necessity.

About a third of the narratives in this study are framed, a literary device that offers the writer scope for diverse worldviews to be presented in the one story. Pardo Bazán's employment of the female voice in three of the stories we have read, "El encaje roto", "Remordimiento" and "La santa de Karnar", is particularly notable. Each of the three voices offers a feminist point of view and at the same time delivers a subversive statement on social justice. The first is on the right of a woman to personal freedom and privacy during a courtship; the second, a questioning of an older Don Juan's right to lust after his young ward, even after her marriage; and the third, a reflection on the right of a woman to her own considered opinion in a verbal challenge with a male doctor.

Cultural allusions and intertexts are a powerful tool for a writer. Pardo Bazán used them judiciously to convey implicit and often subversive meanings to the reader in order to lead them beyond the immediate story. Literary allusions in these stories include well-known fairytales, subverted in Pardo Bazán's re-telling, and two plays, Chekov's *El cerezal* and López de Ayala's *Consuelo*, which subtly comment on societal values of the time. There are allusions to Goya's artwork and one of these works, etching 24 from *Caprichos*, could well have been used to illustrate the untold end to a tale; it features a woman riding to her death at the stake with the flame-embossed *capirote* of the condemned heretic on her head.

Spain's double moral standard, which Pardo Bazán so vehemently denounced, is the obvious focus of Chapter 4, where stories relate the downfall of six Don Juans, self-admitted serial womanizers, but a surprising number of the stories in other chapters also refer to this behavior. In "El árbol rosa" and "Comedia" the male protagonists are presented as opportunists ready to befriend and entice their potential victims. Donjuanesque behavior is addressed directly in "Los pendientes", where the protagonist is willing to overlook her *novio's* behavior. Seduction is implied in "Las cutres" and exposed in "La dama joven" where the suffering that the encounter caused in the protagonist's sister's life is evident. In "El mascarón", the reader is led to believe that the male protagonist is intent on seduction, but his behavior proves to be a ruse that covers up his more sinister aim. I suggest that this repeated inclusion of donjuanesque behavior in so many of these tales reflects Pardo Bazán's concern about the implicit acceptance by some sections of her society of the actions of these men. Again, she illustrates through fiction the point she so eloquently made in "The Women of Spain", as she repeatedly illustrates the "elastic moral system" that Spanish men devised for their own self-indulgences ("Women" 884).

A female protagonist's defiance of male expectations is the focus of many stories. For a middle-class woman defiance is seen as an "unangelic" lack of submission. This attitude is also evident in "Dalinda", where the protagonist is forced to justify her self-defense, while female violence is suggested in "Saletita", implied in "La hoz", and is overt in both "La capitana" and "Un destripador de antaño".

The final chapter closes with a quote from Medeiros to the effect that, of all the Galician writers, Pardo Bazán stood out as the most authentic, both in her reflection of the province and of its people. Almost half of the stories detailed in this book are, in fact set in Galicia, but in the purely urban stories— "La dama joven", "Saletita" "Cenizas", and "Dalinda"—there is very little content that is peculiar to the province. It is in Pardo Bazán's rural stories, however, (and arguably, "La redada" could be seen as one) that its underdevelopment, poverty and widespread beliefs in superstition are exposed. Agricultural practices are shown to be labor-intensive and primitive, *campesinos* seldom own their own land, and there is an extreme lack of manpower. This was due largely to emigration, with its dreams of a world that seemingly offered both an escape from immediate problems and the possibility of wealth; this surfaces unexpectedly in "El molino" and "La hoz" as an option for the male protagonists to conveniently sidestep an imminent problem. Pardo Bazán makes it clear that in her stories, as in real life, rural Galician women step up to do the work of these absent men.

The analysis of every one of these stories has contributed to the answers to the question posed by the title "Challenge or Surrender". In the majority of these stories, Pardo Bazán has drawn protagonists who feel they have good reason to challenge the gendered power imbalances in their society, and, indeed, to challenge the men in their lives themselves as they wield this power: the trio of fiancées who break their engagements; the protagonist of "Posesión", convinced of her need to remain unshriven before her imminent death; the operetta singer in "Apólogo" who realizes the danger that she is in; the female protagonist of "El pajarraco" who refuses a would-be seducer's advances before tricking him, and the mother in "La santa de Karnar" who calmly expresses her point of view in contradiction with that of the doctor. Other women are victims, either directly or indirectly, of their own decisions: the protagonists of "Comedia", "El mascarón", "Cenizas", and "Remordimiento"; by contrast, most of the Galician women make their own decisions without reference to any man. Here I would also include María, the older woman in "La santa de Karnar", whose female-oriented theology is far from orthodox.

In "El cinco de copas" and "Saletita" neither young female protagonist is entirely honest with her parent(s): admittedly not an enormous misdemeanor when compared with some of the other actions that we have seen in these narratives, nevertheless, these protagonists do fall short of societal expectations. "La dama joven" portrays a young woman faced with two alternatives, both with unseen pitfalls. "Los pendientes" is the one story here that cannot be said to depict reality. Prefaced by a caution, it depicts a protagonist who does represent the "ideal angel", a young woman unconditionally obedient to every whim of her *novio*, patiently forgiving his relationships with other women. It is a brutal and dark tale in which Pardo Bazán herself directly challenges and undermines the unreality of the patriarchal expectations of *fin de siècle* womanhood. There are, however three stories where the female protagonists act chastely—"El árbol rosa", "Dalinda" and "El aviso". The first young woman is saved from dishonor by the man's impatience and frustration with her refusals, the second by her self-defensive reflexes and the third by the matter of honor between men being unexpectedly introduced into the narrative. These narratives are drawn from the relatively few Pardo Bazán feminist-oriented stories where, from the woman's point of view, there appears to be a satisfactory ending.

Twenty-five of Pardo Bazán's stories, all with at least one female protagonist, have been analyzed. With a few exceptions, these fictional women paint a picture of everyday life in *fin de siècle* Spanish society and the narratives vividly illustrate the challenges that their society's gendered inequities pose. They also emphasize the impossibility of a Spanish woman measuring up to the prevailing *ángel del hogar* exemplar who existed, as she had done for some three centuries, only in the male imagination.

By way of a final word, I return to "Un matrimonio del siglo XIX", written when Pardo Bazán was sixteen. She sought her father's opinion about the story and received a rebuke: "Me dijo severamente: No te da el naipe por ahí. No sirves para ese género. Debes renunciar a escribir cuentos para toda la vida; es indudable que careces de las condiciones del cuentista, que son rapidez, y una gracia especial, como la que posee Alarcón, por ejemplo" [He told me firmly: You are not called to write stories; the genre does not suit you. Give up writing stories, it is obvious that you lack the speed, and the special grace of a storyteller like Alarcón, for example] (Bravo-Villasante 44–45). Twenty-five years later Pardo Bazán proved her father wrong. She had developed her own style, not imitating Alarcón, or any other writer, and she developed her own ethos, particularly concerning the gendered inequalities that women in her society faced daily. This publication has unequivocally demonstrated that Pardo Bazán's feminist-slanted short stories that she placed before the Spanish reading public were among the most influential works of her lifetime.

Works Cited

Abbott, Edith. "Employment of Women in Industries: Cigar-Making: Its History and Present Tendencies." *Journal of Political Economy*, vol. 15, no. 1, pp. 1-25, 1907.
Abbott, H. Porter. *The Cambridge Introduction to Narrative*. 2nd ed., Cambridge UP, 2015.
Abel, D. Herbert. "Euripides' Deus ex Machina: Fault or Excellence." *The Classical Journal*, vol. 50, no. 3, 1954, pp. 127–30.
Acosta, Eva. *Emilia Pardo Bazán: la luz en la batalla*. Lumen, 2007.
Adell, José Antonio. *Bandoleros: Historias y leyendas románticas españolas*. Torre, 2014.
Alberdi, Inés. *Vida de Emilia Pardo Bazán*. Eila, 2013.
Aldana Reyes, Xavier. *Spanish Gothic: National Identity, Collaboration and Cultural Adaptation*. Palgrave, 2017.
Aldaraca, Bridget A. *El ángel del hogar: Galdós and the Ideology of Domesticity in Spain*. U of North Carolina P, 1991.
———. "The Medical Construction of the Feminine Subject in Nineteenth-Century Spain." Vidal, pp. 395-413.
Alonso Montero, Xesús. *Galicia vista por los no gallegos*. Ediciones Jucar, 1974.
Andreu, Alicia G. "El folletín como intertexto en Tormento." *Anales galdosianos*, no. 17, 1982, pp. 55-61.
Arkinstall, Christine. *Spanish Female Writers and the Freethinking Press (1879–1926)*. U of Toronto P, 2014.
Artstor. "Goya's Los Caprichos." https://www.artstor.org/2014/09/29/goyas-los-caprichos-a-magnificent-failure/, accessed 20 February 2020.
Ashley, Melissa. "The First Fairytales were Feminist Critiques of Patriarchy." https://www.theguardian.com/books/2019/nov/11/the-first-fairytales-were-feminist-critiques-of-patriarchy-we-need-to-revive-their-legacy, accessed 6 October 2020.
Auden, W. H. *The Dyer's Hand and Other Essays*. Vintage Books, 1989.
Auerbach, Nina. *Woman and the Demon: The Life of a Victorian Myth*. Cambridge, 1982.

Bakhtin, Mikhail. *Rabelais and His World*. Translated by Helene Iswolsky, Indiana UP, 1984.

Barnes-Karol Gwendolyn. "Religious Oratory in a Culture of Control." Cruz and Perry, pp. 51-77.

Bieder, Maryellen. "Emilia Pardo Bazán and Literary Women: Women Reading Women's Writing in Late 19th-century Spain." *Revista Hispánica Moderna*, vol. 46, no. 1, 1993, pp. 19-33.

———. "Emilia Pardo Bazán y la emergencia del discurso feminista." Breve historia feminista de la literatura española (en lengua castellana). *La literatura escrita por la mujer. Desde el siglo XIX hasta la actualidad*, vol. 5, edited by Iris M. Zavala, Anthropos, 1998, pp. 75-110.

———. "En-gendering Strategies of Authority. Emilia Pardo Bazán and the Novel." Vidal, pp. 473-96.

———. "Pardo Bazán: Family, Feminism and Friendships." Versteeg and Walter, 2017, pp. 31-41.

———. "Plotting Gender/Replotting the Reader: Strategies of Subversion in Stories by Emilia Pardo Bazán." *Indiana Journal of Hispanic Literatures*, vol. 2, no. 1, 1993, pp. 137-57.

———. "The Challenge of Reading Emilia Pardo Bazán's Insolación in the Twenty-First Century." *ALEC*, vol. 41, no. 4, 2016, pp. 899-918.

———. "Women, Literature, and Society: The Essays of Emilia Pardo Bazán." Glenn and Mazquiarán de Rodríguez, 1998, pp. 25-54.

Biggane, Julia. *In a Liminal Space: The Novellas of Emilia Pardo Bazán*. U of Durham P, 2000.

Blanco Aguinaga, Carlos, et al. *Historia social de la literatura española (en lengua castellana)*. Akal, 2000. 4 vols.

Botrel, Jean-François. "La novela por entregas: unidad de creación y consumo." *Creación y público en la literatura española*, edited by J. F. Botrel and S. Salaün, Castalia, 1974.

Boyer, Christian. "Hacía una lectura psicoanalítica del 'cuento cruel' de Emila Pardo Bazán: 'Un destripador de antaño.'" *La Tribuna: Cadernos de estudios da Casa Museo Emilia Pardo Bazán*, no. 7, 2009, pp. 243-59.

Bravo-Villasante, Carmen. *Vida y obra de Emilia Pardo Bazán*. Occidente, 1962.

Bridges-Esser Christine. "Feijoo y Montenegro, Benito Jerónimo (1676–1764): Spanish Philosopher." http://enlightenment-evolution.org/index.php/Feijoo_y_Montenegro%2C_Benito_Jeronimo, accessed 3 July 2020.

Brown, Donald Fowler. The Catholic Naturalism of Pardo Bazán. U of North Carolina P. 1971.

Bungener, L. F. *History of the Council of Trent*. Translated by John McLintock, Harper, 1855.

Burdiel, Isabel. *Emilia Pardo Bazán*. Taurus, 2019.

Byron, George Gordon. *Don Juan* (1819–24). Edited by T. G. Steffan, et al., Penguin, 1973.

Cambridge Dictionary. https://dictionary.cambridge.org/dictionary/english/, accessed 5 Jan 2020.

Cancelo López, Pablo, et al. "Pepa a Loba y el bandolerismo en Galicia: realidad y ficción." *Oceánide*, no. 8, 2016. URL:http://oceanide.netne.net/articulos/art8-5.pdf, accessed 3 March 2019.

Capel Martínez, "Life and Work in the Tobacco Factories: Female Industrial Workers in the Early Twentieth Century." Enders and Radcliff, pp. 131–50.

Carr, Raymond. *Spain 1808-1975*. Clarendon P, 1982.

Castro, Rosalia de. "Follas novas." *Antología poética*. Edited and translated by Mercedes Castro, EDAF, 2004.

Cerda, Juan de la. *Vida politico de todos los estados de mugeres: en el qual se dan muy provechosos y Cristianas documentos y avisos, para criarse y conservarse debidamente las mugeres en sus estados.* Alcalá de Henares: Juan Gratian, 1599.

Charques Gámez, Rocio. *Los artículos feministas en el Nuevo Teatro Crítico de Emilia Pardo Bazán.* Espagrafic, 2003.

Charnon-Deutsch, Lou. *Fictions of the Feminine in the Nineteenth-Century Spanish Press*. Penn State UP, 2010.

———. *Hold That Pose: Visual Culture in the Late-Nineteenth-Century Spanish Periodical*. Penn State UP, 2008.

———. "Naturalism in the Short Fiction of Emilia Pardo Bazán." *Hispanic Journal*, vol. 3, no. 1, 1981, pp. 73-85.

———. "Racial Theory and Atavism in Pardo Bazán's Short Fiction." *La Tribuna: Cadernos de estudios da Casa Museo Emilia Pardo Bazán*, no. 9, 2012-13, pp. 143-54.

———. *The Nineteenth-Century Spanish Short Story: Textual Strategies of a Genre in Transition*. Tamesis, 1985.

Clémessy, Nelly. *Emilia Pardo Bazán como novelista (de la teoría a la práctica)*. Translated by Irene Gambra, Fundación Universitaria Española, 1981. 2 vols.

Coleridge, Samuel Taylor. *Biographia Literaria*, Rest Fenner, vol. 2, 1817.

Conlon, Joy Margaret Ann. *Empire and Emigration: The Representation of the Indiano in Nineteenth- and Twentieth-Century Spanish Literature*. Stanford U, 2002. PhD dissertation.

Cornide Ferrant, Enrique. *Mujeres estelares en la cultura gallega*. Diputación Provincial de A Coruña, 1993.

Cruz, Anne J. "Studying Gender in the Spanish Golden Age." Vidal, pp. 193-222.

———. and Mary Elizabeth Perry. *Culture and Control in Counter-Reformation Spain*. U of Minnesota P, 1987.

Cuddon, J. A., editor. *The Penguin Dictionary of Literary Terms and Literary Theory*. 3rd ed., Penguin, 1991.

Cuesta, Luis F. "Sports-Themed Kiosk Novelettes and the Silver Age Debate on Tradition and Modernity." Zamostny, pp. 329-52.

Davies, Rhian. "'La cuestión femenina' and *La España Moderna* (1889–1914)." *Bulletin of Spanish Studies: Hispanic Studies and Research on Spain, Portugal and Latin America*, vol. 89, no. 1, 2012, pp. 61-85.
De Beauvoir, Simone. *The Second Sex*. Translated by H. M. Parshley, Knopf, 1961.
Dendle, Brian J. "The Racial Theories of Emilia Pardo Bazán." *Hispanic Review*, vol. 38, no. 1, 1970, pp. 17-31.
Desvois, Jean-Michel. *The Illustrated Press in Spain*. Madrid, 1966.
Dickinson, Emily. *Emily Dickinson's Poems: As She Preserved Them*. Edited by Cristanne Miller, Harvard UP, 2016.
Dougherty Dru. "Theater and culture, 1868-1936." *The Cambridge Companion to Modern Spanish Culture*, edited by David T. Gies, Cambridge UP, 1999, pp. 211-21.
Drayson, Elizabeth. "Televising Boabdil, Last Muslim King of Granada." *Premodern Rulers and Postmodern Viewers: Gender, Sex, and Power in Popular Culture*, Edited by Janice North, et al., Palgrave, 2018.
DuPont, Denise. *Whole Faith: The Catholic Ideal of Emilia Pardo Bazán*. The Catholic U of America P, 2018.
Dutton, Brian. "The Semantics of Honor." *Revista Canadiense de Estudios Hispánicos*, vol. 4, no. 1, 1979, pp. 1-17.
"El Caballero Audaz" [José María Carretero Novillo]. "Nuestras vistas: La Condesade Pardo Bazán", *La Esfera*, no. 7, 1914. pp. 6-8. https://hemerotecadigital.bne.es/hd/es/viewer?id=865b64a4-da39-48d5-bbd5-88b9d1855647&page=8, accessed 8 January 2022.
Eliot, Thomas Stearns. *Four Quartets*. Harcourt 1943.
Enders, Victoria Loreé, and Pamela Beth Radcliff, editors. *Constructing Spanish Womanhood: Female Identity in Modern Spain*. State U of New York P, 1999.
Espinosa, Juan de. *Diálogo en laude de las mujeres*. Edited by Angela González Simón, Bermejo, 1946.
Espronceda, José de. "El estudiante de Salamanca." Alicante 1999. Biblioteca Virtual Miguel de Cervantes, http://www.cervantesvirtual.com/nd/ark:/59851/bmcjd4s2, accessed 16 April 2019.
———. "The Student of Salamanca." Translated by Salvador Ortiz-Carboneres, https://warwick.ac.uk/fac/arts/languagecentre/about/staff/salvador/studentofsalamanca/*Poesías de don José de Espronceda*, Yemes, 1840.
Ezama Gil, Ángeles. "Santidad, Heroísmo y estética en la narrativa de Emilia Pardo Bazán." *Simposio*, edited by José Manuel González Herrán, et al., Casa-Museo de Emilia Pardo Bazán, 2004, pp. 233-258.
Fariña Busto, María Jesús. "De vindicadoras a vengadoras: respuestas frente a la violencia, algunos ejemplos en discursos literarios y artísticos hispánicos." *Investigación y género, logros y retos: III Congreso Universitario Nacional Investigación y Género*, 2011, pp. 571-87.
Faus, Pilar. *Emilia Pardo Bazán: su época, su vida, su obra*. Fundación Pedro Barrié de la Maza, 2003, 2 vols.

Federico, Annette. "Close Reading, Critical Reading." *Engagements with Close Reading*. Routledge, 2016, pp. 1-30.

Feeny, Thomas. "Illusion and the Don Juan Theme in Pardo Bazán's *Cuentos de amor*." *Hispanic Journal*, vol. 1, no. 2, 1980, pp. 67-71.

———. "Pardo Bazán's Pessimistic View of Love as Revealed in *Cuentos de amor*." *Hispanófila*, vol. 64, 1978, pp. 7-14.

Feijóo y Montenegro, Benito Jerónimo. *Obras escogidas del Padre Fray Benito Jerónimo Feijoo y Montenegro*. Rivadeneyra, 1863.

Fernández Cubas, Cristina. *Emilia Pardo Bazán*. Omega, 2001.

Foucault, Michel. "Eye of Power." *Power/Knowledge: Selected Interviews and Other Writings 1972-1977*, edited by Colin Gordon. Pantheon, 1980.

Fórmica, Mercedes. *La hija de don Juan de Austria: Ana de Jesús en el proceso al pastelero de Madrigal*. Occidente, 1973.

Friedman, Edward H. "Redressing the trickster: *El burlador de Sevilla* and critical transitions." *Revista Canadiense de Estudios Hispánicos*, vol. 29, no. 1, 2004, pp. 61-77.

Friedman, Norman. "Point of View in Fiction: The Development of a Critical Concept." *PMLA*, vol. 70, no. 5, 1955, pp. 1160-1184.

———. "What makes a Short Story Short?" *Modern Fiction Studies*, vol. 4, no. 2, 1958, pp. 103-17.

Fuchs, Barbara. *Exotic Nation: Maurophilia and the Construction of Early Modern Spain*. U Penn P, 2009.

Fuentes, Carlos. *The Buried Mirror: Reflections on Spain and the New World*. Houghton Mifflin, 1992.

Furst, Lilian R. *Romanticism*. Longman, 1992.

Gabilondo, Joseba. "Towards a Postnational History of Galician Literature: On Pardo Bazán's Transnational and Translational Position." *Bulletin of Hispanic Studies*, vol. 86, no. 2, 2009, pp. 249-69.

García Santo-Tomás, Enrique. "On Speed and Restlessness: Calderón's Urban Kaleidoscope." *Companion to Early Modern Hispanic Theatre*, edited by Hilaire Kallendorf, Brill, 2014, pp. 165-83.

Garza, Efraín E. *Las manifestaciones del amor en cuentos de Pardo Bazán*. Alexandria, 2014.

Gil y Carrasco, Enrique, editor. *Los españoles pintados por sí mismos*. Gaspar y Roig, 1851.

Gilbert, Sandra, and Susan Gubar. *The Madwoman in the Attic: The Woman Writer and the Nineteenth-Century Literary Imagination*. Yale UP, 1979.

Gilmore David D. *Aggression and Community: Paradoxes of Andalusian Culture*. Yale UP, 1984.

———. *Carnival and Culture: Sex, Symbol, and Status in Spain*. Yale UP, 1998.

Gilmour, Nicola M. *Transvestite Narratives in Nineteenth- and Twentieth-Century Hispanic Authors: Using the Voice of the Opposite Gender*. Edward Mellen, 2008.

Glenn, Kathleen M., and Mercedes Mazquiarán de Rodríguez. Introduction to Glenn and Mazquiarán de Rodríguez, pp. 1-5.

———. *Spanish Women Writers and the Essay: Gender, Politics, and the Self*. U of Missouri P, 1998.

Gold, Hazel. *The Reframing of Realism: Galdós and the Discourses of the Nineteenth-Century Spanish Novel*. Duke UP, 1993.

Gonzáles Arias, Francisca. "Pardo Bazán's Galicia: Representations of Gender, Nature, and Community." Versteeg and Walter, pp. 105-12.

González Herrán, José Manuel. "Doña Emilia en Compostela." *La Tribuna: Cadernos de estudios da Casa Museo Emilia Pardo Bazán*, no. 9, 2013, pp. 121-42.

González Pérez, Clodio. "Trinta anos sen comer nin beber." 2008. http://www.galiciahoxe.com/opinion/gh/trinta-anos-sen-comer-nin-beber/idNoticia-295599/, accessed 5 April 2020.

Gottleib, Marlene. "Don Juan from a Feminist Perspective." *West Virginia Philological Papers*, vol. 44, 2011, pp. 29-38.

Guia, Aitana. "Migrations" Shubert and Álvarez Junco, pp. 292-307.

Hanson, Clare, editor. *Re-reading the Short Story*. St Martin's P, 1989.

———. *Short Stories and Short Fictions, 1880-1890*. Macmillan, 1985.

Harris, Max. "Muhammed and the Virgin: Folk Dramatizations of Battles between Moors and Christians in Modern Spain." *Drama Review*, vol. 38, no. 1, 1994, pp. 45-61.

Haviland, John Beard. *Gossip, reputation, and knowledge in Zinacantan*. U of Chicago P, 1977.

Hemeroteca Digital de la Biblioteca Nacional de España. http://hemerotecadigital.bne.es/.

Hemingway, Maurice. *Emilia Pardo Bazán: The Making of a Novelist*. Cambridge UP, 1983.

———. "The Religious Content of Pardo Bazán's La sirena negra." *Bulletin of Hispanic Studies*, vol. 49, 1972, pp. 369-82.

Henn, David. *The Early Pardo Bazán: Theme and Narrative Technique in the Novels of 1879-89*. Cairns, 1988.

Hills, Ann K. "Dos arquetipos femeninos en los cuentos de Emilia Pardo Bazán." *Romance Quarterly*, vol. 44, no. 3, 1997, pp. 171-80.

Hilton, Ronald. "Doña Emilia Pardo Bazán, Neo-Catholicism and Christian Socialism." *The Americas*, vol. 11, no. 1, 1954, pp. 3-18.

———. "Emilia Pardo-Bazán's Concept of Spain." *Hispania*, vol. 34, no. 4, 1951, pp. 327-42.

———. "The Centenary of Emilia Pardo Bazán." *Books Abroad*, vol. 26, no. 4, 1952, pp. 345-47.

Hoeveler, Diane Long. *The Gothic Ideology: Religious Hysteria*. U of Wales P, 2014.

Hoffman, Joan M. "Ángel del hogar." *The Feminist Encyclopaedia of Spanish Literature*, edited by Janet Pérez and Maureen Ihrie, Greenwood Press, 2000, pp. 27-28.

———. "Torn Lace and Other Transformations: Rewriting the Bride's Script in Selected Stories by Emilia Pardo Bazán." *Hispania*, vol. 82, no. 2, 1999, pp. 238-45.

Hoffmann, E. T. A. "The Sandman." *Best Tales of Hoffmann*, Dover, 1979, pp. 323-71.

Holquist, Michael. Prologue. Bakhtin, pp. xiii-xxiii.

Iarocci, Michael. "Romantic Prose, Journalism and *costumbrismo*." *The Cambridge History of Spanish Literature*, edited by David T. Gies, Cambridge UP, 2004, pp. 381-91.

Ilie, Paul. "Goya's Teratology and the Critique of Reason." *Eighteenth-Century Studies*, vol. 18, no. 1, 1984, pp. 35-56.

Jackson, Rosemary. *Fantasy*. Routledge, 2002.

Jagoe, Catherine. *Ambiguous Angels: Gender in the Novels of Galdós*. U of California P, 1994.

———. "La enseñanza femenina en la España decimonónica." *La mujer en los discursos de género: textos y contextos en el siglo XIX*, edited by Catherine Jagoe, et al., Icaria, 1998, pp. 105-46.

James, Henry. *The Art of the Novel: Critical Prefaces*. Scribner's, 1934.

Jiménez, Javier. "*Costumbrista* Description, Romantic Gaze: The Insufficiencies of Literary Discourse in Sab." *Romance Studies*, vol. 33, no. 1, 2015, pp. 56-67.

Johnson, Roberta. *Gender and Nation in the Spanish Modernist Novel*. Vanderbilt UP, 2003.

———. *Major Concepts in Spanish Feminist Theory*. SUNY P, 2019.

Kilgour, Maggie. *The Rise of the Gothic novel*. Routledge, 1995.

Kirkpatrick, Susan. *Las Románticas: Women Writers and Subjectivity in Spain 1835-1850*. U of California P, 1989.

———. "The Female Tradition in Nineteenth-Century Spanish Literature." Vidal, pp. 343-370.

Lanser, Susan Sniader. *The Narrative Act*. Princeton UP, 1981.

———. "Toward a Feminist Narratology." *Style*, vol. 20, no. 3, 1986, pp. 341-63.

Leggott, Sarah. *History and Autobiography in Contemporary Spanish Women's Testimonial Writings*. Edwin Mellen P, 2001.

León, Fray Luis. *La perfecta casada*. Madrid, 1583. Biblioteca Virtual Miguel de Cervantes, 2003, https://www.cervantesvirtual.com/nd/ark:/59851/bmcopow9, accessed 6 March 2017.

Leppihalme, Ritva. *Culture Bumps: An Empirical Approach to the Translation of Allusions*. Multilingual, 1997.

Levack, Brian P. *Possession and Exorcism in the Christian West*. Yale UP, 2013.

Logú y Zelada, Justo. *Examen médico-filosófico de los padecimientos de la enferma de Santa María de Gonzar en Galicia*. Sánchez, 1840.

López Quintáns, Javier. "Mito y realidad en un 'destripador de antaño.'" *Actas del II Simposio Emilia Pardo Bazán: Los cuentos*, edited by José Manuel González Herrán, et al., Real Academia Galega, 2005, pp. 279-86.

López Teijeiro, Iria. *Keys to Becoming a Better Writer: How to Improve Your Writing Skills*. Translated by Iraide Talavera, Literautas, 2016.

Lother, Gloria et al. "Deus ex Machina." *Encyclopaedia Britannica*, 2017. https://www.britannica.com/art/deus-ex-machina, accessed 23 May 2019.

Lüddecke Tim, et al. "A Salamander's Toxic Arsenal." *The Science of Nature*, 2018. https://doi.org/10.1007/s00114-018-1579-4, accessed 6 September 2020.

McKenna, Susan M. *Crafting the Female Subject: Narrative Innovation in the Short Fiction of Emilia Pardo Bazán*. The Catholic U of America P, 2009.

Magiorkinis, Emmanouil, et al. "Highlights in the History of Epilepsy: The Last 200 Years." *Epilepsy Research and Treatment*, 2014. Article ID 582039, 2014. http://dx.doi.org/10.1155/2014/582039, accessed 10 October 2019.

Mandrell, James. *Don Juan and the Point of Honor*. Penn. State UP, 1992.

———. "Realism in Spain: Galdós, Pardo Bazán, Clarín and the European Context." *Neohelicon*, vol. 15, no. 2, 2005, pp. 83-112.

Martí-López, Elisa. "The folletín: Spain looks to Europe." *The Cambridge Companion to the Spanish Novel*, edited by Harriet Turner and Adelaida López de Martínez, Cambridge UP, 2003, pp. 65-80.

Martínez Arnaldos, Manuel. "Estrategia de la titulación en los cuentos de E. Pardo Bazán." *Homenaje al profesor Trigueros Cano*, vol. 2, edited by Pedro Luis Ladrón de Guevara Mellada, et al., U de Murcia, 1999, pp. 439-57.

Medeiros, António. *Two Sides of One River: Nationalism and Ethnography in Galicia and Portugal*. Translated by Martin Earl, Berghahn, 2013.

Mendlesohn, Farah. "The Immersive Fantasy." *Rhetorics of Fantasy*, Wesleyan UP, 2008, pp. 59-113.

Menon, Patricia. *Austen, Eliot, Charlotte Brontë and the Mentor-Lover*. Palgrave, 2003.

Meyer Spacks, Patricia. "In Praise of Gossip." *The Hudson Review*, vol. 35, no. 1, 1982, pp. 19-38.

Miguélez-Carballeira, Helena. Introduction to *Galicia a Sentimental Nation: Gender, Culture and Politics*. U of Wales P, 2013.

Miller, Stephen. "The Realist novel." *The Cambridge History of Spanish Literature*, edited by David T. Gies, Cambridge UP, 2004, pp. 410-22.

Mitchell, Timothy. *Violence and Piety in Spanish Folklore*. U of Penn P, 1988.

Moran, Bruce T. *Distilling Knowledge: Alchemy, Chemistry and the Scientific Revolution*. Harvard UP, 2005.

Moger, Angela S. "Narrative Structure in Maupassant: Frames of Desire." *PMLA*, vol. 100, no. 3, 1985, pp. 315-27.

Morris, Pam. *Realism*. Routledge, 2003.

Mortimer, Armine Kotin. "Second Stories." *Short Story Theory at a Crossroads*, edited by Susan Lohafer and Jo Ellen Clarey, Louisiana State UP, 1989, pp. 276-298.
Myers, Diana T. "Feminist Theories of Agency." https://www.britannica.com/topic/philosophical-feminism/Feminist-theories-of-agency, accessed 10 December 2020.
Nash, Mary. "Un/Contested Identities: Motherhood, Sex Reform and the Modernization of Gender Identity in Early Twentieth-Century Spain." Enders and Radcliff, pp. 25-50.
Neumeyer, Peter F. "Teaching the Short Story: Plot." *The Journal of Aesthetic Education*, vol. 9, no. 4, 1975, pp. 5-18.
Nimetz, Michael. *Humor in Galdós: A Study of the Novelas contemporáneos*. Yale UP, 1968.
Nora, Pierre. "Between Memory and History: Les Lieux de Mémoire." *Representations*, no. 26, pp. 7-24, 1989.
Noya Taboada, Ruth. *La violencia en los cuentos de Emilia Pardo Bazán*. U de Compostela de Santiago, 2016. PhD dissertation.
Ojea Fernández, María Elena. "Narrativa feminista en los cuentos de la condesa de Pardo Bazán." *EPOS*, vol. 14, 2000, pp. 157-76.
Ordóñez, Elizabeth J. "Mapping Modernity: The *Fin de Siècle* Travels of Emilia Pardo Bazán." *Hispanic Research Journal*, vol. 5, no. 1, 2004, pp. 15-25.
Owen, Christopher, and Amy Crawford. Introduction to *Special Issue: The Two-Hundred-Year Legacy of E. T. A. Hoffmann: Transgressions of Fantastika.*" *Marvels & Tales*, vol. 34, no. 1, 2020, pp. 13-22.
Pardo Bazán, Emilia. "Apuntes autobiográficos." *Los pazos de Ulloa*. Barcelona, 1886, pp. 5-92. Google Books, https://www.google.co.nz/books/edition/Los_Pazos_de_Ulloa/Q1kTAAAAQAAJ?hl=en&gbpv=1&dq=pardo+bazan+apuntes+autobiogr%C3%A1ficos&printsec=frontcover, accessed 1 April 2017.
———. "Concepción Arenal y sus ideas acerca de la mujer." *La mujer española y otros escritos*, pp. 198-214.
———. *Cuadros religiosos*. Pueyo, 1925.
———. *Cuentos completos*. Edited by Paredes Núñez. Galicia Editorial, 1990. 4 vols.
———. "La cuestión académica." *La mujer española y otros escritos*, pp. 75-82.
———. *La cuestión palpitante*. 1883. Edited by Rosa de Diego. Biblioteca Nueva, 1998.
———. *De mi tierra*. 1893. Kessinger, 2010.
———. "Del amor y la amistad." *La mujer española y otros escritos*, pp. 184-91.
———. "Ex momo." *La Ilustración Artística*, no. 738, 1896, p. 146. https://hemerotecadigital.bne.es/hd/es/viewer?id=903dc62a-1977-47cd-9a9f-82177cd53160&page=2, accessed 3 October 2019.
———. "La educación del hombre y la de la mujer." *La mujer española y otros escritos*, pp. 149-77.

———. "La gallega." *Las mujeres españolas, americanas y lusitanas, pintadas por su mismas*, edited by Da Faustina Saez de Melgar, Juan Pons, 1884, pp. 124-28.

———. *Insolación* (1889). Espasa, 2002.

———. *La mujer española y otros artículos feministas*. Edited by Leda Schiavo. Nacional, 1976.

———. *La mujer española y otros escritos*. Edited by Guadalupe Gómez-Ferrer. Cátedra, 1999.

———. "La mujer española." *La mujer española y otros escritos*, pp. 83-115.

———. *La obra periodística completa en La Nación de Buenos Aires (1897-1921)*. Vol. 2, edited by Juliana Sínovas Maté. A Coruña: Diputación Provincal de A Coruña, 1999.

———. *"Náufragas" y otros cuentos*. Edited by Linda M. Willem, Cervantes & Co., 2010.

———. *Obras completas*. Edited by Fundación José Antonio de Castro, Biblioteca Castro, 2004, 2012. 12 vols.

———. "On Spanish Realism." *Documents of Modern Literary Realism*, edited by George J. Becker, Princeton UP, 1963, pp. 261–65. *JSTOR*, http://www.jstor.org/stable/j.ctt183pfvq.27. Accessed 16 Jan. 2022.

———. *Los pazos de Ulloa*. Barcelona, 1886.

———. Prefacio to *Cuentos de amor*. *OC*, vol. 8, pp. 346-607, 2012.

———. *Retratos y Apuntes Literarios*. Prieto, 1908.

———. *San Francisco de Asís (Siglo XIII)*. Casa, 1882, 2 vols. Biblioteca Virtual Miguel de Cervantes, 2003, https://www.cervantesvirtual.com/portales/pardo_bazan/obra/san-francisco-de-asis-siglo-xiii-tomo-segundo-983471/, accessed 6 May 2020.

———. "Sobre los derechos de la mujer." *La mujer española y otros escritos*, pp. 258-67.

———. "Stuart Mill." *La mujer española y otros escritos*, pp. 215-30.

———. "The Women of Spain." *Fortnightly Review*, vol. 51, 1889, pp. 879-904.

———. *Torn Lace and Other Stories*. Translated by María Cristina Urruela, MLA P, 1996.

———. "Tristana." *La mujer española y otros escritos*, pp. 178-83.

———. *Un viaje de novios*. Edited by Marisa Sotelo Vázquez, Alianza, 2003.

Paredes Núñez, Juan. Estudio preliminar to *Cuentos completos*, vol. 1, Pedro Barrie, 1990, pp. 5-49.

———. *La realidad gallega en los cuentos de Emilia Pardo Bazán, (1851-1921)*. Castro, 1983.

Parr, James A. *Don Quixote, Don Juan and Related Subjects: Form and Tradition in Spanish Literature 1339-1630*. Susquehanna UP. 2004.

Patiño Eirín, Cristina. "Goyas a oscuras: el bandido Mahmed Casanova entre la historia y el mito." *Anales de la literatura española contemporánea*, vol. 31, no. 3, 2006, pp. 889-911.

Pattison, Walter T. *Emilia Pardo Bazán*. Twayne, 1971.

Penas Valera, Ermita. "Fantasía en algunos cuentos de E. Pardo Bazán." *Sobre literatura fantástica: Homenaxe ó profesor Anton Risco*, edited by Antonio Risco, U de Vigo, 2001.

Percoco, Cristina Maria. *The Seduction of Objects: Understanding Desire and Material Culture in Emilia Pardo Bazán's Short Fiction*. U of Virginia, 2008. PhD dissertation.

Pereira-Muro, Carmen. *Género, nación y literatura: Emilia Pardo Bazán en la literatura gallega y española*. Purdue UP, 2013.

Pérez, Janet. "Subversion of Victorian Values and Idea Types: Pardo Bazán and the Ángel del hogar." *Hispanófila*, vol. 113, 1995, pp. 31-44.

———. "Winners, Losers and Casualties in Pardo Bazán's Battle of the Sexes." *Letras Peninsulares,* vol. 5, 1992, pp. 347-56.

Pérez Galdós, Benito. "El coleccionista." (1893). *Fisonomías Sociales, Obras Inéditos*, Renacimiento, 1923.

———. "Observaciones sobre la novela contemporánea en España (1870)." *Ensayos de crítica literaria*, edited by Laureano Bonet, Ediciones Península, 1990, pp. 105-08.

Pérez Mateo, Soledad. "El sentido de lo museístico en el Realismo y Naturalismo de la novela española del siglo XIX." *Congreso Internacional Imagen y Apariencia a Murcia,* edited by María Concepción de la Peña Velasco, et al., U de Murcia,

Perry, Mary Elizabeth. "Magdalens and Jezebels in Counter-Reformation Spain." Cruz and Perry, pp. 124-44.

Phelan, James. *Living to Tell about It: A Rhetoric and Ethics of Character Narration*, Cornell UP, 2005.

Phillips, Walter Alison. "Papal Dispensations." https://en.wikisource.org/wiki/1911_Encyclopædia_Britannica/Dispensation, accessed 3 April 2019.

Piglia, Ricardo. "Theses on the Short Story." *New Left Review*, vol. 70, 2011, pp. 63-66.

Poe, Edgar Allan. "Twice-Told Tales by Nathaniel Hawthorne: A Review." *Graham's Magazine*, vol. 10, no. 5, 1842, pp. 125-131.

Ponterotto, Joseph G. "Brief Note on the Origins, Evolution, and Meaning of the Qualitative Research Concept 'Thick Description.'" *The Qualitative Report*, vol. 11, no. 3, 2006, pp. 538-54. Academic OneFile, http://link.galegroup.com/apps/doc/A172554568/AONE?u=vuw&sid=AONE&xid=9e510a29, accessed 30 June 2019.

Prince, Gerald. *Dictionary of Narratology*. U of Nebraska P, 1987.

Quesada Novás, Ángeles. *El amor in los cuentos de Emilia Pardo Bazán*. U of Alicante, 2005.

Ramos, Carlos. "Poseídas y desposeídas: A propósito de un cuento de Emilia Pardo Bazán." *Brujas, demonios y fantasmas en la literatura fantástica hispánica*, U de Lleida, 1999, pp. 217-226.

Rank, Otto. *The Don Juan Legend*. Princeton UP, 1975.

Rawlings, Helen. *The Spanish Inquisition*. Blackwell, 2006.

Real Academia Española. *Diccionario de la lengua española*. Madrid, 1992.
Reigosa Carlos G. *Pepa A Loba*. Xerais, 2006.
Revilla y Moreno, Manuel de la. "Revista bibliográfia." *El Globo*, no. 1, 1879, p.1, https://hemerotecadigital.bne.es/hd/es/viewer?id=d2b3e7b2-9632-4e3b-94dc-7e88d27c5aeb, accessed 18 July 2021.
Rey, Alfonso. "El cuento sicológico en Pardo Bazán." *Hispanófila*, no. 59, 1977, pp. 19-30.
Ribao Pereira, Montserrat. "Soy una voluntad: La cuestión de la mujer en los cuentos por las Américas de Emilia Pardo Bazán." *REI, UNED*, 2016, pp. 43-74.
Richards, I. A. *Principles of Literary Criticism*. Routledge, 1967.
Richardson, Ronald B. *Narrative Madness*. Omar Rodríguez, 2014.
Richardson Durham, Caroline. "Subversion in Two Short Stories by Emilia Pardo Bazán." *Letras peninsulares*, vol. 2, no. 1, 1989, pp. 55-64.
Rodríguez Gonzáles, Olivia. "Catalan and Galician Literatures in Iberian and European Contexts." *New Trends in Iberian Galician Comparative Literature*, edited by María Teresa Vilariño Picos and Anxo Abuín Gonzáles, vol 13, no. 5, Purdue UP, 2011, https:// https://docs.lib.purdue.edu/cgi/viewcontent.cgi?article=1913&context=clcweb, accessed 20 June 2021.
Romar García, Raúl. "La santa de Gonzar, el primer caso documentado de anorexia." *La Voz de Galicia*, 3 March 2014. https://www.lavozdegalicia.es/noticia/sociedad/2014/03/16/santa-gonzar-primer-documentado-anorexia/0003_201403G16P32991.htm, accessed 16 June 2019.
Romero López, Alicia. *Lo fantástico hoffmaniano en ochos cuentos de Emilia Pardo Bazán*. Peter Lang, 2019.
Ross, Marlon B. "Romantic Quest and Conquest: Troping Masculine Power in the Crisis of Poetic Identity." *Romanticism and Feminism*, edited by Anne K. Mellor, Indiana UP, 1988, pp. 26-51.
Rutherford, J. D. "Realism in Spain and Portugal." *The Age of Realism*, edited by F. W. J. Hemmings, Penguin, 1974, pp. 265-322.
Salustio, Doctor. *Carta a una joven sobre lo que debe saber antes de casarse*. Madrid, 1865. Google Books, https://www.google.co.nz/books/edition/Carta_a_una_joven_sobre_lo_que_debe_sabe/iOJzQwAACAAJ?hl=en, accessed 3 May 2017.
Sánchez-Alonso, Blanca. "Those Who Left and Those Who Stayed Behind: Explaining Emigration from the Regions of Spain, 1880-1914." *The Journal of Economic History*, vol. 60, no. 3, 2000, pp. 730-55.
Sánchez Cantón, Francisco Javier. "La 'espiritada' de Gonzar en una miniatura, en una novela romántica y en un cuento 'fin de siglo.'" *Cuadernos de estudios gallegos*, vol. 4, 1949, pp. 328-35.
Sánchez, Porfirio. "How and Why Pardo Bazán Went From the Novel to the Short Story." *Romance Notes*, vol. 11, no. 2, 1969, pp. 309-314.

Sancho Dobles, Leonardo. "Texto/carnaval/escritura: A propósito de 'El discurso de la Edad de Oro.'" *Káñina*, vol. 7, no. 2, 1983, pp. 59-68.
Scanlon, Geraldine. "Gender and Journalism: Pardo Bazán's *Nuevo Teatro Crítico*." *Culture and Gender in Nineteenth-Century Spain*, edited by Lou Charnon-Deutsch and Jo Labanyi, OUP, 1995.
———. *La polémica feminista en la España contemporánea*. Translated by Rafael Mazarrasa, Akal, 1986.
Senabre, Ricardo. "*Obras Completas* XI-XII. Cuentos dispersos: Emilia Pardo Bazán." *El Español*, 22 February 2013, https://www.elespanol.com/el-cultural/letras/20130222/obras-completas-xi-xii-cuentos-dispersos/6499801_0.html, accessed 3 August 2020.
Seoane Couceiro, María Cruz and María Dolores Saíz. *Historia del periodismo español*. Vol. 2, Alianza, 1983.
Shubert, Adrian. *A Social History of Modern Spain*. Unwin Hyman, 1987.
Shubert, Adrian, and José Álvarez Junco, editors. *The History of Modern Spain: Chronologies, Themes, Individuals*, Bloomsbury, 2018.
Sieburth, Stephanie. *Inventing High and Low: Literature, Mass Culture and Uneven Modernity in Spain*. Duke UP, 1994.
Sinclair Knight, Lorna, editor. *Collins Spanish Dictionary*. 8th ed., Collins, 2005.
Singer, Armand E. "The Present State of Studies on the Don Juan Theme." *Tirso's Don Juan: The Metamorphosis of a Theme*, edited by Josep M. Sola Solé and George E. Gringras, The Catholic U of America P, 1998, pp. 1-31.
Sinués de Marco, María del Pilar. *El ángel del hogar*. San Martín, 1881.
Six, Abigail Lee. *Gothic Terrors: Incarceration, Duplication, and Bloodlust in Spanish Narrative*. Bucknell UP, 2010.
Slattery, Sister Mary Francis. "What is Literary Realism?" *The Journal of Aesthetics and Art Criticism*, vol. 31, no. 1, 1972, pp. 55-62.
Smith Jennifer. *Women, Mysticism and Hysteria in Fin-de-Siècle Spain*. Vanderbilt UP, 2021.
———, editor. *Modern Spanish Women as Agents of Change: Essays in Honor of Maryellen Bieder*. Bucknell UP, 2019.
Sotelo Vázquez, Marisa. "Emilia Pardo Bazán y el folklore gallego." *Garoza: revista de la Sociedad Española de Estudios Literarios de Cultura Popular*, no. 7, 2007, pp. 293-314.
Sousa Saramago, José. *The Stone Raft*. Translated by Giovanni Pontiero, Harvill P, 2000.
Spender, Dale. *Man Made Language*. Routledge, 1985.
Summers, Montague. *The Gothic Quest: a History of the Gothic Novel*. Russell and Russell, 1938.
Taboada Chivite, Xesús. "Cultura, material y espiritual." *Los Gallegos*, edited by Gustavo Fabro Barreiro, Istmo, pp. 149-218.
Taylor, Scott K. *Honor and Violence in Golden Age Spain*. Yale UP, 2008.

Templin, W. H. "The Mother in the Comedia of Lope de Vega." *Hispanic Review*, vol. 3, no. 2, 1935, pp. 219-44.

Tenriero Prego, José. *Gothic, Gender and Regenerationism in Emilia Pardo Bazán's Galicia*, U of Exeter, 2013. PhD dissertation.

The Holy Bible: New International Version. Holman, 1984.

Thomas, Bronwen. *Narrative: The Basics*. Routledge, 2016.

Tirso de Molina. *El burlador de Sevilla y convidado de piedra*. Edited by Begoña Alonso Mondero. Santillana, 1995.

Tolliver, Joyce. *Cigar Smoke and Violet Water: Gendered Discourse in the Stories of Emilia Pardo Bazán*. United UP, 1998.

———. "Colonialism, Collages, and Thick Description: Pardo Bazán and the Rhetoric of Detail." *Imagined Truths: Realism in Modern Spanish Literature and Culture*, edited by Mary L. Coffey and Margot Versteeg, U of Toronto P, 2019.

———. "Knowledge, Desire and Syntactic Empathy in Pardo Bazán's 'La novia fiel.'" *Hispania*, vol. 72, no. 4, 1989, pp. 909-18.

———. "'My Distinguished Friend and Colleague Tula': Emilia Pardo Bazán and Literary-Feminist Polemics." *Recovering Spain's Feminist Tradition*, edited by Lisa Vollendorf, MLA P, 2001, pp. 217-37.

Torrecilla, Jesús. "Power and Resistance: The Reality of Spanish Realism." Translated by Margarita Pillado, *A Quarterly Journal in Modern Literatures*, vol. 67, no. 2, 2013, pp. 98-110.

Tortella Casares, Gabriel. *The Development of Modern Spain: An Economic History of the 19th and 20th Centuries*. Translated by Valerie Herr, Harvard UP, 2000.

Troncoso Durán, Dolores. "La santa de Karnar, un cuento fin de siglo." *Estudios sobre Pardo Bazán: In memoriam Maurice Hemingway*, edited by José Manuel González Herrán, U de Santiago, 1997.

Uspensky, Boris. *A Poetics of Composition: The Structure of the Artistic Text and Typology of a Compositional Form*. Translated by Valentina Zavarin and Susan Wittig, U of California P, 1973.

Varela Jácome, Benito. "Pardo Bazán y su 'Nuevo Teatro Crítico.'" *Cuadernos de estudios gallegos*, vol. 7, 1952, pp. 159-64.

Verea y Aguiar, D. José. *Historia de Galicia*. Ferrol, 1838.

Versteeg, Margot, and Susan Walter, editors. *Approaches to Teaching the Writings of Emilia Pardo Bazán*. MLA P, 2017.

Versteeg, Margot "'A Most Promising Girl': Gender and Artistic Future in Emilia Pardo Bazán's 'La dama joven.'" Smith, pp. 126-44.

Vidal, Hernán, editor. *Cultural and Historical Grounding for Hispanic and Luso-Brazilian Feminist Literary Criticism*. Institute for the Study of Ideologies and Literature, 1989.

Villanueva, Darío, and José Manuel González Herrán. Introducciones to *Obras Completas*. 10 vols.

Walter, Susan. *From the Outside Looking in: Narrative Frames and Narrative Spaces in the Short Stories of Emilia Pardo Bazán*. Juan de la Cuesta, 2009.

———. "Images of the femme fatale in Two Short Stories by Emilia Pardo Bazán." *Romance Notes*, vol. 55, no. 2, 2015, pp. 177-89.

Webber, Andrew J. *The Doppelgänger: Double Visions in German Literature*. Clarendon, 1996.

Weinstein, Leo. *The Metamorphoses of Don Juan*. AMS P, 1967.

Wharton, Edith. *The Writing of Fiction*. Simon and Schuster, 1997.

White, Sarah L. "Liberty, Honor, Order: Gender and Political Discourse in Nineteenth-Century Spain." Enders and Radcliff, pp. 233-57.

Wilson, Margaret. *Spanish Drama of the Golden Age*. Pergamon, 1969.

Willem, Linda M. "The Twice-Told and the Unsaid in Emilia Pardo Bazán's 'Presidento', 'En coche-cama', 'Confidencia', and 'Madre.'" Smith, pp. 90-105.

Winther, Per, et al. "Dialogues." *Narrative*, vol. 20, no. 2, 2012, pp. 239-53.

Wood, Gareth. "Sugaring the Pill: Emilia Pardo Bazán, John Stuart Mill and the Biblioteca de la Mujer." *Bulletin of Spanish Studies*, vol. 95, no. 6, 2018, pp. 605-31.

Woolf, Virginia. "How Should One Read a Book?" *Essays on the Self: Selected Essays of Virginia Woolf*, edited by Joanna Kavenna, Notting Hill Editions, 2014, pp. 64-80.

Young, Francis. *A History of Exorcism in Catholic Christianity*. Palgrave 2016.

Zamostny, Jeffrey, and Susan Larson, editors. *Kiosk Literature of Silver Age Spain: Modernity and Mass Culture*, Intellect, 2017.

Zárate, Martha. *Emilia Pardo Bazán's Articles in* La Nación, El Imparcial *and* La Epoca: *A Bibliographic Guide*. UP of America, 2002.

Ziomek Henryk. *A History of Spanish Golden Age Drama*. UP of Kentucky, 1984.

Zorrilla, José. *Don Juan Tenorio*. Edited by Begoña Alonso Mondero, Santillana, 1995.

Appendix: Publication Details

Chapter 2:
"El árbol rosa." 1921. *Cuentos completos*, vol. 3, pp. 333-36.
"Comedia." 1904. *Cuentos completos*, vol. 3, pp. 352-54.
"El zapato." 1911. *Cuentos completos*, vol. 3, pp. 424-27.
"La redada." 1900. *Cuentos completos*, vol. 2, pp. 92-94.
"El encaje roto." 1897. *Cuentos completos*, vol. 1, pp. 331-33.
"Los pendientes." 1909. *Cuentos completos*, vol. 4, pp. 250-52.
"Posesión." 1895. *Cuentos completos*, vol. 1, pp. 394-97.

Chapter 3:
"Apólogo." 1898. *Cuentos completos*, vol. 1, pp. 337-40.
"La dama joven." 1885. *Obras completas*, vol. 7, pp. 11-58.
"Las cutres." 1910. *Cuentos completos*, vol. 3, pp. 364-68.
"Coleccionista." 1910. *Cuentos completos*, vol. 1, pp. 233-35.
"Saletita." 1898. *Cuentos completos*, vol. 2, pp. 90-92.
"El mascarón." 1915. *Cuentos completos*, vol. 4, pp. 35-37.

Chapter 4:
"Cenizas." 1902. *Cuentos completos*, vol. 4, pp. 133-36.
"Remordimiento." 1892. *Obras completas*, vol. 8, pp. 69-75.
"Dalinda." 1906. *Cuentos completos*, vol. 2, pp. 327-30.
"El aviso." 1897. *Cuentos completos*, vol. 1, pp. 400-03.
"El cinco de copas." 1893. *Cuentos completos*, vol. 1, pp. 138-45.
"El pajarraco." 1912. *Cuentos completos*, vol. 3, pp. 166-70.

Chapter 5:
"El molino." 1900. *Cuentos completos*, vol. 2, pp. 187-91.
"La santa de Karnar." 1891. *Cuentos completos*, vol. 2, pp. 77-85.
"El aire cativo." 1919. *Cuentos completos*, vol. 3, pp. 299-302.

"La capitana." 1902. *Cuentos completos*, vol. 2, pp. 343-46.
"La hoz." 1922. *Cuentos completos*, vol. 3, pp. 290-94.
"Un destripador de antaño." 1890. *Cuentos completos*, vol. 2, pp. 5-21.

Index

References of the form "XnY" refer to footnote Y on page X.

Abbott, Edith 128
Acosta, Eva 15
Adriana 155n7
agency 14–15, 17–18, 25–6, 28; in fairytales 48; highlighted in stories 35, 63, 66, 77–8, 100; and wisdom 93
age of consent 65
agricultural workers 17; in Galicia 182, 185–6, 189, 193–4, 225, 233
"El aire cativo" 25, 189–206, 211, 217, 225, 231
Alas, Leopoldo 37
Aldaraca, Bridget A. 33–4, 120
allusions 20, 29, 48, 50
Amar y Borbón, Doña Josefa 33
ambiguity 10, 71, 73, 94, 199, 215, 222
analepses 54
andaluzas 51
ángel del hogar 9, 15–16, 18, 22, 64, 227; antithesis of 26; in *Apólogo* 110; and *bandida* 211; development in Spain 29–35; and Don Juan 156, 158; and *mujer fuerte* 190, 192; and New Woman 120; Pardo Bazán on 28; parody of 91; and women writers 55
angel in the house *see ángel del hogar*
anger 12
"Apólogo" 14, 17, 23, 54n14, 80n17, 104, 185n116, 233; atavism in 51; female protagonist of 105–20; jealousy in 80n17; seducer in 141; as story of small compass 54n14
"Apuesta" 155n7
"El árbol rosa" 22, 101, 227, 232; arranged marriage in 65n2; atavism in 52; female protagonist of 66–78, 234; seducer in 141
Arenal, Concepción 28
Ashley, Melissa 48
atavism 17, 50–1, 51n11, 105–6, 141
Auden, W. H. 13–14
Auerbach, Erich 53
Auerbach, Nina 32, 126
auto-da-fé 96–7
"La aventura" 65n2, 136n22

aventurine 107n2
"El aviso" 161–70, 181, 222–3, 227, 229–30, 234; allusions in 49; *deus ex machina* in 24, 150; as framed story 45; narrative voice in 55
azucena 168, 175, 182

"Bajo la losa" 196, 202n21
Bakhtin, Mikhail 137–8
bandits 182, 206–10
"Barbastro" 132n19
Barnes-Karol, Gwendolyn 29
Barthes, Roland 50
bats 49, 75
Beauvoir, Simone de 31
Biblioteca de la Mujer 21, 28, 38–42, 40n7, 44, 63, 228
Bieder, Maryellen 16–18, 44, 52, 55, 79, 87, 156
Biggane, Julia 16, 112
Blanco y Negro 10n2, 72, 91, 106, 122, 132n20, 151, 162, 206, 210
Bobadilla, Emilio 37
"La boda" 65n2
bodily disfigurement, voluntary 90
bodily transformations 94
La Borgoñona 43n9
bourgeois angel-woman 86, 120
Bravo-Villasante, Carmen 15
Bridges-Esser, Christine 202n23
Brión 218, 218n33, 219n34
"Bucólica" 111
Burdiel, Isabel 15, 32n11, 65n1, 111

El burlador de Sevilla y convidado de piedra (Tirso de Molina) 57, 74, 78n14, 144–5
Busto, Fariña 213

"La caja de oro" 217
Calderón de la Barca, Pedro 72–3, 124n14
Campá, F. de P. 85
campesinos 187, 189–90, 195, 220, 222–5, 230, 233
Campoamor, Ramón 39
"La capitana" 26, 58, 189, 192n9, 206–25, 231, 233
Caras y Caretas 193, 211–12
"La careta rosa" 80n17, 136n22
Carlists 132, 163n15
Carnival 24, 49, 114, 136–41, 136n24
Carretero Novillo, José Mariá 27
Casanova, Mahmed 210
Castro, Rosalia de 62
Catholic Church 30, 32, 206
Catholicism 29; feminine view of 202; imaginative 197
Catholic theology, orthodox 34, 95n31
Celts 185
"Cenicienta" 48, 82, 195
"Cenizas" 24, 87, 149–50, 181, 233; allusions in 50; as carnival story 136n22; female protagonist of 151–61; as framed story 45, 198; Gothic tropes in 58
Cervantes, Miguel de 112
"Champaña" 65n2, 98n35
chaperoning 84, 86, 228

character narrators 121, 162–3, 167, 230
"La charca" 136n22
Charcot, Jean-Marie 33
Charnon-Deutsch, Lou 20, 26; on "Apólogo" 112; on atavism 51; on Naturalism 56, 119, 216
chastity 32, 114, 124, 126, 147, 163, 180, 192, 234
Chaucer, Geoffrey 56n15
Chekhov, Anton 82n18
choices, life-defining 105–20
chulas 18, 139
cigar boxes 128n18
"El cinco de copas" 24, 40, 150, 161–70, 181, 222, 233; as framed story 45; Gothic tropes in 58; scope of 54n14
El cisne de Vilamorta 56n15, 113n9
Clémessy, Nelly 15
clerical opinions 29
close reading 13
"Coleccionista" 23, 104, 142; and *costumbrismo* 58; female protagonists in 120–31; as framed story, as framed story 45; narrator in 230
Coleridge, Samuel Taylor 94n29
"Comedia" 22, 101, 125, 129, 230, 232–3; allusions in 49–50; female protagonist of 66–78; working women in 33
comedia urbana 73
"La compaña" 191n7
Consuelo (López de Ayala) 49, 105, 115–16, 118–19, 232

"Contra treta" 132n19
control: culture of 29; male 35, 82
convidada 86
costumbrismo 20, 58, 60, 230; in "Coleccionista" 127; in Galician stories 25, 185, 200, 208, 218–19; in "El molino" 189, 192; and Realism 52
Counter-Reformation 29
courtship tales 67, 69, 106
Crawford, Amy 60
crimes of passion 93n27, 109n5
Cruz, Anne 31
"Cuadros religiosos" 196
Cuaresmal 198n133
Cuddon, J. A. 13
"Cuento primitivo" 39
Cuentos de amor 14, 44, 85n20, 106, 155–6
Cuentos de la tierra 193, 206
Cuentos del terruño 171, 184, 206
Cuentos de Marineda 184
"cuentos directos" 59
Cuentos dramáticos 190
Cuentos nuevos 155–6
Cuentos sacroprofanos 95, 162
Cuentos Trágicos 14, 176, 181
La cuestión palpitante 42, 52, 56n15, 57, 113, 229
curandero 217, 219, 225
curiosity 71, 87, 122–3, 127–8
"Las cutres" 23, 104, 142, 227, 230; female protagonists in 120–31; as framed story 45

"Dalinda" 24, 87n21, 170–81, 232, 234; allusions in 50; working women in 33

"La dama joven" 13n6, 21, 23, 227, 231, 233; allusions in 48, 50; arranged marriage in 65n2; and Carnival 137n25; female protagonist of 104–20; as *folletín* 60, 129; and Naturalism 56; working women in 33

La dama joven y otros cuentos 111

d'Aurevilly, Jules Amédée Barbey 96

deaths, female 76

La de Bringas (Peréz Galdós) 129

de la Cerda, Juan 30

"Del amor y la Amistad" 41

Dendle, Brian J. 51

"Der Sandmann" 49, 58n16, 223n36

"Desde afuera" 155n7

"Un destripador de antaño" 13n6, 26, 185n3, 186, 189, 197, 206–25, 230, 233; allusions in 48, 50; and *costumbrismo* 58; as framed story 45; Gothic tropes in 58; narrative voice in 55; priests in 96n32

deus ex machina 24, 150, 161, 166, 168, 170

Dickinson, Emily 44

Díez Canedo, Enrique 109n4

direct speech 108, 113, 139, 171, 193

domesticity 35

"Los dominós de encaje" 136n22

"El dominó verde" 136n22

"El don Juan" 180n23

Don Juan 20, 35; and code of honor 127; familial retribution against 180n23; foiled by female protagonists 170–81; intertextual allusions to 49–50, 92; as old man 151, 153–5, 157–60, 232; Pardo Bazán's narratives of 142, 181–2; real-life inspiration for 144n1; and Romanticism 57; Spanish female critics of 148n4; Spanish Golden Age tropes of 74, 77, 144–50; thwarted by miracles 161–70

donjuanesque behavior 25, 40, 147, 152, 156, 163, 182, 232

Don Juan Tenorio (Zorrilla) 78n14

doubles 90, 100

"Drago" 155n7

Drayson, Elizabeth 110n6

Dulce dueño 196

DuPont, Denise 204

Dutton, Brian 162

"La educación del hombre y de la mujer" 149

Eliot, T. S. 120

el qué dirán 9, 22–3, 28, 35–6, 89, 177, 227; in Galician stories 189–90, 193

embedded narrator 45–6, 86, 163, 197–8

embedding narrator 45–6, 156–8

emotion 23–4; destructive 66; as feminine trait 92, 103, 105, 130–1, 142; in Realism 54; in Romanticism 57

"El encaje roto" 13n6, 22, 69, 98n35, 101; female protagonist in 66, 78–89; first person narrator in 229; as framed story 45, 231
enchoyadas 189, 191, 191n120
enclosure of women 30
environmental determinism 112
epilepsy 109
La Época 111
"El escapulario" 136n22, 139
"Los escarmentados" 77, 125
La Esfera 132n20, 136, 141
La España Moderna 15n9, 38, 216
Espinosa, Juan de 30
Espronceda, José de 145–6, 148, 152
exorcisms 96, 98

fairytales 48, 82–3, 195, 209, 232
faith 25, 56, 100, 196–7, 203–6
fallen women 126
Fantastic mode 20, 60, 79n16, 91–4, 132
fantasy: immersive 60, 92, 95, 98; sexual 153
Faus, Pilar 15
Federico, Annette 13
Feijóo y Montenegro, Benito Jerónimo 39, 42, 96n33, 202, 204–5
female protagonists 12–17, 22–6, 47, 66, 227, 229, 231, 234; and betrothals 85; condemned 49, 66; and Don Juan 150, 172, 181; fending for themselves 101, 103, 142; in *folletín* 61; in Galician stories 188–90, 206, 224, 226;

as *Nueva Mujer Moderna* 120; questioning men of standing 40; unconventional behavior of 80; as working women 33
female voices 46, 197, 231; narrative 86, 156, 160, 197
feminine voices 21, 110, 197n130
femininity 32, 38, 85, 92, 131, 205
feminism 10, 14; in Pardo Bazán's stories 142, 229; Pardo Bazán's views on 27, 35, 38, 40–1
"Feminista" 65n2, 87, 156
feminist sub-texts 19, 29, 44, 181, 206, 216, 229
femme fatale 135
Fernández Cubas, Cristina 10, 15, 24
ficelle 122
first-person narration 21, 80, 83, 85, 122, 127, 208–9, 229; female 98n35; male 79, 89
flattery 134, 175n22
folletín 20, 23, 50, 60; parody of 105, 112–13, 119
forastero 174
Formica, Mercedes 144n1
fortune telling 166n17
Foucault, Michel 97n34
Fourier, Charles 42
framed stories 29, 45
Franciscans 30, 161, 166, 168–9, 196, 199n20
Francis of Assisi, Saint 113, 196, 199n20
Fray Luis de León 30, 32–3
free direct discourse 69
free indirect discourse 68

Friedman, Norman 54, 121, 176
Furst, Lilian 57

galán 73–4, 76, 78, 230
galego see Galician language
Galicia: attitudes to Pardo Bazán in 61; Pardo Bazán's stories set in 21, 25, 29, 182, 185, 188, 225–6, 233; reputation for crime 211, 217
Galician language 25, 61–2, 188–90
Galician legends 26, 189–91, 193, 195, 207, 216, 225
Galician women 25–6, 186–8, 195, 203, 206, 225, 231, 233
"La gallega" 185–6
García Gutiérrez, Antonio 145
La gaviota 59
gaze 97, 97n34, 99, 140, 153; female 158
gendered inequalities 9–11, 14, 26, 90, 93n27; Pardo Bazán's challenge to 46, 50, 63, 125
gendered stereotypes 85
gender-neutral narrator 122, 156n8, 208
gender reversals 48, 110, 158, 179, 189, 194
genres 20, 52–61
Gilbert, Sandra M. 46
Gilmore, David D. 36, 137, 140
Gilmour, Nicola M. 38
Goethe, Wolfgang 157
Gold, Hazel 129
Gómez de Avellaneda, Gertrudis 58
Gómez-Ferrer, Guadalupe 16

González Herrán, José Manuel 83, 152, 171, 207
gossip 9, 28, 35–6; in "Las cutres" 104, 123; in "La dama joven" 115; and odd behavior 121; in "Saletita" 133–4, 136; and sexual double standard 228; *see also el qué dirán*
Gothic 20, 26, 50, 58, 60; and "Un destripador de antaño" 206, 216–17, 219, 221, 223–4, 231
Goya, Francisco José de 49, 75, 164, 232
"El guardapelo" 80n17
Gubar, Susan 46
gullibility 99, 101, 133n21

Hadley, Tessa 87
Hanson, Clare 63
Haviland, John Beard 121
Hemingway, Ernest 151
Hemingway, Maurice 16, 196
Henn, David 112
"Heno" 80n17
heresy 23, 95–6, 100
"Los hilos" 155n7
Hilton, Ronald 9, 11
Historias y cuentos de Galicia 83, 132, 184, 197, 216
Hoffman, Joan M. 32
Hoffmann, E. T. A. 49, 58, 218, 221, 223n36, 231
Holquist, Michael 136
honor: female 31, 73, 122–6, 180; male 165, 170; *see also* Spanish code of honor

honor killings 76–7
"La hoz" 26, 185n3, 189, 206–25, 231, 233
Hugo, Victor 218
"Humano" 80n17
humiliation 24, 82, 84, 161, 179–80, 182, 192
hysteria 33–4, 95n31, 204n25

idealism 20
ideal woman 17, 90, 101, 131, 145, 154
ignorance, consequences for women 23, 78
Ilie, Paul 75
La Ilustración Artística 38, 49, 189–90, 217, 231
La Ilustración de la Mujer 42
La Ilustración Española y Americana 80, 127, 132n20
El Imparcial 10n2, 16, 95, 155, 171
indiano 24n10, 105, 131–2
indirect speech 212, 215
"El indulto" 36n3, 43n9
infidelity 32, 66, 92
inheritance patterns, gendered 125
Insolación 37, 106
internal narrator 45, 151
intertexts 20, 29, 48–9, 105, 116, 231–2
irony 60, 159, 161, 169, 175, 211

Jackson, Rosemary 94
Jack the Ripper 217–18
James, Henry 122
jealousy 12, 23, 26; male 66, 78, 80, 83, 85, 89, 105–6
Jiménez, Javier 59
Johnson, Roberta 33, 147
Josefa de la Torre 197–8, 205n26
Judas trees 68

Kant, Immanuel 42
Kilgour, Maggie 58, 217
Kirkpatrick, Susan 57

Leo XIII, Pope 95
Leppihalme, Ritva 48
libertines 145, 155, 175n22
literary styles 19, 21, 43–4, 52–61
literary techniques 24, 29
lo fantástico 60
Lohafer, Susan 178
loitas 189–90, 192
Lopez Teijeiro, Iria 167
love, pessimistic view of 155
love stories 80, 106
lower-class speech 139
loyalty 131; among men 165, 172, 175
lust 28, 90, 92, 169, 232

McKenna, Susan M. 12, 16, 46, 121, 126, 215
Madrazo, Pedro de 58
La madre naturaleza 11, 56n15, 113n9
Madrid 18; in "El árbol rosa" 68; in "Comedia" 72; *comedia urbana* in 73; Pardo Bazán living in 38, 61
madrileñas 51, 68, 127

Maisonneuve, Louis 109
Málaga 167n18
male bodies 84
male voice 29, 46, 197; narrative 55, 79–80, 85, 89, 122
Mandrell, James: on *costumbrismo* 52, 59; on Don Juan 145, 147, 154; on honor 31, 73; on Naturalism 56
marriage 14, 23; critique of 48; in "La dama joven" 112–16, 119; in Don Juan stories 150, 159–60, 165, 181; exemplary 165; in *fin de siècle* Spain 65, 87; refusing 80, 82–3, 85, 87–9, 101; *see also* Pardo Bazán, Emília, marriage of
Martínez Arnaldos, Manuel 50
Martínez Veiga, Ubaldo 33
Mary Magdalene 95, 126n16, 167–9, 196
"La máscara" 136n22
"El mascarón" 23–4, 105, 131–42, 185n116, 232–3; atavism in 52; illustrations for 49
masculine voice 230
masculinity 111, 131, 147, 205
mask narration 163
"Un matrimonio del siglo XIX" 228, 234
"La mayorazga de Bouzas" 43n9, 192n9
Medeiros, António 61
"Las medias rojas" 187, 213
Mendlesohn, Farah 60
Mesonero Romanos, Ramón de 60

middle-class behavior 80, 82, 89, 105
middle-class women 21, 26; social conventions for 28, 32, 34
migration, from Galicia 186–7, 190, 214
Miguélez-Carballeira, Helena 186
Mill, John Stewart 41–2
miracles 24, 161–70, 197, 201–6, 220
mirroring 100
Mitchell, Timothy 162
modernity 132
Moger, Angela S. 45
"El molino" 25, 185n3, 188–206, 225, 233; and *costumbrismo* 58, 230; illustrations for 49
Monsedá de Maciá, Dolores 42
Moors 107, 109–11, 110n6
morality 56; and Don Juan 161, 166, 176, 182
Morrión y Boina 43n9
Mortimer, Armine Kotin 151
mujeres fuertes 18, 29, 47, 49, 63, 135; in Galician stories 187, 190, 192–3, 195, 210–11, 224–5
murder 231; in "Apólogo" 106; in "Un destripador de antaño" 189, 206, 216, 221–5; in "La hoz" 26, 212; in "El mascarón" 131, 136, 141
Murgía, Manuel de 61–2, 186
museums, private 122, 129–30
Myers, Diana T. 35

narrative techniques 44–7
narrative voice, in framed stories 45
narrator persona 45

narrator-witness 167
Naturalism 20, 37, 56; and atavism 107; in "La dama joven" 119; in Galician stories 211, 216, 220
Naturalists 56
neckline, low 116–18
Neumeyer, Peter F. 178
New Woman 47, 120
Nimetz, Michael 61, 119
"No lo invento" 39
non-narrative text 178
nonstandard behavior 120–31
nostalgia 53, 139
novelas 111–12, 119
"La novia fiel" 96n32, 163n14, 202n22
Nueva Mujer Moderna see New Woman
Nuevo Teatro Crítico 21, 28, 39, 41–2, 63, 155–6, 166, 197, 228
nuns 66, 99–100, 146, 150, 152–4, 160, 173, 181–2

Obras Completas (Pardo Bazán) 9n1, 91, 128, 156n8, 193
observer-narrator 121, 167, 169
odd behavior 121
Ojea Fernández, María Elena 47
omniscient narrator 60, 106–7, 169, 171, 176, 209
Ordóñez, Elizabeth J. 51, 61
ostracism, social 152, 161
Owen, Christopher 60

"El pajarraco" 14, 24, 150, 170–81, 233

Pardo Bazán, Carmen 196
Pardo Bazán, Emilia 9–11; approaches to œuvre 11–15; biographies of 15; class position of 79; as *cuentista* 43–4; and Don Juan 148–9; eulogies for 68; feminist publishing ventures 38–43; as Galician writer 61–3, 185; marriage of 61, 65; public persona of 37–8; separation from husband 111; on Spanish women 28, 34
"Un parecido" 155n7
Paredes Núñez, Juan 12, 78, 90n23, 156n8; on Carnival 137; on *costumbrismo* 59–60; on Galicia 184–5, 187, 211, 217, 225
Parr, James A. 145
Pascual López: Autobiografía de un estudiante de medicina 37, 113n9, 164n16
Patmore, Coventry 31
patriarchy 15, 18, 28; and Don Juan 147; and *el ángel del hogar* 29, 32; and honor 166; in Pardo Bazán's stories 46–8, 126; and religious faith 206
Pattison, Walter T. 15
Los pazos de Ulloa 11, 113n9, 152n5, 166n17, 231; and Naturalism 37, 56n15
pejorative words 98n36
Penas Varela, Ermitas 205
"Los pendientes" 23, 101, 231–2, 234; atavism in 52; female protagonist in 66; female

protagonists in 90–101; Gothic tropes in 58; and *lo fantástico* 60
"La penetencia de Dora" 202n21
Percoco, Cristina Maria 128n18
Pereda, Jose María de 37, 53–4
Pérez, Janet 11, 12n5
Pérez de Deza, José Quiroga 65
Pérez Galdós, Benito 53, 119, 122, 128–30
Pérez Mateo, Soledad 129–30
perfection 16
Perry, Mary Elizabeth 30
Phelan, James 167, 199
Phelps, William Lyon 57
philosophical discourse 74
Piglia, Ricardo 133
Poe, Edgar Allan 13n8
"Por dentro" 196, 202n21
Por Francia 106
"Posesión" 23, 29, 233; allusions in 49; female protagonist in 49, 66, 90–101; and *lo fantástico* 60
post-romantic imaginary 99
poverty 114, 122; consequences for women 23, 78; in Galicia 188, 233
Pradilla Ortiz, Francisco 110n6
pregnancy 114, 126
priests: corrupt 219, 223; subversive voice of 230; virtuous 60, 114
priest's niece 173, 182
"Primer amor" 43n9
Prince, Gerald 167
private narrator 45
prolepses 54

prostitutes 90, 100
public narrator 45
Pujol de Collado, Josefa 42
"La puñalada" 80n17

"querer", use of term 71
Quesada Novás, Ángeles 12, 16, 69, 71, 80, 80n17, 105

race, Pardo Bazán on 185
Rank, Otto 149
rationality 54, 103, 164n16, 197, 203, 205–6
Raza Española 67
Realism 19, 23, 29, 52–4, 56, 229; in "El aviso" 162, 164–5; in "El cinco de copas" 167; in "Comedia" 50, 74; and "La dama joven" 119; and *folletín* 113; in Galician stories 209, 211, 216; in "El mascarón" 139; and narrative voice 229–30; and other genres 58, 60, 101; Pardo Bazán's use of 44, 52, 78, 90, 229; and "Los pendientes" 94; in "Saletita" 132
"La redada" 22, 54n14, 70, 80n17, 101; female protagonist in 66, 78–89; first person narrator in 229; jealousy in 80n17; as story of small compass 54n14
red shoes 213–15
refundiciones 50, 78, 145
"Remordimiento" 13n6, 24, 40, 149, 181, 231, 233; arranged marriage in 65n2; female protagonist of

151–61; as framed story 45, 198, 231; scope of 54n14
remorse 149, 154, 159–62
repentance 96–8, 150, 155, 165, 175n22
reported speech 177
Retratos y apuntes literarios 42, 158n10
Revilla y Moreno, Manuel de la 37
"El revólver" 80n17, 87
Rexurdimento 62n19, 186
Rey, Alfonso 212
rhetoric of the retelling 209
Ribao Pereira, Montserrat 212
"El rival" 98n35, 155n7
Romanticism 20, 56–7; and Don Juan 147–8; and Realism 53
rosaries 198, 201, 204–5
Ross, Marlon B. 57

saints 25, 169; in Galician stories 182, 189, 196, 198, 201, 205, 219, 222
salamanders 193–5
"Saletita" 23, 105, 131–41, 233
Sánchez-Alonso, Blanca 187
Sancho Dobles, Leonardo 137
Sand, George 57, 147–8
San Martín, Alejandro 33
La Santa Compaña 25, 189–91
"La santa de Karnar" 25, 40, 189–206, 211, 225, 233; and *costumbrismo* 58; first person narrator in 229; as framed story 45, 231; Gothic tropes in 58

Santiago de Compostela 152n6, 171n21, 197, 200, 218–20
Satan 67, 90–1, 95–6, 98–100
Scanlon, Geraldine 39
Schiavo, Leda 16
"La sed de Cristo" 95–6, 100
seduction 66, 230, 232; in "El árbol rosa" and "Comedia" 67–78; in "Cenizas" 151–2; in "La dama joven" 114; in Don Juan stories 146–50; double standard for 127; failed 175, 177–9; friends complicit in 172; in "El mascarón" 140; in "Los pendientes" 91; in "Remordimiento" 155
self-centeredness 147, 159, 161, 169
self-pity 85, 131, 139
Senabre, Ricardo 128, 130
sentimentalism 20, 113
sexual activity: and female honor 73; illicit 31, 124
sexual double standard 9, 17, 22, 28, 67, 92, 94, 227; and Catholic faith 163; of religious observance 206
short stories 13n8, 43; and the Gothic 58n16; handling of time in 54; in *Nuevo Teatro Crítico* 39; Poe on 13n8; telling two stories 133–4, 151, 159, 218; women writers of 63
Sieburth, Stephanie 112
single women, rights of 22
Sinués de Marco, María del Pilar 32
Six, Abigail Lee 58, 218
Slattery, Sister Mary Francis 19

sleep deprivation 168–9
small compass, stories of 54
Smith, Jennifer 34
smooth talk 175n22
social class 17, 21, 23, 179; and Carnival 137; Pardo Bazán on 43; and women 33
Sociedad del Folklore Gallega 185, 193
"Sor Aparición" 98n35, 148, 169n20
Spacks, Patricia Meyer 121
Spain, counter-reformation period 29
Spanish code of honor 9, 15, 22, 28–9, 31–2, 227; in "Las cutres" 124, 126; and Don Juan 147, 162, 172
Spanish Golden Age 72–4, 124n14, 129, 144, 230
Spanish Inquisition 96
Spanish language: gender markers 156n8; Pardo Bazán using 61
Spanish Realism 19, 53–4
Spanish women 10–11, 14, 16; gendered norms for 22, 28, 30–1, 33–5, 67, 89, 93; and predatory males 24; social control of 36
spas 87, 151
subjectivity 99
submission, female 15, 82, 92
sucedidos 44, 197
suicide 67, 77, 81, 99, 181
Summers, Montague 218n31
superstition 188–9, 195, 202, 217–18, 224, 233

Taboada, Ruth Noya 12
Taylor, Scott K. 124
temporal ellipsis 169, 174
"El tetraca en la aldea" 132n19
theatre 74–5, 104, 108–9, 113–19
thick description 87, 171
third-person narration 21, 54, 167, 230
Tirso de Molina 127, 144, 147, 217
titles 50
tobacco factories 128n18
Tolliver, Joyce 12, 14, 16, 86–7, 98n35, 197
Torrecilla, Jesús 53
"Travesura" 136n22
La Tribuna 56n15, 113n9
Twain, Mark 178

"La última ilusión de Don Juan" 148
understanding 13
upper-class behavior 84, 86, 159
urban-rural dichotomy 172
Uspensky, Boris 122

Valera y Alcalá, Juan 39
Valle-Inclán, Ramon 171
Vega, Lope de 72
venereal disease 55, 163
Verea y Aguiar, José 186
Versteeg, Margot 16, 112
Un viaje de novios 56n15, 112, 113n9
Vicetto, Benito 198n18, 205
"El vidrio roto" 132n19
Villanueva, Dario 83, 171, 208
violence: female 186, 206, 232; in Galician stories 188; male 86, 88–9

virginity 31, 67, 73, 93
Virgin Mary 126, 196

Walter, Susan 12, 16, 45, 86–7, 135
Webber, Andrew J. 221
weddings 83, 87–8
Weinstein, Leo 147, 149
Wells, H. G. 63
White, Sarah L. 124
wife-murders 76
Willem, Linda M. 16, 79
Wilson, Margaret 73
witches 217
Woman, patriarchal view of 103
"The Women of Spain" (essay) 15–16, 18, 79, 185–6, 197, 206, 227, 229, 231–2
Woolf, Virginia 13
working-class women 17, 33, 77, 120, 130

"El zapato" 22, 80n17, 101, 195; allusions in 48; female protagonist in 66, 78–90; first person narrator in 229; jealousy in 80n17
Zarate, Martha 16
Zola, Émile 20, 56
Zorrilla, José 49, 78n14, 145–6, 149, 153

www.ingramcontent.com/pod-product-compliance
Lightning Source LLC
Chambersburg PA
CBHW021940290426
44108CB00012B/907